THE ESSENTIAL WRITINGS
OF
MAHATMA GANDHI

THE
ESSENTIAL WRITINGS
OF
MAHATMA GANDHI

edited by
RAGHAVAN IYER

OXFORD
UNIVERSITY PRESS

OXFORD
UNIVERSITY PRESS

YMCA Library Building, Jai Singh Road, New Delhi 110001

Oxford University Press is a department of the University of Oxford. It furthers the
University's objective of excellence in research, scholarship, and education
by publishing worldwide in

Oxford   New York
Athens   Auckland   Bangkok Bogota Buenos Aires Calcutta
Cape Town   Chennai   Dar es Salaam   Delhi   Florence   Hong Kong   Istanbul
Karachi   Kuala Lumpur   Madrid   Melbourne   Mexico City   Mumbai
Nairobi Paris Sao Paolo Singapore Taipei Tokyo Toronto Warsaw

with associated companies in

Berlin   Ibadan

The Writings of M. K. Gandhi
© Navajivan Trust, Ahmedabad 380 014, India, 1990
Compilation © Raghavan N. Iyer 1991
Oxford India Paperbacks 1993
Third impression 1999

ISBN 0 19 563208 7

Printed at Rekha Printers Pvt. Ltd., New Delhi 110 020
and published by Manzar Khan, Oxford University Press
YMCA Library Building, Jai Singh Road, New Delhi 110 001

Preface

Despite the vast amount of proliferating literature on Mahatma Gandhi, there has as yet been no accessible and coherent record of his essential writings. During his lifetime he wrote weekly articles for the journals he edited—*Indian Opinion, Young India, Harijan,* and *Navajivan.* He was also unusually conscientious about replying to all of his correspondents in South Africa, England, India, and elsewhere, writing as many as seventy letters a day for over four decades. The enormous quantity of his correspondence is the main reason why his *Collected Works* (initiated by the Indian Government soon after his death and now drawing to its completion) has run into ninety volumes. His actual books were few, short, and somewhat inconclusive—*Hind Swaraj, The Story of My Experiments With Truth, Satyagraha in South Africa,* and *Ashram Observances in Action,* together with small tracts on the *Bhagavad Gita,* the Constructive Programme, and on health. His unfinished autobiography and several popular biographies remain the chief—and rather misleading—sources of public knowledge about the personality and impact of Gandhi. While a significant number of mostly perfunctory or fragmentary anthologies have been published, they have largely obscured the richness of his thought.

On the suggestion of G. D. H. Cole, John Plamenatz, and others at Oxford, I began my exploration of Gandhi's unpublished writings when hardly two volumes of the *Collected Works* had appeared. Fortunately, Professor K. Swaminathan was persuaded by Vinoba Bhave to undertake the editorship and production of the *Collected Works.* Professor Swaminathan willingly assumed this onerous task and recently completed it with extraordinary patience, scrupulousness, and care. With his generous help, I was able to consult the corpus of materials in his office and in several libraries. This enabled me to complete *The Moral and Political Thought of Mahatma Gandhi,* published by Oxford University Press in 1973.

Since then, it has become evident that Gandhi has been most inadequately represented by the older anthologies. In attempting to rescue Gandhi's essential writings from the wealth of detail (and ephemera) in the *Collected Works,* I realized that there was no way of doing justice to the subtlety and scope of Gandhi's thought in less than three volumes of materials drawn from the entire corpus. It became necessary to sift every volume of the *Collected Works* and apply the most stringent criteria to produce a comprehensive, balanced, and accessible collection.

While the materials in this one-volume abridgement rely on the definitive versions of the *Collected Works*, there are minor modifications. The entries are given apt titles, and the original titles provided by Gandhi or his associates are cited at the end of each entry. Footnotes have been kept a bare minimum so that the reader is unencumbered by extraneous detail in reading the texts. The selections drawn from the entire lifework of Gandhi are organized under self-explanatory heads. They show the refinement of his thought over many years and also the underlying consistency of his commitments and perspectives.

This concise collection could help a variety of people in different countries—including India itself—to form a fuller and more just appreciation of Gandhi's significant and compelling contribution to the twentieth century and to the future.

R. N. I.

Acknowledgements

I am grateful to the Navajivan Press, for permission to use materials from *The Collected Works of Mahatma Gandhi* (90 volumes); to Professor K. Swaminathan, for valuable suggestions concerning this volume; and to the editorial staff of Oxford University Press.

Contents

IX Conscience, Heroism, and Humility — 210

X *Satya*—Absolute and Relative Truth — 222

Abbreviations

I
Introduction

The Angels keep their ancient places; –
Turn but a stone, and start a wing!
'Tis ye, 'tis your estranged faces,
That miss the many-splendoured thing.

But (when so sad thou canst not sadder)
Cry; – and upon thy so sore loss
Shall shine the traffic of Jacob's ladder
Pitched betwixt Heaven and Charing Cross.

FRANCIS THOMPSON

My heart has become capable of every form;
It is a pasture for gazelles and a convent for Christian monks,
And a temple for idols and the pilgrim's Ka'ba
And the tables for the Torah and the book of the Qur'an
I follow the religion of Love: whatever way
Love's camels take, that is my religion and my faith.

IBN AL-'ARABI

NON-VIOLENT SOCIALISM, GLOBAL TRUSTEESHIP AND SELF-REGENERATION

Mahatma Gandhi held that all human beings are always responsible
to themselves, the entire family of man and to God, or Truth (*sat*),
for their continual use of all the goods, gifts and talents that fall
within their domain. Nature and man are alike sustained and
renewed by the Divine. There is a luminous spark of noetic
intelligence in the action of each atom and in the eyes of every man,
woman and child upon this earth. This is the enduring basis of
effective self-regeneration at all levels—individual, social, national
and global. Men and women can fully incarnate their latent divinity
by deliberately and joyously putting their abilities and assets to
practical use for the sake of all (*sarvodaya*). The finest exemplars of
global trusteeship are, therefore, those who treat all possessions as

though they were sacred or priceless, beyond any pecuniary or earthly scale of valuation.

It is only through daily moral choices and the meritorious and sagacious employment of limited resources in the social sphere that individuals sustain their inherited and acquired entitlements. For this very reason, the divisive and dangerous notion of exclusive ownership is systematically misleading and, at worst, a specious and subtle form of violence. This engenders assertive rights or claims, and even privileged access, that far exceed the legitimate bounds of actual human need—even though protected by statutory law or social custom. It also obscures the generous bounty of nature and the potential fecundity of human resourcefulness and innovation, which together can readily provide enough for all inhabitants of the globe, if only each person would hold in trust whatever he has to meet his essential needs, without profligate excess or any form of exploitation. This is the basic presupposition behind *sarvodaya*, non-violent socialism, which is as old as the communal sharing taught by Buddha and Christ.

Ancient Indian thought viewed the entire cosmos and all human souls as continually sustained by the principle of harmony (*rta*), the principle of sacrifice (*yajna*), and the principle of universal inter-dependence, solidarity and concord. This is enshrined in the Golden Rule which is found in all the major religions of mankind and is mirrored in the codes and norms of all cultures at different stages of development. Vedic chants portrayed heaven and earth as indissolubly linked through the mighty sacrificial ladder of being, which is also found in Pythagorean philosophy and memorably conveyed in Shakespeare's *Troilus and Cressida*. Similarly, Jacob's celestial ladder of angels between heaven and earth signifies the indispensable linkage or Leibnizian continuity between the universal and the particular, the unconditional and the contextually concrete, the divine and the human, the Logos and the cosmos, the macrocosm and the microcosm.

Jacob sensed, in his celebrated dream, that this vital connection provides a shining thread of hope for souls in distress. He also saw that it provides a helpful clue to action by binding together profound contemplation and the apt choice of available means—not because he claimed any supernatural wisdom or superhuman power, but only because he was content to remain an ardent seeker and a constant learner. Philo Judaeus saw in Jacob a transparently good man who had gained the talismanic insight that everyone learns best by emulating noble exemplars instead of merely repeating the words of the wise. Philo also saw the true statesman as a disguised soothsayer, who could interpret the deepest dreams of ordinary men and women, their irrepressible longings for the greater good. He stated in his *De Congressu Eruditionis Gratia*:

It is characteristic of the learner that he listens to a voice and to words, for by these alone is he taught, but he who acquires the good through practice and not through teaching pays attention not to what is said but to those who say it, and imitates their life in its succession of blameless actions. Thus it is said in the case of Jacob, when he is sent to marry one of his kin, 'Jacob hearkened to his father and mother, and journeyed to Mesopotamia' (*Genesis* 28:7), not to their voice or words, for the practicer must be the imitator of a life, not the hearer of words, since the latter is characteristic of one who is being instructed, the former of one who struggles through to the end.[1]

Jacob was perhaps a *karma yogin* (or its rabbinical equivalent), who conscientiously sought to translate what he knew into the concrete discipline of moral conduct. He deeply cherished his vision of the celestial bridge between *theoria* and *praxis*, the invisible arch (or ark of salvation) linking the rarefied empyrean of scriptural ethics and the actual pathway each human being must trace and tread in his life on earth. To Jacob it was given to discern the divine ladder upon which the angels tread (depicted like a spinal column in the kabbalistic tree of life), and to salute the old men who dream dreams as well as the young who see visions (*Joel* 2:28). This is poignantly suggestive of the profound statement of Aleksandr Herzen, which contemporary detractors of perestroika and glasnost ignore at their peril, that political leaders do not change events in the world by rational demonstrations or by syllogisms, but rather by 'dreaming the dreams of men'.

Doubtless, this is easier said than done, but it would indeed be an elitist form of defeatism to abandon the very attempt in a world bedevilled by obsolete *isms* and rigid ideologies, even as it trembles on the brink of nuclear annihilation and global disintegration. As Mikhail Gorbachev frankly conceded:

---

[1] Philo of Alexandria (Philo Judaeus), *The Contemplative Life, The Giants and Selections*, David Winston, trans., (New York: Paulist Press, 1981), p. 215.

The restructuring doesn't come easily for us. We critically assess each step we are making, test ourselves by practical results, and keenly realize that what looks acceptable and sufficient today may be obsolete tomorrow. . . . There is a great thirst for mutual understanding and mutual communication in the world. It is felt among politicians, it is gaining momentum among the intelligentsia, representatives of culture, and the public at large. . . . The restructuring is a must for a world overflowing with nuclear weapons; for a world ridden with serious economic and ecological problems; for a world laden with poverty, backwardness and disease; for a human race now facing the urgent need of ensuring its own survival. . . . We want people of every country to enjoy prosperity, welfare and happiness. The road to this lies through proceeding to a nuclear-free, non violent world.[2]

Whilst Gandhi was much closer in spirit to Jacob and Philo than to Herzen and Lenin, he would have endorsed the self-critical spirit behind perestroika and glasnost.

Mohandas Karamchand Gandhi saw himself essentially as a *karma yogin*, who, without claiming any special or supernatural wisdom, was unusually receptive in his readiness to honour remarkable men such as Naoroji, Gokhale and Rajchandra as rare models of probity. He himself showed consistent fidelity to the paradigm of the self-governed sage, portrayed in eighteen *shlokas* which were daily chanted at his *ashram*.[3] He took this classical model as the basis for assiduous self-study, ever seeking to correct himself whenever he saw that he had erred, especially when he made what he called, with playful hyperbole, 'Himalayan blunders'. He keenly preserved his hard-won awareness that sensitive leaders must always share the trials and travails of the human condition, that ubiquitous suffering is the common predicament of humanity, whilst all earthly pleasures and intellectual joys are ephemeral and deceptive.

Gandhi, like Gautama, did not try to escape the evident truth of human suffering through mindless oblivion or neurotic distractions, nor did he choose to come to terms with it through spiritual ambition or conventional religious piety. Rejecting the route of cloistered monasticism, he pondered deeply and agonizingly upon

[2] Mikhail Gorbachev, *Perestroika*, (New York: Harper and Row, 1987), pp. 53–4.

[3] *The Bhagavad Gita*. Raghavan Iyer, ed. (Santa Barbara: Concord Grove Press, 1985), pp. 84–90.

the human condition, and sought to find the redemptive function and therapeutic meaning of human misery. He translated his painful insights into daily acts of *tapas*—self-chosen spiritual exercises and the repeated renewal of lifelong meditation in the midst of his fervent social activity. He came to see the need for a continual rediscovery of the purpose of living by all those who reject the hypnosis of bourgeois society, with its sanctimonious hypocrisy and notorious 'double standards' for individual and public life.

Gautama Buddha had taught his disciples in the Sangha that *bodhichitta*, the seed of enlightenment, may be found in the cleansed heart and controlled mind, and that it may be quickened by diligent practice of meditative altruism and honest self-examination. As stressed in the later Mahayana schools of India, China and Tibet, *bodhichitta* can serve, like the Upanishadhic *antahkarana* or mediating principle of intellection, as a reliable bridge between fleeting sense-experience and enduring spiritual aspiration. It is also an indispensable aid and stimulus to the ascent of consciousness to its highest possible elevation and even to the plane of *svasamvedana*, universal self-consciousness in the midst of *shunyata*, the voidness released through persistent philosophical negation.

Spiritual striving towards enlightenment can help to raise a ladder of contemplation along which the seeker may ascend and descend, participating in the worlds of eternity and time, perfecting the sense of timing in the sphere of action. In most people, alas, the seed is not allowed to sprout or grow owing to chaotic and contradictory aims and desires, intensified by vain longings and false expectations, fantasies and fears, which block any vibrant encounter with the realities of this world as well as any possibility of envisioning Jacob's ladder, 'pitched betwixt Heaven and Charing Cross'. Gandhi's own spiritual conviction, growing with the ripening of age, was that social reformers and non-violent revolutionaries must radically cleanse their sight and remove all self-serving illusions by placing themselves squarely within the concrete context of mass suffering.

Satyagraha and *sarvodaya* were Mahatma Gandhi's most significant and revolutionary contributions to contemporary political thought. The fundamental concepts of *satya* and *ahimsa*, truth and non-violence, can be found in all the world's major religious and philosophical traditions. Gandhi's originality lay in the way he fused them in both theory and practice. His doctrines of *satyagraha* (or non-violent resistance) and *sarvodaya* (or universal welfare) were at once the logical corollaries of his fundamental premises about human perfectibility, and the mature fruit of his repeated experiments with political action and social reform. If absolute values can never be upheld on utilitarian grounds, adherence to them can none the less lead to desirable results which may be extolled in the language of expediency. Whilst speaking of *satya* in the language of faith, even in terms of total conviction, Gandhi often advocated *ahimsa* as a creed, regardless of results, though capable at times of producing concrete advantages.

Heroism is a quality of the heart, free of every trace of fear and anger, determined to exact instant atonement for every breach of honour. More than any rule-governed morality, heroism can enable a person to stand alone in times of trial and isolation. It can also promote deep concord between like-minded men and women, loyal to their conscience. But for Gandhi, the greatest obstacle to the incarnation of the heroic ideal in society is, paradoxically, the absence of humility. When human beings do not adequately recognize their fallibility, they will make insufficient effort to arouse individual conscience. Foundering in a false sense of security , they will be trapped in a mobocratic state of collective helplessness. Only after the heart is touched by the enormity of divine truth will the distance between the ideal and the real become painfully evident. And only then will genuine humility flow. Whilst heroism is refined skill in action (*karma yoga*), humility is the virtue of effortlessness (*buddhi yoga*).

Just as humility is the natural accompaniment of true heroism, *ahimsa*, or non-violence, is the necessary correlate of fearlessness. In Gandhi's vision, the maintenance of moral stature and spiritual dignity must be based upon the practice of *ahimsa*. He conceived of *ahimsa* as an integral part of *yajna* (or sacrifice), a practice rooted in the Indian presupposition of a beneficent cosmic order and a humane discipline requiring self-purification and self-examination. The moral force generated by *ahimsa* was held by Gandhi to be infinitely greater than any force founded upon selfishness. The intrinsic power of non-violence was viewed alternatively by Gandhi as being 'soul-force' and 'truth-force'. The two terms are essentially equivalent, and differ only in their psychological or ontological emphasis. For Gandhi *ahimsa* represented not a denial or power but a renunciation of all forms of coercion and compulsion. Although

Gandhi was noted for his advocacy of *ahimsa* in social and political arenas, its most fundamental and intimate use lay for him in the moral persuasion of free souls.

Ahimsa, in the widest sense, means a willingness to treat all beings as oneself. Thus *ahimsa* is the basis of (*anasakti*), selfless action. *Ahimsa* cannot be realized alone; it has meaning only in the context of universal human interaction and uplift. Like truth, *ahimsa*, when genuine, carries conviction in every sphere. Unlike many forms of love, however, *ahimsa* is enacted by a truth-seeker not out of longing or lack, but out of a sense of universal obligation. It is only when one takes the vow of *ahimsa* that one has the capacity to assess apparent failures in terms of one's own moral inadequacies. *Ahimsa* means, at the very least, a refusal to do harm. 'In its positive form, *ahimsa* means the largest love, the greatest charity.'[4] Gandhi's refusal to set different standards for saints and ordinary people, combined with his concern to give *ahimsa* a practical social function rather than a purely mystical use, led him to extend and employ the word in novel ways. The political strength which *ahimsa* can summon is greater and deeper than the impact of violence precisely because *ahimsa* is consubstantial with the immortal soul. Any programme of social and political reform, including civil disobedience, must, therefore, begin with the heroic individual, for only when such pioneers radiate the lustre of *ahimsa* will all humanity be uplifted.

Gandhi's concept of *satya*, with *ahimsa* as the means, gave rise to his complex doctrine of *satyagraha*; his concept of *ahimsa*, with *satya* as the common goal, enabled him to develop the doctrine of *sarvodaya* or non-violent socialism. Self-dependence, when rightly understood and embodied, becomes the crucial lever for non-violent social transformation. 'Self-dependence is a necessary ideal so long as, and to the extent that it is an aid to one's self-respect and spiritual discipline.'[5] It is not an end in itself, for those who become responsible through moral and spiritual renewal are those who can awaken a new impulse in the hidden depths of social life. Though he had no detailed plan for social transformation, Gandhi cherished the ideal of *Ramarajya* at the heart of his political vision, and firmly

[4] M. K. Gandhi, 'On *Ahimsa*', *Modern Review*, October 1916; in Raghavan Iyer, ed., *The Moral and Political Writings of Mahatma Gandhi* (hereafter MPWMG), 3 volumes, (Oxford: Clarendon Press, 1986–7), vol. 2, p. 212.

[5] M. K. Gandhi, 'Our Helplessness', *Young India*, 21 March 1929; MPWMG, vol. 3, p. 228.

believed that *ahimsa* would eventually win global acceptance as a universal criterion of civilized life. This conviction, together with his faith in the magical power of millions striving in a common cause, gave him a clear, if intuitive, sense of direction.

Since the doctrine of *satyagraha* is a comprehensive social and political application of *satya* and *ahimsa*, it inevitably reflects the deontic logic of those metaphysical concepts. *Satyagraha* is an ethical imperative: one cannot justifiably claim to adhere to *ahimsa* and *a fortiori* to *satya* without making appropriate efforts to apply *satyagraha* to social conflicts. In this sense, *satyagraha* connotes 'truth-force', the luminous power of truth directed towards the promotion of social welfare. At the same time, because it confronts injustice and its attendant hostility through an effective appeal to conscience, *satyagraha* is a policy for action and a stimulus for social reform. In this sense, it is 'non-violent resistance'. These two dimensions of *satyagraha* are indivisible aspects of a single standpoint, for truth-force is a ceaseless witness to justice in its transcendental and immanent implications, and it must resist injustice whenever and wherever it occurs. Just as light by its presence delimits darkness and makes it evident, so too the *satyagrahi* by his suffering exposes injustice around him. And just as light dispels shadow, yet destroys nothing, so the *satyagrahi* dissolves injustice without harming its agents.

Sarvodaya was predicated upon the diffusion of power, yoked to a firm recognition of the moral priority of social virtue over sectional interest. Competition must make way for concord. To be effective, this shift in social and political perspective must be understood as a spiritual requirement in a civilized world, a revolutionary enterprise which would eventually benefit all humanity. As a macrocosm of the individual seeker, society as a whole must come to renounce everything not supported by the concept of mutual responsibility. In practical terms, therefore, pioneering witnesses to truth and non-violence are obliged to teach through example the necessity of shifting the axis of social life from an aggressive emphasis on rights to an active concern with obligations. They must exemplify a spirit of fellowship that has nothing to do with levelling up or down, since every person's *dharma* is unique to himself. They must also renounce the material and psychological exploitation that causes poverty. The votaries of *sarvodaya* need not repudiate the innovativeness of the technological age; they must merely shun soulless mechanization and trivial gadgetry.

Gandhi envisaged a radical reformulation of the elusive conception of collective welfare. Unlike utilitarians, he was unwilling to accept the principle of the greatest good of the greatest number. Instead, he pleaded for a more synergistic notion of collective welfare, wherein the suffering of the least and the lowest inevitably interacts with the supposed well-being of the most prosperous so as to negate completely the alleged social value of such prosperity. He saw collective social welfare as a chain no stronger than its weakest link. Since institutions possess neither cognitive flexibility nor fidelity to conscience, Gandhi was convinced that social systems essentially depend upon, and cannot rise beyond, the creative individuals who participate in them. Neither political associations nor social movements can be better in practice than their typical adherents, and systems which seek to elevate the general condition of humanity can succeed only to the extent that their supporters meet ethical and intellectual requirements which nurture freedom of initiative and fearless self-criticism.

Rejecting every form of exploitation and viewing all human beings as equally responsible for the welfare of all, Gandhi sought to lay the basis of a redistribution of wealth that would be consistent with the sacrificial moral order (*rta*) of the cosmos. However inequitable the distribution of material and mental resources among human beings, he held that all men and women could act as trustees, rather than as owners, of their resources, and could thus consider themselves as the partners of all their fellows in society. He had no objection to a large measure of society's wealth flowing through the hands of individuals, but he warned that this involved facing a moral temptation, which would require a spirit of non-possession and the deliberate adoption of the principle of trusteeship. He advised every individual to weigh his circumstances in the court of conscience according to the criteria of truth and non-violence and the obligations of *sarvodaya*. Such a radical redefinition of both the means and the ends of production could serve as the basis of a fundamental reform of society.

Gandhi's belief that any sharp distinction between means and ends was theoretically dubious and practically unhelpful confirmed his basic conviction that violence, in any form and for any end whatsoever, had to be explicitly repudiated in principle. He was not burdened by the reductionist and historicist inheritance that weighed heavily on Marx, and to the degree that he grasped its general tenets, he rejected most of them, especially utilitarian conceptions of social amelioration arising out of capitalist econo-mics. In 1928 he was asked whether the economics of Bolshevism was an appropriate model for India. Replying that the abolition of private property was an economic application of the ethical principle of *aparigraha* or non-possession, he insisted that it had to be undertaken voluntarily as a result of moral choice.[6] Reiterating his rejection of all violence to achieve even the most desirable ends, he also commended the sacrificial idealism of many heroic spirits such as Lenin.[7]

Mahatma Gandhi did not see any significant distinction between true communism and real socialism.

My communism is not very different from socialism. It is a harmonious blending of the two. Communism, as I have understood it, is a natural corollary of socialism.[8]

None the less, though he sometimes called the same principles communist or socialist depending on the context, he made subtle distinctions in practice. He tended to restrict his spiritual commun-ism to the *ashram*, or intentionally constituted community, wherein it was devoid of ideological content and was based upon voluntary vows of truthfulness, non-possession, non-stealing, sexual restraint and non-violence. Each of these was given a precise, if extensive, application and enshrined as an ideal, at once practicable and exacting even for the most committed adherents. The *ashram* was the centre of his communist experiments, many of which were candidly described in *Ashram Observances in Action*.

When Gandhi advocated non-violent socialism as a wider political and social ideal, rooted in the philosophy of *yajna* or sacrificial action, *aparigraha* or non-possession and responsible trusteeship, and *sarvodaya* or universal uplift, with a primary emphasis upon the emancipation of the least favoured in society, he could never look to the State as the chief instrument for furthering the socialist ideal. Rather, the masses should be enlightened by the exemplary leadership of the morally committed.

[6] M. K. Gandhi, 'The Students' Interrogatives', *Young India*, 15 Novem-ber 1928.

[7] M. K. Gandhi, 'My Notes', *Navajivan*, 21 October 1928; *Young India*, 15 November 1928; in the present volume (hereafter G.E.), p. 395.

[8] M. K. Gandhi, 'Interview to Louis Fischer', *Harijan*, 4 August 1946; MPWMG, vol. 3, p. 578.

I shall bring about economic equality through non-violence, by converting the people to my point of view by harnessing the forces of love against hatred. I will not wait till I have converted the whole society to my view but will straightaway make the beginning with myself.[9]

Gandhi remained sceptical of imposing even social reformation, let alone a revolution, from the top, and he parted company with ideological and State socialists on this crucial point. To them, his bold attempts at non-violent resistance at least had the merit of being national in scope even when local in origin; yet the Constructive Programme seemed to them like pouring water through a sieve into local villages and small community groups. Gandhi respected innate intelligence and acquired scholarship, but he felt that urban intellectuals could be useful as creative leaders in social reform only when they identified and merged themselves with the rural masses. They could not, as Marx thought, conveniently command the proletariat from revolutionary cloisters and then be drawn along by the mass fervour they had helped to kindle. Replying to a critic who maintained a Marxian perspective on the strategic role of intellectuals in the social revolution, Gandhi said:

Whereas you have before your mind's eye that microscopic minority, the educated Indian, I have before my mind's eye the lowliest illiterate Indian living outside the railway beat. Important as the former class undoubtedly is, it has no importance in my estimation except in terms of the latter and for the sake of the latter. The educated class can justify its existence only if it is willing to sacrifice itself for the mass.[10]

Non-violent revolution has to come from the bottom up if it is to be truly effective and enduring. Neither ingenious permutations of existing elements in the social structure nor the wholesale reassignment of roles and offices in the political system can make any substantial difference to the human situation. If disgruntled intellectuals genuinely wish to help, they must not merely preach to the multitudes, stirring up incendiary reactions whilst remaining monkishly aloof from the murky arena of impassioned conflict. Instead, they must truly merge with the disinherited masses and initiate constructive programmes through their own heroic labours.

[9] M. K. Gandhi, 'Answers to Questions at Constructive Workers' Conference, Madras', *The Hindu*, 26 January 1946; *Harijan*, 31 March 1931.

[10] M. K. Gandhi, 'Letter to Captain J. W. Petavel', SN 12648, Sabarmati Sangrahalaya; Ahmedabad: MPWMG, vol. 3, p. 534.

Gandhi could not endorse any theory of revolution tending towards the formation of a new class of exploiters which replaced the old strata without changing the inherently unjust and inequitable social structure. A revolution from the bottom—since all who desired to share in it had to start anew by renouncing every vestige of class and privilege—could not only produce a genuinely socialist society, but could also avoid the class war which some feared, many desired, and ideologists saw as inevitable. Class war was unacceptable on the principle of *ahimsa*, and it was unnecessary and even irrelevant in a revolution from the bottom. Gandhi could not countenance the possibility of class war on theoretical grounds because it violated his unshakeable conviction that ends never ethically surpass their means. He rejected it in practice owing to the triple criteria of his holistic socialism. First of all, social reform must include everyone—oppressor as well as oppressed, capitalist as well as worker. Secondly, such inclusion must be voluntary and not coerced. And thirdly, it must distinguish between the inequities that will necessarily remain even in the best of societies, whilst utterly abolishing eradicable inequalities.

Inequalities in intelligence and even opportunity will last till the end of time. A man living on the banks of a river has any day more opportunity of growing crops than one living in an arid desert. But if inequalities stare us in the face the essential equality is not to be missed. Every man has an equal right to the necessaries of life even as birds and beasts have. And since every right carries with it a corresponding duty and the corresponding remedy for resisting any attack upon it, it is merely a matter of finding out the corresponding duties and remedies to vindicate the elementary fundamental equality. The corresponding duty is to labour with my limbs and the corresponding remedy is to non-cooperate with him who deprives me of the fruits of my labour. And if I would recognize the fundamental equality, as I must, of the capitalist and the labourer, I must not aim at his destruction.[11]

Socio-economic reform necessitates a radical change in perspective on the part of workers and owners alike. If the latter had to see ownership in a new light, so too the workers had to realize their inalienable power, the power not of destruction but of creation.

By the non-violent method we seek not to destroy the capitalist, we seek to destroy capitalism. We invite the capitalist to regard himself as trustee for

[11] M. K. Gandhi, 'Questions and Answers', *Young India*, 26 March 1931; GE, p. 396.

those on whom he depends for the making, the retention and the increase of his capital. Nor need the worker wait for his conversion. If capital is power, so is work. Either power can be used destructively or creatively. Either is dependent on the other. Immediately the worker realizes his strength, he is in a position to become a co-sharer with the capitalist instead of remaining his slave. If he aims at becoming the sole owner, he will most likely be killing the hen that lays golden eggs.[12]

If class revolution fails to alter the condition of society, however much it may elevate the formerly oppressed and denigrate the overthrown masters, conversion will fail to maintain a viable political and economic system without a *modus operandi* that merges the requirements of social reform with those of economic improvement. This invaluable method was, for Gandhi, rooted in a fundamental reformulation of the classical ideal of universal trusteeship, a powerful concept which, if honestly instantiated, could avert potential class conflict, link comprehensive social reform with stable economic growth, and utilize every available talent and creative skill. Owing to its intrinsic applicability to all sectors of society, affording each the opportunity to contribute constructively to an equitable and harmonious social order, Gandhi was convinced that its consistent and authentic application could demonstrate the practicability of the principle of non-violent social transformation.

The principle of trusteeship and its application to the equitable distribution of wealth, as well as the non-violent socialist revolution it underpins, is feasible because it does not require everyone to undertake it all at once. Unlike most socialists, who reason that they must seize the power of the State before instituting effective reforms, Gandhi held that enlightened individuals could initiate the process of divesting themselves of what is unnecessary, whilst becoming true trustees of their own possessions.

It is perfectly possible for an individual to adopt this way of life without having to wait for others to do so. And if an individual can observe a certain rule of conduct, it follows that a group of individuals can do likewise. . . . Men generally hesitate to make a beginning if they feel that the objective cannot be had in its entirety. Such an attitude of mind is in reality a bar to progress.[13]

[12] M. K. Gandhi, 'Questions and Answers', *Young India*, 26 March 1931; GE,

[13] M. K. Gandhi, 'Equal Distribution', *Harijan*, 25 August 1940; GE, p. 387.

Once the barrier in consciousness is broken, the principle of trusteeship can be made to work by letting go of the demand for a mechanically equal distribution, which Gandhi doubted could ever be realized. Instead, he held to the equally revolutionary idea of equitable distribution, which would be not only possible, but necessary, in the non-violent socialist State.[14]

Mahatma Gandhi's genius as a social reformer lay in his uncommon ability to fuse timeless principles with evolving strategies. This is best seen in the array of activities he initiated under the umbrella of the Constructive Programme. From the twenties until his death in 1948 Gandhi gradually shifted the emphasis of his work from non-violent resistance to constructive schemes for the social good. For Gandhi, non-violent resistance (*satyagraha*) and the Constructive Programme—an embodiment of *sarvodaya*—were corollaries of the same philosophical perspective. Non-violent resistance, however, aimed to rectify entrenched abuses or to abolish patently unfair laws and practices. But non-co-operation with perceived evils cannot by itself create a socialist society. Cessation of wrongdoing is a prerequisite for positive social welfare, but is not identical with it. The Constructive Programme did not rule out non-violent resistance or non-co-operation, but relied upon constructive ways of rebuilding a demoralized society. If civil disobedience and and non-violent resistance could arouse the conscience of others, the Constructive Programme could channel that awakened sensitivity in beneficial ways. It virtue lay in its generality, both because it avoided the psychological defeatism that readily emerges when rigid objectives are not met, and because it gave generous recognition to the intangible and unquantifiable elements of human progress.

The Constructive Programme was designed not only to disseminate Gandhi's basic principles but also to ensure that a variety of shifting opportunities could be taken to secure modest successes wherever possible. A mere succession of violent thrusts at the existing social structure would not be acceptable. Gandhi preferred modest gains, each of which stood a reasonable chance of lasting. Leaving the dramatic action of demolishing the old social structure

---

[14] 'My ideal is equal distribution, but so far as I can see, it is not to be realized. I, therefore, work for equitable distribution.' M. K. Gandhi, *Young India*, 17 March 1927.

to those who preferred what he saw as misguided activity, he sought to build a new edifice brick by brick. The Constructive Programme could slowly build upon every success whilst leaving the future open to bold experimentation, in which there are invariably errors, but errors that do not undermine the benefits. Since each facet of the Constructive Programme is related directly to trusteeship, the various programmes are coherently if loosely associated with one another.

If Gandhi had little faith in the presumed capacity of centralized institutions or violent revolutions to ameliorate human misery and mass deprivation, he was also fully aware that ambitious projects of rural reconstruction would not miraculously transform most social and political workers. Just as he had powerfully employed the novel methods of mass *satyagraha* on a national scale, so too he found that individual *satyagraha* and the spirit of *sarvodaya* could be applied at a micro-level to foster cohesiveness and a sense of direction amongst voluntary workers in the Constructive Programme. When critics wrote to him of the manifold ways in which dedicated workers seemed to succumb to the enticements of power, he advised appropriate forms of non-cooperation. But, he warned,

During my long experience, I also noticed that those who complain of others being ambitious of holding power are no less ambitious themselves, and when it is a question of distinguishing between half a dozen and six, it becomes a thankless task.[15]

Except for strict adherence to non-violence as a principle and a policy, Gandhi did not dispute the socialist and communist ideals of any society in which basic social, economic and political equity sustained a living spirit of equality and fraternity amongst all citizens. He questioned, however, whether a centralized State could serve these ends unless it had actually arisen amongst a people already dedicated to them in practice. Like Marx, he thought that a people so dedicated would not need the centralized nation State in its contemporary forms, since much of its elaborate and elephantine apparatus would have become irrelevant. The radical moral and psychological transformation of a society could not be achieved by a central chain of command, if for no other reason than that the

[15] M. K. Gandhi, 'Some Important Questions', *Harijan*, 2 March 1947; MPWMG, vol. 3, p. 174.

diffusion of political authority cannot be wholly disentangled from the dispersion of social and economic initiative.

Gandhi was deeply convinced that political power itself could be brought to bear constructively on corrupt institutionalized practices which subvert social and economic ends. But just as his radical ideas of comprehensive reform require that all arenas of social interaction be purified and understood in a new light, so too politics must be purified and understood anew. When criticized for his political action, he once responded, 'Is not politics too a part of *dharma*!'[16] but he thought of political power—like all power—as a means and not end.

Political power, in my opinion, cannot be our ultimate aim. It is one of the means used by men for their all-round advancement. The power to control national life through national representatives is called political power. Representatives will become unnecessary if the national life becomes so perfect as to be self-controlled. It will then be a state of enlightened anarchy in which each person will become his own ruler. . . . In an ideal State there will be no political institution and therefore no political power. That is why Thoreau has said in his classic statement that that government is the best which governs the least.[17]

Recognizing that 'enlightened anarchy' was a remote ideal, Mahatma Gandhi none the less held that only the loftiest ideal could effectively motivate the spiritual and ethical advancement of a people. Gandhi was closer to Marx than to Weber in his insistence upon an open-textured vision of human nature, a fundamental standpoint which allowed him to point to social perfectibility without the arbitrary restraint of predetermined time limits. In practice, he was always ready to settle for much less, provided it did not foreclose further progress or actually negate the ideal. Thus Gandhi divorced *sattvic* or noetic politics from the expediencies of political pragmatism. Fusing the political art with the gospel of selfless service, he sought to restore to contemporary politics the classical concern with the common good, the *agathon* or *lokasangraha*. He was wholly convinced that the exemplary sacrifices of non-violent revolutionaries would generate a more lasting, if less

[16] M. K. Gandhi, 'A Letter', *Bihar Pacchi Dilhi*, p. 350; MPWMG, vol 3. p. 548.
[17] M. K. Gandhi, 'Enlightened Anarchy—A Political Ideal', *Sarvodaya*, January 1939; GE, p. 402.

dramatic, transformation of society than any amount of ideological propaganda, terrorist intimidation or inquisitorial persecution.

Gandhi's earnest dialogues with socialists and communists, as well as his ready application of their basic vocabulary to much of his political work, reveal a ·deep insight into the methodology of social transformation. In addition to the need for a bold vision, which all social reformers accept, and the principle of non-violence, which many socialists and all traditional communists would reject, Gandhi discerned the ethical preconditions for permanent social reform. He clearly saw that the potent ideal of voluntary sacrifice for a larger common good had to become mandatory common sense within the social system. If trusteeship is to bring about social reform without bitter conflict, a broad conception of stewardship must command the allegiance of leaders and the people alike. Socialist and communist systems have already demonstrated the awesome capacity of the masses to sacrifice in vain for a vague ideological promise of a glorious future. Gandhi uncompromisingly insisted that those who would be responsible leaders of a socialist society must lead the way in making tangible sacrifices. Failure to do this voided all claims to wisdom, insight and credibility. Sacrificing freely amidst the people demonstrated minimal and authentic understanding of equity and equality, and every honest effort could foster a contagious change in all arenas of society.

Reformers need the very reforms they sought for others. For Gandhi, there were not two species of human being—those who needed reform in a socio-economic context and those who advocated reform and yet had marvellously remained untouched by the societies in which they lived. Though he recognized the rich resources of some individuals in wisdom and knowledge, and even in experience, he held strictly to the equality of all in the common need to transform thinking, motivation and action. This powerful realization came from a penetrating insight into the complexities of human nature and social structures. Gandhi expressed it in Euclidean terms: the ideal society is not a closed circle, but an open one, in which all its citizens work towards extending the horizons of human perfectibility, knowing that they can always do much better.

Whilst Gandhi cherished the grand vision of social transformation offered by optimistic socialists and communists, and indeed expressed a distinct vision of his own that they found daring in its long-term faith in the human race, he could not concede the practicability of magisterial demands for total reformation all at once. His embryonic plan for social transformation is properly called revolutionary not in respect to time but rather to its texture. The revolution he projected must be total but progressive and cumulative. It is essential to nurture the revolution by degrees, however vast the whole picture might be. Gandhi felt that many self-styled revolutionaries were not really committed to a transformation they would not live to see. The willingness to labour patiently for incremental gains towards an end which one would not live to share was for him part of the sacrifice required of all, especially those who would lead.

It is only through pain and patience that we learn to enjoy giving freely without expectation. However, if we readily recognize that trusteeship is a form of sacrificial action (*yajna*) natural to man, then it can truly help us to release the exhilarating sense of soul-satisfaction and soul-emancipation taught by the *Ishopanishad* and exemplified by Mahatma Gandhi. Our daily sacrifices merge into the mighty stream of *adhiyajna* or cosmic sacrifice. Such ungrudging contributions cannot be measured and meted out in the meagre coinage of material rewards. Voluntary sacrifice (*tapas*) releases its own incomparable spiritual elixir. The sacramental yearning to use everything wisely for the greater good of humanity could progressively dissolve the insidious sense of 'mine' and 'thine'. The raging fires of rampant greed, insatiable desire and fierce possessiveness could gradually subside because there would be less and less fuel to sustain them. There would then arise, phoenix-like, the incandescent spirit of love and longing for *lokasangraha*, universal welfare, the whole-hearted celebration of excellence and promise. Meanwhile, courageous pioneers could light up all over the globe the sacred fires of creativity and concord in the common cause of *lokasangraha*, global enlightenment and emancipation.

Gandhi knew that his ideas and ideals were difficult to instantiate precisely because of their inherent simplicity. He recognized, therefore, that he could only clarify and illustrate them to all who sought his counsel. Those others would, through *tapas*, have to assimilate and apply them for themselves. But the hero and villain jostle in the very soul. The morally sensitive individual must learn to detect self-deception with firmness and forbearance, mellowness and maturity. He must come to know the obscuration of light within, before he can ferret out evil at is roots. Eventually, 'a man with intense spirituality may without speech or gesture touch the hearts of millions who have never seen him and whom he has never seen'.[18] Through meditation, man can attain a noetic plane on which thought becomes the primary and most potent mode of action. Gandhi unwaveringly affirmed that living out this conviction would bring sacrificial suffering, as well as an inner joy which cannot be conveyed in words.

On his seventy-eighth birthday in 1947, when well-wishers showered him with lavish and affectionate greetings, Gandhi thought only of the violence and suffering of his recently independent and hastily partitioned motherland:

I am not vain enough to think that the divine purpose can only be fulfilled through me. It is as likely as not that a fitter instrument will be used to carry it out and that I was good enough to represent a weak nation, not a strong one. May it not be that a man purer, more courageous, more far-seeing, is wanted for the final purpose? Mine must be a state of complete resignation to the Divine Will. . . . If I had the impertinence openly to declare my wish to live 125 years, I must have the humility, under changed circumstances, openly to shed that wish. . . . In that state, I invoke the aid of the all-embracing Power to take me away from this 'vale of tears' rather than make me a helpless witness of the butchery by man become savage, whether he dares to call himself a Mussalman or Hindu or what not. Yet I cry, 'Not my will but Thine alone shall prevail'.[19]

Gandhi was sometimes apt to speak of God in the language of Christian mystics, despite his explicit commitment to a more philosophical view of deity, as given in the most advanced Hindu schools of thought and practice. He wavered at times between the standpoints and terminologies of contemplative monists and ecstatic dualists, but he never abandoned his early axiom that Truth is God, which he preferred to the statement that God is Truth, and he also held that Truth is the root of pure love and unconditional compassion. His lifelong faith in God as Truth (*sat*) implied a concrete, if inviolable, confidence in the spiritual and ethical potential of all Humanity, far surpassing the historicist and immanentist beliefs of reductionist sociological doctrines and rival

---

[18] M. K. Gandhi, *Young India*, 22 March 1928.
[19] M. K. Gandhi in *Mahatma: Life of Mohandas Karamchand Gandhi*, V. K. Jhaveri and D. G. Tendulkar (Bombay: 1951–4), vol. 8, p. 144; MPWMG, vol. 1, pp. 10–11.

political ideologies. He could, he felt, honestly call himself a socialist or a communist, although he explicitly repudiated their materialistic assumptions, violent methods, utilitarian programmes, and totalistic claims.

He spoke of socialism of the heart and invoked the Ishopanishadhic injunction to renounce and enjoy the world, which nourished his Tolstoyan conviction that the Kingdom of God is attainable on earth and is, in any event, a feasible, life-sustaining ideal. He knew, especially in his last decade, moods of pessimism and even moments of despair, when his inner voice would not speak, which lent a poignant and heroic quality to his life, reminiscent of the passion of Jesus Christ, the psychological martyrdom of saints, and the early strivings of the wandering monk, Siddhartha Kapilavastu, who became the enlightened Buddha. But always he returned to the conviction that it is presumptuous to deny human perfectibility or the possibility of human progress, let alone to take refuge in the fashionable armchair doctrine that *Ramarajya* is irrelevant to *Kali Yuga*, that the Kingdom of God is wholly unattainable in the world of time.

He held firmly to the view which Vinoba Bhave, his leading disciple, made his lifelong motto, that the social reformer and spiritual anchorite must be committed to the gospel of the *Gita* and to a life of ceaseless, selfless service of the weak. He must choose to become a *Satyayugakari*, an exemplar and witness of *Ramarajya* even in the midst of *Kali Yuga*, the Age of Iron. He could thus serve as a heroic pioneer and a patient builder, contributing bricks to the invisible, ideational endeavour to rebuild Solomon's temple, to re-establish the reign of Truth and Love even in the small circles of human fellowship. As a *karma yogin*, he could yoke a microcosmic approach to social experimentation with a macrocosmic vision of universal peace, human solidarity, and a global 'civilization of the heart'. This requires a staunch refusal to think in terms of nations, tribes, castes and classes, or the tedious distinctions made by the insecure in terms of race and creed, sex and status. What is needed at all times is a purgation of the psyche, a restoration of purity of the heart, and a release of the spiritual will in simple acts consecrated to the good of all. This was strongly stressed by Søren Kierkegaard and Simone Weil. It was powerfully exemplified by many a legendary hero and heroine of the Indian epics and *Puranas*, extolled in song and story to this day among millions of impoverished but indefatigable peasants in thousands of Indian villages, and also known to homeless and dispossessed exiles in chaotic cities and decaying townships.

Towards the close of his extraordinarily eventful life, so crowded with petitioners and visitors of every sort from all over the globe and from the farthest corners of rural India as well as from the towering Himalayas, he reaffirmed his inward vision of the 'Himalayas of the plains' and the inextinguishable integrity of socialist *sannyasa* and *Bodhisattvic* compassion. He ever recalled the formative early influences in his life, the *Vaishnava* ideal of Narsinh Mehta, *The Key to Theosophy* of Helena Petrovna Blavatsky, and the telling instructions of Bishop Butler, William Salter and Henry Drummond. He evidently knew the vivid encomiums of Drummond to Jesus as the Man of Sorrows, though he never explicitly cited the most memorable of such statements:

Christ sets His followers no tasks. He appoints no hours. He allots no sphere. He himself simply went about and did good. He did not stop life to do some special thing which should be called religious. His life was His religion. Each day as it came brought round in the ordinary course its natural ministry. Each village along the highway had someone waiting to be helped. His pulpit was the hillside, His congregation a woman at a well. The poor, wherever He met them, were His clients; the sick, as often as He found them, His opportunity. His work was everywhere; His workshop was the world.[20]

In his *ashrams* and during the periods of abstention from politics, which were longer and more frequent than many imagined, Gandhi was fortunate to experience the secret joy of living in the *atman*, which he early saw in Rajchandra, the jeweller and theodidact. Gandhi's demanding conception of his *svadharma*, his self-chosen obligations, repeatedly thrust him back into the arena of political conflict and conciliation, as well as into the wider forums of the Constructive Programme, social reform and nationwide rural reconstruction. Even here his quintessential philosophy of (*anasakti*) *yoga*, the gospel of selfless, disinterested action taught by Krishna in the *Gita*, came to his aid in distilling non-violent socialism to its irreducible core, as construed by Henry Drummond:

[20] Henry Drummond, 'The Ministry of Christ', in *The Jewel in the Lotus*, Raghavan Iyer, ed., (Santa Barbara: Concord Grove Press, 1983), p. 201.

The most obvious lesson in Christ's teaching is that there is no happiness in having and getting anything, but only in giving. . . . And half the world is on the wrong scent in the pursuit of happiness. They think it consists in having and getting, and in being served by others. It consists in giving and serving others. He that would be great among you, said Christ, let him serve. He that would be happy, let him remember that there is but one way—it is more blessed, it is more happy, to give than to receive.[21]

This is the secret of *sarvodaya*, the doctrine of non-violent socialism which Gandhi fused with his prescription of global trusteeship and his lifelong experience of the reality and relevance of radical self-regeneration through selfless service. Krishna's sovereign remedy of *buddhi yoga*, the *yoga* of divine discernment, points to the crucial connection between *viveka*, discrimination, and *vairagya*, detachment, between self-chosen duty and voluntary sacrifice, *dharma* and *yajna*, individual self-conquest, *swaraj*, and the welfare of the world, *lokasangraha*. Even a little of this practice, as taught in the *Gita* and realized by Gandhi, is invaluable.

In this path of *yoga* no effort is ever lost, and no harm is ever done. Even a little of this discipline delivers one from great danger.[22]

In the words of Dnyaneshwar, the foremost saint and poet of Maharashtra, 'Just as the flame of a lamp, though it looks small, affords extensive light, so this higher wisdom, even in small measure, is deeply precious'.

This is the ideal of the suffering servant of Isaiah, the means of entry into the wider human family as shown by Ibn al-'Arabi in his haunting poems, the evocative vision of the monkish revolutionaries known to the Russian Populists, the basis of inspiration of many a Christian socialist and even the Christian communists of the thirties, the demanding conception of Philo, who concluded from his observation of the Therapeutae and other small communes that 'every day is a festival', let alone the ancient Hindu ideal of the true Mahatma or self-governed sage, the *Jivanmukta* or spiritually free man, for whom every day is like unto a new incarnation, and every incarnation like unto a *manvantara*, the vast epoch of cosmic manifestation.

Gandhi prophesied that for thirty years after his death, his ideas

---

[21] Henry Drummond, 'Happiness', ibid., p. 71.

[22] *The Bhagavad Gita* (2.40), Raghavan Iyer, ed., p. 79.

would be largely forgotten, but that, generations later, the *tapas* of millions would bear fruit, and that out of his ashes 'a thousand Gandhis will arise'.[23] Even though this is still an elusive hope, it is indeed encouraging that intrepid pioneers have emerged from the host of the disillusioned who find the world of today too ghastly to contemplate, a world of mindless mass consumerism induced by the rising curve of shallow expectations, a world in which there is a widespread alienation of lonely individuals from disintegrating societies, of conscience from the intellect, of angry rebels from the agonies of the compassionate heart, of impotent politicians from the global imperatives of radical reconstruction and genuine coexistence among all nations, peoples, creeds and ideologies. Ragnarok, the end of the gods and of the world, is the sole alternative in Nordic mythology to the supernal rainbow bridge between heaven and earth, Bifrost. After crossing this bridge one camps at the boundary of a new land, a new frontier, a new settlement.

Whether or not a New Jerusalem is attainable on earth, there is much wisdom in Gandhi's own well tested message in times of trial. In 'One Step Enough for Me' he said:

When, thousands of years ago, the battle of Kurukshetra was fought, the doubts which occurred to Arjuna were answered by Shri Krishna in the *Gita*; but that battle of Kurukshetra is going on, will go on, forever within us; the Prince of Yogis, Lord Krishna, the universal *Atman* dwelling in the hearts of us all, will always be there to guide Arjuna, the human soul, and our Godward impulses represented by the Pandavas will always triumph over the demoniac impulses represented by the Kauravas. Till, however, victory is won, we should have faith and let the battle go on, and be patient meanwhile.[24]

Those who cannot share this testament of faith—rooted as it is in the spiritual convictions of antiquity concerning the periodic descent of *Avatars* (or Divine Redeemers), the immortality of the soul and the inexorable law of *karma*, the law of ethical causation and moral retribution—may, none the less, actively respond to 'the still, sad music of humanity'. After all, even agnostics and atheists, socialists, humanists and communists, may share a living faith in the future of

---

[23] M. K. Gandhi, 'Message to Students', *Harijan*, 16 January 1937; MPWMG, vol. 1, p. 35.
[24] M. K. Gandhi, 'One Step Enough for Me', Speech at Wardham Ashram, *Navajivan*, 27 December 1925; GE, p. 33.

civilization and hold a truly open view of human nature, social solidarity and global progress. All alike may ponder upon Mahatma Gandhi's life-message. Towards the end of his days on earth, he delivered a deeply moving and testable challenge to theo-philanthropists everywhere:

I will give you a talisman. Whenever you are in doubt, or when the self becomes too much with you, apply the following test. Recall the face of the poorest and weakest man whom you may have seen, and ask yourself if the step you contemplate is going to be of any use to him. Will he gain anything by it? Will it restore him to a control over his own life and destiny? In other words, will it lead to *swaraj* [self-rule] for the hungry and spiritually starving millions? Then you will find your doubts and yourself melting away.[25]

[25] M. K. Gandhi, in *Mahatma: Life of Mohandas Karamchand Gandhi*, V. K. Jhaveri and D. G. Tendular (Bombay: 1951–4), vol. 8, p. 89, GE, p. 418.

Volume One
Civilization, Politics, and Religion

II

Gandhi on Himself and His Mission

1. THE OCHRE ROBE

[19 January 1921]

I am always eager to meet *sadhus*. When I visited the Kum-
bhmela[1] in Hardwar, I tried to go into all *akhadas*[2] of *sadhus* in
search of a *sadhu* who would gladden my heart. I met every
sadhu who had acquired some reputation but I must say I was
disappointed. I am convinced that *sadhus* are an ornament to
India and that, if the country lives, it will be thanks to them.
But I see very little of the goodness of *sadhus* today. On the
last day in Hardwar, I spent the whole night thinking what
I could do so that *sadhus* in the country would be real *sadhus*.
Finally, I took a hard vow.[3] I shall not say what it is, but
many believe that it is a difficult one to keep. By God's grace,
I have still kept it inviolate.

Some friends suggested to me that I should become a *sannyasi*. However, I have not become one. My conscience did
not approve of such a step then and does not do so today. I
am sure you will not believe that the reason for my not doing
so is love of enjoyments. I am struggling to the best of my
ability to conquer the desire for them. But in the very process
of struggling, I see that I am not worthy of the ochre robe. I
cannot say I always practise truth, non-violence and *brahmacharya* in action, speech and thought. Whether I want or no,
I feel attachments and aversions, feel disturbed by desire; I
try to control them with an effort of mind and succeed in
repressing their physical manifestation. If I could practise
them to perfection, I would be in possession today of all the
supernatural powers they speak of; humble myself, the world
would be at my feet and no one would ever want to laugh me
out or treat me with contempt.

But I have not come here to persuade you to give up your dress. I would have failed in my duty if, in gratitude for the straightforwardness which I have found in the Swaminarayana sect and the love with which you have invited me here, I did not tell you what I feel. I submit to you, therefore, that you should bring credit to your outward garb of *sadhus* through the virtues of *sadhus*, and thus shine in lustre yourselves and shed lustre on the Swaminarayana sect.

Speech at Meeting of *Sadhus*, Vadtal (G.)
Navajivan, 23 Jan. 1921

¹ Gandhi visited this fair in 1915 and joined a volunteer corps for the service of the pilgrims.
² Centres for *sadhus* of particular sects.
³ To have only five articles of food.

2. STRIVING AFTER *MOKSHA*

November 1, 1921

It is dawn. Your letter is lying before me. Why should you apologize for what you wrote?

There may be an element of egoism in my article or conduct without my being aware of it. The word *klesha* here should be interpreted in a different way, though I cannot say how. I feel pain when I see others suffer. It is the nature of compassion that whenever one is unable to relieve the suffering of others one suffers unbearably. Logic will not avail when one is describing the condition of one's mind. I have given a graphic description of my feelings. It may be that these feelings were not quite pure. However, my state of mind at the time of writing the article had also in it a yearning for *moksha*—my aspiration for *moksha* was by no means weak then—but the fact is that I am no more than an aspirant after *moksha*. But I am not yet fit for *moksha* in this life. My *tapascharya* is not intense enough. I can control my passions no doubt, but I have not yet become completely free from them. I can control the palate, but the tongue has not yet ceased relishing good food.

He who can restrain the senses is a man of self-control; but the man whose senses have become, through constant practice, incapable of enjoying their objects has transcended self-control, has in fact attained *moksha*. I would not be tempted to give up my striving after *moksha* even for the sake of *swaraj*, but that does not mean that I have attained *moksha*. You will, therefore, notice many defects in my language. For me, even the effort for attaining *swaraj* is a part of the effort for *moksha*. Writing this to you is also a part of the same effort. If I find it a hindrance in the path of *moksha*, my pen would drop down this very moment, such is my yearning for *moksha*. Nevertheless, the mind is like a drunken monkey; mere effort is not enough for controlling it. Our actions also must be coming in our way.

In my article 'Optimism' I have suggested a rule of conduct, viz., that we should cease to have any dealings with a person who breaks a promise. This is the sign of a detached person. If even next year I find that the atmosphere in India is unfavourable and still we go on harping the same tune, it would be an outrage. In that case, I must first acquire the necessary fitness. This is why silence has been considered the best speech. Whatever I may do will be, I am sure, quite natural to me, for I will say and act upon nothing but what I believe to be the truth.

But 'Enjoy what you get today, who ever has seen tomorrow?' has been accepted as their motto alike by libertines and the self-controlled.

May the new year bring happiness to you.

Letter to Mathuradas Trikumji (G.)
Bapuni Prasadi, pp. 38–9

3. THE KINGDOM OF HEAVEN

Pundit Ghasita Ram, 'President, All-India, Sub-Assistant Surgeons Association, Punjab Province, Amritsar', sent to the Editor some days ago an 'open letter' addressed to me. After omitting from it laudatory phrases and sentences of good wishes and after correcting obvious grammatical errors, the letter reads:

I am a *Brahman*, a doctor and an old man like you. It will not be out of courtesy if I in this triple capacity offer you a piece of counsel. If you see wisdom and truth in it and if it appeals to your common sense and sentiments, kindly take it to heart.

You have seen much of the world; you have read much of it. Consequently you possess a wonderful experience of it, but in this world of mortals none till now has been able to accomplish the task he has undertaken in his lifetime. Buddha in spite of his high morality could not convert the whole of India to Buddhism.

Shankaracharya in spite of his high intellectuality could not make all India Vedantist. Christ in spite of his high spirituality could not bring into the fold of Christianity the whole Jewish nation. I do not think, and I am not prepared to believe for a single moment about the accomplishment of your task. Still in face of these historical facts, if you believe in its accomplishment in your lifetime, then Sir, I venture to say that it is nothing but a dream.

This world is a place of trials, troubles and turmoils. The more a man sinks into it the more he is restless and, eventually, he loses his spiritual calmness and peace of mind. Consequently, the *mahatmas* of olden time kept themselves aloof from worldly worries, anxieties and cares and strove to gain perfect peace and true quality of mind and enjoyed an everlasting happiness and bliss thereby.

The Jail life has brought a great change in your life and vigour and the disease has reduced you much. Therefore, in the fitness of things, you may live a calm life and spin the thread of your remaining days in a certain solitary cave in the meditation of God, and in realization of your own self in perfect spiritual tranquillity and calmness, because your health will not allow you to bear the burden of the worldly cares any more. It shall not be out of place to mention that you are absolutely convinced of the goodwill, mercy and sympathy of good officers. That very system of European medicines and surgery, which you condemned more than once, has saved you from the jaws of monstrous death. The English officers helped you in time of your troubles and needs.

'A friend in need is a friend indeed.' Now it remains for you to show your true friendship and to become the true ally of the British Raj in gratitude for the safety of your life and your release from the jail. If anyhow you cannot do so by your words and deeds, then pray do not come into the arena of political activity, but still if your restless soul does not allow you to sit in rest, then in this *bhumi*, the motherland of great sages and saints, *rishis* and *munis*, take up the task of spiritualizing your brother Indians, teach them a lesson of true realization of the self. By doing so, instead of gaining this Kingdom of Earth, you will gain the Kingdom of Heaven.

In my opinion, the writer is desperately in earnest and merits an answer on that account if for nothing else. But it enables me, too, to clear up certain misapprehensions about my mission in life.

Let me first, however, dispose of the advice about my views on medicine. I have not *Indian Home Rule*[1] before me, but I recollect sufficient to be able to say that I have nothing to revise about the views set forth there. If I had written it for English readers and in English, I would have put the same thought in a manner that would have been more acceptable to the English ear. The original is in Gujarati and was written for the Gujarati readers of *Indian Opinion* of Natal. Moreover, what is written there has reference to an ideal state. It is a common error to think that condemnation of measures involves that of men. Medicine does often benumb the soul of the patient. It may, therefore, be considered evil, but not, therefore, necessarily medicine-men. I had precious medical friends when I wrote the book and did not hesitate to seek their advice in times of need. That was, as the writer implies, inconsistent with my belief regarding the use of medicine. Several friends have said to me the same thing in so many words. I plead guilty. But that is to admit that I am not a perfect man. Unfortunately for me, I am far from being perfect. I am an humble aspirant for perfection. I know my way to it also. But knowing the way is not reaching its end.

If I was perfect, if I had acquired full control over all my passions even in thought, I should be perfect in body. I am free to confess that daily I am obliged to expend a great amount of mental energy in acquiring control over my thoughts. When I have succeeded, if I ever do, think what a storehouse of energy would be set free for service. As I hold that appendicitis was a result of infirmity of thought or mind, so do I concede that my submission to the surgical operation was an additional infirmity of mind. If I was absolutely free of egoism, I would have resigned myself to the inevitable; but I wanted to live in the present body. Complete detachment is not a mechanical process. One has to grow to it by patient toil and prayer. As for gratitude, I have more than once publicly expressed my gratitude to Col. Maddock and his staff for the kindness with which they overwhelmed me. But there

is no connection between the kind treatment I received from
Col. Maddock and the system of Government I condemn. Col
Maddock himself would think little of me, if I revised my
views about Dyerism because he, Col. Maddock, was a com-
petent surgeon and did his duty as such. Nor have I any cause
to be thankful to the Government for providing me with best
surgical assistance or for prematurely releasing me. The
former they were bound to provide for every prisoner. The
latter has embarrassed me. I knew my course in prison
whether well or ill. Outside the prison-walls, although I am
slowly regaining my health, I do not know with certainty how
to shape my course.

Now for the central point of the letter. The confusion in the
writer's mind has arisen because of his misconception of the
work of the prophets he names and of an awkward comparison
between them and me. I do not know that Buddha did not
accomplish his task which was to reach *Nirvana*. Tradition has
it that he did. Conversion of others was a by-product, if one
may so describe a sacred function. The Gospels record it of
Jesus that he testified on the Cross of his own work, 'It is
finished.'[2] Nor has their work of love died after them. The
truest part of it will live for ever. The two or three thousand
years that have gone by since their ministry are but a speck
in the vast time circle.

I do not consider myself worthy to be mentioned in the
same breath with the race of prophets. I am an humble seeker
after truth. I am impatient to realize myself, to attain *moksha*
in this very existence. My national service is part of my training for freeing my soul from the bondage of flesh. Thus considered, my service may be regarded as purely selfish. I have
no desire for the perishable kingdom of earth. I am striving
for the Kingdom of Heaven which is *moksha*. To attain my
end it is not necessary for me to seek the shelter of a cave. I
carry one about me, if I would but know it. A cave-dweller
can build castles in the air, whereas a dweller in a palace like
Janak has no castles to build. The cave-dweller who hovers
round the world on the wings of thought has no peace. Janak,
though living in the midst of 'pomp and circumstance', may
have peace that passeth understanding. For me the road to
salvation lies through incessant toil in the service of my coun-

try and therethrough of humanity. I want to identify myself
with everything that lives. In the language of the *Gita* I want
to live at peace with both friend and foe. Though, therefore,
a Mussalman or a Christian or a Hindu may despise me and
hate me, I want to love him and serve him even as I would
love my wife or son though they hate me. So my patriotism is
for me a stage in my journey to the land of eternal freedom
and peace. Thus it will be seen that for me there are no
politics devoid of religion. They subserve religion. Politics
bereft of religion are a death-trap because they kill the soul.

'My Mission'
Young India, 3 Apr. 1924

1 Translation of *Hind Swaraj*.
2 John 19: 30.

4. ONE STEP ENOUGH FOR ME

[21 December 1925]

Ten years have passed since I left South Africa. I have received hundreds of letters, and have replied to them. I have
explained this matter a hundred times over in *Young India* and
in *Navajivan*, and yet, when I come to the Wardha Ashram I
am being asked the very same questions. This has revived old
memories for me and distressed me very much. I do not say
that such questions should not occur to anyone, but, if they
do, people may approach Vinoba and have their doubts
answered. However, the reason for my being distressed was
that it has become a widespread disease to ask such questions.
We should resist the temptation to ask them. Please understand my words properly. What I wish to say is that such
questions may certainly occur to us, but, they should be kept
back in one's mind.

When, thousands of years ago, the battle of Kurukshetra
was fought, the doubts which occurred to Arjuna were
answered by Shri Krishna in the *Gita*; but that battle of Kurukshetra is going on, will go on, for ever within us, the Prince
of Yogis, Lord Krishna, the universal *atman* dwelling in the
hearts of us all, will always be there to guide Arjuna, the

human soul, and our Godward impulses represented by the
Pandavas will always triumph over the demoniac impulses
represented by the Kauravas. Till, however, that victory is
won, we should have faith and let the battle go on, and be
patient meanwhile. This does not mean that we should suppress our inner urge for fear of anyone; it means that if such
an urge takes the form of the question 'Who created God?',
we should curb it, tell ourselves that it is impious to ask such
a question and have faith that the question will answer itself
by and by.

This physical frame which God has given us is a prison, but
it is also the door leading to deliverance and, if we wish that
it should serve only that purpose, we should understand its
limitations. We may well desire to clutch the stars in the
heavens, but we should note that it is beyond our power to do
so; for our soul is imprisoned in a cage, its wings, therefore,
have been clipped and it cannot fly as high as it would. It can
secure a great many occult powers, but it will fail in its aim
of winning deliverance if it goes after such powers. Hence, the
kind of abstract questions which were put to me the other day
should be avoided—in the conviction that in the course of
time the soul will become strong enough and know the
answers to them.

Instead of discussing such abstract questions, we should follow the advice of the poet: 'Let us spend today to some purpose, for who knows what tomorrow will bring?' This line may
seem to come from the pen of Charvak, who also says: 'Live
in ease while you live, drink ghee even if you have to borrow
money for it, for the body will never return to life after it is
cremated.' But the line is not by Charvak. Its author was a
devotee and, when he advised us to spend today profitably,
he meant that we should discharge the duty which lies before
us today. We do not know if we shall be alive tomorrow,
though a little later he says that we shall be born again. This
duty is what was explained by Vinoba the other day, 'ending
the misery of all creatures that suffer', destroying the chain of
ever-recurring birth and death. The only means for this is
bhakti. An Englishman named Newman, a great devotee,
wrote in a poem of his 'One step enough for me.'

This half line is the quintessence of all philosophy. That one step means patient, unswerving *bhakti*. If a sick person gets up and tries to walk down a staircase, he would feel giddy and fall. If we do not understand our limitations and try to get knowledge which is beyond us, we would not only not be able to digest it but would be sick with surfeit.

We should, therefore, cure ourselves of the disease of asking abstract questions, should attend to the immediate duty before us today and leave these questions for some other day. The couplet from a *bhajan* which was sung here today teaches us the very same thing, that instead of talking about *mukti* all the time we should spend our time in *bhakti*. Without *bhakti* there can be no deliverance. Only he, therefore, wins deliverance who is devoted to duty and fills his heart with love of God— he alone wins deliverance who never thinks about it.

Bhakti, moreover, does not imply ineptitude in practical affairs. That which produces such ineptitude cannot be called *bhakti*. It may, of course, be that, looking at the way we conduct our affairs, people will think of us as simpletons. A true devotee, though fully attentive to practical affairs, brings the spirit of *bhakti* into them. His conduct will always be in harmony with *dharma*. It is because Krishna acted in this manner that he is looked upon as the *Purnavatara*. A devotee finds no difficulty in attending to the practical affairs of life.

Ashrams like this one are established so that such a way of life in complete harmony with *dharma* may prevail everywhere. I have, therefore, always cherished the hope that these Ashrams will serve as instruments for raising the country and teaching and spreading true *dharma*. I do not worry whether that hope will be fulfilled in the present or after many generations—it is sufficient for us that we go on doing our duty along the path we have chalked out for ourselves. For this, we should strive to cultivate the qualities of both a *Brahmin*— truth and faith—and a *Kshatriya*—strength and non-violence. It is my faith that this Ashram will help its inmates to cultivate both these types of qualities. I do not suggest, of course, that other Ashrams cannot do that. I believe that this Ashram, at any rate, will do some good.

If we realize that truth and non-violence have a particular value for us and practise them in our lives, if we have the faith that there is no principle in this world which admits of an exception, we shall in the course of time understand the meaning of perfect truth and perfect non-violence. The peace which I have enjoyed here during the past ten days on observing that the inmates of the Ashram perform their duty in the spirit I have explained, I have enjoyed nowhere else, and you can very well imagine what my feelings must be now that I shall have to leave this peaceful atmosphere and go back to a world full of turmoil. But, as I told a friend, our study of the *Gita* would have been to no purpose if we get frightened of the turmoil in the world; we should get our peace not from the external environment, but from within us, and so I do not worry.

Speech at Wardha Ashram (G.)
Navajivan, 27 Dec. 1925

5. MEETING KINDRED SPIRITS

It is not without deep sorrow that I am now able to announce that the much-talked-of visit of mine to Europe is not to come off this year at any rate. To those in Austria, Holland, England, Scotland, Denmark, Sweden, Germany and Russia who had sent me kind invitations I can only say that their disappointment will be no greater than mine.

Somehow or other I dread a visit to Europe and America. Not that I distrust the peoples of these great Continents any more than I distrust my own, but I distrust myself. I have no desire to go to the West in search of health or for sightseeing. I have no desire to deliver public speeches. I detest being lionized. I wonder if I shall ever again have the health to stand the awful strain of public speaking and public demonstrations. If God ever sent me to the West, I should go there to penetrate the hearts of the masses, to have quiet talks with the youth of the West and have the privilege of meeting kindred spirits—lovers of peace at any price save that of Truth.

But I feel that I have as yet no message to deliver personally to the West. I believe my message to be universal but as yet I feel that I can best deliver it through my work in my own country. If I can show visible success in India, the delivery of the message becomes complete. If I came to the conclusion that India had no use for my message, I should not care to go elsewhere in search of listeners even though I still retained faith in it. If, therefore, I ventured out of India, I should do so because I have faith, though I cannot demonstrate it to the satisfaction of all, that the message is being surely received by India be it ever so slowly.

Thus whilst I was hesitatingly carrying on the correspondence with friends who had invited me, I saw that there was need for me to go to Europe, if only to see M. Romain Rolland. Owing to my distrust of myself over a general visit, I wanted to make my visit to that wise man of the West the primary cause of my journey to Europe. I therefore referred my difficulty to him and asked him in the frankest manner possible whether he would let me make my desire to meet him the primary cause of my visit to Europe. In reply I have a noble letter from him through Mirabai[1] wherein he says that in the name of truth itself, he will not think of letting me go to Europe if a visit to him is to be the primary cause. He will not let me interrupt my labours here for the sake of our meeting. I read in his letter no false humility. I read in it a most genuine expression of truth. He knew when he wrote his reply that my desire to go to Europe to meet him was not for a mere courteous discussion but in the interest of the cause as dear to him as to me. But evidently he was too humble to bear the burden of calling me merely so that in furtherance of the common interest we might by mutual talks understand each other better. And I wanted him to shoulder that very burden, if he felt that truth required us to meet each other face to face. His reply therefore I have taken as a clear answer to my prayer. Apart from this visit, I felt within me no imperative call.

I have taken the public into my confidence as, against my wish, the fact that a visit to Europe during this season was under serious contemplation was published in the papers. I regret my decision but it seems to be the correct one. For whilst there is no urge within to go to Europe, there is an incessant call within for so much to do here. And now the death of my best comrade seems to keep me rooted to the Ashram.

But I may say to the many friends in Europe, that next year, if all is well and if they still will have me I shall try to undertake the postponed tour, under the strict limitations mentioned by me and this I shall do whether I am ready to deliver my message or not. To see my numerous friends face to face will be no small privilege. But let me conclude this personal explanation by saying that if ever I am privileged to visit the West, I shall go there without changing my dress or habits, save in so far as the climate may require a change and self-imposed restrictions may permit. My outward form is I hope an expression of the inward.

'To European Friends'
Young India, 26 Apr. 1928

 ¹ Miss Madeleine Slade (1892–1982).

6. NO MIRACULOUS POWERS

Satyagraha Ashram, Sabarmati,
July 13, 1928

Dear Friend,

I have your letter. I don't know how the story about miraculous powers possessed by me has got abroad. I can only tell you that I am but an ordinary mortal susceptible to the same weakness, influences and the rest as every other human being and that I possess no extraordinary powers.

Yours sincerely,

Miss Barbara Bauer
Big Spring, Texas, U.S.A.

Letter to Barbara Bauer
SN 14349

7. THE CALL TO LEAD

[1 November 1928]

I could still lead India. I shall only lead India when the nation comes to me to be led, when there is a national call.

I shall not go before then. I shall not go unless I am certain of my power over the masses. I could not lead India again until I realized that they are numerous enough to pursue a policy of non-violence, nor until I could control them. But I see nothing on the horizon at the moment. That would not make me at all anxious to take that position. Perhaps it will not be in my lifetime. It may be in the time of my successor.

I cannot name one at this moment. There must be one who could lead India today but I cannot name him. Truly I should be ashamed to remain inactive but it may be necessary in my lifetime. It may be there will come a man, but not now.

Interview with *Civil and Military Gazette*
Hindustan Times, 3 Nov. 1928

8. OUT OF MY ASHES

[Faizpur,
26 December 1936]

What new message can I give you at the age of 68? And where is the use of my giving you a message if you pass a resolution there of assassinating me or burning my effigy? Assassinating the body of course does not matter, for out of my ashes a thousand Gandhis will arise. But what if you assassinate or burn the principles I have lived for?

'Message to Students'
Harijan, 16 Jan. 1937

9. WORDS AND MEANINGS

Mahabaleshwar,
May 31, 1945

Chi. Kishorelal,

You work wonders. I have gone through your Preface or whatever you call it. It is all right. However, I do not intend to write in that way. I will not involve myself and my readers in the controversy. I will try to give the key for reading my writings. You have written on the basis of my writings, so it would perhaps be better if it is published as it is, under your name. I would, however, know about it only after I finish writing.

I understand about *paricharya*. It is like this. I have already written—haven't I?—that words like men need growth. As knowledge grows, the meaning of a word becomes wider, which it should. Why should we stick to the meanings of the critics? Even then, what you say seems correct from the point of view of language. The pity is that I am not a linguist and therefore whatever occurred to me on the spur of the moment, I wrote down. Enough, as it is time to go for a walk.

Blessings from
BAPU

Letter to Kishorelal G. Mashruwala (G.)
Pyarelal Papers

10. MY LIFE IS MY MESSAGE

[Mahabaleshwar,
On or before 30 May 1945]

Q. Gandhiji, is there any special message you would care to send to the Negro people of America?

A. My life is its own message. If it is not, then nothing I can now write will fulfil the purpose.

When asked to comment on the probable trend of the race relations, Mr. Gandhi said:

My faith burns brighter today, even brighter than it has in the past; we are fast approaching a solution to troublesome race problems.

This he feels will be accomplished in spite of present-day discouraging symptoms. And he still feels that the best weapon for use by under-privileged peoples is non-violence.

Pointing to his recent statement made at the beginning of the San Francisco Conference, he indicated that India's freedom was closely identified with the welfare of all other under-privileged peoples. At that time he had said: 'The freedom of India will demonstrate to all exploited races of the earth that their freedom is very near and that in no case will they be exploited.'

Interview with Denton J. Brooks[1]
The Hindu, 15 June 1945

[1] Far Eastern correspondent of *Chicago Defender*, in which the interview appeared on 10 June 1945. Brooks reported: ' ... in the exclusive interview given to me last week ... Gandhiji was observing silence, with the exception of an hour after evening prayers .... I asked questions and he hurriedly jotted down his answers.'

11. ACTION IS MY DOMAIN

A friend suggests that I should resume writing my autobiography from the point where I left off and, further, that I should write a treatise on the science of *ahimsa*.

I never really wrote an autobiography. What I did write was a series of articles narrating my experiments with truth which were later published in book form. More than twenty years have elapsed since then. What I have done or pondered during this interval has not been recorded in chronological order. I would love to do so but have I the leisure? I have resumed the publication of *Harijan* in the present trying times as a matter of duty. It is with difficulty that I can cope with this work. How can I find time to bring the remainder of my experiments with truth up to date? But if it is God's will that I should write them, He will surely make my way clear.

To write a treatise on the science of *ahimsa* is beyond my powers. I am not built for academic writings. Action is my domain, and what I understand, according to my lights, to be my duty, and what comes my way, I do. All my action is actuated by the spirit of service. Let anyone who can systematize *ahimsa* into a science do so, if indeed it lends itself to such treatment. In the event of my inability, the correspondent has suggested three names in order of preference for this task: Shri Vinoba, Shri Kishorelal Mashruwala, Shri Kaka Kalelkar. The first named could do it, but I know he will not. Every hour of his is scheduled for his work and he would regard it as sacrilege to take a single moment therefrom for writing a *shastra*. I would agree with him. The world does not hunger for *shastras*. What it craves, and will always crave, is sincere action. He who can appease this hunger will not occupy his time in elaborating a *shastra*.

Shri Kishorelal has already written an independent treatise. If his health permits, I know he would like to write further. It may not be correct to call his work a *shastra*, but it may be said to be very near to one. In his present state of health, however, I do not think he can shoulder the burden, and I would be the last person to lay it on him. Like Shri Vinoba he too does not allow a moment of his time to be wasted. Much of it is given to help solve the personal problems of large circle of friends. The end of the day leaves him utterly exhausted.

Shri Kakasaheb, like Shri Thakkar, is an incorrigible nomad. Just now he has made the propagation and development of the national and provincial languages his special concern. Even if he wanted to divert a moment of his time to the writing of a *shastra*, I would try to prevent him from doing so.

From the above it may be concluded that there is no need at present for the treatise in question. Any such during my lifetime would necessarily be incomplete. If at all, it could only be written after my death. And even so let me give the warning that it would fail to give a complete exposition of *ahimsa*. No man has ever been able to describe God fully. The same holds true of *ahimsa*. I can give no guarantee that I will do or believe tomorrow what I do or hold to be true today. God alone is omniscient. Man in the flesh is essentially imperfect. He may be described as being made in the image of God, but he is far from being God. God is invisible, beyond the reach of the human eye. All that we can do, therefore, is to try to understand the words and actions of those whom we regard as men of God. Let them soak into our being and let us endeavour to translate them into action, but only so far as they appeal to the heart. Could any scientific treatise do more for us?

'Two Requests' (G.)
Harijan, 3 Mar. 1946

12. POTENCY OF THOUGHT

New Delhi,
[On or before 28 October 1946][1]

I do not know what I shall be able to do there. All I know is that I won't be at peace with myself unless I go there.

There are two kinds of thoughts—idle and active. There may be myriads of the former swarming in one's brain. They do not count. But one pure, active thought proceeding from the depth and endowed with all the undivided intensity of one's being, becomes dynamic and works like a fertilized ovum.

Talk with a Friend
Harijan, 10 Nov. 1946

[1] According to Pyarelai, Gandhi was having an argument with a very esteemed friend who tried to dissuade him from setting out on such a long journey just then. Gandhi did leave Delhi on 28 Oct. 1946. He undertook a four-month pilgrimage on foot in East Bengal to quell riots which had broken out there.

13. THE VALUE OF CRITICS

New Delhi,
October 20, 1947

Perhaps you don't know that I greatly value people who abuse me. Thereby their anger is spent and their hearts are cleansed. I like such critics a thousand times better than those who worship me, applaud me, but at the same time commit murders and disregard what I say. For those who abuse me are candid and if I can convince them they work wonders. In my life I have often had such experience.

Note to Manu Gandhi (G.)[1]
Dilhiman Gandhiji, Vol. I, pp. 124-5

[1] The addressee wanted to know why Gandhiji should care to reply to a man who only heaped abuses on him.

14. THOUGHT AS ACTION

New Delhi,
October 16, 1947

A correspondent writes:

In your article 'My Duty' you say that you have not reached that
state. The sentence looks simple enough but I would like you to
expand the meaning a little.

There is a stage in life when a man does not need even to
proclaim his thoughts, much less to show them by outward
action. Mere thoughts act. They attain that power. Then it
can be said of him that his seeming inaction constitutes his
action. I must confess that I am far from that state. All I can
say is that my striving is in that direction.

'Action in Inaction'
Harijan, 26 Oct. 1947

15. SAINT OR POLITICIAN?

A kind friend has sent me the following cutting from the April
number of *East and West*:

Mr. Gandhi has the reputation of a saint but it seems that the
politician in him often dominates his decisions. He has been making
great use of *hartals* and there can be no gainsaying that under his
direction *hartal* is becoming a powerful political weapon for uniting
the educated and the uneducated on a single question of the day.
The *hartal* is not without its disadvantages. It is teaching direct
action, and direct action, however potent, does not work for unity.
Is Mr. Gandhi quite sure that he is serving the highest behests of
ahimsa, harmlessness? His proposal to commemorate the shooting at
Jallianwala Bagh is not likely to promote concord. It is a tragic
incident into which our Government was betrayed, but is the
memory of its bitterness worth retaining? Can we not commemorate

the event by raising a temple of peace, to help the widows and orphans to bless the souls of those who died without knowing why? The world is full of politicians and pettifoggers who, in the name of patriotism, poison the inner sweetness of man and, as a result, we have wars and feuds and such shameless slaughter as turned Jallian-wala Bagh into a shambles. Shall we not now try for a larger sym-biosis such as Buddha and Christ preached, and bring the world to breathe and prosper together? Mr. Gandhi seemed destined to be the apostle of such a movement, but circumstances are forcing him to seek the way of raising resistances and group unities. He may yet take up the larger mission of uniting the world.

I have given the whole of the quotation. As a rule I do not notice criticism of me or my methods except when thereby I acknowledge a mistake or enforce still further the principles criticized. I have a double reason for noticing the extract. For, not only do I hope further to elucidate the principles I hold dear, but I want to show my regard for the author of the criticism whom I know and whom I have admired for many years for the singular beauty of his character. The critic regrets to see in me a politician, whereas he expected me to be a saint. Now I think that the word 'saint' should be ruled out of present life. It is too sacred a word to be lightly applied to anybody, much less to one like myself who claims only to be a humble searcher after truth, knows his limitations, makes mistakes, never hesitates to admit them when he makes them, and frankly confesses that he, like a scientist, is making ex-periments about some of 'the eternal verities' of life, but can-not even claim to be a scientist because he can show no tan-gible proof of scientific accuracy in his methods or such tangible results of his experiments as modern science demands. But though by disclaiming sainthood I disappoint the critic's expectations, I would have him to give up his regrets by answering him that the politician in me has never dominated a single decision of mine, and if I seem to take part in politics, it is only because politics encircle us today like the coil of a snake from which one cannot get out, no matter how much one tries. I wish therefore to wrestle with the snake, as I have been doing, with more or less success, consciously since 1894, unconsciously, as I have now discovered, ever since reaching the years of discretion.

Quite selfishly, as I wish to live in peace in the midst of a bellowing storm howling round me, I have been experimenting with myself and my friends by introducing religion into politics. Let me explain what I mean by religion. It is not the Hindu religion, which I certainly prize above all other religions, but the religion which transcends Hinduism, which changes one's very nature, which binds one indissolubly to the truth within and which ever purifies. It is the permanent element in human nature which counts no cost too great in order to find full expression and which leaves the soul utterly restless until it has found itself, known its Maker and appreciated the true correspondence between the Maker and itself.

It was in that religious spirit that I came upon *hartal*. I wanted to show that it is not a knowledge of letters that would give India consciousness of herself, or that would bind the educated together. The *hartal* illuminated the whole of India as if by magic on the 6th of April, 1919. And had it not been for the interruption of the 10th of April, brought about by Satan whispering fear into the ears of a Government conscious of its own wrong and inciting to anger a people that were prepared for it by utter distrust of the Government, India would have risen to an unimaginable height. The *hartal* had not only been taken up by the great masses of people in a truly religious spirit but it was intended to be a prelude to a series of direct actions.

But my critic deplores direct action. For, he says, 'it does not work for unity.' I join issue with him. Never has anything been done on this earth without direct action. I rejected the word 'passive resistance', because of its insufficiency and its being interpreted as a weapon of the weak. It was direct action in South Africa which told and told so effectively that it converted General Smuts to sanity. He was in 1906 the most relentless opponent of Indian aspirations. In 1914 he took pride in doing tardy justice by removing from the statute-book of the Union a disgraceful measure which in 1909 he had told Lord Morley would be never removed, for he then said South Africa would never tolerate repeal of a measure which was twice passed by the Transvaal Legislature. But what is more, direct action sustained for eight years left behind it not only no bitterness, but the very Indians who put up such a stubborn fight against General Smuts, ranged themselves round his banner in 1915 and fought under him in East Africa. It was direct action in Champaran which removed an age-long grievance.

A meek submission when one is chafing under a disability or a grievance which one would gladly see removed, not only does not make for unity, but makes the weak party acid, angry and prepares him for an opportunity to explode. By allying myself with the weak party, by teaching him direct, firm, but harmless action, I make him feel strong and capable of defying the physical might. He feels braced for the struggle, regains confidence in himself and knowing that the remedy lies with himself, ceases to harbour the spirit of revenge and learns to be satisfied with a redress of the wrong he is seeking to remedy.

It is working along the same lines that I have ventured to suggest a memorial about Jallianwala Bagh. The writer in *East and West* has ascribed to me a proposal which has never once crossed my mind. He thinks that I want 'to commemorate the shooting at Jallianwala Bagh'. Nothing can be further from my thought than to perpetuate the memory of a black deed. I dare say that before we have come to our own we shall have a repetition of the tragedy and I will prepare the nation for it by treasuring the memory of the innocent dead. The widows and the orphans have been and are being helped, but we cannot 'bless the souls of those who died without knowing why', if we will not acquire the ground which has been hallowed by innocent blood and there erect a suitable memorial for them. It is not to serve, if I can help it, as a reminder of the foul deed but it shall serve as an encouragement to the nation that it is better to die helpless and unarmed and as victims rather than as tyrants. I would have the future generations remember that we who witnessed the innocent dying did not ungratefully refuse to cherish their memory. As Mrs. Jinnah truly remarked when she gave her mite to the fund, the memorial would at least give us an excuse for living. After all it will be the spirit in which the memorial is erected that will decide its character.

What was the 'larger symbiosis' that Buddha and Christ preached? Buddha fearlessly carried the war into the enemy's camp and brought down on its knees an arrogant priesthood. Christ drove out the money-changers from the temple of Jerusalem and drew down curses from Heaven upon the hypocrites and the Pharisees. Both were for intensely direct action. But even as Buddha and Christ chastised they showed unmistakable gentleness and love behind every act of theirs. They would not raise a finger against their enemies, but would gladly surrender themselves rather than the truth for which they lived. Buddha would have died resisting the priesthood, if the majesty of his love had not proved to be equal to the task of bending the priesthood. Christ died on the Cross with a crown of thorns on his head defying the might of a whole Empire. And if I raise resistances of a non-violent character I simply and humbly follow in the footsteps of the great teachers named by my critic.

Lastly, the writer of the paragraph quarrels with my 'grouping unities' and would have me take up 'the larger mission of uniting the world'. I once told him under a common roof that I was probably more cosmopolitan than he. I abide by that expression. Unless I group unities I shall never be able to unite the whole world. Tolstoy once said that if we would but get off the backs of our neighbours the world would be quite all right without any further help from us. And if we can only serve our immediate neighbours by ceasing to prey upon them, the circle of unities thus grouped in the right fashion will ever grow in circumference till at last it is co-terminus with that of the whole world. More than that it is not given to any man to try or achieve. *Yatha pinde, tatha brahmande*[1] is as true today as ages ago when it was first uttered by an unknown *rishi*.

'Neither a Saint nor a Politician'
Young India, 12 May 1920

---

[1] 'As with the body, so with the universe.'

16. IDENTIFICATION WITH LABOUR

[8 August 1925]

I have great pleasure in being able to visit these great steel works. I have been thinking of coming to this place ever since 1917, the year in which I was trying to serve the Champaran agriculturists. It was then that Sir Edward Gait told me that I ought not to leave Bihar without having seen these works. But man proposes and God disposes and with me God had disposed otherwise. I made many attempts to see this place.

As you know I am a labourer myself, I pride myself on calling myself a scavenger, weaver, spinner, farmer and what not, and I do not feel ashamed that some of these things I know but indifferently. It is a pleasure to me to identify myself with the labouring classes, because without labour we can do nothing. There is a great Latin saying of which the meaning is 'to labour is to pray', and one of the finest writers of Europe has said that a man is not entitled to eat unless he labours, and by labour he does not mean labour with the intellect, but labour with the hands. The same thought runs throughout Hindu religion. 'He who eats without labour eats sin, is verily a thief.' This is the literal meaning of a verse in *Bhagavad Gita*. I therefore pride myself on the fact that I can identify myself with labour throughout the world.

It was my ambition to see one of the greatest—if not the greatest—Indian enterprises in India, and study the conditions of work there. But none of my activities is one-sided, and as my religion begins and ends with truth and non-violence, my identification with labour does not conflict with my friendship with capital. And believe me, throughout my public service of 35 years, though I have been obliged to range myself seemingly against capital, capitalists have in the end regarded me as their true friend. And in all humility I may say that I have come here also as a friend of the capitalists—a friend of the Tatas. And here it would be ungrateful on my part if I do not give you a little anecdote about how my connection with the Tatas began.

In South Africa, when I was struggling along with the
Indians there in the attempt to retain our self-respect and to
vindicate our status, it was the late Sir Ratan Tata who first
came forward with assistance. He wrote me a great letter and
sent a princely donation,—a cheque for Rs. 25,000 and a
promise in the letter to send more, if necessary. Ever since I
have a vivid recollection of my relations with the Tatas and
you can well imagine how pleasurable it has been for me to
be with you, and you will believe me when I say that, when
I part company with you tomorrow, I shall do so with a heavy
heart, because I shall have to go away without having seen so
many things, for it would be presumption on my part to say
at the end of two days that I had really studied things here.
I know well enough the magnitude of the task before one who
wants to study this great enterprise.

I wish to this great Indian firm all the prosperity that it
deserves and to this great enterprise every success. And may
I hope that the relations between this great house and
labourers who work here under their care will be of the friendliest character? At Ahmedabad I have had much to do with
the capitalists and workmen, and I have always said that my
ideal is that capital and labour should supplement and help
each other. They should be a great family living in unity
and harmony, capital not only looking to the material welfare
of the labourers but their moral welfare also,—capitalists
being trustees for the welfare of the labouring classes under
them.

I am told that though so many Europeans and Indians live
here, their relations are of a happy character. I hope the
information is literally true. It is the privilege of both of you
to be associated in this great enterprise and it is possible for
you to give India an object-lesson in amity and goodwill. You
will, I hope, have best relations with one another not only
under the roofs of the huge workshops you work in, but you
will also carry your amity outside your workshops and both
of you will realize that you have come to live and work here
as brothers and sisters, never regarding another as inferior, or
oneself as inferior. And if you succeed in doing that you will
have a miniature *swaraj*.

I have said that I am a non-co-operator, I call myself a

civil resister—and both words have come to possess a bad odour in the English language like so many other English words—but I non-co-operate in order that I may be able to co-operate. I cannot satisfy myself with false co-operation—anything inferior to 24 carats gold. My non-co-operation does not prevent me from being friendly even to Sir Michael O'Dwyer and General Dyer. It harms no one, it is non-co-operation with evil, with an evil system and not with the evil-doer.

My religion teaches me to love even an evil-doer, and my non-co-operation is but part of that religion. I am saying these things not to soothe the ears of any one—I have in my life never been guilty of saying things I did not mean—my nature is to go straight to the heart, and if often I fail in doing so for the time being, I know that truth will ultimately make itself heard and felt, as it has often done in my experience. The wish, therefore, that the relations between you should be of the friendliest character is a desire from the bottom of my heart. And it is my deep prayer that you may help in delivering India from evil and bondage and help her to give the message of peace to the outside world. For this meeting of Indians and Europeans in India must have or can be made to have a special meaning, and what can be better than that we two may live together so as to spread peace and goodwill on earth? May God grant that, in serving the Tatas, you will also serve India and will always realize that you are here for a much higher mission than merely working for an industrial enterprise.

Speech at Indian Association, Jamshedpur
Amrita Bazar Patrika, 14 Aug. 1925
Young India, 20 Aug. 1925

17. SERVICE OF HUMANITY

It is a privilege for me to enjoy the friendship of so many unknown American and European friends. It pleases me to note that the circle is ever widening, perhaps more especially in America. I had the pleasure of receiving a warm invitation about a year ago to visit that continent. The same invitation has now been repeated with redoubled strength and with the offer to pay all expenses. I was unable then as I am now, to respond to the kind invitation. To accept it is an easy enough task, but I must resist the temptation, for I feel that I can make no effective appeal to the people of that great continent unless I make my position good with the intellectuals of India.

I have not a shadow of doubt about the truth of my fundamental position. But I know that I am unable to carry with me the bulk of educated India. I can therefore gain no effective help for my country from the Americans and Europeans so long as I remain isolated from educated India. I do want to think in terms of the whole world. My patriotism includes the good of mankind in general. Therefore, my service of India includes the service of humanity. But I feel that I should be going out of my orbit if I left it for help from the West. I must be satisfied for the time being with such help as I can get from the West, speaking to it from my smaller Indian platform. If I go to America or to Europe, I must go in my strength, not in my weakness, which I feel today,—the weakness I mean, of my country. For the whole scheme for the liberation of India is based upon the development of internal strength. It is a plan of self-purification. The peoples of the West, therefore, can best help the Indian movement by setting apart specialists to study the inwardness of it.

Let the specialists come to India with an open mind and in a spirit of humility as befits a searcher after Truth. Then, perhaps, they will see the reality instead of a glorified edition that, in spite of all my desire to be absolutely truthful, I am likely to present if I went to America. I believe in thought-power more than in the power of the word, whether written or spoken. And if the movement that I seek to represent has vitality in it and has divine blessing upon it, it will permeate the whole world without my physical presence in its different parts. Anyway, at the present moment I see no light before me. I must patiently plod in India until I see my way clear for going outside the Indian border.

After pressing the invitation, the American friend puts a number of questions for my consideration. I welcome them and gladly take the opportunity of answering them through these columns. He says:

Whether you decide, now or later, to come here or not to come, I trust you will find the following questions worth considering. They have developed insistently in my mind for a long time.

His first question is:

Has the time arrived—or is it coming—when your best way to help India will be by moving the whole world—and especially England and America—to a new consciousness?

I have partly answered the question already. In my opinion the time has not yet arrived—it may come any day—for me to go out of India to move the whole world to a new consciousness. The process, however, is even now indirectly and unconsciously going on though slowly.

Are not the present-day interests of all mankind, everywhere, so inextricably interwoven that no single country, like India, can be moved far out of its present relationships to the others?

I do believe with the writer that no single country can remain in isolation for any length of time. The present plan for securing *swaraj* is not to attain a position of isolation but one of full self-realization and self-expression for the benefit of all. The present position of bondage and helplessness hurts not only India, not only England, but the whole world.

Is not your message and method essentially a world gospel—which will find its power in responsive souls, here and there, in many countries, who will thereby, gradually, remake the world?

If I can say so without arrogance and with due humility, my message and methods are indeed in their essentials for the whole world and it gives me keen satisfaction to know that it has already received a wonderful response in the hearts of a large and daily-growing number of men and women of the West.

If you demonstrate your message in the language only of the East and in terms only of Indian emergencies, is there not grave danger that inessentials will be confused with fundamentals—that some features which correspond only to extreme situations in India will be wrongly understood to be vital in the universal sense?

I am alive to the danger pointed out by the writer, but it seems to be inevitable. I am in the position of a scientist who is in the midst of a very incomplete experiment and who, therefore is unable to forecast large results and larger corollaries in a language capable of being understood. In the experimental stage, therefore, I must run the risk of the experiment being misunderstood as it has been, and probably still is, in many places.

Ought you not to come to America (which in spite of all her faults is perhaps, potentially, the most spiritual of all living peoples) and tell the world what your message means in terms of Western, as well as Eastern, civilization?

People in general will understand my message through its results. The shortest way, therefore, perhaps of making it effectively heard is to let it speak for itself, at any rate for the time being.

For example, should the Western followers of your inspiration preach and practise the spinning-wheel?

It is certainly not necessary for the Western people to preach and practise the spinning-wheel unless they will do so out of sympathy or for discipline or with a view to applying their matchless inventive faculty to making the spinning-wheel a better instrument while retaining its essential characteristic as a cottage industry. But the message of the spinning-wheel is much wider than its circumference. Its message is one of simplicity, service of mankind, living so as not to hurt others, creating an indissoluble bond between the rich and the poor, capital and labour, the prince and the peasant. That larger message is naturally for all.

Is your condemnation of railroads, doctors, hospitals and other features of modern civilization essential and unalterable? Should we not, first, try to develop a spirit great enough to spiritualize the machinery and the organized, scientific and productive powers of modern life?

My condemnation of railroads, etc., whilst true where it stands, has little or no bearing on the present movement which disregards none of the institutions mentioned by the writer. In the present movement, I am neither attacking railroads nor hospitals; but in an ideal State they seem to me to have little or no place. The present movement is just the attempt the writer desires. Yet it is not an attempt to spiritualize the machinery—because that seems to me an impossible task—but to introduce, if it is at all possible, a human or the humane spirit among the men behind the machinery. Organization of machinery for the purpose of concentrating wealth and power in the hands of a few and for the exploitation of many I hold to be altogether wrong. Much of the organization of machinery of the present age is of that type.

The movement of the spinning-wheel is an organized attempt to displace machinery from that state of exclusiveness and exploitation and to place it in its proper state. Under my scheme, therefore, men in charge of machinery will think not of themselves or even of the nation to which they belong but of the whole human race. Thus Lancashire men will cease to use their machinery for exploiting India and other countries but, on the contrary, they will devise means of enabling India to convert in her own villages her cotton into cloth. Nor will Americans under my scheme seek to enrich themselves by exploiting the other races of the earth through their inventive skill.

Is it not possible, in conditions so favourable as America's, to clarify and advance the evolution of the best human consciousness into such purpose and power, courage and beneficence, as shall liberate the souls of India's millions—and of all men everywhere?

It is undoubtedly possible. Indeed, it is my hope that America will seek the evolution of the best human consciousness; but that time is perhaps not yet. Probably it will not be before India has found her own soul. Nothing will please me more than to find America and Europe making the difficult path of India as easy as it is possible for them to do. They can do so by withdrawing the temptations in India's way and by encouraging her in her attempt to revive her ancient industries in her own villages.

Why is it that people like myself, in every country, are grateful to you and eager to follow you? Is it not for two reasons chiefly: first; Because the next [*sic*] and basic need throughout the world is for a new spiritual consciousness—a realization, in the thought and feeling of average people, of the equal divinity of all human beings and the unity, brotherhood, of all; second, because you, more than any other widely known man, have this consciousness—together with the power to arouse it in others?

I can only hope that the writer's estimate is true.

It is a world need—is it not?—to which you have the best answer that God has vouchsafed to man? How can your mission be fulfilled in India alone? If my arm or leg could be vitalized to an extent far beyond the balance of my body, would that make for my general health—or even for the permanent best good of the one favoured member?

I am fully aware that my mission cannot be fulfilled in India alone, but I hope I am humble enough to recognize my limitations and to see that I must keep for the time being, to my restricted Indian platform till I know the result of the experiment in India itself. As I have already replied, I would like to see India free and strong so that she may offer herself as a willing and pure sacrifice for the betterment of the world. The individual, being pure, sacrifices himself for the family, the latter for the village, the village for the district, the district for the province, the province for the nation, the nation for all.

May I even submit,—with deep reverence for your message—that possibly your own vision and inspiration would benefit by adjustment to the world instead of only, or chiefly, to India?

I recognize the considerable force of the foregoing statement. It is not at all impossible that a visit to the West may give me not a wider outlook—for I have endeavoured to show that it is the widest possible but it may enable me to discover new methods of realizing the outlook. If such is my need, God will open the way for me.

Is the political form of government, in India or anywhere, so important as the average individual's soul-force—his courageous expression of the best inspiration he can derive from the divine spirit within and all about him?

The average individual's soul-force is any day the most important thing. The political form is but a concrete expression of that soul-force. I do not conceive the average individual's soul-force as distinguished and existing apart from the political form of government. Hence I believe that after all a people has the government which it deserves. In other words self-government can only come through self-effort.

Is not the basic need, everywhere, for the clarification and development of this soul-force in individuals—beginning, possibly, with a few people and spreading like a divine contagion to the many?

It is, indeed.

You teach, rightly, that the faithful development of such soul-force in India will assure India's freedom. Will it not everywhere shape all political, economic and international institutions including the issues of Peace or War? Can those forms of human civilization be made radically superior in India to the rest of the world—now, when all mankind are neighbours?

I have already answered this question in the preceding paragraphs. I have claimed in these pages before now that India's freedom must revolutionize the world's outlook upon Peace and War. Her impotence affects the whole of mankind.

You know, better than I or anyone, how all these questions should be answered. I chiefly seek to express my eager faith in your gospel, my hungry desire for your leadership in solving the urgent problems of America and of all mankind. Therefore, will you graciously remember that, if (or when) the time may come that India's progress in the directions you have so inspiringly outlined appears to pause— waiting for the Western world to come up alongside—then we of the West stand urging you to give us a few months of your time and your personal presence. My own feeling is that if you will call us and instruct us, we (your uncounted followers scattered obscurely over the wide earth) will join our lives to yours in the discovery and realization of a new and noble, worldwide Commonwealth of the Spirit in which man's age-old dreams of brotherhood, democracy, peace and soul progress shall characterize the daily life of average people—in India, England, America and everywhere.

I wish I had confidence in my leadership on the world platform. I have no false modesty about me. If I felt the call within, I would not wait a single second but straightway respond to an invitation so cordial as this. But with my limitations of which I am painfully conscious, I feel somehow that my experiment must be restricted to a fragment. What may be true of the fragment is likely to be true of the whole. It is true indeed that India's progress in the direction I desire seems to have come to a pause but I think that it only seems so. The little seed that was sown in 1920 has not perished. It is, I think, taking deep root. Presently it will come out as a stately tree. But if I am labouring under a delusion, I fear that no artificial stimulus that my visit to America may temporarily bring can revive it. I am pining for the assistance of the whole world. I see it coming. The urgent invitation is one of the many signs. But I know that we shall have to deserve it before it comes upon us like a mighty flood, a flood that cleanses and invigorates.

'To American Friends'
Young India, 17 Sept. 1925

18. BROTHERHOOD OF MAN

[9 March 1929]

Mr. Chairman and Friends, I propose to speak to a certain length in Hindustani and as your address is worded in English, I propose to make a brief reply first in English and then say

my say in Hindustani. I thank you for this warmth of reception and the kindly sentiments expressed in your address. I
am not able just now to appropriate, much less to assimilate,
all the compliments that you have paid me. But I could certainly claim two things of which you have made kind mention.
The first thing is that my mission is not merely brotherhood
of Indian humanity. My mission is not merely freedom of
India, though today it undoubtedly engrosses practically the
whole of my life and the whole of my time. But through
realization of freedom of India I hope to realize and carry on
the mission of brotherhood of man. My patriotism is not an
exclusive thing. It is all-embracing and I should reject that
patriotism which sought to mount upon the distress or the
exploitation of other nationalities. The conception of my patriotism is nothing if it is not always in every case, without
exception, consistent with the broadest good of humanity at
large. Not only that but my religion and my patriotism derived from my religion embrace all life.

I want to realize brotherhood or identity not merely with
the beings called human, but I want to realize identity with
all life, even with such beings as crawl on earth. I want, if I
don't give you a shock, to realize identity with even the crawling things upon earth, because we claim common descent from
the same God, and that being so, all life in whatever form it
appears must be essentially one. I can therefore safely claim
all the credit that you may choose to give me in describing
my mission of brotherhood of man. As a necessary corollary
you may naturally mention, as you have kindly mentioned,
untouchability. I have said times without number that untouchability is a serious blot on Hinduism and, I think, in the
long run, in the race for life in which all the religions of the
world are today engaged, either Hinduism has got to perish
or untouchability has to be rooted out completely, so that the
fundamental principle of Advaita Hinduism may be realized
in practical life. Beyond these two things among those that
you have mentioned in your address I am unable today to
appropriate or assimilate anything. It will be time enough to
pronounce a verdict upon my work after my eyes are closed
and this tabernacle is consigned to the flames.

You have very kindly asked me to give the indigenous population of Burma some advice. I must own to you that I regard myself as altogether unfit for giving you any advice. My study of your great traditions is merely superficial. My study of your present-day problems is still more superficial, although I yield to none in my love and admiration for you to which I gave expression yesterday at two meetings. I wish I had all the facts before me. I wish that all the different parties in Burma could meet me and I could gain access to your hearts. My heart is there open to receive you, but it is for you to call and certainly that call will not be in vain. And if I find I have enough material before me to give you even provisional limited advice I should be at your disposal

Speech at Public Meeting, Rangoon
Amrita Bazar Patrika, 10 Mar. 1929
Young India, 4 Apr. 1929

19. UNIVERSAL MESSAGE

June 11, 1937

Dear Friend,

I thank you for your letter of the 20th May last. I have no message to give except this that there is no deliverance for any people on this earth or for all the people of this earth except through truth and non-violence in every walk of life without any exceptions. And this is based on an unbroken experience extending practically over half a century.

Yours sincerely,
M. K. GANDHI

Daniel Oliver, Esq.
Hammana
Lebanon, Syria

Letter to Daniel Oliver
Pyarelal Papers

20. ISMS AND FOLLOWERS

July 16, 1945

Chi. Shanta,

I got your letter yesterday. I am writing this after the morning prayer. Address your reply at Sevagram.

You have remained as crazy after becoming a communist and a mother as you were as a child.

Which Ashram has boycotted you? Where is the Ashram? Who has boycotted you? Many communists have stayed with me. In the same way you also can stay. You know that Jayanti had stayed with me.

You should know that I have received many complaints, but I have not acted on any of them. I am in correspondence with the Secretary. He had asked me for my permission to publish the letters and I have granted it. Whether he has published them or not I do not know.

The Working Committee has taken no step. There has been no time to consider the matter.

If Jawaharlalji goes against them, all the communists will have to sit up and think. For he has a soft corner for the Party but he will not tolerate anything unworthy. I myself have not been able to come to a final decision. I have received quite a few complaints. I have sent them to the Head Office.

You have written your letter without thinking. If you calm down and think before writing, you can help the communist cause.

You must learn to distinguish between communism and communists. Besides, Marx stands for one thing, Lenin for another and Stalin for a third. The followers of the last are again divided into two groups. Gandhi is one thing, Gandhism is another and Gandhi-ites are a third thing. There are always, and will remain, such differences. Immature people may identify themselves with one or the other group.

Blessings from
BAPU

Letter to Shanta Patel (G.)
CW 4287

21. PROPOUNDER OF NO ISM

Mussoorie,
June 7, 1946

Chi. Rameshwari,

I know Ratnamayidevi very well. I have no objection to your taking her in. I do not know myself who is a Gandhian. Gandhism is a meaningless word for me. An ism follows the propounder of a system. I am not one, hence I cannot be the cause for any ism. If an ism is built up it will not endure, and if it does it will not be Gandhism. This deserves to be properly understood.

I like your work, it is neat and clean. It is you who have built up the Balika Ashram, you conduct it and I would be pleased if Ratnamayidevi gave you full satisfaction.

Blessings from
BAPU

Letter to Rameshwari Nehru (H.)
CW 3110

III

Influences and Books Read

---

22. THE *VAISHNAVA* IDEAL

A true *Vaishnava* is he
　Who is moved by others' sufferings;
Who helps people in distress,
　And feels no pride for having done so.
Respectful to everyone in the world,
　He speaks ill of none;
Is self-controlled in action, speech and thought—
　Twice-blessed the mother who bore such a one.
He has an equal-seeing eye, and is free from all craving,
　Another's wife is to him a mother;
His tongue utters no untruth,
　And never his hand touches another's wealth.
Moha and *maya* have no power over him,
　In his mind reigns abiding detachment;
He dances with rapture to Rama's name—
　No centre of pilgrimage but is present in his person.
A man he is without greed and cunning,
　And purged of anger and desire;
Offering reverence to such a one, says Narasainyo,[1]
　Will bring release to seventy-one generations of one's forbears.[2]

From the marks of a *Vaishnava* described by Narasinh
Mehta we see that he is a man who
　1. is ever active in bringing relief to the distressed,
　2. takes no pride in doing so,
　3. is respectful to all,
　4. speaks ill of none,
　5. is self-controlled in speech,
　6. in action and
　7. in thought,

8. holds all in equal regard,
9. has renounced desires,
10. is loyal to one woman, his wife,
11. is ever truthful,
12. keeps the rule of non-stealing,
13. is beyond the reach of *maya*,
14. is, in consequence, free from all desire,
15. is ever absorbed in repeating Rama's name,
16. and, as a result, has been sanctified,
17. covets nothing,
18. is free from guile,
19. from the urge of desire and
20. from anger.

Here Narasinh, the best among the *Vaishnavas*, has given pride of place to non-violence. This means that a man who has no love in him is no *Vaishnava*. One who does not follow truth and has not acquired control over all his senses is not a *Vaishnava*. He teaches us in his *prabhatiyan* that one does not become a *Vaishnava* simply by studying the Vedas, by following the rules of *varnashram*, by wearing a string of basil seeds or the *tilak* mark. All these things can be the origin of sin. Even a hypocrite may wear a string of beads or put the *tilak* mark or study the Vedas or keep repeating Rama's name with his lips. But such a one cannot follow truth in his life, cannot, without giving up his hypocrisy, help people in distress or be self-controlled in speech, action and thought.

I invite everyone's attention to these principles, since I still continue to receive letters regarding *Antyajas*. The advice I receive from one and all is that, if I do not exclude *Antyajas* from the national schools, the movement for *swaraj* will end in smoke. If I have even a little of the true *Vaishnava* in me, God will also vouchsafe me the strength to reject the *swaraj* which may be won by abandoning the *Antyajas*.

The resolution, to the effect that the *Antyajas* cannot be excluded from any place which is open to members of other classes or communities, is not mine but that of the senate as a whole. I welcome the resolution. Had the senate not passed it, it would have been guilty of *adharma*.

The resolution lays down nothing new. One to the same effect is actually in operation in the existing schools. The

Congress, a body which the *Vaishnavas* respect, has also passed such a resolution. They have not opposed it. I realize, however, that they honour me by criticizing me for having a hand in a resolution of this kind. The point of their argument is that others may violate *dharma* but that I, especially, should not do so. This is very gratifying to me.

I have been endeavouring to show that *dharma* requires that we do not look upon *Antyajas* as untouchables. Old veils prevent us from seeing that we are guilty of *adharma* in acting to the contrary. Just as, through such veils, British rule cannot see its own Satanism, so also, thanks to them, some of us are unable to see the chains of slavery which bind us. I think it my duty to reason with such people patiently.

But I cannot stand hypocrisy and sophistry. I saw in *Gujarati* an account of a talk I had with Maharajshri,[3] as also the comments on it. I have been very much pained by both. I seldom comment on views expressed in newspapers. In fact I scarcely read papers. But the *Gujarati* is a widely read paper and it claims to present the *sanatan dharma* in its true nature. Hence I am pained whenever I find in it even the least element of unfairness. A friend has sent me a cutting giving the report of my talk with Maharajshri and the criticism on it. I see in both an attempt, deliberate or otherwise, to prove *adharma* to be *dharma*. I shall explain next time what this is.

'To *Vaishnavas*' (G.)
Navajivan, 5 Dec. 1920

[1] Narasinh Mehta (1414–79); saint-poet of Gujarat.
[2] This poem formed part of the daily prayers at the Ashram.
[3] Goswami Shri Gokulnathji Maharaj, religious head of the *Vaishnavas* in Bombay.

23. THEOSOPHY, RENUNCIATION, AND ATHEISM

Towards the end of my second year in England I came across two Theosophists, brothers, and both unmarried. They talked to me about the *Gita*. They were reading Sir Edwin Arnold's translation—*The Song Celestial*—and they invited me to read the original with them. I felt ashamed, as I had read the divine poem neither in Sanskrit nor in Gujarati. I was constrained to tell them that I had not read the *Gita*, but that I would gladly read it with them, and that though my knowledge of Sanskrit was meagre, still I hoped to be able to understand the original to the extent of telling where the translation failed to bring out the meaning. I began reading the *Gita* with them. The verses in the second chapter

> If one
> Ponders on objects of the sense, there springs
> Attraction; from attraction grows desire,
> Desire flames to fierce passion, passion breeds
> Recklessness; then the memory—all betrayed—
> Lets noble purpose go, and saps the mind,
> Till purpose, mind, and man are all undone.

made a deep impression on my mind, and they still ring in my ears. The book struck me as one of priceless worth. The impression has ever since been growing on me with the result that I regard it today as the book *par excellence* for the knowledge of Truth. It has afforded me invaluable help in my moments of gloom. I have read almost all the English translations of it, and I regard Sir Edwin Arnold's as the best. He has been faithful to the text, and yet it does not read like a translation. Though I read the *Gita* with these friends, I cannot pretend to have studied it then. It was only after some years that it became a book of daily reading.

The brothers also recommended *The Light of Asia* by Sir Edwin Arnold, whom I knew till then as the author only of *The Song Celestial*, and I read it with even greater interest than I did the *Bhagavad Gita*. Once I had begun it I could not leave off. They also took me on one occasion to the Blavatsky Lodge and introduced me to Madame Blavatsky and Mrs. Besant. The latter had just then joined the Theosophical Society, and I was following with great interest the controversy about her conversion. The friends advised me to join the Society, but I politely declined saying, 'With my meagre knowledge of my own religion I do not want to belong to any religious body.'

I recall having read, at the brothers' instance, Madame Bla-vatsky's *Key to Theosophy*. This book stimulated in me the desire to read books on Hinduism, and disabused me of the notion fostered by the missionaries that Hinduism was rife with superstition.

About the same time I met a good Christian from Man-chester in a vegetarian boarding house. He talked to me about Christianity. I narrated to him my Rajkot recollections. He was pained to hear them. He said, 'I am a vegetarian. I do not drink. Many Christians are meat-eaters and drink, no doubt; but neither meat-eating nor drinking is enjoined by Scripture. Do please read the Bible.' I accepted his advice, and he got me a copy. I have a faint recollection that he himself used to sell copies of the Bible, and I purchased from him an edition containing maps, concordance, and other aids. I began reading it, but I could not possibly read through the Old Testament. I read the book of Genesis, and the chapters that followed invariably sent me to sleep. But just for the sake of being able to say that I had read it, I plodded through the other books with much difficulty and without the least interest or understanding. I disliked reading the book of Numbers.

But the New Testament produced a different impression, especially the Sermon on the Mount which went straight to my heart. I compared it with the *Gita*. The verses, 'But I say unto you, that ye resist not evil: but whosoever shall smite thee on thy right cheek, turn to him the other also. And if any man take away thy coat let him have thy cloak too', delighted me beyond measure and put me in mind of Shamal Bhatt's 'For a bowl of water, give a goodly meal', etc. My young mind tried to unify the teaching of the *Gita*, *The Light of Asia* and the Sermon on the Mount. That renunciation was the highest form of religion appealed to me greatly.

This reading whetted my appetite for studying the lives of other religious teachers. A friend recommended Carlyle's *Heroes and Hero-worship*. I read the chapter on the Hero as a prophet and learnt of the Prophet's greatness and bravery and austere living.

Beyond this acquaintance with religion I could not go at the moment, as reading for the examination left me scarcely any time for outside subjects. But I took mental note of the fact that I should read more religious books and acquaint myself with all the principal religions.

And how could I help knowing something of atheism too? Every Indian knew Bradlaugh's name and his so-called atheism. I read some book about it, the name of which I forget. It had no effect on me, for I had already crossed the Sahara of atheism. Mrs. Besant who was then very much in the limelight, had turned to theism from atheism, and that fact also strengthened my aversion to atheism. I had read her book *How I Became a Theosophist.*

It was about this time that Bradlaugh died. He was buried in the Woking Cemetery. I attended the funeral, as I believe every Indian residing in London did. A few clergymen also were present to do him the last honours. On our way back from the funeral we had to wait at the station for our train. A champion atheist from the crowd heckled one of these clergymen. 'Well, Sir, you believe in the existence of God?'

'I do,' said the good man in a low tone.

'You also agree that the circumference of the Earth is 28,000 miles, don't you?' said the atheist with a smile of self-assurance.

'Indeed.'

'Pray tell me then the size of your God and where he may be?'

'Well, if we but knew, He resides in the hearts of us both.'

'Now, now, don't take me to be a child,' said the champion with a triumphant look at us.

The clergyman assumed a humble silence.

This talk still further increased my prejudice against atheism.

'Acquaintance With Religions', *The Story of My Experiments With Truth*, Ch. XX (G.)
Navajivan, 18 Apr. 1926

24. THE GOSPEL OF SERVICE

[23 October 1927]

In declaring the *Gita* class open Mahatmaji advised the students to get up at 4 o'clock in the morning and regularly read the *Bhagavad*

Gita daily. He was anxious that they should begin the study of the *Gita* in right earnest. If they could not read Sanskrit they could go in for a Tamil translation of the *Gita*, but not the English one, because the English rendering could not impart the true significance of the *Gita*. He said that the third chapter is an important one in the *Gita*.

The *Gita* contains the gospel of *karma* or work, the gospel of *bhakti* or devotion and the gospel of *jnana* or knowledge. Life should be a harmonious whole of these three. But the gospel of service is the basis of all, and what can be more necessary for those who want to serve the country than that they begin with the chapter enunciating the gospel of work? But you must approach it with the five necessary equipments, viz., *ahimsa* (non-violence), *satya* (truth), *brahmacharya* (celibacy), *aparigraha* (non-possession), and *asteya* (non-stealing). Then and then only will you be able to reach a correct interpretation of it. And then you will read it to discover in it *ahimsa* and not *himsa*, as so many nowadays try to do. Read it with the necessary equipment and I assure you you will have peace of which you were never aware before.

Speech to Students, Tiruppur
The Hindu, 25 Oct. 1927
Young India, 3 Nov. 1927

25. NON-ATTACHMENT

It is more than forty years since I have been reading, pondering and following the *Gita*. Friends expressed a desire that I should put before the Gujaratis my understanding of that work. I embarked on translating it. From the point of view of scholarship my qualifications for attempting the translation would seem to be nil, but as one following its teaching I may be considered to be fairly well qualified. The translation has now been published. Many editions of the *Gita* carry the Sanskrit text also. It has been intentionally left out in this one. I would like it if all knew Sanskrit, but all will never learn Sanskrit. Moreover, many cheap editions with Sanskrit are available. I, therefore, decided to leave out the Sanskrit text and reduce both the size and the price. This edition has 19 pages of introduction and 187 pages of translation so that it can be easily carried in one's pocket. Ten thousand copies have been printed.

My aspiration is that every Gujarati will read this *Gita*, ponder it and practise its teaching. An easy way to ponder it is to try and understand the meaning without referring to the Sanskrit text and then to conduct oneself accordingly. For example, those who interpret the teaching of the *Gita* to mean that one ought to kill the wicked without making a distinction between one's kinsmen and others, should kill their parents or other relatives if they are wicked. In practice, they will not be able to do so. Naturally, then, it would occur to the reader that where destruction is prescribed the work contemplates some other form of destruction.

Almost every page of the *Gita* advises us not to make a distinction between our own people and others. How is this to be done? Reflection will lead us to the conclusion that we should perform all our acts in a spirit of non-attachment. In the very first chapter we find Arjuna facing the troublesome question of one's own people and others. In every chapter the *Gita* brings out how such a distinction is false and harmful. I have called the *Gita* 'Anasaktiyoga'. The interested reader will be able to learn from the work what that is, how non-attachment is to be cultivated, what its characteristics are, etc. Trying as I do to live according to the teaching of the *Gita*, I could not avoid the present struggle. As a friend says in his telegram to me, this is a holy war for me. It is a happy augury for me that this book is being published just as the holy war is entering its last phase in the form of the present struggle.

Bhagavad Gita (Anasaktiyoga) (G.)
Navajivan, 16 Mar. 1930

26. READING THOREAU

Camp Hardoi,
October 12, 1929

Dear Friend,

I was agreeably surprised to receive your letter. Yes, indeed your book[1] which was the first English book I came across on vegetarianism was of immense help to me in steadying my faith in vegetarianism. My first introduction to Thoreau's writings was I think in 1907 or later when I was in the thick of passive resistance struggle. A friend sent me Thoreau's essay on civil disobedience. It left a deep impression upon me. I translated a portion of that essay for the readers of *Indian Opinion* in South Africa which I was then editing and I made copious extracts from that essay for that paper. That essay seemed to be so convincing and truthful that I felt the need of knowing more of Thoreau and I came across your life of him, his 'Walden' and other short essays all of which I read with great pleasure and equal profit.

Yours sincerely,

Henry S. Salt, Esq.
21 Cleveland Road
Brighton (England)

Letter to Henry S. Salt
SN 15663

---

[1] *A Plea for Vegetarianism.*

27. RUSKIN ON EDUCATION

March 28, 1932

John Ruskin was a great writer, teacher and religious thinker. He died about 1880.[1] I suppose most inmates of the Ashram know that one book[2] of his had a great effect on me and that it was this book which inspired me to introduce an important change in my life practically on the instant. He started in 1871 writing monthly letters addressed to factory workers. I had read praise of these letters in some article of Tolstoy, but I had not been able to secure them till now. I had brought with me from England a book about Ruskin's work and his efforts in the field of constructive activities. I read it here. This book also mentioned the letters referred to above. So I wrote to a woman disciple of Ruskin in England, who was none else but the author of that book. Being a poor woman, she could not send me the volumes of these letters. Through foolishness or false courtesy, I had not asked her to write to the Ashram for the money. This good woman sent my letter to a friend of hers who was comparatively in better circumstances. This friend was the editor of *The Spectator*. I had even met him while in England. He sent me the four volumes in which these letters had been published. I have been reading the first part. The thoughts expressed in these letters are beautiful and resemble some of our own ideas, so much so that an outsider would think that the ideas which I have set forth in my writings and which we try to put into practice in the Ashram, I had stolen from these letters of Ruskin. I hope readers will understand what is meant by 'stolen'. If an idea or ideal of life is borrowed from somebody but is presented as one's own conception, it is said to be stolen.

Ruskin has discussed many matters. Here I will mention only a few of his ideas. He says that it is a sheer error to suppose, as is generally done, that some education however little or however faulty is better than no literary education at all. It is his view that we should strive for real education alone. And then he says that every human being requires three things and three virtues. Anyone who fails to cultivate them does not know the secret of life. These six things should therefore form the basis of education. Every child, whether boy or girl, should learn the properties of pure air, clean water and clean earth, and should also learn how to keep air, water and earth pure or clean and know their benefits. Likewise, he has mentioned gratitude, hope and charity as the three virtues. Anybody who does not love truth and cannot recognize goodness or beauty lives in his own self-conceit and remains ignorant of spiritual joy. Similarly, he who has no hope, who has, in other words, no faith in divine justice, will never be cheerful in heart. And he who is without love, that is, lacks the spirit of *ahimsa*, who cannot look upon all living things as his kith and kin, will never know the secret of living.

Ruskin has explained these ideas at great length in his wonderful language. I hope I shall be able to write about them some time in a language which all the inmates of the Ashram can understand. Today I rest content with the brief precis given above. But I will say one thing, that what Ruskin has explained in his finished and cultivated prose with English readers in view, is practically the same ideas which we discuss in our rustic language and which we have been trying to put into practice. I am comparing here not two languages, but two writers. I cannot hope to equal Ruskin's mastery of language. But a time will certainly come when the love of our language will have become universal and we shall have writers like Ruskin who will have dedicated themselves heart and soul to it and will write as powerful Gujarati as the English of Ruskin.

'Some Reflections on Education' (G.)
MMU/II (Microfilm)

[1] Actually in 1900.
[2] *Unto This Last.*

28. TOLSTOY ON NON-RETALIATION

S.S. Kildonan Castle,
November 18, 1909

The letter[1] translated below calls for an explanation.

Count Tolstoy is a Russian nobleman. He has had his full share of life's pleasures, and was once a valiant soldier. He has no equal among European writers. After much experience and study, he has come to the conclusion that the political policies generally followed in the world are quite wrong. The chief reason for that, according to him, is that we are vengeful, a habit unworthy of us and contrary to the tenets of all religions. He believes that to return injury for injury does harm both to ourselves and to our enemy. According to him, we should not retaliate against anyone who may injure us, but reward him with love instead. He is uncompromising in his loyalty to the principle of returning good for evil.

He does not mean by this that those who suffer must seek no redress. He believes rather that we invite suffering on ourselves through our own fault. An oppressor's efforts will be in vain if we refuse to submit to his tyranny. Generally, no one will kick me for the mere fun of it. There must be some deeper reason for his doing so. He will kick me to bend me to his will if I have been opposing him. If, in spite of the kicks, I refuse to carry out his orders, he will stop kicking me. It would make no difference to me whether he did so or not. What matters to me is the fact that his order is unjust. Slavery consists in submitting to an unjust order, not in suffering ourselves to be kicked. Real courage and humanity consist in not returning a kick for a kick. This is the core of Tolstoy's teaching.

The letter translated below was originally written in Russian. It was rendered into English by Tolstoy himself and sent to the editor of *Free Hindustan* in reply to a letter of his. This editor holds different views from Tolstoy's and hence he did not publish the letter. It reached my hands and a friend asked me whether or not it should be published. I liked the letter. What I saw was a copy of the original letter. I sent it to Tolstoy and sought his permission to publish it, asking him at the same time whether the letter was in fact written by him. His permission having been received, both the English version of the letter and a Gujarati translation are being published in *Indian Opinion*.

To me Tolstoy's letter is of great value. Anyone who has enjoyed the experience of the Transvaal struggle will perceive its value readily enough. A handful of Indian *satyagrahis* have pitted love or soul-force against the might of the Transvaal Government's guns. That is the central principle of Tolstoy's teaching, of the teaching of all religions. Khuda-Ishwar has endowed our soul with such strength that sheer brute force is of no avail against it. We have been employing that strength against the Transvaal Government not out of hatred or with a view to revenge, but merely in order to resist its unjust order.

But those who have not known what a happy experience *satyagraha* can be, who have been caught up in the toils of this huge sham of modern civilization, like moths flitting round a flame, will find no interest in Tolstoy's letter all at once. Such men should pause for a moment and reflect.

Tolstoy gives a simple answer to those Indians who appear impatient to drive the whites out of India. We are our own slaves, not of the British. This should be engraved in our minds. The whites cannot remain if we do not want them. If the idea is to drive them out with firearms, let every Indian consider what precious little profit Europe has found in these.

Everyone would be happy to see India free. But there are as many views as men on how that can be brought about. Tolstoy points out a simple way to such men.

Tolstoy has addressed this letter to a Hindu and that is why it cites thoughts from Hindu scriptures. Such thoughts, however, are to be found in the scriptures of every religion. They are such as will be acceptable to all, Hindus, Muslims and Parsis. Religious practices and dogmas may differ, but the principles of ethics must be the same in all religions. I therefore advise all readers to think of ethics.

No one should assume that I accept all the ideas of Tolstoy. I look upon him as one of my teachers. But I certainly do not agree with all his ideas. The central principle of his teaching is entirely acceptable to me, and it is set out in the letter given below.

In this letter, he has not spared the superstitions of any religion. That is, however, no reason why any proud follower of Hinduism or of any other religion should oppose his teaching. It should suffice for us that he accepts the fundamental principles of every religion. When irreligion poses as religion, as it so often does, even true religion suffers. Tolstoy points this out repeatedly. We must pay the utmost attention to his thought whatever the religion we belong to.

In translating, I have endeavoured to use the simplest possible Gujarati. I have been mindful of the fact that readers of *Indian Opinion* prefer simple language. Moreover, I want Tolstoy's letter to be read by thousands of Gujarati Indians, and difficult language may prove tedious reading to such large numbers. Though all this has been kept in mind, slightly difficult words may have been occasionally used when simpler ones were not available, for which I apologize to the readers.

MOHANDAS KARAMCHAND GANDHI

Preface to Leo Tolstoy's 'Letter to a Hindoo' (G.)
Indian Opinion, 25 Dec. 1909

[1] Not reproduced here.

29. THE SIMPLICITY OF NAOROJI

The birth anniversary of the Grand Old Man of India, Dadabhai Naoroji, fell on 4th September; but the National Women's Council arranged the function on the 30th August to suit my convenience since I had to be present in Poona on the 4th. Dadabhai led the life of a *rishi*. I have many sacred memories of him. This Grand Old Man of India was, and continues to be, one of the great men who have moulded my life. I think the memories that I recounted before the sisters are worth being reported to the readers.

I had the privilege to see Dadabhai in 1888 for the first time. A friend of my father's had given me a letter of introduction to him, and it is worth noting that this friend was not at all acquainted with Dadabhai. He, however, took it for granted that anyone from the public could write to such a saintly person. In England, I found that Dadabhai came in contact with all students. He was their leader and attended their gatherings. Ever since, I have seen his life flowing in the same rhythm till the end. I was in South Africa for twenty years, and exchanged hundreds of letters with Dadabhai during the period. I was astonished at the regularity with which his replies came. My letters used to be typed, but I do not remember any typed reply from him. The replies were all in his own hand, and moreover, as I came to know subsequently, he would himself make copies of his letters on a tissue-paper book. I could find that most of my letters were replied to by the return of post. Whenever I met him I tasted nothing but love and sweetness.

Dadabhai would talk to me exactly like a father to a son, and I have heard from others that their experience was the same as mine. The thought uppermost in his mind all the time was how India could rise and attain her freedom. My first acquaintance with the extent of Indian poverty was through Dadabhai's book;[1] I learnt from that book itself that about three crores of men in our country are half-starved. Today this number has increased. His simplicity was without limit. It so happened that someone criticized him in 1908. I found it extremely intolerable and yet I was unable to prove that it was wrong. I was troubled by many doubts.

I thought that it was sinful to entertain doubts about a great patriot like Dadabhai. Therefore I sought an appointment and went to see him with the consent of the critic. That was the first time I went to his private office. It was made up of a very small room with only two chairs. I entered. He asked me to sit in a vacant chair but I went and sat near his feet. He saw distress on my face and questioned me, asking me to speak out whatever weighed on my mind. With great hesitation I reported to him the criticisms of his detractors and said, 'I was troubled by doubts on hearing these things and, because I worship you, I consider it a sin to keep them back.' Smilingly, he asked me, 'What reply do I give you? Do you believe this thing?' His manner, his tone and the pain that was so apparent in his words, were enough for me. I said, 'I do not now want to hear anything more. I have no trace of a doubt left in me.' Even then he told me many things relating to this matter, which it is not necessary to recapitulate here. After this event I realized that Dadabhai was an Indian living in the simple style of a *fakir*. A *fakir*'s style does not imply that a man should not have even a farthing; but Dadabhai had forsaken the luxuries and standards which other people of his stratum were enjoying during those days.

I myself and many others like me have learnt the lessons of regularity, single-minded patriotism, simplicity, austerity and ceaseless work from this venerable man. At a time when criticism of the Government was considered sedition and hardly anyone dared to speak the truth, Dadabhai criticized the Government in the severest terms and boldly pointed out the shortcomings of the administration. I have absolutely no doubt that the people of India will remember Dadabhai affectionately as long as India endures as an entity in the world.

'Birth Anniversary of Dadabhai Naoroji' (G.)
Navajivan, 7 Sept. 1924

[1] *Poverty and Un-British Rule in India.*

30. THE MESSAGE OF GOKHALE

[20 February 1915]

My one desire tonight is that my heart may reach your hearts and that there should be a real at-one-ment between us.

You have all learnt something about Tulsidas's *Ramayana*. The most stirring part is that about the companionship of the good. We should seek the company of those who have suffered and served and died. One such was Mr. Gokhale. He is dead, but his work is not dead, for his spirit lives.

The masses came to know of Gokhale's efficiency in work. All know Gokhale's life of action. But few know of his religious life. Truth was the spring of all his actions.

This was behind all his works, even his politics. This was the reason he founded the Servants of India Society, the ideal of which was to spiritualise the political as well as the social life of the nation.

It was fearlessness which ruled all the actions of his life. But as he was fearless he was also thorough. One of his favourite *shlokas* from the Shastras says: Real wisdom is not to begin a thing but to see the thing through to the end. This characteristic of thoroughness may be seen from this incident. He once had to speak to a large audience and he spent three days in order to prepare a short speech for this meeting and he asked me to write out a speech for him. I wrote out the speech. He took it and smiled his heavenly smile, discussed it with me and said, 'Give me something better, rewrite it.' For three days he worried over it. When the speech was given, it thrilled the whole audience. He delivered his speeches without notes, but he did so, because he was so thorough, that one might say he wrote his speeches with his own blood. As he was thorough and fearless, so he was gentle. He was human from top to toe in all his dealings. He was sometimes impatient, but he would ask forgiveness, coming forward with his smile, whether to a servant or a great man, saying, 'I know you will forgive me, won't you?'

He had a great struggle during the latter days of his life, a struggle with his conscience. He had to decide whether he should continue to take part in a struggle at the expense of his health. His conscience ruled every action of his life. He did not wear it on his sleeve, he wore it in his heart. Therefore he is living still, and may we all have the strength to carry out his last wish. His last word to those members of the Servants of India Society who were with him were: 'I do not want any memorial or any statue. I want only that men should love their country and serve it with their lives.' This is a message for the whole of India and not only for them. It was through service that he learnt to know his own nature and to know his country. His love for India was truthful and therefore he wanted nothing for India which he did not want for humanity also. It was not blind love, for his eyes were open to her faults and failings. If we can love India in the same way that he did, we have done well in coming to Shantiniketan to learn how to live our lives for India's sake. Copy the zeal which he showed in all he took up, the love that was the law of his life, the truthfulness which guided every action and the thoroughness which was characteristic of all his work.

Remember that our *shastras* teach us that these simple virtues are the stepping stones to the higher state of life, without which all our worship and works are useless.

I was in quest of a really truthful hero in India and I found him in Gokhale. His love and reverence for India were truly genuine. For serving his country, he completely eschewed all happiness and self-interest. Even while lying on his sick-bed, his mind was occupied in thinking about the welfare of India. A few days ago, when at night he was under the grip of a painful ailment, he called for some of us and began talking about the bright future of India, as envisaged by him. Doctors repeatedly advised him to retire from work but he would not listen to them. He said, 'None but death can separate me from work.' And death at last brought peaceful rest to him. May God bless his soul!

Speech at Shantiniketan on Gokhale's Death
The Ashram, June–July 1915

31. FREEDOM FROM ATTACHMENT

When shall I know that state supreme,
When will the knots, outer and inner, snap?
When shall I, breaking the bonds that bind us fast,
Tread the path trodden by the wise and the great?

Withdrawing the mind from all interests,
Using this body solely for self-control,
He desires nothing to serve any ulterior end of his own,
Seeing nothing in the body to bring on a trace of the darkness of
    ignorance.

These are the first two verses of Raychandbhai's inspired ut-
terance at the age of eighteen.

During the two years I remained in close contact with him,
I felt in him every moment the spirit of *vairagya* which shines
through these verses. One rare feature of his writings is that
he always set down what he had felt in his own experience.
There is in them no trace of unreality. I have never read any
line by him which was written to produce an effect on others.
He had always by his side a book on some religious subject
and a note-book with blank pages. The latter he used for
noting down any thoughts which occurred to him. Sometimes,
it would be prose and sometimes poetry. The poem about the
'supreme state' must have been written in that manner.

Whatever he was doing at the moment, whether eating or
resting or lying in bed, he was invariably disinterested towards
things of the world. I never saw him being tempted by objects
of pleasure or luxury in this world.

I watched his daily life respectfully, and at close quarters.
He accepted whatever he was served at meals. His dress was
simple, a *dhoti* and shirt, an *angarakhun* and a turban of mixed
silk and cotton yarn. I do not remember that these garments
used to be strikingly clean or carefully ironed. It was the same
to him whether he squatted on the ground or had a chair to
sit on. In the shop, he generally squatted on a *gadi*.

He used to walk slowly, and the passer-by could see that he
was absorbed in thought even while walking. There was a
strange power in his eyes; they were extremely bright, and

free from any sign of impatience or anxiety. They bespoke single-minded attention. The face was round, the lips thin, the nose neither pointed nor flat and the body of light build and medium size. The skin was dark. He looked an embodiment of peace. There was such sweetness in his voice that one simply wanted to go on listening to him. The face was smiling and cheerful; it shone with the light of inner joy. He had such ready command of language that I do not remember his ever pausing for a word to express his thoughts. I rarely saw him changing a word while writing a letter. And yet the reader would never feel that any thought was imperfectly expressed, or the construction of a sentence was defective or the choice of a word faulty.

These qualities can exist only in a man of self-control. A man cannot become free from attachments by making a show of being so. That state is a state of grace for the *atman*. Anyone who strives for it will discover that it may be won only after a ceaseless effort through many lives. One will discover, if one struggles to get rid of attachments, how difficult it is to succeed in the attempt. The Poet made me feel that this state of freedom from attachment was spontaneous to him.

The first step towards *moksha* is freedom from attachment. Can we ever listen with pleasure to anyone talking about *moksha* so long as our mind is attached to a single object in this world? If at any time we seem to do so, it is only the ear which is pleased, in the same way, that is, as we may be pleased merely by the musical tune of a song without following its meaning. It will be a long time before such indulgence of the ear results in our adopting a way of life which could lead towards *moksha*. Without genuine *vairagya* in the mind, one cannot be possessed with a yearning for *moksha*. The poet was possessed by such yearning.

'*Vairagya*'
Shrimad Rajchandra, Ch. 3

32. DISCOVERY OF MEANING

August 21, 1932

Awake and arise, O traveller, it is morning now;
It is no longer night that you still slumber.

If anybody understands these lines to mean simply: 'O traveller, arise, it is morning now. Is it night that you are still
sleeping?'—then he has read the lines but not reflected over
their meaning. For such a reader will rise early at dawn and
feel satisfied. But a reader who wishes to think will ask: Who
is this traveller? What is meant by 'It is morning'? What does
the poet mean when he says that it is no longer night? What
does sleeping mean? He will then discover daily new meanings
in every line, and understand that the traveller represents
every human being. For one who has faith in God, it is always
morning. Night may also signify ignorance. This line applies
to any person who is negligent, be it in ever so small a degree.
Anybody who tells a lie also slumbers. The line is a call to
such a person to wake up. We may thus read a wide meaning
in the line and learn peace of mind through it. In other words,
meditation on this single line can supply enough provision to
a man for his spiritual journey, whereas a person who has
memorized the four Vedas and also studied their meaning
may find them a useless burden. I have given here but one
illustration which occurred to me. If all of us decide in what
direction we wish to progress and start thinking, we would
discover new meanings in life and daily experience a new joy.

'Reading and Reflection—II' (G.)
MMU/II (Microfilm)

IV

Modern Civilization and Moral Progress

33. DESTRUCTIVE MATERIALISM

M. K. Gandhi
Agent for The Esoteric Christian Union
& The London Vegetarian Society

Durban,
January 21, 1895

TO

The Editor
The Natal Advertiser

Sir,

You will oblige me by letting me draw the attention of your readers to the notice that appears in your advertisement columns about the Esoteric Christian Union and the London Vegetarian Society.

The system represented by the Union establishes the unity and common source of all the great religions of the world, and points out, as the books advertised will amply show, the utter inadequacy of materialism which boasts of having given the world a civilization which was never witnessed before, and which is alleged to have done the greatest good to humanity, all the while conveniently forgetting that its greatest achievements are the invention of the most terrible weapons of destruction, the awful growth of anarchism, the frightful disputes between capital and labour and the wanton and diabolical cruelty inflicted on innocent dumb, living animals in the name of science, 'falsely so called'.

There seem to be, however, signs of reaction setting in—the almost phenomenal success of the Theosophical Society, the gradual acceptance by the clergy of the doctrine of holiness, and what is more, the acceptance by Professor Max Muller of the doctrine of reincarnation so conclusively demonstrated in

The Perfect Way, his statement that it was gaining ground
among the thinking minds in England and elsewhere, and the
publication of *The Unknown Life of Jesus Christ*. It is not possible to secure these works in S. Africa. My knowledge of them
is, therefore, confined to their reviews. All these and many
such facts are, I submit, unmistakable signs of a return from
the materialistic tendencies, which have made us so cruelly
selfish, to the unadulterated esoteric teachings of not only
Jesus Christ, but also of Buddha, Zoroaster and Mahomed,
who are no longer so generally denounced by the civilized
world as false prophets, but whose and Jesus's teachings are
beginning to be acknowledged to be complementary of one
another.

I regret that I am unable yet to advertise books on vegetarianism, as they have, by mistake, been forwarded to India,
and will, therefore, take some time before they arrive in Durban. I may, however, state one valuable fact with regard to
the efficacy of vegetarianism. There is no more potent instrument of evil than drunkenness, and I may be allowed to say
that all those who suffer from the craving for drink, but would
like really to be free from the curse, have only to give a trial
for at least one month to a diet chiefly consisting of brown
bread and oranges or grapes, to secure an entire freedom from
the craving. I have myself carried on a series of experiments,
and can testify that on a vegetarian diet, without any condiments and consisting of a liberal supply of juicy fresh fruits, I
have lived comfortably, without tea, coffee, or cocoa, and
even water, for days together. Hundreds in England have
become vegetarian for this reason, and having once been inveterate tipplers, have now reached a stage when the very
smell of grog or whisky is an offence to their tastes. Dr. B.W.
Richardson, in his *Food for Man*, recommends pure vegetarianism as a cure for drunkenness. In a comparatively hot country like Natal, where there is a plentiful supply of fruits and
vegetables, a bloodless diet should prove very beneficial in
every way, apart from its immeasurable superiority to flesh
foods, on grounds scientific, sanitary, economical, ethical, and
spiritual.

It is, perhaps, needless to mention that the sale of E.C.U.
books is not at all a money-making concern. In certain cases
the books have even been given away. They will be gladly

lent in some cases. I shall be very happy to correspond with any of your readers who may want any further information, either about the E.C.U. or the L.V.S., or to have a quiet chat on these (to me at any rate) momentous questions.

I would conclude with what Rev. John Pulsford, D.D., has to say with regard to the teaching of the E.C.U.:

It is impossible for a spiritually intelligent reader to doubt that these teachings were received from within the astral veil. They are full of the concentrated and compact wisdom of the Holy Heavens, and of God. If the Christians knew their own religion, they would find in these priceless records Lord Christ and His vital process abundantly illustrated and confirmed. That such communications are possible, and are permitted to be given to the world, is a sign, and a most promising sign, of our age.

I am, etc.

M. K. GANDHI

'Inadequacy of Materialism'
Natal Advertiser, 1 Feb. 1895

34 . INSTABILITY OF CIVILIZATION

The catastrophe at Paris[1] must have filled all the portions of the globe where the news reached with gloom. We can well imagine the feelings of the victims and the survivors. To us, these untoward happenings are not merely accidents but we look upon them as divine visitations from which we, if we chose, may learn rich lessons. To us, they show a grim tragedy behind all the tinsel splendour of the modern civilization. The ceaseless rush in which we are living does not leave any time for contemplating the full results of events such as have placed Paris in mourning for the time being. The dead will be soon forgotten, and in a very short time, Paris will again resume its usual gaiety as if nothing whatsoever had happened. Those, however, who will give the accident, if so it may be called, more than a passing thought, cannot fail to realize that behind all the splendour and behind all the glittering appearances there is something very real which is missed altogether. To us, the meaning is quite clear, namely, that all of us have to live the present life merely as a preparation for a future, far more certain and far more real. Nothing that the modern civilization can offer in the way of stability can ever make any more certain that which is inherently uncertain; that, when we come to think of it, the boast about the wonderful discoveries and the marvellous inventions of science, good as they undoubtedly are in themselves, is, after all, an empty boast. They offer nothing substantial to the struggling humanity, and the only consolation that one can derive from such visitations has to come from a firm faith not in the theory, but in the fact, of the existence of a future life and real Godhead. And that alone is worth having or worth cultivating which would enable us to realise our Maker and to feel that, after all, on this earth we are merely sojourners.

'Accident?'
Indian Opinion, 20 Aug. 1903

---

[1] A disastrous fire in the underground Electric Railway on 10 Aug. 1903, in which eighty-four persons were killed and many injured.

35. UNION OF EAST AND WEST

[LONDON,
13 October 1909]

Mr. Gandhi[1] said that the question of East and West presented a vast and complex problem. He had had 18 years' experience of contact between East and West and had endeavoured to study the question, and he felt that he might give an audience such as the present one the results of his observations. As he thought of the subject, his heart sank within him. He would have to say many things which would seem repugnant to his audience, and use hard words. He would also have to speak against a system under which he had been brought up. He hoped they would bear with him if he hurt their feelings. He would have to break many idols which he and his countrymen had worshipped, and which his audience may have worshipped. He then referred to the lines in Kipling's poem, that 'East is East and West is West and never the twain shall meet', and said he considered that doctrine to be a doctrine of despair, and inconsistent with the evolution of humanity.

He felt it utterly impossible to accept a doctrine of that nature. Another English poet, Tennyson, had in his 'Vision' clearly foretold the union between East and West and it was because he (the lecturer) believed in that vision that he had cast in his lot with the people of South Africa, who were living there in very great difficulties. It was because he thought it possible for the two peoples to live together in perfect equality that he found himself in South Africa. If he had believed in Kipling's doctrine, he would never have lived there. There had been individual instances of English and Indian people living together under the same rule without a jarring note, and what was true of individuals could be made true of nations. To a certain extent it was true that there was no meeting place between civilizations. The barriers between the Japanese and the Europeans were daily vanishing, because the Japanese assimilated Western civilization. It seemed to him that the chief characteristic of modern civilization [was that it] worshipped the body more than the spirit, and gave everything for the glorifying of the body. Their railways, telegraphs and telephones, did they tend to help them forward to a moral elevation? When he cast his eyes upon India, what was represented there today under British rule?

Modern civilization ruled India. What had it done? He hoped he would not shock his hearers when he said that civilization had done no good to India. There was there a network of railways and telegraphs and telephones; we had given them a Calcutta, a Madras, a Bombay, a Lahore and a Benares—these were symbols of slavery rather than of freedom. He noticed that these modern travelling facilities had reduced their holy places to unholy places. He could picture to himself Benares of old, before there was a mad rush of civilization, and he had seen the Benares of today with his own eyes, an unholy city. He saw the same thing here as in India. The mad activity had unhinged us and, although he was living under the system, it seemed to him desirable that he should speak to them in that strain. He knew it was impossible for the two peoples in India to live together until the British changed their ways. We had offended the religious susceptibilities of the Hindus by sport in their sacred places. Unless this mad rush was changed, a calamity must come. One way would be for them to adopt modern civilization; but far be it from him to say that they should ever do so. India would then be the football of the world, and the two nations would be flying at each other. India was not yet lost, but had been immersed in lethargy. There were many things which could not be understood, for which we must be patient; but one thing was certain, and that was that, so long as this mad rush lasted, with its glorification of the body, the soul within, which was imperishable, must languish.

Speech at Friends' Meeting House, Hampstead
India, 22 Oct. 1909

<hr>

[1] Gandhi spoke on 'East and West' at a meeting held under the auspices of the Hampstead Peace and Arbitration Society at the Friends' Meeting House. C. E. Maurice presided.

36. CIVILIZATION AND CONSCIENCE

May 10, 1910

Dear Mr. Wybergh,[1]

I am exceedingly obliged to you for your very full and valuable criticism of the little pamphlet on Indian Home Rule. I shall with very great pleasure send your letter to *Indian Opinion* for publication, and shall treat this reply likewise.

I entirely reciprocate the sentiments you express in the last paragraph of your letter. I am quite aware that my views will lead to many differences of opinion between my staunchest friends and those whom I have come to regard with respect and myself, but these differences, so far as I am concerned, can neither diminish respect nor affect friendly relations.

I am painfully conscious of the imperfections and defects you point out in your letter, and I know how unworthy I am to handle the very important problems dealt with in the booklet. But, having had the position of a publicist practically forced upon me by circumstances, I felt bound to write for those for whom *Indian Opinion* caters. The choice lay between allowing the readers of *Indian Opinion*, anxious though they were for guidance, to drift away in the matter of the insane violence that is now going on in India, or giving them, no matter how humble, a lead that they were asking for. The only way I saw of mitigating violence was the one sketched in the pamphlet.

I share your views that a superficial reader will consider the pamphlet to be a disloyal production, and I admit, too, that those who will not distinguish between men and measures, between modern civilization and its exponents, will come to that conclusion. And I accept your proposition that I discourage violence only because I think it to be both wrong and ineffective, and not because the object sought to be attained is wrong, that is to say, if it were ever possible, which I hold it is not, to detach the object from the means adopted to attain it. I hold that Home Rule obtained by violence would be totally different in kind from that obtained by the means suggested by me.

I have ventured utterly to condemn modern civilization because I hold that the spirit of it is evil. It is possible to show that some of its incidents are good, but I have examined its tendency in the scale of ethics. I distinguish between the ideals of individuals who have risen superior to their environment, as also between Christianity and modern civilization. Its activity is by no means confined to Europe. Its blasting influence is now being exhibited in full force in Japan. And it now threatens to overwhelm India. History teaches us that men who are in the whirlpool, except in the cases of individuals, will have to work out their destiny in it; but I do submit that those who are still outside its influence, and those who have a well-tried civilization to guide them, should be helped to remain where they are, if only as a measure of prudence. I claim to have tested the life which modern civilization has to give, as also that of the ancient civilization, and I cannot help most strongly contesting the idea that the Indian population requires to be roused by 'the lash of competition and the other material and sensuous, as well as intellectual, stimuli'; I cannot admit that these will add a single inch to its moral stature. Liberation in the sense in which I have used the term is undoubtedly the immediate aim of all humanity. It does not, therefore, follow that the whole of it can reach it in the same time. But if that liberation is the best thing attainable by mankind, then, I submit, it is wrong to lower the ideal for anyone. All the Indian Scriptures have certainly preached incessantly liberation as an immediate aim, but we know that this preaching has not resulted in 'activity in the lower worlds' being abandoned.

I admit that the term 'passive resistance' is a misnomer. I have used it because, generally speaking, we know what it means. Being a popular term, it easily appeals to the popular imagination. The underlying principle is totally opposed to that of violence. It cannot, therefore, be that 'the battle is transferred from the physical to the mental plane'. The function of violence is to obtain reform by external means; the function of passive resistance, that is, soul-force, is to obtain it by growth from within; which, in its turn, is obtained by self-suffering, self-purification. Violence ever fails; passive resistance is ever successful. The fight of a passive resister is none the less spiritual because he fights to win. Indeed, he is obliged to fight to win, that is, to obtain the mastery of self. Passive resistance is always moral, never cruel; and any activity, mental or otherwise, which fails in this test is undoubtedly not passive resistance.

Your argument tends to show that there must be complete divorce between politics and religion or spirituality. That is what we see in everyday life under modern conditions. Passive resistance seeks to rejoin politics and religion and to test every one of our actions in the light of ethical principles. That Jesus refused to use soul-force to turn stones into bread only supports my argument. Modern civilization is at present engaged in attempting that impossible feat. The use of soul-force for turning stones into bread would have been considered, as it is still considered, as black magic. Nor can I hold with you that motives alone can always decide the question of a particular act being right or wrong. An ignorant mother may, from the purest motives, administer a dose of opium to her child. Her motives will not cure her of her ignorance, nor, in the moral world purge her of the offence of killing her child. A passive resister, recognising this principle and knowing that, in spite of the purity of his motives, his action may be utterly wrong, leaves judgment to the Supreme Being, and, in attempting to resist what he holds to be wrong, suffers only in his own person. Throughout the *Bhagavad Gita*, I can see no warrant for holding that a man who can only control 'the organs of action' but cannot help 'dwelling in his mind on the objects of the senses' had better use the organs of action until the mind, too, is under control. In ordinary practices, we call such use an indulgence, and we know, too, that, if we can control the flesh even while the spirit is weak, always wishing that the spirit were equally strong, we will certainly arrive at a right correspondence. I think the text you have quoted refers to a man who, for making a show, appears to be controlling the organs of action, whilst deliberately in his mind dwelling on the objects of the senses.

I agree with you entirely that a pure passive resister cannot allow himself to be regarded as a martyr nor can he complain of the hardships of prison or any other hardships, nor may he make political capital out of what may appear to be injustice or ill-treatment, much less may he allow any matter of passive resistance to be advertised. But all action unfortunately is mixed. Purest passive resistance can exist only in theory. The anomalies you point out only emphasize the fact that the Indian passive resisters of the Transvaal are, after all, very fallible human beings and yet very weak, but I can assure you that their object is to make their practice correspond with pure passive resistance as nearly as possible, and, as the struggle progresses, pure spirits are certainly rising in our midst.

I am free to admit also that all passive resisters are not fired with the spirit of love or of truth. Some of us are undoubtedly not free from vindictiveness and the spirit of hatred; but the desire in us all is to cure ourselves of hatred and enmity. I have noticed, too, that those who simply became passive resisters under the glamour of the newness of the movement or for selfish reasons have fallen away. Pretended self-suffering cannot last long. Such men never were passive resisters. It is necessary to discuss the subject of passive resistance somewhat impersonally. If you say that physical sufferings of soldiers have vastly exceeded those of the Transvaal passive resisters, I agree with you entirely; but the sufferings of world-known passive resisters who deliberately walked into funeral pyres or into boiling cauldrons were incomparably greater than those of any soldier it is possible to name.

I cannot pretend to speak for Tolstoy, but my reading of

his works has never led me to consider that, in spite of his merciless analysis of institutions organised and based upon force, that is governments, he in any way anticipates or contemplates that the whole world will be able to live in a state of philosophical anarchy. What he has preached, as, in my opinion, have all world-teachers, is that every man has to obey the voice of his own conscience, and be his own master, and seek the Kingdom of God from within. For him there is no government that can control him without his sanction. Such a man is superior to all government. And can it be ever dangerous for a lion to tell a number of other lions who in their ignorance consider themselves to be merely lambs that they, too, are not lambs but lions? Some very ignorant lions will no doubt contest the knowing lion's proposition. There will, no doubt, on that account be confusion also, but, no matter how gross the ignorance may be, it will not be suggested that the lion who knows should sit still and not ask his fellow-lions to share his majesty and freedom.

It has indeed occurred to me that an anti-Asiatic league which from pure though entirely misguided motives wishes to deport Asiatics from the Transvaal, because it may consider them to be an evil, would be certainly justified, from its own view-point, in violently attaining its object. It is not open to passive resisters, if they are not weak, to complain of such, in their opinion, high-handed action, but for them deportation and worse must be a welcome relief from having to submit to a course of action which is repugnant to their conscience. I hope you will not fail to see the beauty of passive resistance in your own illustration. Supposing that these deportees were capable of offering physical violence against forcible deportation, and yet from pure choice elected to be deported rather than resist deportation, will it not show superior courage and superior moral fibre in them?

Yours sincerely,

M. K. GANDHI

Letter to W. J. Wybergh
Indian Opinion, 21 May 1910

[1] Member of the Legislative Assembly, Transvaal.

37. ECONOMIC AND MORAL PROGRESS

[22 December 1916]

Mr. M. K. Gandhi delivered an instructive lecture on 'Does economic progress clash with real progress?' at a meeting of the Muir Central College Economic Society held on Friday evening in the physical science theatre. The Hon. Pandit Madan Mohan Malaviya presided ... Mr. Gandhi delivered the following lecture:

When I accepted Mr. Kapildeva Malaviya's invitation to speak to you upon the subject of this evening, I was painfully conscious of my limitations. You are an economic society. You have chosen distinguished specialists for the subjects included in your syllabus for this year and the next. I seem to be the only speaker ill-fitted for the task set before him. Frankly and truly, I know very little of economics, as you naturally understand them. Only the other day, sitting at an evening meal, a civilian friend deluged me with a series of questions on my crankisms. As he proceeded in his cross-examination, I being a willing victim, he found no difficulty in discovering my gross ignorance of the matters. I appeared to him to be handling with a cocksureness worthy only of a man who knows not that he knows not. To his horror and even indignation, I suppose, he found that I had not even read books on economics by such well-known authorities as Mill, Marshall, Adam Smith and a host of such other authors. In despair, he ended by advising me to read these works before experimenting in matters economic at the expense of the public. He little knew that I was a sinner past redemption.

My experiments continue at the expense of trusting friends. For, there come to us moments in life when about some things we need no proof from without. A little voice within us tells us, 'You are on the right track, move neither to your left nor right, but keep to the straight and narrow way.' With such help we march forward slowly indeed, but surely and steadily. That is my position. It may be satisfactory enough for me, but it can in no way answer the requirements of a society such as yours. Still it was no use my struggling against Mr. Kapildeva

Malaviya. I knew that he was intent upon having me to engage your attention for one of your evenings. Perhaps you will treat my intrusion as a welcome diversion from the trodden path. An occasional fast after a series of sumptuous feasts is often a necessity. And as with the body, so, I imagine, is the case with the reason. And if your reason this evening is found fasting instead of feasting, I am sure it will enjoy with the greater avidity the feast that Rao Bahadur Pandit Chandrika Prasad has in store for you for the 12th of January.

Before I take you to the field of my experiences and experiments, it is perhaps best to have a mutual understanding about the title of this evening's address: *Does economic progress clash with real progress?* By economic progress, I take it, we mean material advancement without limit and by real progress we mean moral progress, which again is the same thing as progress of the permanent element in us. The subject may therefore be stated thus: 'Does not moral progress increase in the same proportion as material progress?' I know that this is a wider proposition than the one before us. But I venture to think that we always mean the larger one even when we lay down the smaller. For we know enough of science to realise that there is no such thing as perfect rest or repose in this visible universe of ours. If therefore material progress does not clash with moral progress, it must necessarily advance the latter. Nor can we be satisfied with the clumsy way in which sometimes those who cannot defend the larger proposition put their case. They seem to be obsessed with the concrete case of thirty millions of India stated by the late Sir William Wilson Hunter to be living on one meal a day. They say that before we can think or talk of their moral welfare, we must satisfy their daily wants. With these, they say, material progress spells moral progress. And then is taken a sudden jump: what is true of thirty millions is true of the universe. They forget that hard cases make bad law. I need hardly say to you how ludicrously absurd this deduction would be. No one has ever suggested that grinding pauperism can lead to anything else than moral degradation. Every human being has a right to live and therefore to find the wherewithal to feed himself and where necessary to clothe and house himself. But, for this very simple performance, we need no assistance from economists or their laws.

'Take no thought for the morrow'[1] is an injunction which finds an echo in almost all the religious scriptures of the world. In well-ordered society, the securing of one's livelihood should be and is found to be the easiest thing in the world. Indeed, the test of orderliness in a country is not the number of millionaires it owns, but the absence of starvation among its masses. The only statement that has to be examined is whether it can be laid down as a law of universal application that material advancement means moral progress.

Now let us take a few illustrations. Rome suffered a moral fall when it attained high material affluence. So did Egypt and so perhaps most countries of which we have any historic record. The descendants, kinsmen of the royal and divine Krishna, too, fell when they were rolling in riches. We do not deny to the Rockefellers and the Carnegies possession of an ordinary measure of morality but we gladly judge them indulgently. I mean that we do not even expect them to satisfy the highest standard of morality. With them material gain has not necessarily meant moral gain. In South Africa, where I had the privilege of associating with thousands of our countrymen on most intimate terms, I observed almost invariably that the greater the possession of riches, the greater was their moral turpitude. Our rich men, to say the least, did not advance the moral struggle of passive resistance as did the poor. The rich men's sense of self-respect was not so much injured as that of the poorest. If I were not afraid of treading on dangerous ground, I would even come nearer home and show you that possession of riches has been a hindrance to real growth. I venture to think that the scriptures of the world are far safer and sounder treatises on laws of economics than many of the modern text-books.

The question we are asking ourselves this evening is not a new one. It was addressed to Jesus two thousand years ago. St. Mark[a] has vividly described the scene. Jesus is in his solemn mood; he is earnest. He talks of eternity. He knows the world about him. He is himself the greatest economist of his time. He succeeded in economising time and space—he transcended them. It is to him at his best that one comes running, kneels down, and asks: 'Good Master, what shall I do that I may inherit eternal life?' And Jesus said unto him: 'Why callest thou me good? There is none good but one, that is God. Thou knowest the commandments. Do not commit adultery, Do not kill, Do not steal, Do not bear false witness, Defraud not, Honour thy father and mother.' And he answered and said unto him: 'Master, all these have I observed from my youth.' Then Jesus beholding him, loved him and said unto him: 'One thing thou lackest. Go thy way, sell whatever thou hast and give to the poor, and thou shalt have treasure in heaven—come take up the cross and follow me.' And he was sad at that saying and went away grieved—for he had great possessions. And Jesus looked round about and said unto his disciples: 'How hardly shall they that have riches enter into the kingdom of God.' And the disciples were astonished at his words. But Jesus answereth again and saith unto them: 'Children, how hard it is for them that trust in riches to enter into the kingdom of God. It is easier for a camel to go through the eye of a needle than for a rich man to enter into the kingdom of God!'

Here you have an eternal rule of life stated in the noblest words the English language is capable of producing. But the disciples nodded unbelief as we do even to this day. To him they said as we say today: 'But look how the law fails in practice. If we sell all and have nothing, we shall have nothing to eat. We must have money or we cannot even be reasonably moral.' So they state their case thus. 'And they were astonished out of measure saying among themselves: "Who then can be saved?"' And Jesus looking upon them saith: 'With men it is impossible but not with God, for with God all things are possible.' Then Peter began to say unto him: 'Lo, we have left all, and have followed thee.' And Jesus answered and said: 'Verily I say unto you there is no man that has left house or brethren or sisters, or father or mother, or wife or children or lands for my sake and the Gospels, but he shall receive one hundred fold, now in this time houses and brethren and sisters and mothers and children and lands with persecutions and in the world to come eternal life. But many that are first shall be last and the last first.' You have here the result or reward, if you prefer the term, of following the law.

I have not taken the trouble of copying similar passages from the other non-Hindu scriptures and I will not insult you by quoting in support of the law stated by Jesus passages from the writings and sayings of our own sages, passages even stronger if possible than the Biblical extracts I have drawn your attention to. Perhaps the strongest of all the testimonies in favour of the affirmative answer to the question before us are the lives of the greatest teachers of the world. Jesus, Mahomed, Buddha, Nanak, Kabir, Chaitanya, Shankara, Dayanand, Ramkrishna were men who exercised an immense influence over and moulded the character of thousands of men. The world is the richer for their having lived in it. And they were all men who deliberately embraced poverty as their lot.

I should not have laboured my point as I have done, if I did not believe that, in so far as we have made the modern materialistic craze our goal, in so far are we going downhill in the path of progress. I hold that economic progress in the sense I have put it is antagonistic to real progress. Hence the ancient ideal has been the limitation of activities promoting wealth. This does not put an end to all material ambition. We should still have, as we have always had, in our midst people who make the pursuit of wealth their aim in life. But we have always recognised that it is a fall from the ideal. It is a beautiful thing to know that the wealthiest among us have often felt that to have remained voluntarily poor would have been a higher state for them. That you cannot serve God and Mammon is an economic truth of the highest value. We have to make our choice. Western nations today are groaning under the heel of the monster-god of materialism. Their moral growth has become stunted. They measure their progress in £.s.d. American wealth has become standard. She is the envy of the other nations. I have heard many of our countrymen say that we will gain American wealth but avoid its methods. I venture to suggest that such an attempt if it were made is foredoomed to failure.

We cannot be 'wise, temperate and furious'[3] in a moment. I would have our leaders teach us to be morally supreme in the world. This land of ours was once, we are told, the abode of the gods. It is not possible to conceive gods inhabiting a land which is made hideous by the smoke and the din of mill chimneys and factories and whose roadways are traversed by rushing engines dragging numerous cars crowded with men mostly who know not what they are after, who are often absent-minded, and whose tempers do not improve by being uncomfortably packed like sardines in boxes and finding themselves in the midst of utter strangers who would oust them if they could and whom they would in their turn oust similarly. I refer to these things because they are held to be symbolical of material progress. But they add not an atom to our happiness. This is what Wallace, the great scientist, has said as his deliberate judgement.

In the earliest records which have come down to us from the past, we find ample indications that general ethical considerations and conceptions, the accepted standard of morality, and the conduct resulting from these were in no degree inferior to those which prevail to-day.

In a series of chapters, he then proceeds to examine the position of the English nation under the advance in wealth it has made. He says:

This rapid growth of wealth and increase of our power over nature put too great a strain upon our crude civilization, on our superficial Christianity, and it was accompanied by various forms of social immorality almost as amazing and unprecedented.

He then shows how factories have risen on the corpses of men, women and children, how as the country has rapidly advanced in riches, it has gone down in morality. He shows this by dealing with insanitation, life-destroying trades, adulteration, bribery and gambling. He shows how, with the advance of wealth, justice has become immoral, deaths from alcoholism and suicide have increased, the average of premature births and congenital defects has increased, and prostitution has become an institution. He concludes his examination by these pregnant remarks:

The proceedings of the divorce courts show other aspects of the result of wealth and leisure, while a friend who had been a good deal in London society assured me that both in country houses and in London various kinds of orgies were occasionally to be met with which would hardly have been surpassed in the period of the most dissolute emperors. Of war, too, I need say nothing. It has always been more or less chronic since the rise of the Roman Empire; but there is now undoubtedly a disinclination for war among all civilized peoples. Yet the vast burden of armaments, taken together with the most pious declarations in favour of peace, must be held to show an almost total absence of morality as a guiding principle among the governing classes.

Under the British aegis, we have learnt much, but it is my firm belief that there is little to gain from Britain in intrinsic morality, that if we are not careful, we shall introduce all the vices that she has been a prey to, owing to the disease of materialism. We can profit by that connection only if we keep our civilization, and our morals, straight, i.e., if instead of boasting of the glorious past, we express the ancient moral glory in our own lives and let our lives bear witness to our past. Then we shall benefit her and ourselves. If we copy her because she provides us with rulers, both they and we shall suffer degradation. We need not be afraid of ideals or of reducing them to practice even to the uttermost. Ours will only then be a truly spiritual nation when we shall show more truth than gold, greater fearlessness than pomp of power and wealth, greater charity than love of self. If we will but clean our houses, our palaces and temples of the attributes of wealth and show in them the attributes of morality, we can offer battle to any combinations of hostile forces without having to carry the burden of a heavy militia. Let us seek first the kingdom of God and His righteousness and the irrevocable promise is that everything will be added with us. These are real economics. May you and I treasure them and enforce them in our daily life.

An interesting discussion followed in the course of which several students put questions to the lecturer....

Prof. Jevons said ... It was necessary for economists to exist. It was not their business to lay down what the end should be. That was the business of philosophers....

Prof. Gidwani, president of the society, thanked the lecturer for his address....

Prof. Higginbottom said that there was no economic problem which could be separated from the moral problem....

Mr. Gandhi in the course of his remarks referred to Mr. Jevons's remark about the need for economists and said that it was said that dirt was matter misplaced. So also when an economist was misplaced, he was hurtful. He certainly thought that the economist had a place in the economy of nature when he occupied the humble sphere for which he was created. If an economist did not investigate the laws of God and show them how to distribute wealth so that there might not be poverty, he was a most unwelcome intrusion on the Indian soil. He would also suggest for the reflection of their economic students and professors that what might be good for England and America need not necessarily be good for India. He thought that most of the economic laws which were consistent with moral laws were of universal application, but there might be in their restricted application some distinction and difference. So he would utter the note of warning that Indian conditions being in some respects so essentially different from the English and American conditions, it was necessary to bring to bear on the matters that presented themselves to the economists a fresh mind. If they did so, both Indians and the economists would derive benefit. Mr. Higginbottom, he said, was studying the real economics that were so necessary for India and reducing his studies inch by inch to practice and that was the safest guide to follow, whether they were students or professors. Referring to a question by a student, he said that a man should not hoard money for selfish ends, but if he wished to hoard money as a trustee for the millions of India, he would say that he might have as much riches as he could. Ordinarily, economists prescribed laws for the rich people. It was against those economists that he would always cry out.

As regards another question, whether factories should not be replaced by cottage industries, Mr. Gandhi spoke approvingly of the suggestion but said that the economists should first of all examine with patience their indigenous institutions. If they were rotten, they must be wiped out and if there were remedies which could be suggested for their betterment, they should improve them.

As regards intercourse with other nations, he said that he did not think that they necessarily advanced one little bit in their moral growth by bringing their masses with others into physical contact and pointed to Indians in South Africa as an instance. The rapid locomotion such as steamers, trains and others dislocated so many of their ideals and created a great deal of mischief.

As regards the question what was the minimum and the maximum wealth a man should have—he would answer in the words of Jesus, Ramkrishna and others who said 'none'.

The Hon. Pandit Madan Mohan Malaviya in his concluding remarks offered a cordial vote of thanks to Mr. Gandhi for his excellent address. The ideals which Mr. Gandhi put before them, he said, were so high that he did not expect that all of them would be prepared to subscribe to all of them. But he was sure they would agree with the main object he put before them, namely, that they should go for the welfare of man as the test of all economic questions with which they dealt....

Speech at Muir College Economic Society, Allahabad
The Leader, 25 Dec. 1916

---

[1] Matthew 6: 34.

[2] Mark 10: 17–31.

[3] 'Who can be wise, amazed, temperate and furious,/Loyal and neutral, in a moment?/No man.' (*Macbeth*, II. iii)

38. FAITH IN INDIAN CIVILIZATION

Indore,
March 30, 1918

We often think that changes of the kind that take place in Europe will also occur in India; that when some big transformation comes about, people who know beforehand how to prepare themselves for it win through and those who fail to take account of this are destroyed; that mere movement is progress and that our advancement lies in it. We think that we shall be able to progress through the great discoveries that have been made in the continent of Europe. But this is an illusion. We are inhabitants of a country which has so long survived with its own civilization. Many a civilization of Europe is destroyed, but India, our country, survives as a witness to its own civilization. All scholars agree in testifying that the civilization of India is the same today as it was thousands of years ago. But, now, there is reason to suspect that we no longer have faith in our civilization. Every morning we do our worship and prayer, recite the verses composed by our forbears, but do not understand their significance. Our faith is turning in another direction.

So long as the world goes on, the war between the Pandavas and the Kauravas will also continue. The books of almost all the religions say that the war between the gods and Satan goes on for ever. The question is how we are to make our preparations. I have come here to tell you that you should have faith in your civilization and keep to it steadfastly. If you do this, India will one day hold sway over the entire world.

Our leaders say that, in order to fight the West, we have to adopt the ways of the West. But please rest assured that it will mean the end of Indian civilization. India's face is turned away from your modern trend; that India you do not know. I have travelled much and so come to know the mind of India and I have discovered that it has preserved its faith in its ancient civilization. The *swaraj* of which we hear will not be achieved the way we are working for it. The Congress League Scheme, or any other scheme which is even better, will not get us *swaraj*. We shall get *swaraj* through the way in which we live our lives. It cannot be had for the asking. We can never gain it through copying Europe.

That European civilization is Satanic we see for ourselves. An obvious proof of this is the fierce war that is going on at present. It is so terrible that the Mahabharata War was nothing in comparison. This should be a warning to us and we should remember that our sages have given us the immutable and inviolate principles that our conduct should be godly and that it should be rooted in *dharma*. We should follow these principles alone. So long as we do not follow *dharma*, our wish will not be fulfilled, notwithstanding all the grandiose schemes we may devise. Even if Mr. Montagu offers us *swaraj* today we can in no way benefit from that *swaraj*. We must make use of the legacy left us by our *rishis* and *munis*.

The whole world knows that the *tapasya* that was practised in ancient India is found nowhere else. Even if we want an empire for India, we can get it through no other method but that of self-discipline. We can be certain that once the spirit of discipline comes to pervade our lives, we shall be able to get anything we may want.

Truth and non-violence are our goal. Non-violence is the supreme *dharma*, there is no discovery of greater import than this. So long as we engage in mundane actions, so long as soul and body are together, some violence will continue to occur through our agency. But we must renounce at least the violence that it is possible for us to renounce. We should understand that the less violence a religion permits, the more is the truth contained in it. If we can ensure the deliverance of India, it is only through truth and non-violence. Lord Willingdon, the Governor of Bombay, has said that he feels greatly disappointed when he meets Indians for they do not express what is in their minds but only what would be agreeable to him, so that he never knows the real position. Many people have this habit of hiding their own sentiments when in the presence of an important person and suiting their talk to his pleasure. They do not realize how cruelly they deceive themselves and harm the truth. One must say what one feels. It is impertinence to go against one's reason. One must not hesitate the least to tell what one feels to anyone, be he a Minister of the Government or even a more exalted person. Deal with all with truth and non-violence.

Love is a rare herb that makes a friend even of a sworn enemy and this herb grows out of non-violence. What in a dormant state is non-violence becomes love in the waking state. Love destroys ill will. We should love all—whether Englishmen or Muslims. No doubt, we should protect the cow. But we cannot do so by fighting with Muslims. We cannot save the cow by killing Muslims. We should act only through love; thus alone shall we succeed. So long as we do not have unshakeable faith in truth, love and non-violence, we can make no progress. If we give up these and imitate European civilization, we shall be doomed. I pray to Suryanarayan that

India may not turn away from her civilization. Be fearless. So long as you live under various kinds of fears, you can never progress, you can never succeed. Please do not forget our ancient civilization. Never, never give up truth and love. Treat all enemies and friends with love. If you wish to make Hindi the national language, you can do so in a short time through the principles of truth and non-violence.

Speech on Indian Civilization (H.)
Mahatma Gandhi

39. ANCIENT GLORY AND PRESENT INERTIA

Editors often have something or other ready at hand to fill space in newspapers. In English this is called 'evergreen', that is, always fresh. You can publish the matter any time. I unexpectedly came across something like this in *The* [*Bombay*] *Chronicle*. It contains the following information.

The Hindus invented the decimal system. Geometry and Algebra were first developed in India, and so too Trigonometry. The first five hospitals to be built were in India. The physicians of ancient Europe used Indian drugs. Hindus investigated the anatomy of the human body in the sixth century B.C. and about the same time acquired the art of surgery. People in ancient India knew the art of casting iron pillars of the same kind which they make now. India specialized in carving caves. Alexander, when he invaded India, found republican states in the Punjab and in Sind. In ancient India, women enjoyed all those rights for which women of Europe are fighting hard at present. Municipalities were in existence in the times of Chandragupta. It was the Hindus who perfected the science of grammar. The *Ramayana* and the *Mahabharata* still remain unrivalled.

I do not know how far these statements are true, but this I know, that, if the late Justice Ranade were alive today and heard such talk of India's past glory, he would certainly have asked, 'So what?' He used to say that no people could progress by merely dwelling on its past glory. If at all we do so, it should be only in order that we may be able to add to it. Where is the man who can write the *Ramayana* today? Where are the morals of ancient times? Where is the ability of those days? And devotion to duty? We have added nothing to the drugs discovered thousands of years ago, nor do we even have adequate knowledge about those mentioned in the ancient books. We witness the same poverty in respect of all the other gifts mentioned above, borrowing as we do everything from Europe. I, at any rate, feel that so long as we have not revived in the present the glory which was ours in the past, wisdom lies in not speaking about it. That wealth which has no exchange value, which the world does not recognize as such, brings not credit, but only humiliation and is in the nature of a burden. If, as we believe, we had these gifts in ancient times, we ought to be able to give evidence of them again. We are indeed heirs of a brave people, but by confessing at the same time our inability to be worthy of that heritage we shall achieve nothing. We shall see hereafter how we can become so worthy.

'Living on the Past' (G.)
Navajivan, 20 June 1920

40. APPEAL TO THE MASSES

A European friend thus writes:

What can be done, what would you suggest that could be tried in favour of the starving millions of the West? By starving millions I mean the masses of the European and American proletariat who are being driven to the abyss, who live a life not worth the name, full of the direst privations, who can nourish no dream of future relief by any form of *swaraj*, who are perhaps more hopeless than the millions of India because the faith in God, the consolation of religion, has left them to be replaced by nothing but hatred.

The iron hands which press down the Indian nation are at work there also. The devilish system is at work in each of these independent countries; politics do not count as there is a close solidarity of greed. Vice is devastating these masses who naturally try to escape the hell of their life at any cost, at the cost of making it a greater hell, and who have no longer the outlet of religious hopes, as Christianity by siding for centuries with the powerful and the greedy has lost all credit.

Of course, I expect Mahatmaji to answer that the only way to salvation for these masses, if there is any left, if the whole Western world is not already doomed, lies in the application of a disciplined non-violent resistance carried on on a large scale. But there are no traditions of *ahimsa* in the European soil and mind. Even the spreading of the doctrine would encounter huge difficulties, what about its right understanding and application!

The problem underlying the question so sincerely put by the friend lies outside my orbit. I, therefore, attempt an answer merely in courteous recognition of friendship between the questioner and myself. I confess that no value attaches to my answer, save what we attach to every considered argument. I know neither the diagnosis of the European disease nor the remedy in the same sense that I claim to know both in the case of India.

I, however, feel that fundamentally the disease is the same in Europe as it is in India, in spite of the fact that in the former country the people enjoy political self-government. No mere transference of political power in India will satisfy my ambition, even though I hold such transference to be a vital necessity of Indian national life. The peoples of Europe have no doubt political power but no *swaraj*. Asian and African races are exploited for their partial benefit, and they, on their part, are being exploited by the ruling class or caste under the sacred name of democracy. At the root, therefore, the disease appears to be the same as in India. The same remedy is, therefore, likely to be applicable. Shorn of all the camouflage, the exploitation of the masses of Europe is sustained by violence.

Violence on the part of the masses will never remove the disease. Anyway, up to now experience shows that success of violence has been short-lived. It has led to greater violence. What has been tried hitherto has been a variety of violence and artificial checks dependent mainly upon the will of the violent. At the crucial moment these checks have naturally broken down. It seems to me, therefore, that sooner or later, the European masses will have to take to non-violence if they are to find their deliverance. That there is no hope of their taking to it in a body and at once does not baffle me. A few thousand years are but a speck in the vast time circle. Someone has to make a beginning with a faith that will not flinch.

I doubt not that the masses, even of Europe, will respond, but what is more emergent in point of time is not so much a large experiment in non-violence as a precise grasp of the meaning of deliverance.

From what will the masses be delivered? It will not do to have a vague generalization and to answer 'from exploitation and degradation'. Is not the answer this that they want to occupy the status that capital does today? If so, it can be attained only by violence. But if they want to shun the evils of capital, in other words, if they would revise the viewpoint of capital, they would strive to attain a juster distribution of the products of labour. This immediately takes us to contentment and simplicity, voluntarily adopted. Under the new outlook multiplicity of material wants will not be the aim of life, the aim will be rather their restriction consistently with comfort. We shall cease to think of getting what we can, but we shall decline to receive what all cannot get.

It occurs to me that it ought not to be difficult to make a successful appeal to the masses of Europe in terms of economics, and a fairly successful working of such an experiment must lead to immense and unconscious spiritual results. I do not believe that the spiritual law works on a field of its own. On the contrary, it expresses itself only through the ordinary activities of life. It thus affects the economic, the social, and the political fields. If the masses of Europe can be persuaded to adopt the view I have suggested, it will be found that violence will be wholly unnecessary to attain the aim and they can easily come to their own by following out the obvious corollaries of non-violence. It may even be that what seems to me to be so natural and feasible for India, may take longer to permeate the inert Indian masses than the active European masses. But I must reiterate my confession that all my argument is based on suppositions and assumptions and must, therefore, be taken for what it is worth.

'What of the West'
Young India, 3 Sept. 1925

41. SIMPLICITY AND ARTIFICIALITY

Satyagraha Ashram,
Sabarmati,
March 21, 1928

Dear Friend.

It was a pleasure to receive your letter after such a long time. I am sending you the two books you mention and I am adding a third—Hand-spinning Essay, the *Guide to Health* and *Takli Teacher.*

Now about the 2nd paragraph. I would just like to say that whilst I am a passionate devotee of simplicity in life, I have also discovered that it is worthless unless the echo of simplicity comes from within. The modern organized artificiality of so-called civilized life cannot have any accord with true simplicity of heart. Where the two do not correspond, there is always either gross self-deception or hypocrisy.

Yours sincerely,

T. de Manziarly

Letter to T. de Manziarly
SN 14267

42. EVERYTHING ON ITS MERITS

March 8, 1945

Forgetting East and West we should consider everything on its own merits.

Note to Gope Gurbuxani (H.)
GN 1324

V

Politics and Religion

43. SPIRITUALIZING POLITICAL LIFE

[8 May 1915]

My dear Countrymen, before I perform this ceremony to which you have called me, I wish to say this to you that you have given me a great opportunity or rather a privilege on this great occasion. I saw in the recitation,[1] the beautiful recitation that was given to me, that God is with them whose garment was dusty and tattered. My thoughts immediately went to the end of my garment; I examined and found that it is not dusty and it is not tattered; it is fairly spotless and clean. God is not in me. There are other conditions attached; but in these conditions too I may fail; and you, my dear countrymen, may also fail; and if we do tend this well, we should not dishonour the memory of one whose portrait you have asked me to unveil this morning. I have declared myself his disciple in the .political field and I have him as my *Rajya Guru*; and this I claim on behalf of the Indian people. It was in 1896 that I made this declaration, and I do not regret having made the choice.

Mr. Gokhale taught me that the dream of every Indian, who claims to love his country, should be to act in the political field, should be not to glorify in language, but to spiritualise the political life of the country, and the political institutions of the country. He inspired my life and is still inspiring [it]; and in that I wish to purify myself and spiritualise myself. I have dedicated myself to that ideal. I may fail, and to what extent I may fail, I call myself to that extent an unworthy disciple of my master.

What is the meaning of spiritualising the political life of the country? What is the meaning of spiritualising myself? That question has come before me often and often and to you it may seem one thing, to me it may seem another thing; it may mean different things to the different members of the Servants of India Society itself. It shows much difficulty and it shows the difficulties of all those who want to love their country, who want to serve their country and who want to honour their country. I think political life must be an echo of private life and that there cannot be any divorce between the two.

I was by the side of that saintly politician to the end of his life and I found no ego in him. I ask you, members of the Social Service League, if there is no ego in you. If he wanted to shine,—he wanted to shine in the political field of his country,—he did so not in order that he might gain public applause, but in order that his country might gain. He developed every particular faculty in him, not in order to win the praise of the world for himself, but in order that his country might gain. He did not seek public applause, but they were showered upon him, they were thrust upon him; he wanted that his country might gain and that was his great inspiration.

There are many things for which India is blamed, very rightly, and if you should add one more to our failure, the blame will descend not only on you but also on me for having participated in today's functions. But I have great faith in my countrymen.

You ask me to unveil this portrait[2] today, and I will do so in all sincerity and sincerity should be the end of your life.

Speech at Government High School, Bangalore
Indian Review, May 1915

[1] From Tagore's *Gitanjali*.
[2] Of G. K. Gokhale.

44. SHADOW AND SUBSTANCE IN POLITICS

Laburnum Road,
Bombay,
August 4, 1919

Dear Mr. Arundale,[1]

I have read and re-read your kind letter for which I thank you. I am publishing the letter in *Young India* together with this reply.

Much as I should like to follow your advice, I feel that I am incompetent for the task set forth by you in your letter. I am fully aware of my limitations. My bent is not political but religious and I take part in politics because I feel that there is no department of life which can be divorced from religion and because politics touch the vital being of India almost at every point. It is therefore absolutely necessary that the political relations between Englishmen and ourselves should be put on a sound basis. I am endeavouring to the best of my ability to assist in the process. I do not take much interest in the reforms because they are in safe hands and because reforms *cum* Rowlatt legislation mean to my mind a stalemate. Rowlatt legislation represents a poisonous spirit. After all, the English civilians can, unless Indian opinion produces a healthy re-action upon them, reduce the reforms practically to a nullity. They distrust us and we distrust them. Each considers the other as his natural enemy. Hence the Rowlatt legislation. The Civil Service has devised the legislation to keep us down. In my opinion, that legislation is like the coil of the snake round the Indian body. The obstinacy of the Government in clinging to the hateful legislation in spite of the clearest pos-sible demonstration they have had of public opinion against it makes me suspect the worst. With the views enunciated above, you will not wonder at my inability to interest myself in the reforms. Rowlatt legislation blocks the way. And my life is dedicated among other things to removing the block.

Let there be no mistake. Civil resistance has come to stay. It is an eternal doctrine of life which we follow consciously or unconsciously in many walks of life. It is the new and extended application of it which has caused misgivings and excitement. Its suspension is designed to demonstrate its true nature, and to throw the responsibility for the removal of the Rowlatt legislation on the Government as also the leaders (you among them) who have advised me to suspend it. But if within a reasonable time the legislation is not removed, civil resistance will follow as surely as day follows night. No weapon in the Government armoury can either overcome or destroy that eternal force. Indeed a time must come when civil resistance will be recognized as the most efficacious, if also the most harmless, remedy for securing redress of grievances.

You suggest the desirability of unity. I think unity of goal we have. But parties we shall always have—and we may not find a common denominator for improvements. For some will want to go further than some others. I see no harm in a wholesome variety. What I would rid ourselves of is distrust of one another and imputation of motives. Our besetting sin is not our differences but our littleness. We wrangle over words, we fight often for shadow and lose the substance. As Mr. Gokhale used to say, our politics are a pastime of our leisure hours when they are not undertaken as a stepping-stone to a career in life.

I would invite you and every editor to insist on introducing charity, seriousness and selflessness in our politics. And our disunion will not jar as it does today. It is not our differences that really matter. It is the meanness behind that is undoubtedly ugly.

The Punjab sentences are inextricably mixed up with the Rowlatt agitation. It is therefore as imperatively necessary to have them revised as it is to have the Act removed. I agree with you that the Press Act requires overhauling. The Government are actually promoting sedition by high-handed executive action. And I was sorry to learn that Lord Willingdon[2] is reported to have taken—the sole responsibility for the—in my opinion unwarranted action[3] against *The Hindu* and the *Swadesha Mitran*. By it, they have not lost in prestige or popularity. They have gained in both. Surely there are judges enough in the land who would convict where a journalist has overstepped the bounds of legitimate criticism and uttered sedition. I am not enamoured of the Declaration of Rights business. When we have changed the spirit of the English civilian, we shall have made considerable headway with the Declaration of Rights. We must be honourable friends, or equally honourable enemies. We shall be neither, unless we are manly, fearless and independent. I would have us to treasure Lord Willingdon's advice and say 'no' when we mean 'no' without fear of consequences. This is unadulterated civil resistance. It is the way to friendliness and friendship. The other is the age-worn method of open violence on honourable lines in so far as violence can be allowed to be honourable. For me the roots of violence are in dishonour. I have therefore ventured to present to India the former, in its complete form called *satyagraha*, whose roots are always in honour.

Yours sincerely,

M. K. GANDHI

Letter to G. S. Arundale
Young India, 6 Aug. 1919

[1] In reply to his letter of 26 July, appealing to Gandhi that, since civil disobedience had been suspended, he should join in working the Montagu-Chelmsford Constitutional Reforms.

[2] 1866-1941; Governor of Bombay; later, Viceroy of India, 1931-6.

[3] The Government demanded a security of Rs 2,000 from each of these Madras newspapers and banned *The Hindu* in the Punjab and in Burma.

45. 'TRUTH EVEN UNTO THE WICKED'

[Delhi,
After 18 January 1920]

I naturally feel the greatest diffidence about joining issue with the Lokamanya[1] in matters involving questions of interpretation of religious works. But there are things in or about which instinct transcends even interpretation. For me there is no conflict between the two texts quoted by the Lokamanya. The Buddhist text lays down an eternal principle. The text from the *Bhagavad Gita* shows to me how the principle of conquering hate by love, untruth by truth, can and must be applied. If it be true that God metes out the same measure to us that we mete out to others, it follows that if we would escape condign punishment, we may not return anger but gentleness even against anger. And this is the law not for the unworldly but essentially for the worldly. With deference to the Lokamanya, I venture to say that it betrays mental laziness to think that the world is not for *sadhus*. The epitome of all religions is to promote *purushartha*, and *purushartha* is nothing but a desperate attempt to become *sadhu*, i.e., to become a gentleman in every sense of the term.

Finally, when I wrote the sentence about 'everything being fair in politics' according to the Lokamanya's creed, I had in mind his oft-repeated quotation.[2]

To me it enunciates bad law. And I shall not despair of the Lokamanya with all his acumen agreeably surprising India one day with a philosophical dissertation proving the falsity of the doctrine. In any case I pit the experience of a third of a century against the doctrine underlying 'wickedness unto the wicked'. The true law is 'truth even unto the wicked'.

M. K. GANDHI

'Note on Tilak's Letter'
Young India, 28 Jan. 1920

[1] An honorific, signifying 'revered by the people'. B. G. Tilak, the militant patriot, came to be widely known as 'the Lokamanya'.

[2] 'Wickedness unto the wicked.'

46. MEN AND SYSTEMS

A journalist has made these remarks . . .[1]

Parliament is indeed barren. I do not imagine that its nature can change in India. I live, however, in the hope that our Parliament will only remain barren and not give birth to a wicked son. I cannot abandon practical considerations. The ideal is one only, namely, *Ramarajya*. But where can we find Rama? The journalist says, 'whom the people approve'. People means Parliament and, in our view, whomsoever the Parliament approves is a virtuous man or woman. I am suggesting many ways to ensure that the voice of Parliament is really the voice of the people and not that of hired voters. With this end in view I am searching for a device which will enable us to listen to the voice of the entire people. All systems are bound to be defective. We are looking for a system which will yield maximum benefit to India. Good men can transform a bad system into a good one—like the wise housewife who transforms dust into grains. Wicked men can misuse the best of systems and make it defective, like a foolish housewife who allows bright food grains to decay into dust. I am therefore on the look-out for good men in India and employing devices to sort out such men. But what can a man do? He can only make an honest effort. The fruit lies in the hands of God. The efforts of many, and not one, are required for securing the desired fruit. Many other factors determine the fruit. Therefore 'one step is enough' for us.

The same journalist says . . .[2]

All this criticism is true; but these errors are unavoidable. Should we abandon truth because falsehood parades under the garb of truth? Man has to cultivate the inner sense. It does not belong to every man as a natural gift. Its cultivation needs spiritual surroundings and constant effort. It is a delicate plant. Children do not have anything like an inner voice. Those who are considered barbarous have no inner sense. The inner sense reflects the impact produced by a cultivated intellect on the heart. It would therefore be ridiculous if every man claimed to possess an inner voice.

Even then, there is not the least cause for apprehension if many people claim it. Injustice cannot be justified in the name

of conscience. Moreover, those who work under the false pretext of an inner voice are not prepared to undergo suffering.
Their activities will come to a halt after a little while. It
would, therefore, not harm the world if any number of people
made this claim. Those who have played pranks with this
delicate device are likely to ruin themselves, not others. Newspapers provide many instances of this truth. Many newspapers
are at present engaged in spreading poison in the name of
public service. This business will not, however, last long. One
day or other, people are bound to get sick of it. The Punjab
is the greatest culprit in this respect. It is surprising that such
dirty journals can manage to pay their way. Why do people
encourage them? As long as moneyed men are there, thieves
would not starve. Similarly, when a section of the people are
prepared to read poisonous writings, such journals are bound
to prosper. The only cure consists in the cultivation of a clean
public opinion.

'My Notes' (G.)
Navajivan, 24 Aug. 1924

¹ Not reproduced here. They were critical of the British parliamentary system.
² Not reproduced here.

47. VOLUNTARY POVERTY

[London,
23 September 1931]

You will be astonished to hear from me that, although to all
appearances my mission is political, I would ask you to accept
my assurance that its roots are—if I may use that term—
spiritual. It is commonly known, though perhaps not believed,
that I claim that at least my politics are not divorced from
morality, from spirituality, from religion. I have claimed—
and the claim is based upon extensive experience—that a man
who is trying to discover and follow the will of God cannot
possibly leave a single field of life untouched. I came also, in
the course of my service, to the conclusion that if there was
any field of life where morality, where truth, where fear of
God, were not essential, that field should be given up entirely.

But I found also that the politics of the day are no longer a concern of kings, but that they affect the lowest strata of society. And I found, through bitter experience that, if I wanted to do social service, I could not possibly leave politics alone.

Do not please consider that I want to speak to you tonight about politics and somehow or other connect voluntary poverty with politics. That is not my intention. I have simply given you an introduction how I came to believe in the necessity of voluntary poverty for any social worker or for any political worker who wanted to remain untouched by the hideous immorality and untruth that one smells today in ordinary politics. The stench that comes from that life has appeared to some to be so suffocating that they came to the conclusion that politics were not for a god-fearing man.

Had that been really so, I feel that it would have been a disaster for mankind. Find out for yourselves, in the light of what I am now saying, whether directly or indirectly every activity of yours today in this one of the greatest cities of the world is not touched by politics.

Well, then, when I found myself drawn into the political coil, I asked myself what was necessary for me in order to remain absolutely untouched by immorality, by untruth, by what is known as political gain.

In the course of my search, I made several discoveries which I must, for tonight, leave alone. But, if I am not mistaken, this necessity for poverty came to me first of all.

I do not propose to take you through all the details of that act or performance—interesting and, to me, sacred though they are—but I can only tell you that it was a difficult struggle in the beginning and it was a wrestle with my wife and—as I can vividly recall—with my children also.

Be that as it may, I came definitely to the conclusion that, if I had to serve the people in whose midst my life was cast and of whose difficulties I was witness from day to day, I must discard all wealth, all possessions.

I cannot tell you with truth that, when this belief came to me, I discarded everything immediately. I must confess to you that progress at first was slow. And now, as I recall those days of struggle, I remember that it was also painful in the begin-

ning. But, as days went by, I saw that I had to throw over-
board many other things which I used to consider as mine,
and a time came when it became a matter of positive joy to
give up those things. And one after another then, by almost
geometric progression, the things slipped away from me. And,
as I am describing my experiences, I can say a great burden
fell off my shoulders, and I felt that I could now walk with
ease and do my work also in the service of my fellowmen with
great comfort and still greater joy. The possession of anything
then became a troublesome thing and a burden.

Exploring the cause of that joy, I found that, if I kept
anything as my own, I had to defend it against the whole
world. I found also that there were many people who did not
have the thing, although they wanted it; and I would have to
seek police assistance also if hungry, famine-stricken people,
finding me in a lonely place, wanted not merely to divide the
thing with me but to dispossess me. And I said to myself: if
they want it and would take it, they do so not from any
malicious motive, but they would do it because theirs was a
greater need than mine.

And then I said to myself: possession seems to me to be a
crime. I can only possess certain things when I know that
others, who also want to possess similar things, are able to do
so. But we know—every one of us can speak from experience—
that such a thing is an impossibility. Therefore, the only thing
that can be possessed by all is non-possession, not to have
anything whatsoever. In other words, a willing surrender.

You might then well say to me: but you are keeping many
things on your body even as you are speaking about voluntary
poverty and not possessing anything whatsoever! And your
taunt would be right, if you only superficially understood the
meaning of the thing that I am speaking about just now. It is
really the spirit behind. Whilst you have the body, you will
have to have something to clothe the body with also. But then
you will take for the body not all that you can get, but the
least possible, the least with which you can do. You will take
for your house not many mansions, but the least cover that
you can do with. And similarly with reference to your food
and so on.

Now you see that there is here a daily conflict between what you and we understand today as civilization and the state which I am picturing to you as a state of bliss and a desirable state. On the one hand, the basis of culture or civilization is understood to be the multiplication of all your wants. If you have one room, you will desire to have two rooms, three rooms, the more the merrier. And similarly, you will want to have as much furniture as you can put in your house, and so on, endlessly. And the more you possess the better culture you represent, or some such thing. I am putting it, perhaps, not as nicely as the advocates of that civilization would put it, but I am putting it to you in the manner I understand it.

And, on the other hand, you find the less you possess the less you want, the better you are. And better for what? Not for enjoyment of this life, but for enjoyment of personal service to your fellow beings; service to which you dedicate yourselves, body, soul and mind.

Well, here you find there is ample room for hypocrisy and humbug, because a man or a woman may easily deceive himself or herself and deceive his or her neighbours also, by saying: 'In spirit I have given up all possessions, and yet externally I am possessing these things; you must not examine my deed, you must examine my intention; and of my intention only I must remain the sole witness.' That is a trap, and a death trap. How are you then to justify the possession even of a piece of cloth two or three or four yards, say, in length and a yard in width? How can you justify even the possession of that piece of cloth in order to cover your body somewhat, when you know that, if you left that piece of cloth alone, even that would be taken over by someone—not maliciously again—but because he would want it for he has not even so much as that piece of cloth? I am witness, eye-witness, of millions of human beings who have not even so much as that piece of cloth. How are you then to justify your act of possessing this thing with your intention not to possess anything at all?

Well, there is a remedy provided for this dilemma, this difficulty, this contradiction in life—that if you must possess these things, you must hold them at the disposal of those who want them. What happens is that, if somebody comes and wants your piece of cloth, you are not going to keep it from him, you are not going to shut any doors, you are certainly not going to the policeman to ask him to help you to keep these things.

And you have also got to be content with what the world will give you. The world may give you that piece of cloth or may not because, if you do not possess anything, naturally you do not possess the token coin with which you may buy clothing or food. You have got then to live purely on the charity of the world. And even when charitable people give you something, that something does not become your possession. You simply retain it with the fullest intention of that thing being surrendered to anybody who wishes to take it. If somebody comes and uses force against you to dispossess you, you may not go and report to the next policeman you meet and say you have been assaulted. You will not have been assaulted.

Well, that, to my mind, is the meaning of voluntary poverty. I have given you an ideal. Dr. Royden[1] has claimed that I am the greatest exponent of voluntary poverty in the world. I must, in all humility, disown any such claim whatsoever. And this I say to you not because of false modesty, but I say it to you sincerely, believing it to be true. I have given you but a little of my conception of voluntary poverty. And I must own to you that I am far from having realized that ideal in its fullness. In order to realize that ideal in its fullness, there must be a definite intention and conviction in my mind that I do not want to, I must not, possess anything on this earth as my property, not even this body, because this body also is a possession.

If you believe with me—as you must believe with me if you are church-goers, that is, if you believe in God—you believe that body and soul are not one and the same thing, but that the body is a house only, a temporary residence for a soul or a spirit within; and if you believe that, as you do believe, I take it—then it follows that even the body is not yours. It has been given to you as a temporary possession, and it can also be taken from you by Him who has given it to you.

Therefore, having that absolute conviction in me, such must be my constant desire, that this body also may be surrendered at the will of God, and while it is at my disposal, must be used not for dissipation, not for self-indulgence, not for pleasure, but merely for service and service the whole of our waking hours.

And if this is true with reference to the body, how much more with reference to clothing and many other things that we use?

Having got that conviction and held it for so many years, I am here to give you my evidence against myself, that I have not reached that perfect state of voluntary poverty. I am a poor man, in the sense you understand of struggling to reach that ideal, not poor in the sense in which we ordinarily use the word poor.

As a matter of fact, when I was once challenged by someone, I was able to claim that to my neighbours, and people in the world I seemed to be the richest man on earth, for the richest man is really one who, possessing nothing, has everything at his disposal.

And those who have actually followed out this vow of voluntary poverty to the fullest extent possible (to reach absolute perfection is an impossibility, but the fullest possible extent for a human being) those who have reached the ideal of that state, they testify that, when you dispossess yourself of everything you have, you really possess all the treasures of the world. In other words, you really get all that is in reality necessary for you, everything. If food is necessary, food will come to you.

Many of you are men and women of prayer, and I have heard from very many Christian lips that they got their food in answer to prayer, that they get everything in answer to prayer. I believe it. But I want you to come with me a step further, and believe with me that those who voluntarily give up everything on earth, including the body, that is to say, have readiness to give up everything (and they must examine themselves critically, rigidly, and give always an adverse judgment against themselves)—those who will follow this out will really find that they are never in want.

And I will confess to you that, when I felt God had given me some portion of the riches of the earth and when I had many possessions, I had not the facilities for possessing things that I have at this time. I had not certainly one-millionth part

of the ability to command money and everything that I need
for service.

A spirit of service had come to me even when I was practising and earning money and was in possession of several
things, but at that time I had certainly not the capacity for
getting whatever I wanted for service. But today (whether it
is good for me or bad for me I do not know, God alone knows)
I can give you this evidence, that I have never been in want.

After a period when I had really dispossessed myself by
intention and had no hankering after anything that I could
call my own, and began to share everything I possessed in
common with my neighbours (I cannot share everything with
the whole world; if I share with my neighbours, I do share
with the whole world, my neighbours also doing likewise; if
we do that, it is all a limited human being can do) but immediately I came to that state to a fair extent, I found that I
was never in want.

Want must not, again, be taken literally. God is the hardest
task-master I have known on this earth, and He tries you
through and through. And when you find that your faith is
failing or your body is failing you and you are sinking, He
comes to your assistance somehow or other and proves to you
that you must not lose your faith and that He is always at
your beck and call, but on His terms, not on your terms. So
I have found. I cannot really recall a single instance when, at
the eleventh hour, He has forsaken me. And I have got this
reputation, which I can repeat to you, a reputation for being
one of the best beggars in India. And, as my critics will tell
you, at one time I collected one crore of rupees; in pounds,
shillings and pence I cannot count it for you, but it is some
horribly large sum (about £750,000), but I had no difficulty
in collecting it. And since then, whenever any emergency has
arisen, not for any consideration, not in the soul of my fundamental being, can I recall a single instance of my failing to
obtain whatever was necessary for service.

But you will say: this is in answer to prayer. It is not just
an answer to prayer, it is a scientific result of this vow of
non-possession or vow of voluntary poverty. You do not want
to possess anything whatever: and the more therefore you
simplify your life, dispossess yourself, the better it is for you.

Immediately you come to that, you can command anything. You can command vanities, but if you only once take
possession of these, this power will immediately be gone; you
must not take for yourself. If you do, you are done for. I have
known this happen in so many instances. Many a man has
said: 'Oh yes, God has now answered my prayer for money or
possessions. I will now keep this—this Koh-i-noor diamond,
or whatever it may be.' That will be the last time. He won't
be able to defend that diamond.

Therefore, all I am just now holding out before you as a
grand thing is that you can command all the resources of the
world for service. To one who does not believe, that may seem
an arrogant statement to make. But, as I believe, it is not an
arrogant thing to say that you can command all the resources
of the earth for service—to the extent of your ability to serve.
If you want to command the whole services of the world, it is
not enough to go down to some of those houses in the East
End, find out the distress of those who live there and fling in
their faces a few coppers; you will not have all the resources
of the world for that; God will fling in your face also a few
coppers.

But if you surrender yourself, body, soul and mind, and
give yourself up to the world, then I say: the treasures of the
world are at your feet, not for your enjoyment, but for the
enjoyment of that service, only yours for that service.

The moral that I would have us to draw from this talk that
I have given to you is really very apposite at this time. I want
you to believe me when I tell you that my whole heart goes
out to this nation in its distress. I cannot possibly present my
solution of your financial difficulty. You are great enough,
resourceful enough, to find out your own remedies. But I
would ask you to elaborate this thought in your own minds in
connection with the present distress.

Mr. C.F. Andrews brought to my notice a letter that was
written by the Prime Minister to a correspondent and which
he told me yesterday was being used as an advertisement
throughout the District Railway, probably in the Tubes also;
it runs somewhat like this: 'You must buy only British goods;
must employ only British labour, and try to buy as much as
you can.' That is one remedy I know. But I want to suggest

to you that, in order to solve the problem of distress in the world, this idea of voluntary poverty is a root idea. No doubt, with your resourcefulness, you will tide over the difficulty and feel that there was nothing wrong. If you will permit me to say so, that would be perhaps short-sighted, for a time perhaps has come for a revision of values.

But again I must not go into deep waters. I can only throw out this hint to those who can appreciate the necessity of voluntary poverty for service. I have not tonight presented this blessed thing for the acceptance of all: though let me add that, in the innermost recesses of my heart, I feel that the world would not go all wrong, would not become a world of idiots, if all of us took the vow of voluntary poverty. But I know that this is almost an impossible thing. Everything is possible for God but, humanly speaking, it is wise to say that it is an impossible thing. But it is not an impossible thing; indeed, I hold it to be absolutely indispensable that those who give themselves wholly to the service of their fellow-beings must take the vow of voluntary poverty.

Try to find out for yourself whether you are not thereby assisting very materially in solving this great national problem that today faces you.

You will not have solved the problem if the people, who do not want to give up their salaries or whatever they are required to give up, are compelled to give them up by law. While they say: 'What can we do? We do not want to resist; we cannot resist', their minds are still hankering after these things.

But imagine that, in the midst of this hankering, there is a body of servants arising, who will themselves become voluntarily poor. They would be like lighthouses to guide the paths of those who do not know what voluntary poverty is because they know only involuntary poverty. I do not go among my fellows who starve and talk of voluntary poverty; I do not tell them how blessed they would be if they changed that involuntary poverty into voluntary. There is no such thing as magic of that character on this earth. It is a painful process, and these men have first of all to have the necessities of life before I can talk to them of voluntary poverty.

What does happen is this: that a man like me going among

them, living in their midst as best he can their life, can bring a ray of hope into their hearts. They will accept remedies that a man like me may suggest to them. At least, if I cannot suggest any immediate remedy, they would find in a man like me a friend. They would say: 'He is happy although he possesses nothing; how is it?' I do not need to argue with them; they begin to argue for themselves.

How can I share these richest treasures from my experience with everybody on earth? I could not. But today, having undertaken to speak on voluntary poverty, I am sharing, to a certain extent only, these treasured experiences of mine not amongst a few hundred people here but amongst millions of people. I tell you that it is beyond description, the bliss, the happiness, and the ability that this voluntary poverty gives one. I can only say: try it and experiment with it, test it for yourselves.

I thank you for giving me your undivided attention. There are still exactly ten minutes left before the hour of prayer, and if any of you wish to ask me any questions, I shall be glad. You need not hesitate to ask anything that is in your mind; you will never offend me by asking any questions, let them be as awkward as they may be.

Q. Can the Mahatma tell us how he can justify collecting large sums of money when Jesus, the Buddha and other great religious teachers who have practised voluntary poverty have never asked for or received large sums of money? I cannot reconcile this with the rest of what he told us.

A. Did these great teachers never ask for or receive moneys? After Jesus many Christians, who believed in poverty also, took moneys and used them for service. And I can speak with better confidence about the Buddha, who is reported in his own lifetime to have founded institutions. He could not possibly found institutions without money. And it is said that they who gave themselves body, soul and mind gave their riches also and placed them at the feet of the Buddha, who gladly accepted them—but not for himself.

Q. Why should we serve our fellow-beings?

A. In order that we may see a glimpse of God through them; because they have got the same spirit as we have, and unless we learn that, there is a barrier drawn between God and ourselves; if we want to demolish that barrier, the beginning is made by complete identification with our fellow-beings.

Speech at Guildhouse Church, under the auspices of the Franciscan Society
The Guildhouse, 23 Sept. 1931

[1] Dr. Maude Royden, progressive social reformer, was in the chair.

48. RELIGION AND IRRELIGION IN POLITICS

May 30, 1932

In my opinion unity will come not by mechanical means but by change of heart and attitude on the part of the leaders of public opinion. I do not conceive religion as one of the many activities of mankind. The same activity may be either governed by the spirit of religion or irreligion. There is no such thing for me therefore as leaving politics for religion. For me, every, the tiniest, activity is governed by what I consider to be my religion.

A Letter
Mahadevbhaini Diary, Vol. 1, p. 189

49. SEEKING OFFICE

Marwar Junction,
February 16, 1929

Dear Swami,

I was sorry I was not able to have more time with you alone than I was able to have. I would now share with you my innermost thoughts through the more imperfect medium of correspondence.

I look to you to discharge your responsibility and shed sweetness around and about you, as you have promised. You have to stoop to conquer. You should become a real *sannyasi* without anger, without malice, without desire for self. I was not unobservant of the fact that you had no power behind you outside the ranks of your own immediate and very limited following. You are evidently unable to command money when you need it for public work. All this must be altered. You have sacrifice behind you. You have courage. What is it that keeps you from possessing greater influence over the people for their own good?

Why do you want office when the office does not want you? The narrow majority by which you may be able to retain office can bring no real satisfaction, can give you no real opportunity for service. If you will interpret office in terms of service, why will you not refuse to hold it unless your opponents too insist upon your holding it?

I have given effect as much as possible to your wishes in so far as I have been able to interpret them. But I would like you after the election is over or even before, if you have the humility, to confer with Jairamdas and others and think of another president whom you will unanimously elect. Anyway I look to you to run the Congress machinery in Sind smoothly and honestly. *Verb. sap.* You will not I hope misunderstand or misinterpret this letter.

Yours sincerely,

[P. S.] I am in Delhi between Sunday and Tuesday care Speaker Patel. Then Sabarmati for a week.

Letter to Swami Govindanand
SN 15339

50. POLITICAL POWER

Sjt. Satyamurti writes:

I write to you about the article 'Substance Not Shadow' by you, in the *Young India*, of the 18th June. The first sentence which causes me some doubt and anxiety is, 'My proposition therefore before the Working Committee was that agreed settlement failing, the Congress should give up the hope of winning a *swaraj* constitution by way of the present Round Table Conference and should wait till all the communities were satisfied to adopt a purely national solution.' Does this not mean a charter for extreme communalists to go on obstructing?...

But the sentence which causes me grave anxiety is that which ends as follows: 'We can gain our end without political power and by directly acting upon the powers that be.' I would add the following sentences also from your article in order to make my doubts clear to you. 'One form of direct action is adult suffrage. The second and more potent form is *satyagraha*. It can easily be shown that whatever is needful and can be gained by political power can perhaps be more quickly and more certainly gained by *satyagraha*.' I venture to join issue with you. I was always and am today under the impression that what the Congress wants is political power more than anything else. And, concretely speaking, prohibition can be more easily brought about by State action than by peaceful picketing. *Khaddar* and *swadeshi* cloth can be spread better and more quickly by State action than by peaceful picketing, and the necessary reforms embodied in the Karachi resolution on Fundamental Rights can be enforced only by a *swaraj* Government.

In any case, I do not see why the nation should not concentrate all its energies today, upon the gaining of political power.

To me, political power is the substance, and all other reforms can and ought to wait....

I am thankful for this letter. It enables me more clearly than I have been able to explain my position.

My implicit faith in non-violence does mean yielding to minorities when they are really weak. The best way to weaken communalists is to yield to them. Resistance will only rouse their suspicion and strengthen their opposition. A *satyagrahi* resists when there is threat of force behind obstruction. I know that I do not carry the Congressmen in general with me in this what to me appears as very sensible and practical point of view. But if we are to come to *swaraj* through non-violent means, I know that this point of view will be accepted.

Now for Sjt. Satyamurti's second difficulty. To me political power is not an end but one of the means of enabling people to better their condition in every department of life. Political power means capacity to regulate national life through national representatives. If national life becomes so perfect as to become self-regulated, no representation is necessary. There is then a state of enlightened anarchy. In such a state everyone is his own ruler. He rules himself in such a manner that he is never a hindrance to his neighbour. In the ideal state therefore there is no political power because there is no State. But the

ideal is never fully realized in life. Hence the classical statement of Thoreau that that Government is best which governs
the least.

If then I want political power, it is for the sake of the
reforms for which the Congress stands. Therefore when the
energy to be spent in gaining that power means so much loss
of energy required for the reforms, as threatens to be the case
if the country is to engage in a duel with the Mussalmans or
Sikhs, I would most decidedly advise the country to let the
Mussalmans and Sikhs take all the power and I would go on
with developing the reforms.

If we were to analyse the activities of the Congress during
the past twelve years, we would discover that the capacity of
the Congress to take political power has increased in exact
proportion to its ability to achieve success in the constructive
effort. That is to me the substance of political power. Actual
taking over of the Government machinery is but a shadow, an
emblem. And it could easily be a burden if it came as a gift
from without, the people having made no effort to deserve it.

It is now perhaps easy to realize the truth of my statement
that the needful can be 'gained more quickly and more certainly by *satyagraha* than by political power'. Legislation in
advance of public opinion has often been demonstrated to be
futile. Legal prohibition of theft in a country in which the vast
majority are thieves would be futile. Picketing and the other
popular activities are therefore the real thing. If political
power was a thing apart from these reforms, we would have
to suspend latter and concentrate on the former. But we have
followed the contrary course. We have everywhere emphasized the necessity of carrying on the constructive activities as
being the means of attaining *swaraj*. I am convinced that
whenever legal prohibition of drinks, drugs and foreign cloth
comes, it will come because public opinion had demanded it.
It may be said that public opinion demands it today but the
foreign Government does not respond. This is only partly
right. Public opinion in this country is only now becoming a
vital force and developing the real sanction which is *satyagraha*.

'Power not an End'
Young India, 2 July 1931

51. POWER AND REPRESENTATION

[26 October 1934]

You have in your affection misread the whole of my position.[1] If you have given me the position of a general commanding an army, you must allow that general to judge whether he serves the army by being at its head or whether he serves the army by retiring and giving place to lieutenants who have served well.

It is always the wisest thing for the general to swing to power or office or withhold that power that came to him unsought, because there are occasions when generals have been found to consider themselves unequal to hold the reins, and in the interests of the army, the interests of the cause for which the army and its chief are fighting to give up the command. If you believe that I have been a fairly wise general, you must believe in my judgment even now when I seem to be deserting you in the hour of your defeat.

I have said times without number that I myself share no feeling of defeat. I am not deserting the cause for which I live, and for which I love to work. I go away from you in order, as I have said, to discover if there are still greater possibilities in experiments that we have been making, and for which you have given me such a generous support. I must express to you that I seem to have come to the end of my resources. I must confess to you that I have not lost faith in the efficacy of the means that I placed at the disposal of the Congress. But I feel there is a body of opinion rising in the country which has begun to question the efficacy of this means, and it is because they question the efficacy of this means that they have the sense of defeat in them.

In the dictionary of a *satyagrahi*, there is no such thing as defeat. To him, the very pursuit of his battle is its own reward. But when I find some of my best companions, who have believed in truthfulness and non-violence with all its implications, are filled with doubt and feeling of helplessness, when I find that I am not able to touch them with my faith, I see all around me an impenetrable darkness. I see no ray of light. I see I cannot infect them with the faith that is in me.

Therefore I would like you not to take me literally when I

say that I go, if I can get your blessing. I go with your blessing in search of greater power to discover means whereby I can give you the faith that is in me. It may be that the search will be in vain. It may be that my roaming in solitude will be in vain. But depend upon it that I shall not wait a moment longer to be called by you, when I feel the necessity. I shall come to you, and once more come to the Congress to register myself as a primary member, and do whatever I can in the interests of the Congress.

I ask you therefore not to feel dispirited, but to feel that you will be able to discharge your duty, that you will have leaders enough to lead you on to victory. When it becomes necessary for me to come to this House, I will be entirely at your disposal. Therefore, I would simply urge not to press the resolution further. You have unanimously passed that resolution. Let that be enough. Somehow or other I believe good, and only good, will come out of this decision. If you yourselves stand for the principle for which I stand, and for which you have given allegiance, which I acknowledge you have given out of your generosity, some of you no doubt blindly, some of you after having considered for yourselves, I have in all humility accepted all these allegiances. Let me now prove to myself, if it is possible, that I am worthy of it, and I invite you to prove it for yourselves also, whether I remain a member of the Congress or not, that the principle that you have more or less followed during all these long or short 14 or 15 years, you have followed because you have believed in it.

I tell you that it gives me still greater joy and pleasure, for I am able to say to myself, and if you are able to say to the world, that although I am gone you believe in the principle that you have fought for and lived for all these years and that you are going to follow them out not loosely, but still more truly and thoroughly than you have done before.

Immediately after his speech dealing with the question of his retirement Gandhiji proceeded to move formally a comprehensive resolution incorporating all the recommendations of the constitution sub-committee and the Congress Working Committee. In commending the whole of the resolution, for the acceptance of the House *in toto*, Gandhiji at the outset referred to the previous day's decision of the House turning down the Working Committee's recommendation relating to the change of the Congress creed.

Mahatma Gandhi delivered a stirring address lasting 90 minutes in which he appealed to the Subjects Committee to adopt the revised constitution.

Mahatma Gandhi referred to Thursday's vote and congratulated the House on the frank way in which they had voted in referring the question of change of creed to provincial committees. He said, when he had read the public and Press criticism of his proposals, he had made up his mind not to take up those amendments, but members of the Working Committee had of their own accord unanimously taken the view that the Committee would sponsor those resolutions. Gandhiji added:

I was surprised to find that members of the Committee devoted two hours this morning to deliberating as to what was their duty in connection with these amendments. I told the Working Committee to carry out your resolution, but my feeling is that Mr. Sidhwa's amendment was wholly unnecessary. You could have rejected the Working Committee's proposal, but there was no use circulating it.

I listened carefully to Mr. Patwardhan's speech. He argued ably, but either he was deceiving himself or he was acting simply as an advocate. He said that we had descended from ideals to realism. But has not socialism its ideals and if I told him to remove even a comma from their ideals he would reject my proposition. Do you suppose you will realize complete independence at any time even after fifty generations? The socialist creed goes even further. I suggest we must have a measuring rod. The day humanity ceases to believe in ideals, it will descend to the level of the beasts. Today if you believe in truthfulness and non-violence say so. It does not mean you will be cent per cent truthful. I am not cent per cent truthful. If I were, my words will pierce you like arrows and come out clean, but I must aspire to attain my ideals. Did Marx live to see his ideal realized? Is it not undergoing changes and are not meanings put to it which Marx himself never dreamt of? If you do not mean by 'legitimate and peaceful' means that they are 'truthful and non-violent', then merely define your creed to be that of attaining your end by whatever means you think legitimate. Then that would be your measuring rod, but you must have a measuring rod. You must be clear about your aims and means. They are convertible terms.

You know that *swaraj* is your goal. It means '*purna swaraj*' but someone said it did not mean complete independence; so we defined it to mean '*purna swaraj*'. Just as you did that you must define your creed so that it may not be open to double interpretation. No one can draw a right angle, yet Euclid drew it up in imagination and gave the engineers a measuring rod by which the world has progressed. There is a right angle which is treasured in the Tower of London.

The Working Committee on Friday asked you to define your measuring rod. You sent it round for circulation. That was not the right course to take. Let us not tell the world that there is one thing on our lips and another in our thoughts.

Mahatma Gandhi next explained the main purpose of the amendments proposed in the constitution. He said:

Do not pass these changes buoyed up with the hope that I will reconsider my decision. If I began my unofficial leadership of the Congress by the constitution for which I was primarily responsible I am also tendering you a humble gift in the shape of this amended constitution so that you may get the benefit of the judgment and experience of one who has endeavoured to live that constitution in closest communication and communion with you and has discovered its faults. I want you, therefore, to pass these amendments after touching them up.

You can take a day for consideration after hearing me and do whatever lobbying you like and give your verdict. You must first make up your mind to reduce your delegates from 6,000 to 1,000. If you reject that, the entire scheme falls through.

The second point is that the delegates should be real representatives of the people. We are indirectly representative of the nation's dumb millions. We are their mouthpiece, their voice and their thought. That is what the Congress has stood for since 1885, but indirectly we are representatives only of our electors.

Can anyone among us say whom he represents, as to

whether he is in living touch with his constituents and knows their feelings? Even the tallest amongst us cannot claim that. Sardar Vallabhbhai is the uncrowned king of Gujarat, but which electorate does he represent, whom do I represent, I do not know. I challenge anyone to produce the Congress register of electors. We must have constituencies and electors and each member shall represent his constituency and be in living touch with it. Then alone you will have your measuring rod.

The third principle I have put forward is that three things be combined in one election. It will not merely mean greater convenience and saving of money; it is rich with promise if you adopt it. Delegates will then be elected by their electorate. They will not assemble as now for three days in a year and then disappear from the horizon. They will remain active Congressmen as members of the A.I.C.C. and will take up work all the year round.

Today only 350 out of 1,530 are members of the A.I.C.C. Then again a body of 1,000 can be accommodated in Sardar Vallabhbhai's Ras or Bardoli. I have got a complete scheme ready for a successful session being held in the village of that character. Those villages can slave for you but they cannot give you money for your Reception Committee. You must have people who know the business of running a Congress meeting and even importing provisions and the Reception Committee shall not waste lakhs on its arrangements.

I question the wisdom of the Reception Committee wasting lakhs on *tamashas* and in building triumphal arches. Where is our triumph? We are a slave nation and all we want the Reception Committee to do is to give us the hospitality, not of pudding and ice-cream, but ordinary food. Our scheme is to relieve the Reception Committees of their heavy burden. If I had been in Nariman's position I would have become a lunatic.

Mahatma Gandhi, reverting to his plea that the matter be not referred to Provincial Committees, said:

Why do you want to refer it to the provinces? Why shirk your duty? You are super-delegates because you are the Subjects Committee. Others are mere delegates, but mere dele-

gates representing 350 millions. Then I say it is for them to
hammer out a constitution and not shirk the duty. I promise
you fair consideration of every criticism you have made. I am
giving you an iron constitution from which not one single man
can go away. If there is any corruption you can detect it
unless everyone becomes a fraud. No constitution can be
robber-proof and thief-proof. I have sufficient faith in my
countrymen that they will never betray their country.

Sri Prakasa says our present constitution is rotten. Then are
we to waste another year in waiting for what we shall do? I
am sure that the position will remain where it is and we will
not receive a single report during the next twelve months.
Make such use as you can of the wisdom you say is possessed
by me whom the world holds as a fool. But wisdom sometimes
does come out of the mouth of fools. I would like you to accept
my suggestions and I will be ready for compromise. Already,
when Mr. Masani came to me, I assured him that I wanted
Socialists to be represented. They are the advance wing. There
is nothing to be feared from their activity. They call themselves Congressmen and while they are Congressmen they are
supposed to believe in the Congress creed and loyally follow
the discipline of the Congress. If they fail to follow the Congress discipline, they will fail in their own creed. I have agreed
to their suggestion regarding the single transferable vote. This
constitution has been revised by able lawyers like Mr. Bhulab-
hai Desai and Mr. K. M. Munshi and many others have been
consulted. I may also make it clear that there will be plural
constituencies in urban areas, but their number is not defined.
The Working Committee is entirely in your hands in these
matters of detail, but do not postpone these matters.

You are going to have a Parliamentary Board. They will
look after the Assembly work. In the Assembly it is not a
battle between men, but between principles; our members
will go to represent the principles which will not require eloquence, but will be enunciated in unequivocal terms.

Hereafter you will have your register of electors and you
will be in living touch with them. Mr. Nageshwara Rao says
that there are 7,000 voters for one seat. My scheme is modest.
It wants only 1,000 voters for one seat. I will be satisfied if
you are the representatives of one million and then we can

have more and more. But I do submit that we will lose one precious year in the life of the nation by referring these matters to Provincial Committees.

Proceeding, Mahatma Gandhi referred to the amendments seeking to incorporate the existing convention of allowing the President to select his colleagues of the Working Committee in the Congress constitution. Gandhiji said that there had been no single instance in the past wherein the President's choice in this matter had been overridden by the A.I.C.C. But he thought it would be better to incorporate this convention in the constitution so as to avoid difficulties attendant on selection of candidates. The President under this amendment would not have to stand the fire of cross-examination at the A.I.C.C.

There must be some occasions in the life of the Working Committee when they would have to say: 'If you want us to carry on then we ask you to arm us with certain powers and if you cannot trust us then you must look for better men to fill our place.' For the same reason he had sought that the Secretaries and the Treasurer should also be the President's choice.[2]

Speech at Subjects Committee Meeting, All India Congress Committee
Home Department, Political, File No. 4/27/36

[1] Earlier the Subjects Committee had unanimously passed a resolution expressing the country's confidence in Gandhi and requesting him to revise his decision to retire.
[2] This appeared in the *Bombay Sentinel*, 27 Oct. 1934.

52. POLITICAL POWER AND SOCIAL REFORM

Among the questions that a correspondent asked me for discussion in *Harijan* there was one which I have kept on my file for some time:

Don't you think that it is impossible to achieve any great reform without winning political power? The present economic structure has also got to be tackled. No reconstruction is possible without a political reconstruction and I am afraid all this talk of polished and unpolished rice, balanced diet and so on and so forth is mere moonshine.

I have often heard this argument advanced as an excuse for failure to do many things. I admit that there are certain things which cannot be done without political power, but there are numerous other things which do not at all depend upon political power. That is why a thinker like Thoreau said that 'that government is the best which governs the least'. This means that when people come into possession of political power, the interference with the freedom of people is reduced to a minimum. In other words, a nation that runs its affairs smoothly and effectively without much State interference is truly democratic. Where such a condition is absent, the form of government is democratic in name.

There is certainly no limit or restraint on the freedom of thought. It may be remembered that many reformers are nowadays laying the greatest emphasis on a new ideology. How few of us are going in for any reform in our opinions? Modern scientists recognize the potency of thought and that is why it is said that as a man thinks so does he become. One who always thinks of murder will turn a murderer, and one who thinks of incest will be incestuous. On the contrary he who always thinks of truth and non-violence will be truthful and non-violent, and he whose thoughts are fixed on God will be godly. In this realm of thought political power does not come into play at all. Even so it must be obvious that political power ·or want of it is of no consequence in many of our activities. I would make a humble suggestion to the correspondent. Let him make a detailed note of all his daily activities and he is sure to find that many of them are performed independently of any political power. Man has to thank himself for his dependence. He can be independent as soon as he wills it.

The correspondent has raised the bugbear of 'great' reform and then fought shy of it. He who is not ready for small reforms will never be ready for great reforms. He who makes the best of his faculties will go on augmenting them, and he will find that what once seemed to him a great reform was really a small one. He who orders his life in this way will lead a truly natural life. One must forget the political goal in order to realize it. To think in terms of the political goal in every matter and at every step is to raise unnecessary dust. Why worry one's head over a thing that is inevitable? Why die before one's death?

That is why I can take the keenest interest in discussing vitamins and leafy vegetables and unpolished rice. That is why it has become a matter of absorbing interest to me to find out how best to clean our latrines, how best to save our people from the heinous sin of fouling Mother Earth every morning. I do not quite see how thinking of these necessary problems and finding a solution for them has no political significance and how an examination of the financial policy of Government has necessarily a political bearing. What I am clear about is that the work I am doing and asking the masses to do is such as can be done by millions of people, whereas the work of examining the policy of our rulers will be beyond them. That it is a few people's business I will not dispute. Let those who are qualified to do so do it as best as they can. But until these leaders can bring great changes into being, why should not millions like me use the gifts that God has given them to the best advantage? Why should they not make their bodies fitter instruments of service? Why should not they clear their own doors and environments of dirt and filth? Why should they be always in the grip of disease and incapable of helping themselves or anyone else?

No, I am afraid the correspondent's question betrays his laziness and despair and the depression that has overtaken many of us. I can confidently claim that I yield to none in my passion for freedom. No fatigue or depression has seized me. Many years' experience has convinced me that the activities that absorb my energies and attention are calculated to achieve the nation's freedom, that therein lies the secret of non-violent freedom. That is why I invite everyone, men and women, young and old, to contribute his or her share to the great sacrifice.

'A Fatal Fallacy'
Harijan, 11 Jan. 1936

53. SILENT SERVICE

New Delhi,
April 15, 1946

The suggestion for not accepting office greatly appeals to me. Carry on silently whatever constructive work, you can. These are difficult times. If all want power who will render silent service?

Note to Baba Raghavdas (H.)
Hindustan, 16 Apr. 1946

VI

Religion

54. THE TRIALS OF HINDUISM

When the Theosophical Society invited me to deliver these speeches, I accepted the invitation on two considerations. It is now nearly twelve years that I have been living in South Africa. Everyone is aware of the hardships suffered by my compatriots in this land. People view with contempt the colour of their skin. I believe all this is due to a lack of proper understanding; and I have continued to stay in South Africa with a view to helping as much as possible in the removal of this misunderstanding. I, therefore, felt that it would to some extent help me in the fulfilment of my duty if I accepted the Society's invitation; and I shall regard myself very fortunate if I am able, through these lectures, to give you a better understanding of the Indians. I am to speak to you no doubt about the Hindus; but the ways and manners of the Hindus and other Indians are all but identical. All Indians have similar virtues and vices and are descended from the same stock. The other consideration was that there was, among the objects of the Theosophical Society, this one, viz., to compare the various religions, find out the truth underlying these and show the people how those religions were only so many roads leading to the realisation of God, and how one ought to hesitate to dub any of them false. I thought that this object, too, would be realised to some extent if I said a few words on the Hindu religion.

Hindus are not considered to be the original inhabitants of India. According to Western scholars, the Hindus as well as most of the European peoples lived at one time in Central Asia. Migrating from there, some went to Europe, some to Iran, others moved south-eastwards down into India through the Punjab, and there spread the Aryan religion. The Hindu population in India exceeds two hundred millions. They are called Hindus because they once lived beyond the river Sindhu (Indus). The Vedas are their oldest scripture. Very devout Hindus believe that the Vedas are of divine origin and without beginning. Western scholars hold that these were composed before 2000 B.C. The famous Mr. Tilak of Poona has shown that the Vedas must be at least 10,000 years old. The main thing that distinguishes the Hindus is their belief that the *Brahman* or oversoul is all-pervading. What we all have to attain is *moksha* or liberation, *moksha* here meaning freeing oneself from the evil of birth and death and merging in the *Brahman*. Humility and even-mindedness are the chief qualities of their ethics, while caste reigns supreme in their temporal affairs.

The Hindu religion underwent its first trial on the advent of Lord Buddha. The Buddha was himself the son of a king. He is said to have been born before 600 B.C. At that time the Hindus were under the glamour of the outward form of their religion, and the *Brahmins* had, out of selfishness, abandoned their true function of defending the Hindu faith. Lord Buddha was moved to pity when he saw his religion reduced to such a plight. He renounced the world and started doing penance. He spent several years in devout contemplation and ultimately suggested some reform in the Hindu religion. His piety greatly affected the minds of the *Brahmins*, and the killing of animals for sacrifice was stopped to a great extent. It cannot, therefore, be said that the Buddha founded a new or different religion. But those who came after him gave his teachings the identity of a separate religion. King Ashoka the Great sent missionaries to different lands for the propagation of Buddhism, and spread that religion in Ceylon, China, Burma and other countries. A distinctive beauty of Hinduism was revealed during this process: no one was converted to Buddhism by force. People's minds were sought to be influenced only by discussion and argument and mainly by the very pure conduct of the preachers themselves. It may be said that, in India at any rate, Hinduism and Buddhism were but one, and that even to-day the fundamental principles of both are identical.

We have seen that Buddhism had a salutary effect on Hinduism, that the champions of the latter were aroused by its impact. A thousand years ago, the Hindu religion came under another influence more profound. Hazrat Mahomed was born 1300 years ago. He saw moral anarchy rampant in Arabia. Judaism was struggling for survival; Christianity was not able to gain a foothold in the land; and the people were given to licence and self-indulgence. Mahomed felt all this to be improper. It caused him mental agony; and in the name of God, he determined to make them realise their miserable condition. His feeling was so intense that he was able immediately to impress the people around him with his fervour, and Islam spread very rapidly. Zeal or passion, then, is a great speciality, a mighty force, of Islam. It has been the cause of many good deeds, and sometimes of bad ones too. A thousand years ago the army of Ghazni invaded India in order to spread Islam. Hindu idols were broken and the invasions advanced as far as Somnath. While, on the one hand, violence was thus being used, the Muslim saints were, on the other, unfolding the real merit of Islam. The Islamic principle that all those who embraced Islam were equals made such a favourable impression on the lower classes that hundreds of thousands of Hindus accepted that faith, and there was great commotion in the whole community.

Kabir was born in Benares. He thought that, according to Hindu philosophy, there could be no distinction between a Hindu and a Muslim. Both of them, if they did good works, would find a place in heaven. Idolatry was not an essential part of Hinduism. Reasoning thus, he attempted to bring about a synthesis between Hinduism and Islam; but it did not have much effect, and his became no more than a distinct sect, and it exists even to-day. Some years later, Guru Nanak was born in the Punjab; he accepted the reasoning of Kabir and made a similar attempt to fuse the two religions. But while doing so, he felt that Hinduism should be defended against Islam, if necessary with the sword. This gave rise to Sikhism, and produced the Sikh warriors. The result of all this is that, despite the prevalence of Hinduism and Islam as the two principal religions of India to-day, both the communities live together in peace and amity and are considerate enough not to hurt one another's feelings save for the bitterness caused by political machinations and excitement. There is very little difference between a Hindu *yogi* and a Muslim *fakir*.

While Islam and Hinduism were thus vying with each other, the Christians landed at the port of Goa about 500 years ago, and set about converting Hindus to Christianity. They also partly resorted to force and [converted] partly through persuasion. Some of their ministers were exceedingly tender-hearted and kind, rather one would call them saintly. Like the *fakirs* they made a deep impression on the lower classes of Hindu society. But later, when Christianity and Western civilisation came to be associated, the Hindus began to look upon that religion with disfavour. And to-day, we see few Hindus embracing Christianity in spite of the fact that the Christians are ruling over a vast kingdom. Nevertheless, Christianity has had a very considerable influence on Hinduism. Christian priests imparted education of a high order and pointed out some of the glaring defects in Hinduism, with the result that there arose among the Hindus other great teachers who, like Kabir, began to teach the Hindus what was good in Christianity and appealed to them to remove these defects. To this category belonged Raja Ram Mohan Roy,[1] Devendranath Tagore, and Keshab Chandra Sen.[2] In Western India we had Dayanand Saraswati.[3] And the numerous reformist associations like the Brahmo Samaj and the Arya Samaj that have sprung up in India today are doubtless the result of Christian influence. Again, Madame Blavatsky[4] came to India, told both Hindus and the Muslims of the evils of Western civilisation and asked them to beware of becoming enamoured of it.

Thus, we have seen how there have been three assaults on Hinduism, coming from Buddhism, Islam and then Christianity, but how on the whole it came out of them unscathed. It has tried to imbibe whatever was good in each of these religions. We should, however, know what the followers of this religion, Hinduism, believe. This is what they believe: God exists. He is without beginning, immaculate, and without any attribute or form. He is omnipresent and omnipotent. His original form is *Brahman*. It neither does, nor causes to be done. It does not govern. It is bliss incarnate, and by it all this is sustained. The soul exists, and is distinct from the body. It also is without a beginning, without birth. Between its original form and the *Brahman*, there is no distinction. But it takes on, from time to time, a body as a result of *karma* or the power of *maya*, and goes on being born again and again into high or low species in accordance with the good or bad deeds performed by it. To be free from the cycle of birth and death and be merged in *Brahman* is *moksha* or liberation. The way to achieve this *moksha* is to do pure and good deeds, to have compassion for all living beings, and to live in truth. Even after reaching this stage, one does not attain liberation, for one has to enjoy embodied existence as a consequence of one's good deeds as well. One has, therefore, to go a step further. We will, however, have to continue to act, only we should not cherish any attachment to our actions. Action should be undertaken for its own sake, without an eye on the fruit. In short, everything should be dedicated to God. We should not cherish, even in a dream, the feeling of pride that we do or can do anything. We should look upon all equally. These are the beliefs or tenets of Hinduism, but there admittedly exist a number of schools. Also, there have arisen a few factions or sects resulting from [differences in] secular practices. But we need not consider them on the present occasion.

If, after listening to this, any one of you has been favourably impressed and has come to feel that the Hindus or the Indians, in whose country the religion expounded above prevails, cannot be altogether an inferior people, you can render service to my countrymen even without becoming involved in political matters.

All religions teach that we should all live together in love and mutual kindness. It was not my intention to preach you a sermon neither am I fit to do so. But if it has produced any favourable impression on your mind, I would appeal to you to let my brethren have its benefit and, as behoves the English people, to defend them, whenever they are maligned.

Lectures on Religion, Johannesburg Lodge, Theosophical Society
Indian Opinion, 15 April 1905

¹ Founder of the Brahmo Samaj.

² Raja Ram Mohan Roy's work was continued by Devendranath Tagore and Keshab Chandra Sen, the former on the lines of pure Hinduism and the latter along those of Christianity.

³ Founder of the Arya Samaj.

⁴ Founder of the Theosophical Society.

55. GOLDEN SAYINGS OF ISLAM

We discussed in previous issues some books in the series *The Wisdom of the East*. The same writers have brought out a book on the subject noted above and have sent us a copy for review. It is hardly necessary to say that the book is in English. It is priced at one shilling only. It contains extracts from the holy Koran, and reproduces the sayings of Arab thinkers on different matters. For instance, with reference to nobility, it is said that 'He who disregards his own honour gets no good from an honourable lineage.... Learning and high principles cover the shame of low origin.' The book is full of rich thoughts having a bearing on our struggle for honour. The poet says: 'Men see no fault in one who respects himself.' Then again: 'Be ashamed in your own sight more than in the sight of men.' Once more: 'He who respects not himself can have no respect for others.' And elsewhere it is said: 'Life has no worth and this world has no happiness for a man who has lost his self-respect and abandoned himself to shamelessness.' Under Character, we have: 'A man is truly religious when he is truly good.' Under Knowledge, we have: 'A man without education is like a brave man without arms.' 'Kings govern men and learned men govern kings.' 'A wise man is not he who considers how he may get out of an evil, but he who sees to it that he does not fall into it.' On Truthfulness, it is said: 'No man's religion can be right unless his heart becomes right, nor can his heart become right unless his tongue is right.... That man is a hypocrite who prays and fasts, but is untruthful in what he says, false to his word, and unfaithful in discharging a trust.' Such are the golden sayings contained in this little book. We advise everyone who can read English to buy this book.

'Arab Wisdom' (G.)
Indian Opinion, 28 Dec. 1907

56. THE BUDDHIST REFORMATION

[Bombay,
18 May 1924]

The only reason for inviting me to preside at this meeting is,
I presume, that I am more than most people endeavouring to
popularize the truth for which Gautama Buddha lived and
died. For, my book-knowledge of Buddhism, I am sorry to
have to confess, is of the poorest type. It is confined to the
fascinating book of Sir Edwin Arnold, which I read for the
first time now nearly thirty-five years ago, and one or two
books during my brief incarceration in the Yeravda Jail. But
that great Buddhist scholar, Professor Kausambi, tells me that
The Light of Asia gives but a faint idea of Buddha's life, and
that at least one incident in the beautiful poem is not to be
found in any authoritative original Buddhist work. Perhaps
some day the learned Professor will give us the results of his
ripe scholarship in the shape of a reliable story of Buddha's
life for the ordinary Indian reader.

For the moment, however, I would like to tell the meeting
what I believe about Buddhism. To me it is a part of Hinduism. Buddha did not give the world a new religion; he gave
it a new interpretation. He taught Hinduism not to take but
to give life. True sacrifice was not of others but of self. Hinduism resents any attack upon the Vedas. It regarded the new
interpretation as such attack. Whilst, therefore, it accepted
the central truth of Buddha's teaching, it fought against
Buddhism regarded as a new and anti-Vedic cult.

It has become the fashion nowadays in some quarters to say
that India's downfall dates from her acceptance of Buddha's
teachings. It is tantamount to saying that love and piety, if
sufficiently practised, will degrade the world. In other words,
according to the critics, evil should triumph in the end. It is
my unalterable belief that India has fallen not because it
accepted Gautama's teaching, but because it failed to live up
to it. The priest has ever sacrificed the prophet. Vedas to be
divine must be a living word, ever growing, ever expanding
and ever responding to new forces. The priest clung to the
letter and missed the spirit.

But we need not despair. The reformation that Buddha

attempted has not yet had a fair trial. Twenty-five hundred years are nothing in the life of the world. If the evolution of form takes aeons, why should we expect wonders in the evolution of thought and conduct? And yet the age of miracles is not gone. As with individuals, so with nations. I hold it to be perfectly possible for masses to be suddenly converted and uplifted. Suddenness is only seeming. No one can say how far the leaven has been working. The most potent forces are unseen, even unfelt, for long. But they are working none the less surely. Religion to me is a living faith in the Supreme Unseen Force. That Force has confounded mankind before, and it is bound to confound us again. Buddha taught us to defy appearances and trust in the final triumph of Truth and Love. This was his matchless gift to Hinduism and to the world.

He taught us also how to do it, because he lived what he taught. The best propaganda is not pamphleteering, but for each one of us to try to live the life we would have the world to live.

Speech at Buddha Jayanti, Bombay
CW 5176

57. THE SERMON ON THE MOUNT

[15 November 1927]

There are some who will not even take my flat denial when I tell them that I am not a Christian.

The message of Jesus, as I understand it, is contained in his Sermon on the Mount unadulterated and taken as a whole, and even in connection with the Sermon on the Mount, my own humble interpretation of the message is in many respects different from the orthodox. The message, to my mind, has suffered distortion in the West. It may be presumptuous for me to say so, but as a devotee of truth, I should not hesitate to say what I feel. I know that the world is not waiting to know my opinion on Christianity.

One's own religion is after all a matter between oneself and one's Maker and no one else's, but if I feel impelled to share my thoughts with you this evening, it is because I want to enlist your sympathy in my search for truth and because so many Christian friends are interested in my thoughts on the teachings of Jesus. If then I had to face only the Sermon on the Mount and my own interpretation of it, I should not hesitate to say, 'Oh yes, I am a Christian.' But I know that at the present moment if I said any such thing I would lay myself open to the gravest misinterpretation. I should lay myself open to fraudulent claims because I would have then to tell you what my own meaning of Christianity is, and I have no desire myself to give you my own view of Christianity. But negatively I can tell you that in my humble opinion, much of what passes as Christianity is· a negation of the Sermon on the Mount. And please mark my words. I am not at the present moment speaking of Christian conduct. I am speaking of the Christian belief, of Christianity as it is understood in the West.

I am painfully aware of the fact that conduct everywhere falls far short of belief. But I don't say this by way of criticism. I know from the treasures of my own experience that although I am every moment of my life trying to live up to my professions, my conduct falls short of these professions. Far therefore be it from me to say this in a spirit of criticism. But I am placing before you my fundamental difficulties. When I began as a prayerful student to study the Christian literature in South Africa in 1893, I asked myself, 'Is this Christianity?' and have always got the Vedic answer, *neti neti* (not this, not this). And the deepest in me tells me that I am right.

I claim to be a man of faith and prayer, and even if I was cut to pieces, God would give me the strength not to deny Him and to assert that He is. The Muslim says He is and there is no one else. The Christian says the same thing and so the Hindu, and if I may say so, even the Buddhist says the same thing, if in different words. We may each of us be putting our own interpretation on the word God—God Who embraces not only this tiny globe of ours, but millions and billions of such globes. How can we, little crawling creatures, so utterly helpless as He has made us, how could we possibly measure His greatness, His boundless love, His infinite compassion, such that He allows man insolently to deny compassion, such that He allows man insolently to deny Him, wrangle about Him, and cut the throat of his fellow-man? How can we measure the greatness of God Who is so forgiving, so divine?

Thus though we may utter the same words they have not the same meaning for us all. And hence I say that we do not need to proselytize or do *shuddhi* or *tabligh* through our speech or writing. We can only do it really with our lives. Let them be open books for all to study. Would that I could persuade the missionary friends to take this view of their mission. Then there will be no distrust, no suspicion, no jealousy and no dissensions.

Gandhiji then took the case of modern China as a case in point. His heart, he said, went out to young China in the throes of a great national upheaval, and he referred to the anti-Christian movement in China, about which he had occasion to read in a pamphlet received by him from the students' department of the Young Women's Christian Association and the Young Men's Christian Association of China. The writers had put their own interpretation upon the anti-Christian movement, but there was no doubt that young China regarded Christian movements as being opposed to Chinese self-expression. To Gandhiji the moral of this anti-Christian manifestation was clear. He said:

Don't let your Christian propaganda be anti-national, say these young Chinese. And even their Christian friends have come to distrust the Christian endeavour that had come from the West. I present the thought to you that these essays written by young men have a deep meaning, a deep truth, because they were themselves trying to justify their Christian conduct in so far as they had been able to live up to the life it had taught them and at the same time find a basis for that opposition. The deduction I would like you all to draw from this manifestation is that you Ceylonese should not be torn from your moorings, and those from the West should not consciously or unconsciously lay violent hands upon the manners, customs and habits of the Ceylonese in so far as they are not repugnant to fundamental ethics and morality. Confuse not Jesus' teachings with what passes as modern civilization, and pray do not do unconscious violence to the people among whom you cast your lot. It is no part of that call, I assure you, to tear the lives of the people of the East by its roots. Tolerate whatever is good in them and do not hastily, with your preconceived notions, judge them.

Do not judge lest you be judged yourselves. In spite of your belief in the greatness of Western civilization and in spite of your pride in all your achievements, I plead with you for humility, and ask you to leave some little room for doubt, in which, as Tennyson sang, there was more truth, though by 'doubt' he no doubt meant a different thing. Let us each one live our life, and if ours is the right life, where is the cause for hurry? It will react of itself.

To you, young Ceylonese friends, I say: Don't be dazzled by the splendour that comes to you from the West. Do not be thrown off your feet by this passing show. The Enlightened One has told you in never-to-be-forgotten words that this little span of life is but a passing shadow, a fleeting thing, and if you realize the nothingness of all that appears before your eyes, the nothingness of this material case that we see before us ever changing, then indeed there are treasures for you up above, and there is peace for you down here, peace which passeth all understanding, and happiness to which we are utter strangers. It requires an amazing faith, a divine faith and surrender of all that we see before us.

What did Buddha do, and Christ do, and also Mahomed? Theirs were lives of self-sacrifice and renunciation. Buddha renounced every worldly happiness, because he wanted to share with the whole world his happiness which was to be had by men who sacrificed and suffered in search of truth. If it was a good thing to scale the heights of Mt. Everest, sacrificing precious lives in order to be able to go there and make some slight observations, if it was a glorious thing to give up life after life in planting a flag in the uttermost extremities of the earth, how much more glorious would it be to give not one life, surrender not a million lives but a billion lives in search of the potent and imperishable truth? So be not lifted off your feet, do not be drawn away from the simplicity of your ancestors.

A time is coming when those who are in the mad rush today of multiplying their wants, vainly thinking that they add to the real substance, real knowledge of the world, will retrace their steps and say: 'What have we done?' Civilizations have come and gone, and in spite of all our vaunted progress I am tempted to ask again and again 'To what purpose?' Wallace, a contemporary of Darwin, has said the same thing. Fifty years of brilliant inventions and discoveries, he has said, has not added one inch to the moral height of mankind. So said a dreamer and visionary if you will—Tolstoy. So said Jesus, and Buddha, and Mahomed, whose religion is being denied and falsified in my own country today.

By all means drink deep of the fountains that are given to you in the Sermon on the Mount, but then you will have to take sackcloth and ashes. The teaching of the Sermon was meant for each and every one of us. You cannot serve both God and Mammon. God the Compassionate and the Merciful, Tolerance-incarnate, allows Mammon to have his nine days' wonder. But I say to you, youth of Ceylon, fly from that self-destroying but destructive show of Mammon.

Speech at YMCA, Colombo
Young India, 8 Dec. 1927

58. RELIGION AND CULTURE

A student of the Gujarat Vidypith[1] writes:

What concrete form ought religious instruction to take in the Vidyapith?

To me religion means truth and *ahimsa* or rather truth alone, because truth includes *ahimsa*, *ahimsa* being the necessary and indispensable means for its discovery. Therefore anything that promotes the practice of these virtues is a means for imparting religious education and the best way to do this, in my opinion, is for the teachers rigorously to practise these virtues in their own person. Their very association with the boys, whether on the playground or in the class-room, will then give the pupils a fine training in these fundamental virtues.

So much for instruction in the universal essentials of religion. A curriculum of religious instruction should include a study of the tenets of faiths other than one's own. For this purpose the students should be trained to cultivate the habit of understanding and appreciating the doctrines of various great religions of the world in a spirit of reverence and broad-minded tolerance. This, if properly done, would help to give them a spiritual assurance and a better appreciation of their own religion. There is one rule, however, which should always be kept in mind while studying all great religions and that is that one should study them only through the writings of known votaries of the respective religions. For instance, if one wants to study the *Bhagavata* one should do so not through a translation of it made by a hostile critic but through one prepared by a lover of the *Bhagavata*. Similarly to study the Bible one should study it through the commentaries of devoted Christians. This study of other religions besides one's own will give one a grasp of the rock-bottom unity of all religions and afford a glimpse also of that universal and absolute truth which lies beyond the 'dust of creeds and faiths'.

Let no one even for a moment entertain the fear that a reverent study of other religions is likely to weaken or shake one's faith in one's own. The Hindu system of philosophy regards all religions as containing the elements of truth in them and enjoins an attitude of respect and reverence towards them all. This of course presupposes regard for one's own religion. Study and appreciation of other religions need not cause a weakening of that regard; it should mean extension of that regard to other religions.

In this respect religion stands on the same footing as culture. Just as preservation of one's own culture does not mean contempt for that of others, but requires assimilation of the best that there may be in all the other cultures, even so should be the case with religion. Our present fears and apprehensions are a result of the poisonous atmosphere that has been generated in the country, the atmosphere of mutual hatred, ill-will and distrust. We are constantly labouring under a nightmare of fear lest someone should stealthily undermine our faith or the faith of those who are dear and near to us. But this unnatural state will cease when we have learnt to cultivate respect and tolerance towards other religions and their votaries.

'Religious Education'
Young India, 6 Dec. 1928

----

[1] An educational institution.

59. TRUE SPIRITUAL TRANSFORMATION

[Before 1 March 1929]

DR. MOTT: What do you consider to be the most valuable contribution that India can make to the progress of the world?

GANDHI: Non-violence, which the country is exhibiting at the present day on a scale unprecedented in history. But for it, there might have been a blaze, for provocation of the gravest kind has not been wanting on the side of the Government. There is no doubt a school in the country that believes in violence, but it is a mere excrescence on the surface and its ideals are not likely to find a congenial soil in the country.

What causes you solicitude for the future of the country?

Our apathy and hardness of heart, if I may use that Biblical phrase, as typified in the attitude towards the masses and their poverty. Our youth are full of noble feelings and impulses but these have not yet taken any definite practical shape. If our youth had a living and active faith in truth and non-violence, for instance, we should have made much greater headway by now. All our young men, however, are not apathetic. In fact without the closest co-operation of some of our educated young men and women, I should not have been able to establish contact with the masses and to serve them on a nationwide scale; and I am sustained by the hope that they will act as the leaven, and in time transform the entire mass.

From this they passed on to the distinctive contributions of Hinduism, Islam and Christianity to the upbuilding of the Indian nation.

The most distinctive and the largest contribution of Hinduism to India's culture is the doctrine of *ahimsa*. It has given a definite bias to the history of the country for the last three thousand years and over and it has not ceased to be a living force in the lives of India's millions even today. It is a growing doctrine, its message is still being delivered. Its teaching has so far permeated our people that an armed revolution has almost become an impossibility in India, not because, as some would have it, we as a race are physically weak, for it does not require much physical strength so much as a devilish will to press a trigger to shoot a person, but because the tradition of *ahimsa* has struck deep roots among the people.

Islam's distinctive contribution to India's national culture is its unadulterated belief in the oneness of God and a practical application of the truth of the brotherhood of man for those who are nominally within its fold. I call these two distinctive contributions. For in Hinduism the spirit of brotherhood has become too much philosophized. Similarly though philosophical Hinduism has no other god but God, it cannot be denied that practical Hinduism is not so emphatically uncompromising as Islam.

What then is the contribution of Christianity to the national life of India? I mean the influence of Christ as apart from Christianity, for I am afraid there is a wide gulf separating the two at present.

Aye, there's the rub. It is not possible to consider the teaching of a religious teacher apart from the lives of his followers. Unfortunately, Christianity in India has been inextricably mixed up for the last one hundred and fifty years with the British rule. It appears to us as synonymous with materialistic civilization and imperialistic exploitation by the stronger white races of the weaker races of the world. Its contribution to India has been therefore largely of a negative character. It has done some good in spite of its professors. It has shocked us into setting our own house in order. Christian missionary literature has drawn pointed attention to some of our abuses and set us athinking.

What has interested me most is your work in connection with the removal of untouchability. Will you please tell me what is the most hopeful sign indicating that this institution is as you say on its last legs?

It is the reaction that is taking place in orthodox Hinduism and the swiftness with which it has come about. As a most illustrious example I will mention Pandit Malaviyaji. Ten years back he was as punctilious in the observance of the rules with regard to untouchability as perhaps the most orthodox Hindu of that day. Today he takes pride in administering the *mantra* of purification to the untouchables by the bank of the Ganges, sometimes even incurring the wrath of unreasoning orthodoxy. He was all but assaulted by the diehard section in Calcutta in December last for doing this very thing. In Wardha a wealthy merchant Sheth Jamnalal Bajaj recently threw open his magnificent temple to the untouchables and that without arousing any serious opposition. The most remarkable thing about it is that from the record kept in the temple of the daily visitors it was found that the attendance had gone up instead of declining since the admission of the untouchables to it. I may sum up the outlook by saying that I expect the tide against untouchability to rise still more swiftly in the near future, astonishingly swift as it has already been.

Where do you find your friends? Do you get the backing of the Mussalmans and the Christians in this work?

The Mussalmans and the Christians can from the very nature of the case render little help in this matter. The removal of untouchability is purely a question of the purification of Hinduism. This can only be effected from within.

But my impression was that Christians would be a great help to you in this connection. The Rev. Whitehead, Bishop of the Church of England Mission, made some striking statements about the effect of Christian mass movement in ameliorating the condition of the untouchables in the Madras Presidency.

I distrust mass movements of this nature. They have as their object not the upliftment of the untouchables but their ultimate conversion. This motive of mass proselytization lurking at the back in my opinion vitiates missionary effort.

There are conflicting opinions on this point. There are some who seriously believe that the untouchables would be better off if they turned Christians from conviction, and that it would transform their lives for the better.

I am sorry I have been unable to discover any tangible evidence to confirm this view. I was once taken to a Christian village. Instead of meeting among the converts with that frankness which one associates with a spiritual transformation, I found an air of evasiveness about them. They were afraid to talk. This struck me as a change not for the better but for the worse.

Do you then disbelieve in all conversion?

I disbelieve in the conversion of one person by another. My effort should never to be undermine another's faith but to make him a better follower of his own faith. This implies belief in the truth of all religions and therefore respect for them. It again implies true humility, a recognition of the fact that the divine light having been vouchsafed to all religions through an imperfect medium of flesh, they must share in more or less degree the imperfection of the vehicle.

Is it not our duty to help our fellow-beings to the maximum of truth that we may possess, to share with them our deepest spiritual experiences?

I am sorry I must again differ from you, for the simple reason that the deepest spiritual truths are always unutterable. That light to which you refer transcends speech. It can be felt only through the inner experience. And then the highest truth needs no communicating, for it is by its very nature self-propelling. It radiates its influence silently as the rose its fragrance without the intervention of a medium.

But even God sometimes speaks through His prophets.

Yes, but the prophets speak not through the tongue but through their lives. I have however known that in this matter I am up against a solid wall of Christian opinion.

Oh, no, even among Christians there is a school of thought—and it is growing—which holds that the authoritarian method should not be employed but that each individual should be left to discover the deepest truths of life for himself. The argument advanced is that the process of spiritual discovery is bound to vary in the case of different individuals according to their varying needs and temperaments. In other words they feel that propaganda in the accepted sense of the term is not the most effective method.

I am glad to hear you say this. That is what Hinduism certainly inculcates.

What counsel do you give to the young men who are fighting a losing battle with their lower selves and come to you for advice?

Simply prayer. One must humble oneself utterly and look beyond oneself for strength.

But what if the young men complain that their prayer is not heard, that they feel like speaking to brass heavens as it were?

To want an answer to one's prayer is to tempt God. If prayer fails to bring relief it is only lip prayer. If prayer does not help nothing else will. One must go on ceaselessly. This then is my message to the youth. In spite of themselves the youth must believe in the all-conquering power of love and truth.

The difficulty with our youth is that the study of science and modern philosophy has demolished their faith and so they are burnt up by the fire of disbelief.

That is due to the fact that with them faith is an effort of the intellect, not an experience of the soul. Intellect takes us along in the battle of life to a certain limit but at the crucial moment it fails us. Faith transcends reason. It is when the horizon is the darkest and human reason is beaten down to the ground that faith shines brightest and comes to our rescue. It is such faith that our youth require and this comes when one has shed all pride of intellect and surrendered oneself entirely to His will.

Interview with Dr John Mott
Young India, 21 Mar. 1929

60. RELIGION AND ART

[London,
14 October 1931]

The movement of artists and poets who are endeavouring to free themselves from the shackles of commercial and industrial influences of this age is a most laudable venture if only they have strength enough to do it. Religion is the proper and eternal ally of art. What religion teaches people the artist brings near to them in form on the plastic plane. I hate 'art for art's sake', which I think is a lamentable aberration of the human mind. Art has a profound similarity with religion inasmuch as the fundamental experience in both of them belongs to the domain of man's relationship with God. Indian art symbolizes this relationship and at the same time expresses the ritual of religious worship. If an artist who thinks he is surrounded by people without any religious sentiment chooses to become a scoffer, he will inevitably frustrate his own vocation. On the other hand if he feels that his is a mission, then a poet or artist has a right to oppose the prevalent creed or

lack of creed and he will be justified by the greater value of
his own revelation. I do not pretend to know anything about
art, but I believe firmly that both religion and art have to
serve the identical aims of moral and spiritual elevation.

The central experience of life will for ever remain the relationship which man has to God and it will never be superseded
or replaced by anything else, just as human bodies will never
free themselves from the law of gravitation. In this relationship
of man to God it is the mysterious forces which matter, not
the meagre texts expressed in words. There may be changes
in this relationship of man to God as represented by the various and successive religions of mankind; but to quote Cardinal
Newman: 'One step enough for me.'

Statement to *The Island*
GN 1055a

61. REALIZATION OF GOD

April 8, 1932

1 and 2. We must believe in God if we believe in ourselves. If
living beings have existence God is the sum total of all life and
this in my view is the strongest proof.

3. The denial of God is injurious in the same way as denial
of ourselves. That is to say, to deny God is like committing
suicide. The fact remains that it is one thing to believe in God
and quite another to realize God emotionally and act accordingly. Truly, no one in the world is an atheist; atheism is
merely a pose.

4. One can realize God only by ridding oneself totally of
attachment, aversion, etc., and in no other way. I hold that
one who claims to have realized God has not truly done so.
Realization can be experienced, but is beyond description. Of
this I have no doubt.

5. I can live only by having faith in God. My definition of
God must always be kept in mind. For me there is no other
God than Truth; Truth is God.

Letter to Hanumanprasad Poddar (H.)
Mahadevbhaini Diary, Vol. I, p. 82

62. THE UNFAILING TEST

April 25, 1932

I wish you will not take to heart what the Bishop[1] has been saying. Your church is in your heart. Your pulpit is the whole earth. The blue sky is the roof of your church. And what is this Catholicism? It is surely of the heart. The formula has its use. But it is made by man. If I have any right to interpret the message of Jesus as revealed in the Gospels, I have no manner of doubt in my mind that it is in the main denied in the churches, whether Roman or English, High or Low. Lazarus has no room in those places. This does not mean that the custodians know that the Man of Sorrows has been banished from the buildings called Houses of God. In my opinion, this excommunication is the surest sign that the truth is in you and with you. But my testimony is worth nothing, if when you are alone with your Maker, you do not hear His voice saying, 'Thou art on the right path.' That is the unfailing test and no other.

Letter to Dr Verrier Elwin
The Diary of Mahadev Desai, Vol. 1, p. 87

[1] A Bishop had called Dr. Elwin a traitor to Christ and had prohibited him from preaching in churches.

63. ACCEPTANCE OF GOD

August 15, 1932

I believe in both Gods,[1] the one that serves us and the one that we serve. It cannot be that we should render service and should not receive service of any kind. But both Gods are of our imagining. There is only one God who is real. The real God is beyond conception. He neither serves nor receives service. He cannot be described by any epithets, being not an external power but something dwelling in our heart. Since we do not understand the ways of God, we have necessarily to think of a power beyond our conception. And the moment we think of it, the God of our imagining is born. The fact is that belief in God is a function not of the intellect but of faith.

Reasoning is of little help to us in this matter and once we accept God the ways of the world cease to bother us. Then we have to accept that no creation of God can be purposeless. Beyond this I cannot go.

Letter to Bhuskute (H.)
Mahadevbhaini Diary, Vol. I, p. 364

---

[1] 'There are two Gods. There is the God people generally believe in, a God who has to serve them sometimes in a very refined way; perhaps merely by giving them peace of mind. This God does not exist. But the God whom we all have to serve does exist and is the prime cause of our existence and of all we perceive.' Referring to these words of Tolstoy, the questioner had asked 'which of these two Gods Gandhiji believed in, for if a man believed in the second God, prayer had no meaning for him'.

64. EVER-GROWING INWARDNESS

November 25, 1932

What a joy it would be when people realize that religion consists not in outward ceremonial but an ever-growing inward response to the highest impulses that man is capable of.

From a Letter to Samuel E. Stokes
Mahadevbhaini Diary, Vol. II, p. 279

65. RELIGION AND SOCIAL SERVICE

[About 23 January 1935]

I have been asked by Sir S. Radhakrishnan to answer the following three questions:
(1) What is your religion?
(2) How are you led to it?
(3) What is its bearing on social life?

My religion is Hinduism which, for me, is the religion of humanity and includes the best of all the religions known to me.

I take it that the present tense in the second question has been purposely used instead of the past. I am being led to my religion through Truth and Non-violence, i.e., love in the broadest sense. I often describe my religion as religion of Truth. Of late, instead of saying God is Truth I have been saying Truth is God, in order more fully to define my religion. I used at one time to know by heart the thousand names of God which a booklet in Hinduism gives in verse form and which perhaps tens of thousands recite every morning. But nowadays nothing so completely describes my God as Truth. Denial of God we have known. Denial of Truth we have not known. The most ignorant among mankind have some truth in them. We are all sparks of Truth. The sum total of these sparks is indescribable, as-yet-Unknown Truth, which is God. I am being daily led nearer to it by constant prayer.

The bearing of this religion on social life is, or has to be, seen in one's daily social contact. To be true to such religion one has to lose oneself in continuous and continuing service of all life. Realization of Truth is impossible without a complete merging of oneself in and identification with this limitless ocean of life. Hence, for me, there is no escape from social service; there is no happiness on earth beyond or apart from it. Social service here must be taken to include every department of life. In this scheme there is nothing low, nothing high. For all is one, though we *seem* to be many.

'Questions and Answers'
S. Radhakrishnan, *Contemporary Indian Philosophy*, p. 21

66. THE ROOT OF ALL RELIGIONS

November 1, 1945

Panditji,

I have had your book read out to me from beginning to end. These days while I spin I have a friend read out to me some book which I think is worth reading. I am disappointed with your book. From what you had said I had expected that I would learn something new from it and at the same time some light would be thrown on the Hindu–Muslim question. Right from my childhood I have lived with Muslims and when I went to London Providence placed me in close association with Christians, Muslims and Parsis. Hindus of course were there. I came into contact with the intellectuals among them and that is how I read the holy books of all the four religions. I came to the conclusion that we could know the true facts about any religion only after reading its sacred books. I also read quite a few criticisms of them. I can say that I have also read the Muslim critics you mention in your letter. I had a talk with Muslims in South Africa about those books and also with an Englishman who had become Muslim. After coming here I read the works of Maulana Shibli. As a result I have realized that every religion contains both truth and untruth. The root of all religions is one and it is pure and all of them have sprung from the same source, hence all are equal. This equality of all religions has been included by Vinoba among the eleven vows in a Marathi *sloka*, which is daily recited in the prayers.

Non-violence, truth, non-stealing, *brahmacharya*, non-possession, body-labour, control of the palate, fearlessness on all occasions, equal respect for all religions, *swadeshi* and *sparshabhavana*[1]—these eleven vows should be observed in a spirit of humility.

I am trying to live in accordance with this and so are my associates.

As it is, the letter has become quite long but since you have taken so much trouble and have also sent to me extra copies of your book, I felt I should at least let you know my stand.

I do not wish to argue with you. I have an answer to what you have suggested but I see no need to give it here. I therefore think that what I have said is enough.

Yours,

M. K. GANDHI

Letter to Mahadevshastri Divekar (H.)
Pyarelal Papers

[1] Refusal to treat anybody as untouchable.

67. THE TRANSCENDENT AND THE IMMANENT

A friend from Baroda, who writes in English, says:

You ask us to pray to God to give light to the whites in South Africa and strength and courage to the Indians there to remain steadfast to the end. A prayer of this nature can only be addressed to a person. If God is an all-pervading and all-powerful force, what is the point of praying to Him? He goes on with His work whatever happens.

I have written on this topic before. However, if one keeps on saying the same thing again and again in different words some new words or phrases used are likely to help someone or other to understand the matter better. In my view, whether called Rama, Rahman, Ormuzd, God or Krishna, He is that Supreme Power that man is ever trying to find a name for. Man, though imperfect, strives after perfection and in so doing is caught up in the tides of thought. Then like a baby learning to toddle, he now stumbles, now stands up. Thus if we say that a reasoning man is only a few months' old child, we shall not in the least be exaggerating, judging by the immensity of cosmic time; we shall be stating a simple truth. Man can express himself only by means of language. But there can be no such medium as language for the Power that is God. Man however can describe this infinite Power only with his imperfect means. If one has grasped this there is nothing left further to ask. Then it would be right to pray to Him in the language of man, for one can comprehend Him somewhat by fitting Him into one's own mould.

One ought always to remember, while dwelling on Him, that one is but a drop, the tiniest of creatures of the ocean that is God. One may experience Him by being in Him, but one can never describe Him. As Madame Blavatsky[1] puts it, man in praying, worships the Great Power residing within. Only he who knows this may pray. He who does not, need not pray. God will not be offended by it, but I can say from experience that that man will be the loser by not praying. So it is immaterial if some worship God as a Person and some others as a Great Power. Both are right, each in his own way. Nobody knows what is intrinsically right and nobody is likely ever to know. The ideal, to be an ideal, must forever remain out of reach. All the other forces are static, while God is the Life Force, immanent and at the same time transcendent.

Sevagram, August 8, 1946

'Is God a Person or a Principle?' (G.)
Harijan, 18 Aug. 1946

[1] *The Key to Theosophy.*

Volume Two
Truth and Non-Violence

VII
Human Nature, Perfectibility, and History

68. MEN ARE GOOD

January 12, 1910

My dear West,

I have often wished to write a personal letter but I have not been able to.

How are you feeling now in body, mind and soul? Are you more at ease than before? How is the home atmosphere? Does the new arrangement satisfy Mrs. West? Is Devi now at peace? How are the other people in the settlement?

For me, I am going through many a battle. Circumstances surrounding me just now are not at all congenial. But I think that my mind is at peace. My mind as you know is extremely active—never at rest. I am now trying bold experiments. Ethics of hawking only foreshadows what is coming in my life. The more I observe, the greater is the dissatisfaction with the modern life. I see nothing good in it. Men are good. But they are poor victims making themselves miserable under the false belief that they are doing good. I am aware that there is a fallacy underneath this. I who claim to examine what is around me may be a deluded fool. This risk all of us have to take. The fact is that we are all bound to do what we feel is right. And with me I feel that the modern life is *not* right. The greater the conviction, the bolder my experiments.

Yours sincerely,
M. K. GANDHI

[P.S.] I am disturbed whilst I am writing this. The above however is enough for the time being.

Letter to A. H. West
CW 4413

69. PREACHING TO EMPTINESS

Sevagram,
August 16, 1946

Downes was a Seventh Day Adventist. He was a quack like
me. He was my guest years ago in Durban. One day he said
he must preach the simple life to those who cared to listen to
him. He succeeded in borrowing a chapel hall for one hour in
Mercury Lane and asked me to preside. I warned him that
with me as chairman in the very early days of my life in South
Africa, probably in 1894, he must not expect an audience. He
would not heed the warning. Precisely at the advertised time
Downes began his address to an audience of one. I asked him
in vain to wait a few minutes for other comers. He would not
be party to stealing God's time and unconcerned, he went on
with his speech. So far as I remember, a few stragglers, under
ten, came in during the speech. I happened to relate this
experience to Horace Alexander whilst I was in Delhi. He
gave me in return the stranger story of Stephen Grellet, a
Quaker, preaching to emptiness. I asked him to give me the
authentic version for the readers of *Harijan*, it being a rich
experience of living faith in God. I reproduce below the story
as sent by Horace Alexander.

'Preaching to Emptiness'
Harijan, 8 Sept. 1946

70. PERFECTION ON EARTH

Motihari,
January 13, 1918

My dear Esther,

Having been wandering about, I have not been able to
reply to your letters. I was in Calcutta, thence went to Bombay and the Ashram and returned only yesterday. I had
varied experiences which I cannot describe for want of time.

To say that perfection is not attainable on this earth is to deny God. The statement about impossibility of ridding ourselves of sin clearly refers to a stage in life. But we need not search scriptures in support of the assertion. We do see men constantly becoming better under effort and discipline. There is no occasion for limiting the capacity for improvement. Life to me would lose all its interest if I felt that I *could* not attain perfect love on earth. After all, what matters is that our capacity for loving ever expands. It is a slow process. How shall you love the men who thwart you even in well-doing? And yet that is the time of supreme test.

I hope that you are now enjoying greater peace of mind. Let your love for the Ashram be a source of strength in your attempt to do your duty there. The Ashram is undoubtedly intended to teach us to do our assigned task with the utmost attention and with cheerfulness. There is meaning in our wishes (however pure) not being fulfilled. Not our will but His will be done.

I hope you are making progress in your Tamil lessons.

Did you receive from Messrs. Natesan & Co. a book they have brought out containing my speeches and writings? I am sending you a copy of my speech in Calcutta on Social Service.

With love,

Yours,
BAPU

Letter to Esther Faering
My Dear Child, pp. 24–5

71. OPTIMISM AND PESSIMISM

Optimism indicates faith; only an atheist can be a pessimist. The optimist lives in fear of God, listens with humility to the inner voice, obeys its promptings and believes that God ordains everything for the best.

The pessimist vainly thinks that it is he who does everything. When he fails in some undertaking, he leaves himself out and blames others; indulges in vain prating about not being sure whether God exists and, finally, concluding that this world is worthless and he alone good, but that his merit is not recognized, puts an end to his life. If he does not do that, he merely endures an existence which is little better than death.

The optimist lives delighting in thoughts of love and charity and, since there is none whom he looks upon as his enemy, he moves without fear whether he is in the forest or in the midst of men. He has no fear of ferocious animals or equally dreadful men, for his soul cannot be bitten by snakes nor pierced by the sinner's sword. Such a one will not give too much thought to his body, will rather look upon it as a fragile vessel of glass which is fated to break some day and will not go roaming all over the world to preserve it in health. The optimist will not kill or harass any human being. With his inner ear ever attuned to the sweet music of his soul, he will live floating on an ocean of joy.

The pessimist, being himself a prey of violent attachments and dislikes, looks upon every person as his enemy and fears him. He has of course no such thing as the inner voice. Like the honey bee, he flits from pleasure to pleasure, daily tiring of them and daily seeking new ones and, finally, dies, unloved, unwept and unsung.

Such being my views, I hope no one will believe that I ever told anyone I would commit suicide if *swaraj* was not won this year. Except for saving oneself from rape, suicide is, according to me, a major sin and an act of cowardice. Why indeed should I commit suicide because India may not have won *swaraj*? If she sincerely desires *swaraj*, let her fight for it and get it. She has realized its value, and has even tasted of it. If now she cares enough for it, let her pay the price and secure it. Whether or not she does so, what reason is that for me to commit suicide?

I did, however, mention one thing before some friends. When asked what I would do if we had not got *swaraj* by January, I said I had so great a faith in the country that till the very end of December I would continue to believe that we would definitely get *swaraj*. What, therefore, I would do in January, I did not know at all, I said. With people's leave, I would retire to a solitary place and live by myself, or would welcome helping the country, to the best of my ability, in drafting its constitution under *swaraj*. I should not like to remain alive next year if we have not won *swaraj* by then. I am, in that event, likely to be pained so deeply that this body may perish—I would desire that it should.

I have seen so much suffering in the country, economic and moral, that, if I have not perished in the flames, it is because of the hope which people have inspired in me. 'We shall have purified ourselves in a day', and 'Today our millions will get some flesh on their skeletons'—I am sustained from day to day by such hopes. I believe that one year is enough in which to realize them. In September 1920, I was the only one who believed and said that this was possible.

In December, others unanimously took up the programme. If now the Congress fails to fulfil its pledge, what would be the position of a person like me? It would surely mean bankruptcy for me no less than for the Congress. If, putting my trust in the Congress, I issue a draft and then find that it is not honoured, where should I turn? I very much desire that in the event of our failing to get *swaraj* in this year, everyone else should suffer on January 1 as much as I would. Everyone should feel the want of *dharma* as much as of food.

A friend asked me if this was not cowardice. I do not think so. I see in it an expression of compassion; it is plain common sense to me. There is no point in continuing to give service when it is not valued as such and none in living if there is no good in it. When the body itself is worn out, would it not be better to live on the Ganga water and let it slowly perish than to keep it alive, a mere skeleton, by treating it with *vasantmalati* or some such stuff? As far as I can see today, I shall never advise any course but 'adopt *swadeshi* and win *swaraj*'. If I cannot think of anything else at all, of what service can I possibly be?

We are now on the last rung of the ladder. To take a step further up without recouping ourselves where we stand would ultimately mean a set-back for us. I remember, when I was climbing the ghat for going up to Sinhgad,[1] a point came beyond which I simply could not continue to climb. I could resume the climb only after I had rested for a while and regained my strength.

We are in the same position. Till we have completely succeeded in the *swadeshi* programme, we shall not get the strength to push forward. My remaining alive, therefore, or continuing to live in society, depends on the success of *swadeshi*.

This is how I see things; this is the state of my mind today. What tomorrow will bring, God alone knows.

'Optimism' (G.)
Navajivan, 23 Oct. 1921

¹ A mountain fort near Poona in Maharashtra.

72. MAN'S DIGNITY AND MISSION

Ashram, Sabarmati,
April 9, 1926

Dear Friend,

I have your letter. I too have seen many a lizard going for cockroaches and have watched cockroaches going for lesser forms but I have not felt called upon to prevent the operation of the law of the larger living on the smaller. I do not claim to penetrate into the awful mystery but from watching these very operations, I learn that the law of the beast is not the law of the Man; that Man has by painful striving to surmount and survive the animal in him and from the tragedy of the *himsa* which is being acted around him he has to learn the supreme lesson of *ahimsa* for himself. Man must, therefore, if he is to realize his dignity and his own mission, cease to take part in the destruction and refuse to prey upon his weaker fellow creatures. He can only keep that as an ideal for himself and endeavour day after day to reach it. Complete success is possible only when he has attained *moksha*, a state in which the spirit becomes and remains independent of physical existence.

Yours sincerely,

Sh. V. N. S. Chary
7, High Road
Egmore

Letter to V. N. S. Chary
SN 19438

73. PERFECTIBILITY

Nandi Hills,
May 28, 1927

My dear Gulzarilal,

I was delighted to hear from you. Whilst lying on my bed, I have constantly thought of so many like you in whom I am deeply interested and from whom, I expect many large and big things if only God will give them the requisite health for the task before them.

Your description of a truly religious life is accurate. I have not a shadow of a doubt that this blessed state of inward joy and freedom from anxiety should last in the midst of the greatest trials conceivable. It admits of no exception whatsoever. Naturally, it is unattainable except by the very fewest. But that it is attainable by human beings, I have also no doubt. That we do not find in history evidence regarding the existence of any such person merely proves to me that all the record that we have has been prepared by imperfect beings, and it is impossible for imperfect beings to give us a faithful record of perfect ones. The same may be said of our own experiences. We have to be very nearly perfect in order to meet perfect souls such as you have described. Nor need you think that I have laid down an absurd proposition inasmuch as it is incapable of being recorded, or being experienced by the average man. To raise such a doubt would be begging the question, for we are here picturing to ourselves extraordinary mortals, though mortals nevertheless, and surely extraordinary powers are required to find out these extraordinary mortals. This statement is true even of much lesser things, things almost ridiculous, and yet very difficult of accomplishment, such, for instance, as the discoveries of Sir J. C. Bose or the finest paintings. Both these, we average beings will have to take on trust. It is only the privileged few who have got the special faculty for understanding and appreciating either those discoveries, or those paintings. These do not appear to us to be incredible and we are able to accept them on faith only because in favour of these we have the testimony of a larger number of witnesses than we can possibly have for the things of permanent value, such as human perfection of the utmost type. Therefore the limitation that you have accepted is quite a workable thing for the time being. For, even inside the limitation, there is ample scope for widening the field for the progress of the state of being and remaining unruffled in the face of the onslaught of sorrows and trials, which before re-generation would have paralysed us.

I am glad you have intensified your devotions. I do not know what you are reading at present. And I do not know whether I told you that we must arrive at a time when we do not need the solace of many books but that we make one book yield us all we want. In the last stage, of course, when life becomes one of perfect surrender and complete self-efface-ment, the support of even one book becomes unnecessary. At the present moment, though I am reading many things, the *Bhagavad Gita* is becoming more and more the only infallible guide, the only dictionary of reference, in which I find all the sorrows, all the troubles, all the trials arranged in the alpha-betical order with exquisite solutions. I think I did tell you that the *Song Celestial* was the best rendering I had come across of the *Bhagavad Gita*. But if you do not know Sanskrit, I know that a knowledge of Sanskrit to enable you to understand the *Bhagavad Gita* is easily within your power. You can almost in a month's time know enough Sanskrit to understand the ori-ginal text. For, though the English rendering is grand and though you might be able to get some Hindi or Urdu transla-tion also, of course there is nothing like the original. The original will enable you to give your own meaning and gloss to the text. That book is not a historical record, but it is a record of the concrete experiences of its author, whether it was really Vyasa or not I am not concerned. And if it is a record of anybody's experience, it must not be beyond us to be able to test the truth of it by repeating the experience. I am testing the truth almost every day in my life and find it never failing. This of course does not mean that I have reached the state described, for instance, at the end of the Second Chapter. But I know that the more we carry out the prescription given in it, the nearer do we answer the description given of the perfect state.

I hope you are keeping good health. I am of course making steady progress.

Yours sincerely,
BAPU

Letter to Gulzarilal Nanda
CW 9641

74. EDUCATION OF THE HEART

Gorakhpore,
October 7, 1929

Sisters,

I am reminded of you on so many occasions. As I see women and observe their condition in the course of my tours, I think of the tasks before you and realize that real education is of the heart. If pure love springs in it, everything else will be added. The field of service is unlimited. Our capacity for service can also be made boundless, for there is no limit to the strength of the soul. If but the doors of one's heart have opened, it can contain everything. Even a little work done by such a person will shine out. On the contrary, he whose heart is sealed may do much work, but it will get little appreciation. This is the significance of the story of Vidura's offering of *bhaji* and Duryodhana's of fruit.

Blessings from
BAPU

Letter to Ashram Women (G.)
GN 3704

75. INDIVIDUALITY AND PERSONALITY

Yeravda Mandir,
September 8, 1930

My dear Mathew,

Human speech is inadequate to express the reality. The soul is unborn and indestructible. The personality perishes, must perish. Individuality is and is not even as each drop in the ocean is an individual and is not. It is not because apart from the ocean it has no existence. It is because the ocean has no existence, if the drop has not, i.e., has no individuality. They are beautifully interdependent. And if this is true of the physical, how much more so of the spiritual world!

Love,

Letter to P. G. Mathew
GN 1544

76. SELF-INDULGENCE AND SELF-CONTROL

March 24, 1932

My Dear,

In working out plans for self-restraint, attention must not for a single moment be withdrawn from the fact that we are all sparks of the divine and, therefore, partake of its nature, and since there can be no such thing as self-indulgence with the divine it must of necessity be foreign to human nature. If we get a hard grasp of that elementary fact, we should have no difficulty in attaining self-control, and that is exactly what we sing every evening. You will recall that one of the verses says that the craving for self-indulgence abates only when one sees God face to face.

Love,
Bapu

A Letter
CW 8961

77. SELF-KNOWLEDGE

June 21, 1932

A craving for things of beauty is perfectly natural. Only there is no absolute standard of beauty. I have therefore come to think that the craving is not to be satisfied, but that from the craving for things outside of us, we must learn to see beauty from within. And when we do that, a whole vista of beauty is opened out to us and the love of appropriation vanishes. I have expressed myself clumsily, but I hope you follow what I mean. . . .

The purpose of life is undoubtedly to know oneself. We cannot do it unless we learn to identify ourselves with all that lives. The sum total of that life is God. Hence the necessity of realizing God living within every one of us. The instrument of this knowledge is boundless selfless service.

A Letter
Mahadevbhaini Diary, Vol. I, pp. 242–3.

78. PEACE AND GODLINESS

[1935]

Not to believe in the possibility of permanent peace is to disbelieve the godliness of human nature. Methods hitherto adopted have failed because rock-bottom sincerity on the part of those who have striven has been lacking. Not that they have realized this lack. Peace is unattainable by part perform-ance of conditions, even as a chemical combination is impos-sible without complete fulfilment of the conditions of attain-ment thereof. If the recognized leaders of mankind who have control over engines of destruction were wholly to renounce their use, with full knowledge of its implications, permanent peace can be obtained. This is clearly impossible without the great Powers of the earth renouncing their imperialistic de-sign. This again seems impossible without great nations ceas-ing to believe in soul-destroying competition and to desire to multiply wants and therefore increase their material posses-sions. It is my conviction that the root of the evil is want of a living faith in a living God. It is a first-class human tragedy that peoples of the earth who claim to believe in the message of Jesus who they describe as the Prince of Peace show little of that belief in actual practice. It is painful to see sincere Christian divines limiting the scope of Jesus' message to select individuals. I have been taught from my childhood and tested the truth by experience that the primary virtues of mankind are possible of cultivation by the meanest of the human species. It is this undoubted universal possibility that distinguishes the humans from the rest of God's creation. *If even one great nation were unconditionally to perform the supreme act of renunciation, many of us would see in our lifetime visible peace established on earth.*

'Answer to *The Cosmopolitan*'
Harijan, 18 June 1938

79. GROWTH FROM WITHIN

May 3, 1935

Faith is not a thing to grasp, it is a state to grow to. And growth comes from within.

A Letter
Mahadev Desai's Diary (MSS)

80. ALL-ROUND DEVELOPMENT

March 23, 1945

One meaning of education is knowledge of the Self and it is perfect in itself. But today it is wrongly interpreted. Hence I would say it is the all-round development of man and a true teacher is one who helps in such development.

Blessings from
BAPU

Note to Gope Gurbuxani (H.)
GN 1331

81. THE SELF AND THE PERSONALITY

March 24, 1945

Personality, i.e., the quality of being oneself, can be good or bad. If it is in conformity with the Self it is good and if it disregards the Self it is bad. It becomes good and develops by meditating on the Self and understanding its attributes.

Blessings from
BAPU

Note to Gope Gurbuxani (H.)
GN 1334

VIII

Principles and Vows

82. CONCERNING ONESELF WITH THE PRESENT

[Before 27 June 1927]

Just as it is useless to brood over the past, even so, it is useless to speculate about the future. 'One step enough for me', says the voice of wisdom. What does it avail us to know the future? Or why not merge both the past and the future into the present? The present or the past does have a future. And when change confronts us from moment to moment, to think of some remote future is building castles in the air. And only a fool builds castles in the air. The present means our duty at this moment. If we put all our strength into doing our duty, as we know it at this moment, we shall have made the highest human effort. Sorrow springs from dreaming of the future and from lamenting the past. Hence one who concerns himself with the present and does his duty has neither birth nor death.

A Letter (G.)
Mahadev Desai's Diary (MSS)

83. PURIFICATION AND SERENITY

Monday [7 November 1927]

Chi. Gangabehn (Senior),

Ramibehn accidentally met me in the train. She travelled with me from Mehmedabad to Nadiad. She talked about you all the time. She feels unhappy because you do not look after the children. I told her that, if the children were entrusted to you on your conditions and if no one interfered with you afterwards, you would certainly agree to take charge of them. She had nothing to say to this. I am sure you write to her from time to time. Her ideals are good. At present, she devotes all her time to acquiring knowledge of the letters.

See that you do not flee from the responsibility which has come upon you. It is now that the knowledge and experience you have gained are being tested. With patience, good temper and generosity of heart, you will be able to overcome all difficulties. Just as the sea accepts the water of all rivers within itself, purifies it and gives it back again, so you too, if you make yourself as the sea, will be able to accept all people. As the sea makes no distinction between good rivers and bad, but purifies all, so one person, whose heart is purified and enlarged with non-violence and truth, can contain everything in that heart and it will not overflow or lose its serenity. Remember that you aim at being such a person.

Blessings from
BAPU

Letter to Gangabehn Vaidya (G.)
CW 8706

84. CONFLICT OF DUTIES

A gentleman writes from Bardoli Satyagraha camp.[1]

The circumstances in which this gentleman is placed confront many in this country. The rule is that one who accepts selfless service as one's duty would sacrifice one's family for its sake. But even though we know this fundamental rule, we do not always find a straight principle to guide us in our conduct. Ordinarily the man oscillates between duty to his family and duty to his country. Under ideal conditions these two duties are not incompatible, but in the present situation we often see only conflict between them. That is so because love of family is based on selfishness and the family members are worshippers of selfishness; therefore, as a normal course it may be suggested that one should plunge into the service of the country after providing for the needs of the family in accordance with the poor living conditions in India. No one can serve the nation by leaving the family to fend for itself. But what can be called a family? And even in a family, who is to be maintained? This article is not meant for him who deceives himself by regarding all his fellow-castemen as his family. Nor is it meant for him who wishes to feed the able-bodied members of the family who sit at home. He who wishes to serve the country will continue his work by remaining above reproach in such matters. It is my experience that the families of such people do not have to starve. It is the right of those who are engaged in the service of the nation to earn enough to meet their needs; and by virtue of that right hundreds of selfless workers support themselves and their dependants.

'A Volunteer's Dilemma' (G.)
Navajivan, 1 July 1928

[1] The correspondent had asked what would happen to his dependants if he took up national work or joined the *satyagraha* fight without a wage.

85. DUTY IS A DEBT

Swaraj Ashram, Bardoli,
August 4, 1928

Dear Friend,

I have your letter.

If you have the strength of mind you will certainly wear *khadi* even if you incur the displeasure of your employers. Our duty is to so act as not to cause injury to others. Duty is a debt and discharge of a debt does not carry any reward with it unless of satisfaction with oneself.

We pray to feel strong and purified.

Yours sincerely,

D. C. Rajagopalachari
L/78/3 Coral Merchant Street, Madras

Letter to D. C. Rajagopalachari
SN 13903

86. REAL NON-ATTACHMENT

Lucknow,
September 28, 1929

Chi. Chhaganlal,

Imamsaheb arrived here this morning. He is fine.

It is quite true that there cannot be real non-attachment without spiritual knowledge. Non-attachment does not include ignorance, cruelty and indifference. The work done by a person filled with the real spirit of non-attachment shines far more and succeeds better than that of a man who works with attachment. The latter may sometimes get upset and forget things because of worries; he may even feel ill will and in the result may spoil the work. The man of non-attachment is free from all these defects. I need not write and explain this to you. But, when a thing we know is brought to our notice by someone else at the right time, it has an altogether different effect on us. I send to you from time to time useful thoughts like these which occur to me in order that you may not get nervous.

The correspondence which you carried on with the *Vidyapith* seems quite all right to me. As a trustee, you could have done nothing else. If your action gives rise to a misunderstanding, bear it in patience as temporary. For, so long as you yourself are certain that you have done a particular thing without ill will or without being carried away by emotion, you need not worry about the matter at all.

Letter to Chhaganlal Joshi (G.)
GN 5448

87. DISCHARGE OF DUTY

April 9, 1932

Chi. Raojibhai,

This is only to acknowledge your letter. Anybody who attempts to do something which is beyond his capacity lacks wisdom. He deserves compliments who does his duty to the best of his ability. Really speaking, a person need not be complimented for his devotion to duty, but when most people

disown their obligations, the few who discharge theirs deserve
compliments.

Blessings from
BAPU

Letter to Raojibhai M. Patel (G.)
CW 9014

88. IGNORANCE OF DUTY

April 18, 1932

Chi.,

We see ignorance all around us. We should not feel de-
pressed on that account, but should try to get rid of our own
ignorance. If we do that, the ignorance of other people also
will probably disappear. Ignorance means ignorance of one's
duty, or disinclination to do one's duty even when one knows
what it is.

Blessings from
BAPU

A Letter (G.)
CW 9030

89. MORALITY IN POLITICS AND BUSINESS

April 22, 1932

Chi. Parasram,

Who helped you to write the letter in Gujarati? Whoever it
was, his handwriting is excellent. I assume that the actual
language was yours.

One may certainly enter into loving rivalry, with a fellow-
disciple of one's guru or with anybody else. That is, we can
take everybody who can do something better than we as our
ideal and advance. There should be no trace of envy in this.
I have used the adjective 'loving' above to suggest this. In
such rivalry, we should wish in our heart that the person

whom we have accepted as our ideal will improve his skill day by day, so that the ideal which we seek to attain will always be rising higher as we progress. Such a wish will have a beneficial result for us too, since we shall be continually advancing.

I am firmly of the view, and it is my experience too, that, if a person has violated a moral principle in any one sphere of his life, his action will certainly have an effect in other spheres. In other words, the belief generally held that an immoral man may do no harm in the political sphere is quite wrong. And so is the other belief that a person who violates moral principles in his business may be moral in his private life or in his conduct in family affairs. Hence, whenever we do an evil we should overcome the tendency towards it.

Blessings from
BAPU

Letter to Parasram Mehrotra (G.)
CW 9437

90. BECOMING A CIPHER

August 4, 1932

Babalbhai,

I got your letter. My experience tells me that, instead of bothering about how the whole world may live in the right manner, we should think how we ourselves may do so. We do not even know whether the world lives in the right manner or in a wrong manner. If, however, we live in the right manner, we shall feel that others also do the same, or shall discover a way of persuading them to do so.

To know the *atman* means to forget the body, or, in other words, to become a cipher. Anybody who becomes a cipher will have realized the *atman*.

BAPU

Letter to Babalbhai Mehta (G.)
SN 9449

91. *DHARMA* AND SELF-PURIFICATION

August 14, 1932

One's respective *dharma* towards one's self, family, nation and the world cannot be divided into watertight compartments. The harm done to oneself or one's family cannot bring about the good of the nation. Similarly one cannot benefit the nation by acting against the world at large. Thus the purport is that we must sacrifice ourselves in the interest of the family, the family must do so for the nation and the nation for the world. But the sacrifice has to be pure. Therefore it all starts from self-purification. When the heart is pure, from moment to moment one's duty becomes apparent effortlessly.

A Letter (H.)
Mahadevbhaini Diary, Vol. I, p. 362

92. ACTIONS COUNT

September 11, 1932

It is our actions which count. Thoughts, however good in themselves, are like false pearls unless they are translated into action.

We should always see our neighbour's virtues and our own defects. A man like Tulsidas described himself as a crooked man despite all his goodness.

A Letter (G.)
Mahadevbhaini Diary, Vol. II, p. 15

93. *SVADHARMA*

November 20, 1933

Bhai Kotwal,

The work which has come to us unsought is *svadharma*. Anybody who is wedded to an institution should not, as a general rule, join the present battle. One's *dharma* cannot be pointed out to one by somebody else. He who has seen it adheres to it despite the opposition of the whole world.

We should not sit in judgment over anybody. Every case should ultimately be judged on its own merits. It is therefore dangerous to be guided by solutions of hypothetical cases.

Blessings from
BAPU

Letter to Kotwal (G.)
GN 3604

94. FATE AND EFFORT

March 16, 1945

Fate is the fruition of *karma*. Fate may be good or it may be bad. Human effort consists in overcoming adverse fate or reducing its impact. There is a continuous struggle between fate and human effort. Who can say which of the two really wins? Let us therefore continue effort and leave the result to God.[1]

BAPU

Note to Gope Gurbuxani (H.)
GN 1327

[1] The addressee had asked: 'What is fate and how is it related to human effort?'

95. NON-INTERFERENCE

October 7, 1945

Chi. Amin,

I have already written to you. It is everyone's duty to destroy sin. But that is for one's own sin. With regard to another's sin our attitude should be one of non-interference, i.e., in that case nothing but non-violence is our duty. My mother used to go to temples. I did not. I did not take away or destroy the idols she used to worship. Let us not sit in judgment on others. Of course I admire your spirit of service. But you are rash and hot-tempered. Get rid of these two short-comings and you will double your capacity for service.

Aminbhai
Anti-cholera Camp
Sindi Khandala
Wardha

Letter to Jatindas M. Amin (G.)
Pyarelal Papers

96. NO MORAL ALIBI

Panchgani,
July 13, 1946

In the song that has just been sung, the world has been aptly described as the valley of sorrow and suffering. God alone enables us to brave it all. The poet, however has proceeded to call the world an illusion and a dream. Joy or what men call happiness may be, or really is, a dream in a fleeting and transitory world, where everything is like a dissolving phantasmagoria. But we cannot dismiss the suffering of our fellow creatures as unreal and thereby provide a moral alibi for ourselves. Even dreams are true while they last and to the sufferer, his suffering is a grim reality. Anyway, whether the world be real or unreal, we have certain duties in life which must be faced, understood and duly performed while we are in this world.

From speech at a Prayer Meeting
Harijan, 21 July 1946
The Hindu, 15 July 1946

97. DRAWING ONE'S OWN COROLLARIES

August 13, 1924

I do believe that it is a mistake, a dangerous thing, to get orders from me in every matter. My answer is bound to be

only according to the way a question is put. I may make a
mistake in giving my answer. Everyone should draw his own
corollaries from general principles.

Letter to Mathuradas Trikumji (G.)
Bapuni Prasadi, p. 74

98. IDEALS AND COMPROMISES

Satyagraha Ashram,
Sabarmati,
March 12, 1928

My dear Friend,

I like the manner in which you are combating my views. I
discovered the difference between us even in Orissa. For me,
there is no difference between the individual and the social
position. At the same time there is ample room for the compromise of the nature suggested by you, for the simple reason
that I ever compromise my own ideals even in individual
conduct not because I wish to but because the compromise
was inevitable. And so in social and political matters I have
never exacted complete fulfilment of the ideal in which I have
believed. But there are always times when one has to say thus
far and no further, and each time the dividing line has to be
determined on merits. Generally speaking where the sum total
of a movement has been evil, I have held non-co-operation to
be the only remedy and where the sum total has been for the
good of humanity, I have held co-operation on the basis of
compromise to be the most desirable thing. If I seem to be
holding myself aloof from some of the political movements just
now, it is because I believe their tendency to be not for the
promotion of *swaraj* but rather its retarding. It may be that I
have erred in my judgment. If so, it is but human and I have
never claimed to be infallible. You will see this point somewhat developed in a recent autobiographical chapter dealing
with my participation in the late War. Tell me now if I have
answered your question, even if I have not solved the puzzle.

Andrews is here and will be for a few days longer. How nice
it would be if you could come and pass a few days of quiet

with me so that we could discuss the important problems you have been raising in your letters. This is however not to say that you may not discuss them through correspondence. Please do, so long as it is necessary.

Yours sincerely,

B. W. Tucker
Calcutta

Letter to B. W. Tucker
SN 13104

99. PRINCIPLES AND FACTS

Wardha,
December 13, 1928

Chi. Mathuradas,

The way before you is not clear. Read the accompanying letter. I have even suggested to Ram Sahay that he should have a talk with you. Show unlimited love. If you exercise patience and do not give up in despair, ultimately victory is yours. Do not be easily satisfied with your work. Show love to both; that is what is meant by an equal mind. When we give bread to a hungry person and advise another suffering from indigestion to fast, in both cases we are prompted by love; this, therefore, is showing an equal mind and treating an ant and an elephant with equal consideration. Do not assume, in dealing with him, that your new method has succeeded completely. If you patiently explain it to those who insist on following the old method and carry them with you, there will be minimum friction.

Whether the method adopted is the old or the new one, it must be followed faithfully. Write to me from time to time about the difficulties which you experience. Never feel worried in the smallest measure. If you feel at any time that my conclusions are based on inadequate data or incorrect reasoning, draw my attention to the fact. You may have faith in the principles which I lay down, but the conclusions which I draw from certain facts cannot be a matter of faith.

Faith has no place in a matter which can be grasped by reason. Hence, whenever you see my ignorance as regards facts and find the reasoning vitiated by that ignorance, please do correct me. If you make this a regular practice, I shall be able to write to you more freely and guide you better.

Blessings from
BAPU

Letter to Mathuradas (G.)
GN 4213

100. STRIVING TO REACH THE IDEAL

Yeravda Mandir,
Silence Day [30 June 1930]

Chi. Gangabehn,

All of us are far away from our ideal and will remain so. Our duty lies in striving to reach it. Man's ideal grows from day to day and that is why it ever recedes from him. You are ever striving and that is all that you can do. Our effort should be pure and unremitting.

Blessings from
BAPU

Letter to Gangabehn Vaidya (G.)
CW 8751

101. RULES OF INNER AND OUTER LIVING

August 15, 1932

Achara means the outward mode of living and it can change from time to time. The rules of inner living must remain the same; that is, one should cling to truth, *ahimsa*, etc. In trying to follow them, we may change the rules of outward mode of living whenever necessary. We need not cling to anything, saying or believing that according to the Shastras *achara* is the first step in *dharma*. All rules given in Sanskrit were not *shastra*.

Even the book entitled *Manavdharmashastra* is not really speaking a *shastra*. *Shastra* is not anything written in a book. It should be a living thing. Hence the words of a wise man of good character whose actions are in accord with his speech are our *shastra*. If we do not have any such lighthouse to guide us, what seems truth to us is our *shastra*, provided our minds and hearts have been purified.

A Letter (G.)
Mahadevbhaini Diary, Vol. I, p. 364

102. EACH CASE ON ITS MERITS

May 13, 1935

Bhai Thakur Prasad Sharma,

Good relations cannot be brought about by concealing our faults. If both the parties jointly appoint an arbitrator, they need not go to the law-court. But if this is not possible I see nothing wrong in making an attempt to obtain justice through the courts. One cannot lay down a fixed principle in such matters. Every case is to be judged on its own merits.

M. K. GANDHI

Shri Thakur Prasad
Jalpa Devi
Benares City

Letter to Thakur Prasad Sharma (H.)
CW 9754

103. REDUCING THEORIES TO PRACTICE

June 18, 1935

My dear Jagannathdas,

You were quite right in writing to me at length on nudism.[1] I have no hesitation in agreeing with you in theory. But theories are not always capable of being reduced to practice. Not even in exact mathematics, like geometry, are theories capable of always being reduced to practice. The imaginary right angle of geometry will not build houses but the nearly perfect right angle which masons and carpenters use is responsible for many marvellous things. In the Western world as well as in India nudism in practice is not permissible. I am convinced that it would be a great error to act as though all men and women were pure-minded. I hold it, therefore, to be dangerous.

Yours sincerely,
BAPU

Sjt. C. G. Jagannathdas
459 Mint Street
Park Town, Madras

Letter to C. G. Jagannathdas
GN 9091

---

¹ The addressee in his letter of 15 June had made out a case for the adoption of nudism. Clothing, he had argued, was unnatural and unhealthy.

104. NO COMPROMISE ON ETERNAL PRINCIPLES

[Before 2 September 1936]

A group of school teachers went to Segaon one morning with that old Platonic problem—Knowledge is virtue—and asked if it was true. Why was it that though we knew very well indeed that a particular course of action was morally wrong, we could not avoid it? Replying to them Gandhiji said:

Human life is a series of compromises and it is not always easy to achieve in practice what one has found to be true in theory. Take this very simple case. The principle is that all life is one and we have to treat the sinner and the saint alike, as the *Gita* says we have to look with an equal eye on a learned pundit and a dog and a dog-eater. But there I am. Though I have not killed the snake, I know I have been instrumental in killing it. I know that I should not have done so. I know, besides, that snakes are *kshetrapals* (guardians of the field), and therefore too I should not have helped in killing it. But as you see I have not been able to avoid it. But it is no use my thinking that I cannot avoid it. I do not give up the principle which is true for all time that all life is one, and I pray to God that He may rid me of the fear of snakes and enable me to achieve the non-violence necessary to handle snakes as we handle other domestics. Take another instance, again a very simple one. I know that as a villager and as one who has made it his business to promote village crafts, I must use a village-made razor, but you see that I am using a foreign one.[1]

I might have got a village-made razor, if I had written to friends to procure one for me. But I thought I must help the village barber, no matter what kind of razor he used. I therefore decided to cultivate him, and put up with his dirty clothes and uncouth instruments. But on one thing I could not possibly compromise. He said he would not shave *Harijans* on the same terms as he was prepared to shave me, and I had to do without his services. Now you find me having a shave with a foreign razor, though it is open to me to procure a village-made one. Here there is obviously an indefensible compromise. And yet there is an explanation. I have been sticking on to a set of shaving tackle given me by a loving sister, whose gift I could not resist and whose feelings I could not hurt by rejecting the foreign razor and insisting on having a village-made one. But there it is, the compromise is there. I do not commend it for imitation. We must be prepared to displease the dearest ones for the sake of principles.

There are eternal principles which admit of no compromise, and one must be prepared to lay down one's life in the practice of them. Supposing someone came and asked you to give up your religion and to embrace another at the point of the sword, would you do it? Supposing someone were to compel you to drink wine or eat beef, or tell a lie, would you not rather lay down your life than yield to the coercion? No. A principle is a principle, and in no case can it be watered down because of our incapacity to live it in practice. We have to strive to achieve it, and the striving should be conscious, deliberate and hard.

Has not our Poet[2] sung for all time that fearless striving is the very condition of freedom?

Where the mind is without fear, and the head is held high . . .

Where tireless striving stretches its arms towards perfection ...
Into that heaven of freedom, Oh Father, let my country awake.

'Discussion with Teachers'
Harijan, 5 Sept. 1936

[1] Gandhi was having a shave when the teachers arrived.
[2] Rabindranath Tagore.

105. VOWS AND SELF-TRAINING

If we resolve to do a thing, and are ready even to sacrifice our lives in the process, we are said to have taken a vow. It is essential for every person to train himself to keep such vows; one can strengthen one's power of will by doing so and fit oneself for greater tasks. One may take easy and simple vows to start with and follow them with more difficult ones. It seems the negroes of the Congo have taken such a vow. For the past three years, the whites have been trying hard to get the negroes over there to extract rubber, but they answer that their forefathers had pledged themselves not to do so. They are, therefore, unable to go against their plighted word. We shall find several examples in history of men undergoing great suffering for the sake of a pledge. To embrace *satyagraha* amounts to taking a great vow. Having taken it, one must die rather than forsake it. Such is the profound import of *satyagraha*, and it is for this reason that *satyagraha* may be said to know no defeat.

'Importance of Vows' (G.)
Indian Opinion, 8 Oct. 1913

106. VOWS AND WRONGDOING

Sabarmati,
March 13, 1926

Bhai Shukhdev Prasad Sinha,

Your letter. A vow applies to only good deeds. One does not resolve to do something wrong. If through ignorance one should make any such vow it is one's duty to break it. For instance if one had vowed to commit adultery, one should withdraw from it promptly, on coming to one's senses. If one does not, one sins.

Yours,
MOHANDAS GANDHI

Letter to Shukhdev Prasad Sinha (H.)
SN 19862

107. VOWS AND HYPOCRISY

[20 March 1926]

To Prabhudas

What you write about my vow regarding a watch is embarrassing not because of the vow but because the mind is not yet trained in *aparigraha*. But I know no other way of training the mind against possessiveness. If a person having any number of watches is indifferent over one of them, that certainly is no great merit in him. His indifference might be at the cost of some other person. If one is not worried about one's watch in spite of such a vow, and in spite of knowing that another cannot be had if this is lost, one has at least a remote chance of attaining *aparigraha*. Again, if a person who has a one-thing vow begins to feel jealous, that is no new failing in him; what was dormant, revives by contact. This then is the virtue of vows. When the mind is cleaned of one thing all the other filth also comes out. And if we succeed with one vow, there is a chance of all other uncleanliness being flushed out. He who has not taken a vow sincerely has taken no vow at all. He is a hypocrite. And we cannot judge the sincere by the standards of the hypocrite.

Ayodhyakanda[1] is such that one is not tired of it after reading it a thousand times. The more you work on it, the more you will be rewarded.

Letter to Prabhudas (G.)
SN 19878-A

[1] The second book of the *Ramayana*.

108. NEVER ACCEPT DEFEAT

A student writes[1] ...

Everyone is impelled sometimes to ask this question. Nevertheless it is based on a misunderstanding. A vow has the effect of raising us exactly because, in spite of it, there is a chance of our falling. If there was no such danger, there would be no scope for striving. A vow serves the same purpose as a lighthouse does. If we keep our eyes fixed on it, we shall come safe through any storm. The lighthouse itself cannot quieten the storm, yet it guides sailors caught in a storm and helps them to fight it, even so a vow is a kind of powerful force which saves a human being from the innumerable waves raging in the heart. This being the case, no way has been found, or is likely to be found, by following which a person taking a vow can be assured that he will never fall. And this is as it should be; otherwise the moral injunctions about truth and so on will lose the great value which is attached to them. One has to exert oneself so much to acquire ordinary knowledge or raise a few lakhs of rupees for a fund. There are many who do not mind risking their lives merely to be able to see a lifeless spot like the North Pole. Why should we, then, wonder or be unhappy if we have to put in a thousand times more difficult effort in order to conquer our powerful foes such as anger, malice and so on. Our success lies in the very struggle for this deathless glory. The effort itself is victory. If those who sail to the North Pole fail in their object, their effort may be considered to have been wasted, but every effort we make in our life to conquer these foes, attachment and aversion, will have taken us forward. Thus, no effort, however slight, towards such an end is ever wasted—that is the Lord's assurance.[2]

The only encouragement, therefore, which I can give this student is that he should go on striving and never lose heart. He should never abandon the vow. He should banish from his dictionary the word 'impossible'. If he forgets his vow at any time, he should do *prayaschitta* and remind himself of the vow. Every time he violates it, he should start again, and have complete confidence that he is bound at last to succeed. No man of spiritual illumination has ever told us of his experience that untruth had ever triumphed; on the contrary, every such person has unanimously proclaimed most emphatically his experience that in the end truth triumphs. We should keep the experience of these persons in mind, and entertain no doubts of any kind when striving for a good end or be afraid to take a vow with a virtuous aim. Pandit Rambhuj Datt Chaudhari has left us a poem in Punjabi with the following refrain:

'Never accept defeat, though you lose your life.'

'Significance of Vows' (G.)
Navajivan, 1 Aug. 1926

[1] The letter is not printed here. The correspondent had asked if there was any way by following which he would always be able to keep a vow.

[2] *Bhagavad Gita* II. 40.

109. ETHICS OF VOW-TAKING

A correspondent who seems to be a regular and careful reader of *Navajivan* writes:

I spin regularly, but the question is whether or not I should bind myself to it by a vow. If I take a vow to spin regularly for one hour every day. I suppose I must do an hour's honest spinning unfailingly, come what may. Suppose now, having taken the vow I am required to go out on a long journey, how can I fulfil my vow about spinning? Or again, suppose I fall seriously ill, even then I must do my spinning, or else be guilty of breaking my vow before man and God. On the other hand if I do not take a vow, what guarantee is there that my resolution would not give way and betray me at a critical moment?

You will perhaps say that one's resolution ought to be made of sterner stuff. But when even the acknowledged leaders of the country are seen hourly breaking their resolutions, what can one expect from the rank and file? What are lesser mortals like myself to do? Would you kindly resolve my dilemma?

Being accustomed from very childhood to taking vows I confess I have a strong bias in favour of the practice. It has come to my rescue in many a crisis; I have seen it save others from many a pitfall. A life without vows is like a ship without anchor or like an edifice that is built on slip-sand instead of a solid rock. A vow imparts stability, ballast and firmness to one's character. What reliance can be placed on a person who lacks these essential qualities? An agreement is nothing but a mutual interchange of vows; simultaneously one enters into a pledge when one gives one's word to another.

In old days, the word of mouth of illustrious persons was regarded as good as a bond. They concluded transactions involving millions by oral agreements. In fact our entire social fabric rests on the sanctity of the pledged word. The world would go to pieces if there was not this element of stability or finality in agreements arrived at. The Himalayas are immovably fixed for ever in their place. India would perish if the firmness of the Himalayas gave way. The sun, the moon and other heavenly bodies move with unerring regularity. Were it not so, human affairs would come to a standstill. But we know that the sun has been rising regularly at its fixed time for countless ages in the past and will continue to do so in future. The cooling orb of the moon will continue always to wax and wane as it has done for ages past with a clockwork regularity. That is why we call the sun and the moon to be witness to our affairs. We base our calendar on their movements, we regulate our time by their rising and setting.

The same law, which regulates these heavenly bodies, applies equally to men. A person unbound by vows can never be absolutely relied upon. It is overweening pride to say, 'This thing comes natural to me. Why should I bind myself permanently by vows? I can well take care of myself at the critical moment. Why should I take an absolute vow against wine? I never get drunk. Why should I forgo the pleasure of an occasional cup for nothing?' A person who argues like this will never be weaned from his addiction.

To shirk taking of vows betrays indecision and want of resolution. One never can achieve anything lasting in this world by being irresolute. For instance, what faith can you place in a general or a soldier who lacks resolution and determination, who says, 'I shall keep guard as long as I can'? A householder, whose watchman says that he would keep watch as long as he can, can never sleep in security. No general ever won a victory by following the principle of 'being vigilant so long as he could'.

I have before me innumerable examples of spinners at will. Every one of them has come to grief sooner or later. On the other hand, sacramental spinning has transformed the entire life of those who have taken to it; mountains of yarn stored up by them tell the tale. A vow is like a right angle. An insignificant right angle will make all the difference between ugliness and elegance, solidity and shakiness of a gigantic structure. Even so stability or instability, purity or otherwise of an entire career may depend upon the taking of a vow.

It goes without saying that moderation and sobriety are of the very essence of vow-taking. The taking of vows that are not feasible or that are beyond one's capacity would betray thoughtlessness and want of balance. Similarly a vow can be made conditional without losing any of its efficacy or virtue. For instance there would be nothing wrong about taking a vow to spin for at least one hour every day and to turn out not less than 200 yards daily except when one is travelling or is sick. Such a vow would not only be quite in form but also easy of observance. The essence of a vow does not consist in the difficulty of its performance but in the determination behind it unflinchingly to stick to it in the teeth of difficulties.

Self-restraint is the very key-stone of the ethics of vow-taking. For instance, one cannot take a vow of self-indulgence, to eat, drink and be merry, in short, to do as one pleases. This warning is necessary because I know of instances when an attempt was made to cover things of questionable import by means of vows. In the heyday of non-co-operation one even heard the objection raised, 'How can I resign from Government service when I have made a covenant with it to serve it?' Or again, 'How can I close my liquor shop since I have bound myself by contract to run it for five years?' Such questions might appear puzzling sometimes. But on closer thinking it will be seen that a vow can never be used to support or justify an immoral action. A vow must lead one upwards, never downwards towards perdition.

The correspondent has concluded by having a fling at the 'acknowledged leaders' of the country and cited their so-called fickleness to justify his position. This sort of reasoning only betrays weakness. One should try to emulate and imitate only the virtues of one's leaders, never their faults. Our national leaders do not claim to be paragons of perfection. They occupy the position of eminence that they do in public life by virtue of certain qualities which they exhibit in their character. Let us ponder over those qualities and try to assimilate them, let us not even think of their shortcomings. No son can be called a worthy son of his father who only imbibes the shortcomings of his parents or pleads inability to keep clear of them. It is the virtues, not the faults of one's parents, that constitute one's true legacy. A son who only adds to the debts of his parents would be written down as unworthy. A worthy son would liquidate their debts and increase the legacy left by them.

'The Efficacy of Vows' (G.)
Navajivan, 11 Aug. 1929
Young India, 22 Aug. 1929

110. VOWS—A SIGN OF STRENGTH

Tuesday morning, October 14, 1930

Chi. Narandas,

In this series, I have dealt cursorily with the importance of vows, but it is perhaps necessary to consider at some length their bearing on a godly life. Now that I have discussed all our vows except that of *swadeshi*, let us consider the necessity of vows. There is a powerful school of thinkers who concede the propriety of observing certain rules but do not acknowledge the necessity of vows. They go even so far as to suggest that vows are a sign of weakness and may even be harmful. Again they say that, if a rule is subsequently discovered to be inconvenient or sinful, to adhere to it after such discovery would be positively wrong. They say: 'It is a good thing to abstain from liquor, but what harm is there in taking it occasionally, say on medical grounds? A pledge of total abstinence would be a needless handicap; and as with liquor, so with other things. Why may we not even speak an untruth for a good end?' This argument does not convince me. A vow means unflinching determination, and helps us against temptations. Determination is worth nothing if it bends before discomfort.

The universal experience of humanity supports the view that progress is impossible without inflexible determination. There cannot be a vow to commit a sin. Such a vow represents a wicked nature. In the case of a vow first thought to be meritorious but later found to be sinful, there arises a clear necessity to give it up. But no one takes, or ought to take, vows about dubious matters. Vows can be taken only on points of universally recognized principles, which, however, we do not habitually act upon. The possibility of sin in such a case is more or less imaginary. A devotee of Truth cannot stop to consider if someone will not be injured by his telling the truth, for he believes that truth can never do harm. So also about total abstinence. The abstainer will either make an exception as regards medicine, or will be prepared to risk his life in fulfilment of his full vow. What does it matter if we happen to lose our lives through a pledge of total abstinence? There can be no guarantee that our lives will be prolonged by liquor, and even if life is thus prolonged for a moment, it may be ended the very next through some other agency. On the other hand, the example of a man who gives up his life rather than his pledge is likely to wean drunkards from liquor and thus become a great power for good in the world. Only they can hope some time to see God who have nobly determined to bear witness to the faith that is in them even at the cost of life itself.

Taking vows is not a sign of weakness but of strength. To do at any cost what one ought to do constitutes a vow. It becomes a bulwark of strength. It makes no difference whether such a resolve is called a vow or known by some other name. A man who says that he will do something 'as far as possible' betrays either his pride or his weakness, though he himself may attribute it to his humility. There is, in fact, not a trace of humility in such an attitude of mind. I have noticed in my own case, as well as in that of others, that the limitation 'as far as possible' provides a fatal loophole. To do something 'as far as possible' is to succumb to the very first temptation. There is no sense in saying that we will observe truth 'as far as possible'. Even as no business man will look at a note in which a man promises to pay a certain amount on a certain date 'as far as possible', so will God refuse to accept a promissory note drawn by a man who will observe truth 'as far as possible'.

God is the very image of the vow. God would cease to be God if He swerved from His own laws even by a hair's breadth. The sun is a great keeper of observances; hence the possibility of measuring time and publishing almanacs. He has created in us the faith that he always rises and will for ever continue to rise, and thereby given us a sense of security. All business depends upon men fulfilling their promises. There could be no commerce if merchants did not regard themselves as bound by their word to one another. We thus see that keeping a vow is a universal practice. Are such promises less necessary in character building or self-realization? We should, therefore, never doubt the necessity of vows for the purpose of self-purification and self-realization.

Blessings from
BAPU

Letter to Narandas Gandhi (G.)
MMU/I

III. PROMISES TO ONESELF

October 31, 1930

My dear Kumarappa,

I am glad you have expressed yourself freely on the question of 'vows'.

You seem to me to misunderstand my meaning. No fault of yours. You have not the original before you. I have not seen the translation. The word 'vow' is also an unsuitable equivalent for the original *vrata*. But the best thing for me is to explain what I mean and then leave you to find the exact word if you endorse my position. If you contest it, you should continue the correspondence till we have thrashed the subject out.

You seem to think of vows publicly administered to audiences. This may or may not be good. The 'vow' I am thinking of is a promise made by one to oneself. We have to deal with two dwellers within: Rama and Ravana, God and Satan, Ormuzd and Ahriman. The one binds us to make us really free, the other only appears to free us so as to bind us tight within his grip. A 'vow' is a promise made to Rama to do or not to do a certain thing which, if good, we want to do, but have not the strength unless we are tied down, and which, if bad, we would avoid, but have not the strength to avoid unless similarly tied down. This I hold to be a condition indispensable to growth. I grant that we are higher than the sun, how much more necessary for us to be at least as true and faithful as the sun if not truer and more faithful? If in matters of commerce, a man who vacillates is useless, why should he fare otherwise in matters spiritual which carry with them infinitely greater consequences? If you hold that I must speak and do the right thing at any cost, you grant my whole position and so you also do·if you grant that, at the peril of my life, I should be faithful to my wife or friend. You can easily multiply such instances. For me Jesus was pre-eminently a man of unshakeable resolution, i.e., vows. His yea was yea for ever. A life of vow is like marriage, a sacrament. It is marriage with God indissoluble for all time. Come let us marry Him. *Verb Sap*.

Love,

BAPU

Letter to J. C. Kumarappa
GN 10081

112. STRENGTH AND WEAKNESS

Yeravda Mandir,
November 16, 1930

My dear Kumarappa,

If a man makes an unalterable decision to do or not to do a particular thing, it is for me a vow. The strongest men have been known at times to have become weak. God has a way of confounding us in our strength. Hence the necessity of vows, i.e., invoking God's assistance to give us strength at the crucial moment. But I must not strive with you. It seems to me that we mean the same thing but express it differently—you in Spanish and I in Italian, shall we say?

Love,

BAPU

Letter to J. C. Kumarappa
GN 10082

113. PURIFICATION THROUGH WORK

August 23, 1932

It does not seem correct to me to say[1] that it is part of man's nature to spend some time in idle thoughts. If there is a single exception to this, we cannot say that it is part of man's nature to do so. Actually, we find many exceptions. It is true that vast numbers of people are always busy thinking about all manner of things which they will do or will not do, and thus may be said to spend time in idle thoughts. If this were not so, it would not be necessary to emphasize the importance of concentration. What is important for us at present is this. We ourselves make all kinds of plans and resolutions, most of which we do not even remember after some time. All such thoughts are mental incontinence. Just as man dissipates his physical strength through ordinary incontinence, so he dissipates his mental strength through mental incontinence, and, as physical weakness affects the mind, so mental weakness affects the body. That is why I have defined *brahmacharya* in a wide sense and described even idle thoughts as violation of it.

By defining *brahmacharya* in a narrow sense, we have made it more difficult to observe. If we accept its wider definition and try to control all the eleven organs,[2] the control of the one most important organ would be much easier. You seem to believe in the heart of your hearts that physical activity prevents or hinders us from watching the progress of our inward purification. My experience is the opposite of this. Without inward purification, work cannot be done in a spirit of non-attachment. Hence the degree of inward purification can be judged mainly by the purity of our work. Anybody who tries to cultivate inward purity without doing work will more likely than not be in danger of falling into a delusion. I have seen many such instances.

I will give an ordinary example. I have known many co-workers making all kinds of good resolutions in jail, and also seen their resolutions broken at the first blow after they were released. In jail they were quite sure that they would never swerve from their resolutions, that they had achieved inward purification, that they had examined themselves in complete peace of mind and that they had acquired concentration in prayer. But I found that the moment they were outside the jail walls all this evaporated into thin air. The fifth verse of Chapter III of the *Gita* states a profound truth. Scientist after scientist has told us that the principle enunciated in it is a universal law. It simply means that no human being can cease from *karma* even for a moment.

Karma or motion is the universal law of all material things and forms of life. Man's spiritual knowledge and his excellence lie in obeying it in a spirit of non-attachment. There are two verses in the *Ishopanishad* which state the same truth, and they are equally profound. Who am I to criticize a great soul like the Buddha? Besides, I love and revere him. But did he himself set up the organization of monasteries or did his followers do so? Whoever did it, the monasteries which were established became, in obedience to this universal law, stagnant and by and by acquired reputation as dens of sloth. Even today we find Buddhist monks in Ceylon, Burma and Tibet sunk in ignorance and the veritable images of sloth. In India, too, the monks known as *sannyasis* are not found to be shining specimens of humanity.

Personally I am convinced, therefore, that man can achieve real and enduring purification of heart only through work. I again feel tempted to quote the *Gita*. Verse 18 of Chapter IV means that he who sees action in inaction and inaction in action is the wise man, he is the true *yogi* and the true man of *karma*. I have, however, explained here what I have found in my own experience. I have quoted the *Gita* verses because I have found the truth of their teaching in my experience. I never quote anything from *shastras* which I have not tested in experience. The experience of others may be different from mine and they may even quote verses from the *Gita* which tend in the opposite direction or they may quote in support of their experience the same verses which I do and interpret them differently. All this is possible. I, therefore, never insist that all people should accept my experience as the sole guide.

Letter to Darbari Sadhu (G.)
Mahadevbhaini Diary, Vol. I, pp. 378–80

¹ The addressee had said in his letter that 'aimless thoughts were certainly burdensome but it seemed as if even the seeker after truth had to pass through the stage of wandering thoughts. It was true that selfless action purified the mind. But after some purification had not the seeker quietly to observe his mental activity? Or was the selfless action sufficient in itself? Buddha recommended a combination of activity and contemplation with some such end in view. Bapu, however, was all for action, which according to him was the royal road to self-perfection. But did it enable the seeker to understand the activity of the soul?'

² Five organs of perception, five of action and the mind.

114. THE USE OF TIME

Some time elapses in merely thinking about a piece of work before it is actually begun. Such time is known as stray moments. We carelessly allow these bits of time to pass. If we add up these stray moments which are thought to be of little account, they make no mean part of our life; and not to make a proper use of them is to waste life itself.

Each one of us talks, more or less, about his education and improvement. We make plans of how best to use our spare time; but, whenever we get a few stray minutes of leisure, we men and women—particularly women—allow them thought-lessly to pass away. We go on cherishing dreams of the many things we would do, if and when we have the time. The time we get is just a quarter or half hour or just a few minutes. Then, we say to ourselves, 'Well, it does not matter, there isn't enough time now.' Thus we go on dreaming and the golden opportunities slip away.

What a fool we shall call the person who, needing £10, does not take care of the few shillings he regularly gets! Never-theless, we behave just like him. We regret that we do not get time; and yet, we idle away the stray minutes, which put together would make a whole day, just as the stray shillings make a Bank-note.

By making regular, daily use of such minutes, a young European lady succeeded in learning Italian. Another was able to collect an astonishingly large sum of money in a year by knitting for charity during such moments of leisure.

'The Value of Stray Moments' (G.)
Indian Opinion, 25 Mar. 1905

115. MENTAL ENERGY AND SLEEP

When a man feels exhausted and is unable to carry on his work, the best remedy is to lie down and sleep and, if possible, to remain in bed for about a week. This is the best means to regain lost energy, particularly mental energy, for during sleep the brain enjoys complete rest, and the brain cells that are consumed during active work are then restored through the supply of blood. Just as every revolution of the wheel of an imposing steamer is the result of fuel burning in the furnace of the boiler, so also every thought arising in the brain is caused by the utilization of its cells during the process of thinking. The brain cells thus spent up can only be restored from the life-giving substance in the blood, which is formed out of the food we eat. The brain is so constituted that it can recover its used up cells only in the quietude of rest or sleep. Intoxicating drinks or drugs cannot give any nourishment to the brain. They only stimulate it and force it to consume more of its cells; so much so that the brain gets ultimately exhausted, and has no strength left even to take in the food needed by it, even as a man about to die of hunger and thirst cannot swallow any food or drink.

'Sleep (Best) Restorer of Energy' (G.)
Indian Opinion, 25 Mar. 1905

116. REFORMING ONESELF

Ashram,
April 14, 1926

Bhai Adamsaleh Alibhai,

You have left me far behind. I have undertaken to reform a single person, and that is my own self. And I realize how difficult it is to reform him. Now, need I answer your questions?

Vande Mataram from
MOHANDAS GANDHI

Sjt. A. A. Patel
Panoli
District Broach

Letter to Adamsaleh A. Patel (G.)
SN 19901

117. NO SELF-SUPPRESSION

Poona,
October 7, 1945

Chi. Munnalal,

I got your letter. You will never find any suggestion for self-suppression in my letters. I would approve of only such non-attachment as involves no self-suppression.

I am putting off the other questions for my next letter.

Blessings from
BAPU

Letter to Munnalal G. Shah (G.)
GN 8630

118. CONTROL OVER TEMPER

February 27, 1946

Chi. Munnalal,

You must learn to exercise control over your language. Even when thinking about individuals one should not pay too much attention to their shortcomings. You yourself should decide whether or not you should remain here. If you cannot decide, it would mean you should not stay here; for the work is so difficult that, if you cannot take full interest in it, you would not be able to do it. This is an important sphere of work for learning to acquire control over one's temper.

Blessings from
BAPU

Letter to Munnalal G. Shah (G.)
CW 5606

119. MENTAL CLEANSING

New Delhi,
August 28, 1946

Chi. Kamala,

If you have really become what you say, you will be able to render a lot of service. When the mind has been thoroughly cleansed, the body also will be all right. There is a saying that if the mind is pure the Ganga flows at one's door-step. In other words, if the mind is steady and *sattvic* the body too must become so.

I am not writing to Anna separately.

Shrimati Kamalabehn Sharma
Sevagram

Letter to Kamala Sharma (H.)
Pyarelal Papers

120. TRUE REPENTANCE

Patna,
April 16, 1947

The way to true repentance lies in making a firm resolve not
to soil one's hand with evil in future. If ever again you happen
to commit a wrong you should not sleep over your confession.
It is human to err. Therefore one is bound to commit an
errror, but that in itself is not a very grave matter. The danger
lies in hiding that error. When a person resorts to untruth to
hide his error he commits another folly. If one continues to
make mistakes one after another, it can be very harmful. If
there is an abscess in the body, one can press it and remove
the pus. But if the poison is not removed and it spreads in the
body it may result in death. The same is true of a person who
commits a sin but does not confess it. A sinner may commit
many sins but if at the last moment there is sincere repentance,
God forgives him. One should pray for the well-being not only
of human beings but of all creatures, which also are the creation of God. And the only way to attain this strength is to
meditate upon God morning and evening. The prayer for the
welfare of all includes our welfare as well.

'A Talk' (G.)
Biharni Komi Agman, pp. 209–10

121. RESPONSIBILITY AND SOUL-FORCE

Gandhi Camp, Patna,
April 17, 1947

Only this morning I poured out my anguish before some sisters. I did not expect that you also would be the cause of

similar pain. It is a bad habit with us that whenever we call a meeting to discuss some work, we start indulging in personal recrimination, lose our tempers and thus waste our time. It seems there is a growing inconsistency between the public and private life of a Congress worker. The result is that *goondaism*, lack of discipline and carelessness are increasing day by day. As preparations are afoot for transferring the Government into our hands, our responsibility is also increasing. We must get rid of anger, intolerance, etc., otherwise we will not be able to stand on our own. Not only this, we might be caught up in a bigger bondage. I want a *swaraj* in which the millions of illiterates in our country will realize its benefits. You have to cultivate the strength to achieve that. The government under *swaraj* should be such that people may clearly see the distinction between the arbitrary and autocratic British rule and the democratic government run on non-violent lines. I am an optimist. I maintain that once the reins of Government are transferred to us we will realize our responsibilities and all the artificial barriers existing at present will vanish.

My faith in non-violence and truth is being strengthened all the more in spite of the increasing number of atom bombs. I have not a shadow of doubt that there is no power superior to the power of truth and non-violence in the world. See what a great difference there is between the two: one is moral and spiritual force, and is motivated by infinite soul-force; the other is a product of physical and artificial power, which is perishable. The soul is imperishable. This doctrine is not my invention; it is a doctrine enunciated in our Vedas and Shastras. When soul-force awakens, it becomes irresistible and conquers the world. This power is inherent in every human being. But one can succeed only if one tries to realize this ideal in each and every act in one's life without being affected in the least by praise or censure.

Talk with Congress Workers (G.)
Biharni Komi Agman, pp. 216-17

IX

Conscience, Heroism, and Humility

---

122. CONSCIENCE AND WILFULNESS

A correspondent says in effect: 'Do you know what you have done by continually harping on conscience. I find youngsters and grown-up people talking utter nonsense under cover of conscience. What is more, youngsters have become impudent and grown-up people unscrupulous; can you not prevent this mischief? If you cannot, please withdraw the word from use and stop the drive that is being said in the name of that sacred but much abused word. Pray tell us who has a conscience? Do all have it? Do cats have a conscience when they hunt to death poor mice?'

I have not given the correspondent's question in his own words. I have endeavoured to paraphrase it. In doing so I hope I have done no injustice to him.

I must confess that the charge is not without substance. But he has presented only the dark side. Every virtue has been known to be abused by the wicked. But we do not on that account do away with virtue. We can but erect safeguards against abuse. When people cease to think for themselves and have everything regulated for them, it becomes necessary at times to assert the right of individuals to act in defiance of public opinion or law which is another name for public opinion. When individuals so act, they claim to have acted in obedience to their conscience. I entirely agree with the correspondent that youngsters as a rule must not pretend to have conscience. It is a quality or state acquired by laborious training. Wilfulness is not conscience. A child has no conscience. The correspondent's cat does not go for the mouse in obedience to the call of conscience. It does so in obedience to its nature. Conscience is the ripe fruit of strictest discipline. Irresponsible youngsters therefore who have never obeyed anything or anybody save their animal instinct have no conscience, nor therefore have all grown-up people. The savages for instance have to all intents and purposes no conscience.

Conscience can reside only in a delicately tuned breast. There is no such thing therefore as mass conscience as distinguished from the consciences of individuals. It is safe therefore to say that when a man makes everything a matter of conscience, he is a stranger to it. It is a truthful saying that 'conscience makes cowards of us all'. A conscientious man hesitates to assert himself, he is always humble, never boisterous, always compromising, always ready to listen, ever willing, even anxious to admit mistakes.

The correspondent is needlessly agitated. What does it matter that fifty thousand people say they act or refrain for conscience's sake? The world has no difficulty in distinguishing between conscience and an arrogant or ignorant assumption of it. Such men would have acted in similar circumstances exactly as they would under cover of conscience. The introduction of conscience into our public life is welcome even if it has taught a few of us to stand up for human dignity and rights in the face of the heaviest odds. These acts will live for ever, whereas those done under shams are like soap-bubbles enjoying a momentary existence.

'Under Conscience's Cover'
Young India, 21 Aug. 1924

123. FREEDOM OF CONSCIENCE

After showing that in this land of many religions, a volunteer is hard put to it to find a common denominator of conduct, a correspondent thus eloquently described the religion of a volunteer.[1]

Stripped of the eloquence, this religion of Truth again resolves itself into its component parts—Hinduism, Islam, Christianity, etc. For Truth will appear to most sincere and conscientious Hindus, Mussalmans and Christians as Hinduism, Islam and Christianity, respectively, *as they believe them*.

The golden rule of conduct, therefore, is mutual toleration, seeing that we will never all think alike and that we shall always see *Truth* in fragment and from different angles of vision. Conscience is not the same thing for all. Whilst, therefore, it is a good guide for individual conduct, imposition of that conduct upon all will be an insufferable interference with everybody else's freedom of conscience. It is a much-abused term. Have all people a conscience? Has a cannibal a conscience? Must he be allowed to act according to the dictates of his conscience which tells him that it is his duty to kill and eat his fellows? Now the etymological meaning of conscience is 'true knowledge'. The dictionary meaning is 'faculty distinguishing between right and wrong and influencing conduct accordingly'. Possession of such a faculty is possible only for a trained person, that is, one who has undergone discipline and learnt to listen to the inner voice. But even amongst the most conscientious persons, there will be room enough for honest differences of opinion. The only possible rule of conduct in any civilized society is therefore mutual toleration. It can be inculcated among and practised by all irrespective of their status and training.

'Religion of Volunteers'
Young India, 23 Sept. 1926

---

[1] The letter is not printed here. The correspondent had emphasized that Truth, as the essence of all religions, should be the religion of the volunteer, and be above all denominational religions.

124. THE INNER VOICE

April 17, 1932

Chi. Prithuraj,

I am addressing this letter c/o the Ashram, as you have not mentioned your address. In your excellent letter you say nothing about the hand.

It is not true that the same person cannot be self-reliant and also owe something to his parents. Just as one inherits certain physical qualities from one's parents, so also one may inherit from them wealth and prestige too. It would be false pride to reject them. A good son's duty is to make good use of them and add to them. In this way, one should see that one's own efforts carry forward what the parents had achieved.

We should listen to everybody's advice, but do only what our conscience tells us. And in order that our conscience may speak, we should observe the *yama-niyamas*. Everybody cannot hear the inner voice. We need divine ears to hear it.

Your handwriting shows considerable improvement, but it has not yet become sufficiently well formed.

Blessings from
BAPU

Letter to Prithuraj L. Asar (G.)
GW 9045

125. REASON AND THE INNER VOICE

May 25, 1932

What do you mean by asserting that there is no guiding force in the universe? How can we make such an assertion? My statement seems to have been somewhat twisted in this context. I have only said that Truth is identical with God and you may take it to be the Moving Spirit. In this context *karta*[1] does not have the meaning we usually attribute to it. Therefore Truth is *karta* as well as *akarta*.[2] But this is only an intellectual explanation. There is nothing wrong in this matter in believing whatever one's heart accepts, as no man has perfect knowledge of God nor can he express whatever little knowledge he has. It is true that I do not depend upon my intellect to decide upon any action. For me the reasoned course of action is held in check subject to the sanction of the inner voice. I do not know if others would call it the mysterious power or whatsoever. I have never deliberated upon this nor analysed it, I have felt no need of doing so either. I have faith, and knowledge, too, that a Power exists beyond reasoning. This suffices for me. I am unable to clarify this any further as I know nothing more in the matter.

Letter to Bhuskute (H.)[3]
Mahadevbhaini Diary, Vol. I, pp. 173-4

[1] Doer.
[2] Non-doer.
[3] He had asked how Gandhi acted according to the dictates of the inner voice while he believed that Truth is God and there is no Creator.

126. FITNESS TO LISTEN AND SELF-DECEPTION

Segaon, Wardha,
September 23/24, 1939

How I wish I had the same enthusiasm that fires you. Of course I have the experience of listening, not merely of trying to listen. The more I listen, the more I discover that I am still far away from God. While I can lay down rules, the observance of which is essential for proper listening, the reality still escapes me. When we say we are listening to God and getting answers, though we say it truthfully, there is every possibility there of self-deception. I do not know that I am myself altogether free from self-deception. People sometimes ask me if I may not be mistaken, and I say to them, 'Yes, very likely, what I say may be just a picture of my elongated self before you.'

And then see how one may claim to be God-guided in taking a particular course of action, and another may make the same claim in taking an opposite course of action. I will give you a good illustration. Rajaji, whom you know, at any rate whose name you have heard, is I think unsurpassed in godliness or God-mindedness. Now when I took the 21 days' purificatory fast in the Yeravda Jail in 1933 and proclaimed that it was in answer to a call from God, Rajagopalachari came all the way from Madras to dissuade me. He felt sure that I was deluding myself and that I should probably die and, if I did not, I should certainly be demented. Well, you see that I am still alive and of a sound mind. And yet perhaps Rajaji still thinks I was deluded and it was by an accident that I was saved, and I continue to think that I fasted in answer to the still small voice within.

I say this in order to warn you how unwise it may be to believe that you are always listening to God. I am not at all against the endeavour, but I warn you against thinking that this is a kind of 'open sesame' which has just to be shown to the millions. No one will contradict me when I say I have tried my very best to make India listen to the way of God. I have had some success but I am still far away from the goal. When I listen to the testimonies you have given I become cautious and even suspicious. In South Africa a preacher came who after his sermon got people to sign their names under a pledge, which was published in a book, binding them not to drink. Well, I have been witness to numerous of these promises being broken. It was no fault of these people. They signed the pledge under the temporary influence of the preacher's moving eloquence.

This I know that all that glitters is not gold, and also that if a man has really heard the voice of God, there is no sliding back, just as there is no forgetting it by one who has learnt to swim. The listening in must make people's lives daily richer and richer.

Let me not appear to damp your enthusiasm; but if it is to be built on solid rock, it is better that listening in is also based on solid rock.

This listening in presupposes the fitness to listen, and the fitness is acquired after constant and patient striving and waiting on God. Shankaracharya has likened the process to the attempt to empty the sea by means of a drainer small as the point of a blade of grass. This process thus necessarily is endless, being carried through birth after birth.

And yet the effort has to be as natural as breathing or the winking of the eyes, which processes happen without our knowing them. The effort coincides with the process of living. I commend to you this process of eternal striving which alone can take us face to face with God.

What is India as a nation to do at this juncture? What would you want her to do? How is she to repent? India may say she has committed many sins for which she is suffering and would pray to be given the strength to wipe them out. Or is there anything else at the back of your minds?

Discussion with Members of Oxford Group
Harijan, 7 Oct. 1939

127. AWAKENING CONSCIENCE

March 4, 1945

Conscience has to be awakened. There are rules and observances for the purpose. Not everyone can be said to have his conscience awakened.

Note to Gope Gurbuxani[1]
GN 1320

[1] The addressee who was staying at the Sevagram Ashram had asked: 'Truth is God, but what is Truth? Is it a thing which appeals to our conscience?'

128. *TAPAS* AND HUMILITY

October 8, 1924

There are instances of *tapas* at every step in Hindu mythology. Parvati desired to win Shankara and she took to *tapas*. Siva did something wrong and so he undertook *tapas*. Vishwamitra was the very incarnation of *tapas*. When Rama went into exile, Bharata plunged into *yoga* discipline, practised austere *tapas* and wore out his body.

God cannot test man in any other manner. If the soul is different from the body, it should remain blissful even when the body is tormented. Food is nourishment for the body, whereas knowledge and meditation are sustenance to the soul. Everyone has to realize this for himself as and when occasion arises.

If, however, the *tapas* is not accompanied by faith, devotion and humility, then all that austerity becomes a futile exercise. It also becomes hypocrisy. A devotee of God who enjoys eating his meal is a thousand times better than such an ascetic.

I have not the strength today to narrate the story of my *tapas* but I may state this much that I cannot possibly live without *tapas*. Once again I am destined to plunge into the stormy ocean. Please, God, know that I am humble and protect me.

'Importance of *Tapas*' (G.)
Navajivan, 12 Oct. 1924

129. MEEK AS A LAMB AND STRONG AS A LION

October 31, 1925

Who acts courageously and for what purpose? One could be courageous in order to be licentious, one could be courageous for the sake of a woman and, even for the sake of wealth. However, all this is like being courageous in order to jump into a well. Courage should be shown for the purpose of swimming across to the other shore. The supreme effort should be made for the sake of self-realization. We should take up a profession in which we offend no one and in which not a single pie has to be borrowed from anyone. Gentlemen with whom I was very familiar and who were like the multi-millionaires with whom I conversed the other day have been reduced to the sort of penury described in the couplet.[1] 'I saw the relations of Shah Alam[2] begging in the streets.' Hence, why should there be all this rush, pretence and fuss about something that is of a fleeting nature? Courage should be shown in having a vision of the glory of God and in singing His praises. True courage consists in losing one's mind in looking around at God's creations. These countless stars which shine in the sky, whose is the lustre they shed? One may spend many lives in trying to solve this riddle. Shrimad Rajchandra lay in insufferable agony before his death; however, he was not aware of it, he only eagerly awaited the vision of God. Today, I have to say harsh things gently; hence I feel I am lucky in being able to recall to memory a man like Shrimad Rajchandra and to praise his non-violence. Let us today derive from the memory of this man the strength to speak out without fear the plain, milk-white truth as seen by the soul. Let us stand in awe of the Self alone; let us be concerned that the Self, which is ever watchful, does not suffer pain. Let us learn endless penance from Rajchandra's life and realize that at the end of such penance, he came to worship *chaitanya*.[3] Let us make our lives meaningful by realizing our insignificance and thus become meek as a lamb and strong as a lion by contemplating the *chaitanya* that is within us.

Speech at Mandvi (G.)
Navajivan, 8 Nov. 1925

¹ By Behramji Malbari, a Parsi poet of Gujarat.
² One of the last Mogul emperors.
³ Universal consciousness.

130. HUMILITY, EGOTISM, AND INERTIA

Tuesday morning, October 7, 1930

Chi. Narandas,

Humility cannot be an observance by itself. For it does not lend itself to being deliberately practised. It is, however, an indispensable test of *ahimsa*. In one who has *ahimsa* in him it becomes part of his very nature. A preliminary draft of the rules and regulations of the Satyagraha Ashram was circulated among friends, including the late Sir Gurudas Banerji. He suggested that humility should be accorded a place among the observances. This suggestion could not then be accepted for the reason that I have just mentioned. But although humility is not one of the observances, it is certainly as essential as, and perhaps even more essential than any of them. Only it has never come to anyone by practice. Truth can be cultivated as well as Love. But to cultivate humility is tantamount to cultivating hypocrisy. Humility must not be here confounded with mere manners or etiquette. One man will sometimes prostrate himself before another although his heart is full of bitterness against him. This is not humility, but cunning. A man may chant *Ramanama* or tell his beads all day long, and move in society like a sage; but if he is selfish at heart, he is not meek but only hypocritical. A humble person is not himself conscious of his humility.

Truth and the like perhaps admit of measurement, but not humility. Inborn humility can never remain hidden, and yet the possessor is unaware of its existence. The story of Vashishtha and Vishwamitra furnishes a very good case in point. Humility should make the possessor realize that he is as nothing. Directly we imagine ourselves to be something, there is egotism. If a man who keeps observances is proud of keeping them, they will lose much, if not all, of their value. And a man who is proud of his virtue often becomes a curse to society. Society will not appreciate it, and he himself will fail to reap any benefit from it. Even a little thought will suffice to convince us that all creatures are nothing more than a mere atom in this universe. Our existence as embodied beings is purely momentary. What are a hundred years in eternity? But if we shatter the chains of egotism and melt into the ocean of humanity, we share its dignity. To feel that we are something is to set up a barrier between God and ourselves; to cease feeling that we are something is to become one with God. A drop in the ocean partakes of the greatness of its parent, although it is unconscious of it. But it is dried up as soon as it enters upon an existence independent of the ocean. We do not exaggerate when we say that life on earth is a mere bubble. How is it possible to cultivate such utter humility? It develops of itself if we understand the spirit of our observances. Can one who aspires to follow truth ever be a proud man?

A life of service must be one of humility. He who would sacrifice his life for others has hardly time to reserve for himself a place in the sun. Inertia must not be mistaken for humility, as it has been in Hinduism. Because it has been so mistaken, lethargy and hypocrisy have often flourished in its name. True humility means most strenuous and constant endeavour entirely directed towards the service of humanity. God is continuously in action without resting a single moment. If we would serve Him or become one with Him, our activity must be as unwearied as His. There may be momentary rest in store for the drop which is separated from the ocean, but not for the drop in the ocean, which knows no rest. The same is the case with ourselves. As soon as we become one with the ocean, in the shape of God, there is no more rest for us, nor indeed do we need rest any longer. Our very sleep is action. For we sleep with the thought of God in our hearts. This restlessness constitutes true rest. This never-ceasing agitation holds the key to peace ineffable.

True humility, therefore, requires us to dedicate ourselves to the service of all living creatures. When we have surrendered our all in this manner, no day in the week is a day of rest for us. This supreme state of total surrender is difficult to describe, but not beyond the bounds of human experience. It has been attained by many dedicated souls, and may be attained by ourselves as well. This is the goal which we of the Satyagraha Ashram have set before ourselves; all our observances and activities are calculated to assist us in reaching it. We shall reach it some day all unawares if we have truth in us. It is unattainable if we consciously strive for it.

Blessings from
BAPU

Letter to Narandas Gandhi (G.)
MMU/I

131. HUMILITY AND EXCLUSIVENESS

Camp Agra,
September 14, 1929

Dear Friend,

I have your letter. My message to the Christians would be to cultivate humility instead of arrogating to themselves the exclusive possession of absolute truth.

The only way I know of bringing about better understanding between different peoples is to treat all as of ourselves.

Yours sincerely,

Allen Melton, Esq.
President, World Fellowship Council, Dallas, Texas

Letter to Allen Melton
SN 15239

132. HUMILITY AND SELF-RESPECT

Yeravda Mandir,
October 18, 1930

Chi. Radhika,

I have your letter. In your previous letter I saw no impropriety. You had only poured out in it the thoughts which agitated your mind and you had a right to do so.

Humility cannot be learnt through formal training, but it grows of itself as one cultivates the spirit of non-violence. Outward humility of behaviour, which we find in royal families, can be learnt in a formal manner. It is, however, not true humility, but is only a part of cultured manners. In the humility which I advise, one has to forget the sense of 'I' and become a mere cipher. Can that be learnt through any lessons? But one who has realized the body's transitoriness and has in some measure become aware of the self soon becomes humble. What fine humility would it be on your part if, even though I should speak in anger to you, you merely listened with lowered eyes like those of a poor cow and did not even feel angry with me? Such humility comes only when you have learnt true self-respect. If you have not understood my meaning, ask me again and again. I shall not get tired of explaining it. Have you completely recovered now?

Blessings from
BAPU

Letter to Radhabehn Gandhi (G.)
CW 8687

133. BRAVERY AND MARTYRDOM

[After 10 October 1938]

We are lucky in having a true, honest, godfearing man like Badshah Khan in our midst here. To his credit stands the miracle of making thousands of Pathans renounce their arms. No one can say what the future will reveal. Maybe that all Khudai Khidmatgars may not prove to be true servants of God as their name implies. But making due allowance for all that, still what has been achieved is nothing short of marvellous. What I shall expect of you is that even if someone subjects you to the most inhuman tortures, you will joyfully face the ordeal and make the supreme sacrifice with God's name on your lips and without a trace of fear or anger or thoughts of revenge in your hearts. That will be heroism of the highest type.

To fight with the sword does call for bravery of a sort. But to die is braver far than to kill. He alone is truly brave, he alone is martyr in the true sense who dies without fear in his heart and without wishing hurt to his enemy, not the one who kills and dies. If our country, even in its present fallen state, can exhibit this type of bravery, what a beacon light will it be for Europe with all its discipline, science and organization! If Europe but realized that, heroic as it undoubtedly is for a handful of people to offer armed resistance in the face of superior numbers, it is far more heroic to stand up against overwhelming numbers without any arms at all, it would save itself and blaze a trail for the world.

Address to the Officers of Red Shirts
A Pilgrimage for Peace, pp. 56-7

134. THE BOOK OF JOB

An anonymous friend has taken the trouble of collecting apposite extracts from the Book of Job and Psalms. As they are a perpetual reminder to all of us, I gladly give them below. The moral I draw from the sheaf is that since man is only dust and at best grass, he had better pass the few moments he is on this earth in the service of his fellow creatures. I am hoping that the sender has not collected the Biblical verses to show the futility of all work, which is a doctrine of laziness and parasitism.

'Good Reminder'
Harijan, 19 May 1946

X

Satya—Absolute and Relative Truth

135. GIVING THE FIRST PLACE TO TRUTH

July, 1920

'The path of truth is for the brave alone, never for a coward.'
I realize the significance of this poem[1] more and more as days

pass. I also see that it is not for grown-ups only to put the idea of this verse into practice; children and students, too, can do so. If we try to know and follow the path of truth right from childhood, then alone, on growing up, shall we be saved from following the path of untruth. Just as a disease, if neglected, becomes chronic and incurable, so also untruth, if permitted to take root in us from childhood, will later grow into a serious disease and, becoming incurable, gradually ruin our health. It is for this reason that we find untruth increasing in us.

So the highest lesson to be learnt during one's student-life is that one should know truth and act on it.

This path has always been for the brave because a much greater effort is required to go up the steep slope of truth than to climb the Himalayas. If at all, therefore, we want to work in this direction and serve ourselves, we should give the first place to truth and march forward with unshakeable faith in it. Truth is God.

MOHANDAS

'Path of Truth for the Brave Alone'[2] (G.)
Madhpudo, I. ii

---

[1] By Pritamdas (*c.* 1720-98), a Gujarati poet.
[2] Gandhi's contribution to 'Madhpudo', the manuscript magazine of the Ashram School, Sabarmati.

136. THE VOW OF TRUTH

There is a story in the gospel, in which a judge inquired, 'What is truth?', but got no answer. The holy books of Hindus tell of Harishchandra who sacrificed his all at the altar of Truth and let himself, his wife, and his son be sold to a *chandala*. (What, by the way, must be the position about untouchability in those early days?) Imam Hassan and Hussein lost their lives for the sake of truth.

The fact remains, however, that the question posed by that judge has not been answered. Harishchandra renounced his all for the sake of the truth as he knew it and so won immortal fame. Imam Hussein gave up his dear life for truth as he understood it. But Harishchandra's truth and Imam Hussein's truth may or may not be our truth.

Beyond these limited truths, however, there is one absolute Truth which is total and all-embracing. But it is indescribable, because it is God. Or say, rather, God is Truth. All else is unreal and false. Other things, therefore, can be true only in a relative sense.

He, therefore, who understands truth, follows nothing but truth in thought, speech and action, comes to know God and gains the seer's vision of the past, the present and the future. He attains *moksha* though still encased in the physical frame.

If we get one single person, before the 31st of December, who would practise truth to such perfection, *swaraj* should be ours this very day.

Some of us are no more than *satya-agrahis*, those, in other words, who aspire to follow truth scrupulously, but they hardly succeed in doing so even in the limited sphere of speech. We thus see that observance of the vow of truth is no easy matter.

A friend remarked: 'You have taken the vow of truth; and yet you misread the telegram from Mr. Das[1] so as to interpret it in your favour and announced Bengal's contribution to be 25 lakhs instead of what it was, 15 lakhs. Were you not, in this case, guilty of a subtle form of untruth?' I did not deliberately interpret the telegram in my favour. I am not in the habit of reading meanings which suit me. But I was certainly hasty in interpreting the telegram. It was received late at night after 12. I state this fact not by way of extenuation but to show that truth must shine as brightly as ever even when one has mounted the gallows. He who yearns to follow the truth at all times and under all conditions must not be guilty of such haste. One who always follows truth is never guilty of untruth in word or deed even unknowingly. In fact such a person becomes incapable of acting in this manner. According to this definition, I certainly lapsed from truth.

My only consolation is that I never claim anything beyond a sincere endeavour to keep the vow of truth. It never happens that I tell a lie deliberately. I do not remember having deliberately told a lie any time in my life, except on one occasion when I cheated my revered father. It has become part of my nature to speak the truth and act in accordance with truth. But it is impossible for me to claim that truth, which I perceive but dimly, has become part of my life. I am not beyond indulgence in unconscious exaggeration or self-praise or taking interest in describing my achievements. There is a shade of untruth in all these and they will not stand the test of truth. A life wholly filled with the spirit of truth should be clear and pure as crystal. Untruth cannot survive even for a moment in the presence of such a person. No one can deceive a man who always follows truth, for it ought to be impossible that untruth will not be exposed in his presence. The most difficult vow to keep is the vow of truth. Out of lakhs who may strive to follow truth, only a rare person will succeed completely in the course of his present life.

When somebody utters a lie before me, I get more angry with myself than with him because I then realize that untruth still exists somewhere deep in me.

The word *satya* comes from *sat*, which means 'to be', 'to exist'. Only God is ever the same through all time. A thousand times honour to him who has succeeded, through love and devotion for this *satya*, in opening out his heart permanently to its presence. I have been but striving to serve that truth. I have, I believe, the courage to jump from the top of the Himalayas for its sake. At the same time, I know that I am still very far from that truth. As I advance towards it, I perceive my weakness ever more clearly and the knowledge makes me humble. It is possible to be puffed up with pride so long as one does not know one's own insignificance. But once a man sees it, his pride melts away. Mine melted away long ago. I can very well understand why Tulsidas called himself a villain. This path is for the brave alone; the timid had better not tread it. He who strives for all the twenty-four hours of the day ever meditating on truth, whether eating, drinking, sitting, sleeping, spinning or easing himself, doing anything whatever, will certainly have his whole being filled with truth. And when the sun of truth blazes in all its glory in a person's heart, he will not remain hidden. He will not, then, need to use speech and to explain. Or, rather, every word uttered by him will be charged with such power, such life, that it will produce an immediate effect on the people. I do not have this truth in me. But, as I happen to be treading this path, I am in the unhappy condition of the castor-oil plant which, as they say, is king on a tree-less heath.

Truth cannot exist without love. Truth includes non-violence, *brahmacharya*, non-stealing and other rules. It is only for convenience that the five *yamas* have been mentioned separately. The man who commits violence after knowing truth falls from truth. That a man who has known truth can be lecherous is as inconceivable as that darkness may exist despite the sun shining. If, we have, before 31st of December, even one person who will follow truth to this perfect degree, *swaraj* is a certainty, for everyone will have to obey his word as law. The sun's light does not need to be pointed out. Truth shines with its own light and is its own proof. In these evil times, it is difficult to follow truth in such perfection but I know it is not impossible. If a large number from among us strive to follow it even in some measure, we can win *swaraj*. We can also win it if a few of us pursue it with utmost consciousness. Only, we must be sincere. It will not do merely to make a show of following truth. It does not matter if we follow truth only to the extent of one anna in a rupee, but it must be truth and not something else. The little measure of it which we follow must not, in any circumstances, be mixed with deliberate falsehood. It is my earnest desire that, in this holy *yajna*, all of us will learn to follow truth as a matter of principle.

'What is Truth?' (G.)
Navajivan, 20 Nov. 1921

¹ C. R. Das.

137. THE QUEST FOR TRUTH

[Sabarmati Jail,]
Thursday Night [16 March 1922]

Chi. Jamnalal,¹

As I proceed in my quest for Truth, it grows upon me that Truth comprehends everything. I often feel that *ahimsa* is in Truth, not vice versa. What is perceived by a pure heart at a particular moment is Truth to it for that moment. By clinging to it, one can attain pure Truth. And I do not imagine that this will lead us into any moral dilemma. But often enough, it is difficult to decide what is *ahimsa*. Even the use of disinfectants is *himsa*. Still we have to live a life of *ahimsa* in the midst of a world full of *himsa*, and we can do so only if we cling to Truth. That is why I can derive *ahimsa* from truth. Out of Truth emerge love and tenderness. A votary of Truth, one who would scrupulously cling to Truth, must be utterly humble. His humility should increase with his observance of Truth. I see the truth of this every moment of my life. I have now a more vivid sense of Truth and of my own littleness than I had a year ago.

The wonderful implication of the great truth *Brahma satyam jaganmithya*[2] grows on me from day to day. We should therefore be always patient. This will purge us of harshness and make us more tolerant. Our lapses will then appear as mountains and those of others as small as mole-hills. The body exists because of our ego. The utter extinction of the body is *moksha*. He who has achieved such extinction of the ego becomes the very image of Truth; he may well be called the *Brahman*. Hence it is that a loving name of God is *Dasanudasa*.[3]

Wife, children, friends, possessions—all should be held subject to that Truth. We can be *satyagrahis* only if we are ready to sacrifice each one of these in our search for Truth. It is with a view to making the observance of this Truth comparatively easy that I have thrown myself into this movement and do not hesitate to sacrifice men like you in it. Its outward form is Indian *swaraj*. Its real inner form is the *swaraj* of particular individuals. This *swaraj* is being delayed because we have not found even one *satyagrahi* of that pure type. This, however, need not dismay us. It should spur us on to greater effort.

You have, indeed, made yourself my fifth son. But I am striving to be a worthy father to you. It is no ordinary responsibility which a man who adopts a son undertakes. May God help me, and may I be worthy of the responsibility in this very life.

Blessings from
BAPU

Letter to Jamnalal Bajaj (G.)
GN 2843

¹ 1889-1942; merchant and banker of Wardha; close associate of Gandhi; social worker and philanthropist; Treasurer of the Congress for a number of years.

² 'Brahma is real, this world is unreal.'

³ Servant of servants.

138. 'TO THINE OWN SELF BE TRUE'

December 1, 1925

Think of last Tuesday, when I began my fast. Why did I take that step? There were three ways open to me:

1. PUNISHMENT: I could have followed the easy road of corporal punishment. Usually a teacher on detecting errors on the part of pupils would flatter himself with having done a good thing if he punished them. I have been a teacher myself, though my preoccupations prevent me from teaching you during these days. As a teacher I had no option but to reject this accepted method for I know by experience it is futile and even harmful.

2. INDIFFERENCE: I could have left you to your fate. Not unoften does a teacher do so. 'It is enough', he argues, 'that the boys do their lessons tolerably well and reproduce what they are taught. Surely I am not concerned with their private behaviour. And even if I was, how am I to keep watch over them?' This indifference could not appeal to me.

3. The third was the method of LOVE. Your character is to me a sacred trust. I must therefore try to enter into your lives, your innermost thoughts, your desires and your impulses, and help you to detect and eradicate impurities, if any. For inward cleanliness is the first thing that should be taught, other things must follow after the first and most important lesson has gone home. I discovered irregularities amongst you. What was I to do? Punishing you was out of the question. Being the chief among the teachers, I had to take the punishment on myself in the form of the fast which breaks today.

I have learnt a lot during these days of quiet thinking. What have you? Could you assure me that you will never repeat your mistake? You may err again but this fast will be lost on you if you do not realize the way out of it. Truthfulness is the master-key. Do not lie under any circumstances whatsoever. Keep nothing secret, take your teachers and your elders into your confidence and make a clean breast of everything to them. Bear ill will to none, do not say an evil thing of anyone behind his back, above all 'to thine own self be true', so that you are false to no one else. Truthful dealing even in the least little things of life is the only secret of a pure life.

You must have noticed that I receive my inspiration on such occasions from the hymn, *Vaishnava Jana to tene kahiye* (He is the true *Vaishnava* etc.). That hymn is enough to sustain me, even if I were to forget the *Bhagavad Gita*. To tell you the truth, however, there is one thing which is even simpler, but which may possibly be difficult for you to understand. But that has been my pole star all along during life's journey—the conviction that Truth is God and untruth a denial of Him.

Speech to Students
Young India, 10 Dec. 1925

139. PURITY OF HEART

Ashram, Sabarmati,
April 2, 1926

I have your letter. A pure heart enables one to find and see truth. Every one of us therefore must aim after purity of heart. All else follows as a matter of course.

Letter to Shah Jamil-Alam
SN 11057

140. GROWING REVELATION OF TRUTH

Ashram, Sabarmati,
April 24, 1926

Dear Friend,

I have your letter and thank you for your good wishes.

The way you have put my position very nearly takes my breath away. For, you say, 'it is quite clear you have never changed from untruth to truth'. The statement is both true and untrue. There was no occasion for me to make a conscious effort to speak the truth or to be able to appreciate truth. But interpreting truth in its broadest sense, I must confess that I am still filled with untruth and am ever striving to rid myself of it. Therefore, I can fully endorse the latter portion of the sentence from which I have quoted; for, I see truth every day clearer and clearer. The process through which the soul has been passing is an effort of the heart. The intellect has been hooked to its service by prayer, meditation and constant watchfulness which are essentially matters of the heart and which have been the predominant factors that have contributed to the growing revelation of truth. I have never felt that whatever knowledge has been gained was imposed from without but that it has come from within. It has been an unfolding, drawing out or perhaps better still removing the hard and ugly crusts that overlay the truth that is within us. In other words, the process has been one of self-purification.

My visit to Mussoorie has been cancelled.

Yours sincerely,

Sjt. Amulya Chandra Sen
Language School
Queen's Hill
Darjeeling

Letter to Amulya Chandra Sen
SN 19504

141. TRUTH THROUGH LOVE

As at the Ashram, Sabarmati,
June 8, 1927

Dear Friend,

Mr. K. T. Paul has just handed your letter personally to me.

Here is my answer to your enquiry:

TRUTH and LOVE have been jointly the guiding principle of my life. If God who is indefinable can be at all defined, then

I should say that God is TRUTH. It is impossible to reach HIM, that is, TRUTH, except through LOVE. LOVE can only be expressed fully when man reduces himself to a cipher. This process of reduction to cipher is the highest effort man or woman is capable of making. It is the only effort worth making, and it is possible only through ever-increasing self-restraint.

Ever at youth's service,

Basil Mathews, Esq.,
Editor, 'World's Youth'
3, Rue Général Dufour
Geneva

Letter to Basil Mathews
SN 12514

142. *SATYA*—A STATE OF BEING

After morning prayers,
July 22, 1930

Chi. Narandas,

There is a suggestion in Vishvanath's letter that every week I should write and send a discourse to be read out at prayer time. I thought about the request and felt that it deserved to be complied with. Treat these discourses as my contribution to the attempt to make the prayers more alive. I am considering with Kakasaheb if we can send anything for the other six days as well. Here is something for this week.

I deal first with truth, as the Satyagraha Ashram owes its very existence to the pursuit and the attempted practice of truth.

The word *satya* is derived from *sat*, which means that which is. *Satya* means a state of being. Nothing is or exists in reality except Truth. That is why *sat* or *satya* is the right name for God. In fact it is more correct to say that Truth is God than to say that God is Truth. But as we cannot do without a ruler or general, the name God is and will remain more current. On deeper thinking, however, it will be realized that *sat* or *satya* is the only correct and fully significant name for God.

And where there is Truth, there also is knowledge which is true. Where there is no Truth, there can be no true knowledge. That is why the word *chit* or knowledge is associated with the name of God. And where there is true knowledge, there is always *ananda*, bliss. There sorrow has no place. And even as Truth is eternal, so is the bliss derived from it. Hence we know God as *Sat-chit-ananda*, one who combines in Himself Truth, knowledge and bliss.

Devotion to this Truth is the sole justification for our existence. All our activities should be centred in truth. Truth should be the very breath of our life. When once this stage in the pilgrim's progress is reached, all other rules of correct living will come without effort and obedience to them will be instinctive. But without Truth it is impossible to observe any principles or rules in life.

Generally speaking, observance of the law of Truth is understood merely to mean that we must speak the truth. But we in the Ashram should understand the word *satya* or Truth in a much wider sense. There should be Truth in thought, Truth in speech and Truth in action. To the man who has realized this Truth in its fullness, nothing else remains to be known, because, as we have seen above, all knowledge is necessarily included in it. What is not included in it is not Truth, and so not true knowledge; and there can be no real bliss without true knowledge. If we once learn how to apply this never-failing test of Truth, we will at once be able to find out what is worth doing, what is worth seeing, what is worth reading.

But how is one to realize this Truth, which may be likened to the philosopher's stone or the cow of plenty? By *abhyasa*, single-minded devotion, and *vairagya*, indifference to all other interests in life—replies the *Bhagavad Gita*. Even so, what may appear as truth to one person will often appear as untruth to another person. But that need not worry the seeker. Where there is honest effort, it will be realized that what appear to be different truths are like the countless and apparently different leaves of the same tree. Does not God Himself appear to different individuals in different aspects? Yet we know that

He is one. But Truth is the right designation of God. Hence there is nothing wrong in every man following Truth according to his lights. Indeed it is his duty to do so. Then if there is a mistake on the part of anyone so following Truth, it will be automatically set right. For the quest of Truth involves *tapascharya*, self-suffering, sometimes even unto death. There can be no place in it for even a trace of self-interest. In such selfless search for Truth, nobody can lose his bearings for long. Directly he takes to the wrong path he stumbles, and is thus redirected to the right path. Therefore the pursuit of Truth is true *bhakti*, devotion. Such *bhakti* is 'a bargain in which one risks one's very life'. It is the path that leads to God. There is no place in it for cowardice, no place for defeat. It is the talisman by which death itself becomes the portal to life eternal.

But now we have come to the border-line beyond which lies *ahimsa*. We shall discuss it next week.

In this connection, it would be well to ponder over the lives and examples of Harishchandra, Prahlad, Ramachandra, Imam Hasan and Imam Husain, the Christian saints, etc. How beautiful it would be if all of us, young and old, men and women, meditated, till next week, on these thoughts at all hours of the day, whether working, eating, drinking or playing, and were rewarded with innocent sleep.

God as Truth has been for me, at any rate, a treasure beyond price. May He be so to every one of us.

Blessings from
BAPU

Letter to Narandas Gandhi (G.)
MMU/I

143. TRUTH AND PURE CONSCIOUSNESS

March 21, 1932

Chi.,

Do you remember my definition of God? Instead of saying that God is Truth, I say that Truth is God. I did not always think thus. I realized this only four years ago. But without knowing it I always acted as if it was so. I have always known God as Truth. There was a time when I doubted the existence of God, but even at that time I did not doubt the existence of Truth. This Truth is not a material quality but is pure consciousness. That alone holds the universe together. It is God because it rules the whole universe. If you follow this idea, it contains the answer to all your other questions. If you have any difficulty, however, put your question to me. For me this is almost a matter of direct experience. I say 'almost' because I have not seen face to face God Who is Truth. I have had only a glimpse of Him. But my faith is unshakeable.

Blessings from
BAPU

Letter to Boys and Girls (G.)
Mahadevbhaini Diary, Vol. I, p. 27

144. TRUTH IN ALL CONDITIONS

June 19, 1932

He alone is a lover of truth who follows it in all conditions of life. Nobody is forced to tell lies in business or in service. One should not accept a job which does so, even if one starves in consequence.

A Letter (G.)
Mahadevbhaini Diary, Vol. I, pp. 231-2

145. TRUTH AND SELF-EXAMINATION

Sunday, July 3, 1932

What I said about *ahimsa* also applies to truth. If we split hairs about issues such as whether one may or may not tell a lie to save a cow and ignore what is daily happening before us, we cannot follow truth. By raising such complicated issues we make truth difficult to discover. If we follow truth today in solving the problems which confront us in our daily life, we shall know instinctively how to act in difficult situations when they arise.

Each of us should examine only himself or herself from this point of view. Do I deceive anybody knowingly? If I believe that B is a bad person but show him that I believe him to be good, I deceive him. Do I try to show, in order to win people's respect or esteem, that I possess certain virtues which in fact I do not possess? Do I exaggerate in my speech? Do I hide my misdeeds from persons to whom I should confess them? If a superior or co-worker puts me any question, do I evade him? Do I keep back what I ought to declare? If I do any of these things, I am guilty of untruth. Everybody should examine his conduct daily in this manner and try to overcome his shortcomings. One to whom truth has become second nature and who has risen to a state so that he can never speak untruth may not do this. But everyone who has the least trace of untruth in him or who can follow truth only with effort should examine himself daily as explained above and put to himself those or any other similar questions which may occur to him and reply to them. Anybody who follows this practice even for a month will clearly observe a change having taken place in himself.

'How to Observe Truth' (G.)
MMU/II

146. FEARLESSNESS AND LOVE

[14 November 1935]

Chi. Avadhesh,

I have your letter after a long time. Why have you not yet taken up some definite work? In order to be fearless we should love all and adhere to the path of truth. The assertion that goodness is easier to come by is based on the fact that all wish to be known as good people and no one wants to be known as a sinner. Therefore it can be said that to be a sinner is difficult!

Blessings from
BAPU

Letter to Avadhesh Dutt Avasthi (H.)
GN 3214

147. TRUTH AND NEGATION

November 7, 1945

Bhai Vamanrao,

I have your beautiful letter. It is interesting too.

I write the truth as I personally see it. Absolute truth alone is God. It is beyond reach. At the most we can say it is *neti, neti*.[1] The truth that we see is relative, many-sided, plural and is the whole truth for a given time. There is no scope for vanity in it and the only way of reaching it is through *ahimsa*. Pure and absolute truth should be our ideal. We can reach the ideal only by constantly meditating on it, and reaching it is attaining *moksha*. For the last sixty years I have been experiencing what I have said above. I am still experiencing it.

Blessings from
BAPU

Letter to Vamanrao Joshi (H.)
Pyarelal Papers

[1] 'Not this, not this.'

XI

Ahimsa—The Scope and Power of Non-Violence

148. NON-VIOLENCE—THE LAW OF OUR SPECIES

In this age of the rule of brute force, it is almost impossible for anyone to believe that anyone else could possibly reject the law of the final supremacy of brute force. And so I receive anonymous letters advising me that I must not interfere with the progress of non-co-operation even though popular violence may break out. Others come to me and assuming that secretly I must be plotting violence, inquire when the happy moment for declaring open violence will arrive. They assure me that the English will never yield to anything but violence secret or open. Yet others, I am informed, believe that I am the most rascally person living in India because I never give out my real intention and that they have not a shadow of a doubt that I believe in violence just as much as most people do.

Such being the hold that the doctrine of the sword has on the majority of mankind, and as success of non-co-operation depends principally on absence of violence during its pendency and as my views in this matter affect the conduct of a large number of people, I am anxious to state them as clearly as possible.

I do believe that where there is only a choice between cowardice and violence I would advise violence. Thus when my eldest son asked me what he should have done, had he been present when I was almost fatally assaulted in 1908, whether he should have run away and seen me killed or whether he should have used his physical force which he could and wanted to use, and defended me, I told him that it was his duty to defend me even by using violence. Hence it was that I took part in the Boer War, the so-called Zulu rebellion and the late War. Hence also do I advocate training in arms for those who believe in the method of violence. I would rather have India resort to arms in order to defend her honour than that she should in a cowardly manner become or remain a helpless witness to her own dishonour.

But I believe that non-violence is infinitely superior to violence, forgiveness is more manly than punishment. *Kshama virasya bhushanam*. 'Forgiveness adorns a soldier.' But abstinence is forgiveness only when there is the power to punish; it is meaningless when it pretends to proceed from a helpless creature. A mouse hardly forgives a cat when it allows itself to be torn to pieces by her. I, therefore, appreciate the sentiment of those who cry out for the condign punishment of General Dyer and his ilk. They would tear him to pieces if they could. But I do not believe India to be helpless. I do not believe myself to be a helpless creature. Only I want to use India's and my strength for a better purpose.

Let me not be misunderstood. Strength does not come from physical capacity. It comes from an indomitable will. An average Zulu is any way more than a match for an average Englishman in bodily capacity. But he flees from an English boy, because he fears the boy's revolver or those who will use it for him. He fears death and is nerveless in spite of his burly figure. We in India may in a moment realize that one hundred thousand Englishmen need not frighten three hundred million human beings. A definite forgiveness would therefore mean a definite recognition of our strength. With enlightened forgiveness must come a mighty wave of strength in us, which would make it impossible for a Dyer and a Frank Johnson to heap affront upon India's devoted head. It matters little to me that for the moment I do not drive my point home. We feel too downtrodden not to be angry and revengeful. But I must not refrain from saying that India can gain more by waiving the right of punishment. We have better work to do, a better mission to deliver to the world.

I am not a visionary. I claim to be a practical idealist. The religion of non-violence is not meant merely for the *rishis* and saints. It is meant for the common people as well. Non-violence is the law of our species as violence is the law of the brute. The spirit lies dormant in the brute and he knows no law but that of physical might. The dignity of man requires obedience to a higher law—to the strength of the spirit.

I have therefore ventured to place before India the ancient law of self-sacrifice. For *satyagraha* and its off-shoots, non-co-operation and civil resistance, are nothing but new names for the law of suffering. The *rishis*, who discovered the law of non-violence in the midst of violence, were greater geniuses than Newton. They were themselves greater warriors than Wellington. Having themselves known the use of arms, they realized their uselessness and taught a weary world that its salvation lay not through violence but through non-violence.

Non-violence in its dynamic condition means conscious suffering. It does not mean meek submission to the will of the evil-doer, but it means the putting of one's whole soul against the will of the tyrant. Working under this law of our being, it is possible for a single individual to defy the whole might of an unjust empire to save his honour, his religion, his soul and lay the foundation for that empire's fall or its regeneration.

And so I am not pleading for India to practise non-violence because it is weak. I want her to practise non-violence being conscious of her strength and power. No training in arms is required for realization of her strength. We seem to need it because we seem to think that we are but a lump of flesh. I want India to recognize that she has a soul that cannot perish and that can rise triumphant above every physical weakness and defy the physical combination of a whole world. What is the meaning of Rama, a mere human being, with his host of monkeys, pitting himself against the insolent strength of ten-headed Ravana surrounded in supposed safety by the raging waters on all sides of Lanka? Does it not mean the conquest of physical might by spiritual strength? However, being a practical man, I do not wait till India recognizes the practicability of the spiritual life in the political world. India considers herself to be powerless and paralysed before the machine-guns, the tanks and the aeroplanes of the English. And she takes up non-co-operation out of her weakness. It must still serve the same purpose, namely, bring her delivery from the crushing weight of British injustice if a sufficient number of people practise it.

I isolate this non-co-operation from Sinn Feinism, for, it is so conceived as to be incapable of being offered side by side with violence. But I invite even the school of violence to give this peaceful non-co-operation a trial. It will not fail through its inherent weakness. It may fail because of poverty of response. Then will be the time for real danger. The high-souled men, who are unable to suffer national humiliation any longer, will want to vent their wrath. They will take to violence. So far as I know, they must perish without delivering themselves or their country from the wrong. If India takes up the doctrine of the sword, she may gain momentary victory. Then India will cease to be the pride of my heart. I am wedded to India because I owe my all to her. I believe absolutely that she has a mission for the world. She is not to copy Europe blindly. India's acceptance of the doctrine of the sword will be the hour of my trial. I hope I shall not be found wanting. My religion has no geographical limits. If I have a living faith in it, it will transcend my love for India herself. My life is dedicated to service of India through the religion of non-violence which I believe to be the root of Hinduism.

Meanwhile I urge those who distrust me, not to disturb the even working of the struggle that has just commenced, by inciting to violence in the belief that I want violence. I detest secrecy as a sin. Let them give non-violent non-co-operation a trial and they will find that I had no mental reservation whatsoever.

'The Doctrine of the Sword'
Young India, 11 Aug. 1920

149. THE GREATEST FORCE IN THE WORLD

Delhi
November 14, 1924

To
The 'World Tomorrow'
396, Broadway
New York
U.S.A.

My study and experience of non-violence have proved to me that it is the greatest force in the world. It is the surest method of discovering the truth and it is the quickest because there is no other. It works silently, almost imperceptibly, but none the less surely. It is the one constructive process of Nature in the midst of incessant destruction going on about us. I hold it to be a superstition to believe that it can work only in private life. There is no department of life public or private to which that force cannot be applied. But this non-violence is impossible without complete self-effacement.

M. K. GANDHI

Message to *World Tomorrow*
Mahadev Desai's Diary (MSS)

150. THE SPIRIT OF NON-VIOLENCE

[15 July 1926]

Non-violence is the greatest force man has been endowed with. Truth is the only goal he has. For God is none other than Truth. But Truth cannot be, never will be, reached except through non-violence.

That which distinguishes man from all other animals is his capacity to be non-violent. And he fulfils his mission only to the extent that he is non-violent and no more. He has no doubt many other gifts. But if they do not subserve the main purpose—the development of the spirit of non-violence in him—they but drag him down lower than the brute, a status from which he has only just emerged.

The cry for peace will be a cry in the wilderness, so long as the spirit of non-violence does not dominate millions of men and women.

An armed conflict between nations horrifies us. But the economic war is no better than an armed conflict. This is like a surgical operation. An economic war is prolonged torture. And its ravages are no less terrible than those depicted in the literature on war properly so called. We think nothing of the other because we are used to its deadly effects.

Many of us in India shudder to see blood spilled. Many of us resent cow-slaughter, but we think nothing of the slow torture through which by our greed we put our people and cattle. But because we are used to this lingering death, we think no more about it.

The movement against war is sound. I pray for its success. But I cannot help the gnawing fear that the movement will fail, if it does not touch the root of all evil—man's greed.

Will America, England and the other great nations of the West continue to exploit the so-called weaker or uncivilized races and hope to attain peace that the whole world is pining for? Or will Americans continue to prey upon one another, have commercial rivalries and yet expect to dictate peace to the world?

Not till the spirit is changed can the form be altered. The form is merely an expression of the spirit within. We may succeed in seemingly altering the form but the alteration will be a mere make-believe if the spirit within remains unalterable. A whited sepulchre still conceals beneath it the rotting flesh and bone.

Far be it from me to discount or under-rate the great effort that is being made in the West to kill the war-spirit. Mine is merely a word of caution as from a fellow-seeker who has been striving in his own humble manner after the same thing, may be in a different way, no doubt on a much smaller scale. But if the experiment demonstrably succeeds on the smaller field and, if those who are working on the larger field have not overtaken me, it will at least pave the way for a similar experiment on a large field.

I observe in the limited field in which I find myself, that unless I can reach the hearts of men and women, I am able to do nothing. I observe further that so long as the spirit of hate persists in some shape or other, it is impossible to establish peace or to gain our freedom by peaceful effort. We cannot love one another, if we hate Englishmen. We cannot love the Japanese and hate Englishmen. We must either let the Law of Love rule us through and through or not at all. Love among ourselves based on hatred of others breaks down under the slightest pressure. The fact is such love is never real love. It is an armed peace. And so it will be in this great movement in the West against war. War will only be stopped when the conscience of mankind has become sufficiently elevated to recognize the undisputed supremacy of the Law of Love in all the walks of life. Some say this will never come to pass. I shall retain the faith till the end of my earthly existence that it shall come to pass.

'Non-Violence—The Greatest Force'
The Hindu, 8 Nov. 1926

151. THE LAW OF LOVE

It takes a fairly strenuous course of training to attain to a mental state of non-violence. In daily life it has to be a course of discipline though we may not like it, like for instance the life of a soldier. But I agree that unless there is a hearty co-operation of the mind, the mere outward observance will be simply a mask, harmful both to the man himself and to others. The perfect state is reached only when mind and body and speech are in proper co-ordination. But it is always a case of intense mental struggle. It is not that I am incapable of anger, for instance, but I succeed on almost all occasions to keep my feelings under control. Whatever may be the result, there is always in me a conscious struggle to follow the law of non-violence deliberately and ceaselessly. Such a struggle leaves one stronger for it.

Non-violence is a weapon of the strong. With the weak it might easily be hypocrisy. Fear and love are contradictory terms. Love is reckless in giving away, oblivious as to what it gets in return. Love wrestles with the world as with itself and ultimately gains a mastery over all other feelings. My daily experience, as of those who are working with me, is that every problem would lend itself to solution if we are determined to make the law of truth and non-violence the law of life. For truth and non-violence are, to me, faces of the same coin.

Whether mankind will consciously follow the law of love I do not know. But that need not perturb us. The law will work, just as the law of gravitation will work whether we accept it or no. And just as a scientist will work wonders out of various applications of the laws of nature, even so a man who applies the law of love with scientific precision can work greater wonders. For the force of non-violence is infinitely more wonderful and subtle than the force of nature, like for instance electricity. The man who discovered for us the law of love was a far greater scientist than any of our modern scientists. Only our explorations have not gone far enough and so it is not possible for every one to see all its workings. Such, at any rate, is the hallucination, if it is one, under which I am labouring. The more I work at this law the more I feel the delight in life, the delight in the scheme of this universe. It gives me a peace and a meaning of the mysteries of nature that I have no power to describe.

'From S. S. Rajputana–III' (Letter from M. D.)[1]
Young India, 1 Oct. 1931

---

[1] Mahadev Desai published the above extract from a discourse given by Gandhi at the evening prayer, during his voyage to London.

152. NON-VIOLENCE AS MEANS AND END

June 26, 1933

My dear Asaf Ali,

I have your long letter for which I thank you. I do not at all mind your having sent it to the Press. You had a perfect right to send me that letter and I appreciate the frankness with which you have expressed your views.

I am, as yet, unable to say anything on the present situation because I am still bed-ridden and have not been able to make an analytical study of it. I want you, however, to understand my fundamental difficulty which constitutes also my limitation. Non-violence for me is not a mere experiment. It is part of my life and the whole of the creed of *satyagraha*, non-co-operation, civil disobedience, and the like are necessary deductions from the fundamental proposition that non-violence is the law of life for human beings. For me it is both a means and an end and I am more than ever convinced that in the complex situation that faces India, there is no other way of gaining real freedom. In applying my mind to the present situation I must, therefore, test everything in terms of non-violence.

Yours sincerely,

M. Asaf Ali, Esq., bar-at-law
Kucha Chelan, Delhi

Letter to M. Asaf Ali
SN 19108

153. LOVE AND BROTHERHOOD

August 4, 1932

Brotherhood is just now only a distant aspiration. To me it is a test of true spirituality. All our prayers, fasting and observances are empty nothings so long as we do not feel a live kinship with all life. But we have not even arrived at that intellectual belief, let alone a heart realization. We are still selective. A selective brotherhood is a selfish partnership. Brotherhood requires no consideration or response. If it did, we could not love those whom we consider as vile men and women. In the midst of strife and jealousy, it is a most difficult performance. And yet true religion demands nothing less from us. Therefore each one of us has to endeavour to realize this truth for ourselves irrespective of what others do.

Letter to Esther Menon[1]
Mahadevbhaini Diary, Vol. I, p. 345

[1] The addressee had asked 'why the idea of brotherhood did not take root among nations in spite of the example set by Bapu, Kagawa, Albert Schweitzer and others' (*The Diary of Mahadev Desai*, Vol. I, p. 270).

154. LOVE OF ALL

May 2, 1935

Love has no boundary. My nationalism includes the love of all the nations of the earth irrespective of creed.

A Letter
Mahadev Desai's Diary (MSS)

155. AXIOMS OF NON-VIOLENCE

Non-violence is at the root of every one of my activities and therefore also of the three public activities on which I am just now visibly concentrating all my energy. These are untouchability, *khadi*, and village regeneration in general. Hindu–Muslim unity is my fourth love. But so far as any visible manifestation is concerned, I have owned defeat on that score. Let the public, however, not assume therefrom that I am inactive. If not during my lifetime, I know that after my death both Hindus and Mussalmans will bear witness that I had never ceased to yearn after communal peace.

Non-violence to be a creed has to be all-pervasive. I cannot be non-violent about one activity of mine and violent about others. That would be a policy, not a life-force. That being so, I cannot be indifferent about the war that Italy is now waging against Abyssinia. But I have resisted most pressing invitation to express my opinion and give a lead to the country. Self-suppression is often necessary in the interest of Truth and non-violence. If India had as a nation imbibed the creed of non-violence, corporate or national, I should have had no hesitation in giving a lead. But in spite of a certain hold I

have on the millions of this country, I know the very grave
and glaring limitation of that hold. India had an unbroken
tradition of non-violence from times immemorial. But at no
time in her ancient history, as far as I know it, has it had
complete non-violence in action pervading the whole land.
Nevertheless, it is my unshakeable belief that her destiny is
to deliver the message of non-violence to mankind. It may
take ages to come to fruition. But so far as I can judge,
no other country will precede her in the fulfilment of that
mission.

Be that as it may, it is seasonable to contemplate the implications of that matchless force. Three concrete questions were,
the other day, incidentally asked by friends:

1. What could ill-armed Abyssinia do against well-armed Italy, if
she were non-violent?
2. What could England, the greatest and the most powerful member
of the League, do against determined Italy, if she (England) were
non-violent in your sense of the term?
3. What could India do, if she suddenly became non-violent in your
sense of the term?

Before I answer the questions let me lay down five simple
axioms of non-violence as I know it:

1. Non-violence implies as complete self-purification as is
humanly possible.

2. Man for man the strength of non-violence is in exact
proportion to the ability, not the will, of the non-violent person to inflict violence.

3. Non-violence is without exception superior to violence,
i.e., the power at the disposal of a non-violent person is always
greater than he could have if he was violent.

4. There is no such thing as defeat in non-violence. The
end of violence is surest defeat.

5. The ultimate end of non-violence is surest victory—if
such a term may be used of non-violence. In reality where
there is no sense of defeat, there is no sense of victory.

The foregoing questions may be answered in the light of
these axioms.

1. If Abyssinia were non-violent, she would have no arms

would want none. She would make no appeal to the League or any other power for armed intervention. She would never give any cause for complaint. And Italy would find nothing to conquer if Abyssinians would not offer armed resistance, nor would they give co-operation willing or forced. Italian occupation in that case would mean that of the land without its people. That, however, is not Italy's exact object. She seeks submission of the people of the beautiful land.

2. If Englishmen were as a nation to become non-violent at heart, they would shed imperialism, they would give up the use of arms. The moral force generated by such an act of renunciation would stagger Italy into willing surrender of her designs. England would then be a living embodiment of the axioms I have laid down. The effect of such conversion would mean the greatest miracle of all ages. And yet if non-violence is not an idle dream, some such thing has some day to come to pass somewhere. I live in that faith.

3. The last question may be answered thus. As I have said, India as a nation is not non-violent in the full sense of the term. Neither has she any capacity for offering violence—not because she has no arms. Physical possession of arms is the least necessity of the brave. Her non-violence is that of the weak. She betrays her weakness in many of her daily acts. She appears before the world today as a decaying nation. I mean here not in the mere political sense but essentially in the non-violent, moral sense. She lacks the ability to offer physical resistance. She has no consciousness of strength. She is conscious only of her weakness. If she were otherwise, there would be no communal problems, nor political. If she were non-violent in the consciousness of her strength, Englishmen would lose their role of distrustful conquerors. We may talk politically as we like and often legitimately blame the English rulers. But if we, as Indians, could but for a moment visualize ourselves as a strong people disdaining to strike, we should cease to fear Englishmen whether as soldiers, traders or administrators, and they to distrust us. Therefore if we became truly non-violent we should carry Englishmen with us in all we might do. In other words, we being millions would be the greatest moral force in the world, and Italy would listen to our friendly word.

The reader has, I hope, by now perceived that my argument is but a feeble and clumsy attempt to prove my axioms which to be such must be self-proved.

Till my eyes of geometrical understanding had been opened, my brain was swimming, as I read and re-read the twelve axioms of Euclid. After the opening of my eyes geometry seemed to be the easiest science to learn. Much more so is the case with non-violence. It is a matter of faith and experience, not of argument beyond a point. So long as the world refuses to believe, she must await a miracle, i.e., an ocular demonstration of non-violence on a mass scale. They say this is against human nature—non-violence is only for the individual. If so, where is the difference in kind between man and beast?

'The Greatest Force'
Harijan, 12 Oct. 1935

156. NON-VIOLENCE AS A CREED AND A POLICY

It was on the 18th instant that I expressed the following hope in *Harijan*:

If my argument has gone home, is it not time for us to declare our changeless faith in non-violence of the strong and say we do not seek to defend our liberty with the force of arms but we will defend it with the force of non-violence?

On the 21st the Working Committee felt unable to enforce such faith in action when the time for it came.[1] For the Committee never before had an occasion to test their faith. At the last meeting they had to lay down a course of action for meeting impending anarchy within and danger of aggression from without.

I pleaded hard with the Committee: 'If you have faith in non-violence of the strong, now is the time to act up to it. It does not matter that many parties do not believe in non-violence whether of the strong or of the weak. Probably that is all the greater reason for Congressmen to meet the emergency by non-violent action. For if all were non-violent, there could be no anarchy and there would be no question of any-body arming for meeting aggression from without. It is because Congressmen represent a party of non-violence, in the midst of parties who do not believe in it, that it becomes imperative for Congressmen to show that they are well able to act up to their faith.'

But the members of the Working Committee felt that Congressmen would not be able to act up to it. It would be a new experience for them. They were never before called upon to deal with such a crisis. The attempt made by me to form peace brigades to deal with communal riots and the like had wholly failed. Therefore they could not hope for the action contemplated.

My position was different. With the Congress non-violence was always a policy. It was open to it to reject it if it failed. If it could not bring political and economic independence, it was of no use. For me non-violence is a creed. I must act up to it whether I am alone or have companions. Since propagation of non-violence is the mission of my life, I must pursue it in all weathers. I felt that now was the time for me to prove my faith before God and man. And so I asked for absolution from the Committee. Hitherto I have been responsible for guiding the general policy of the Congress. I could no longer do so when fundamental differences were discovered between them and me. They readily recognized the correctness of my attitude. And they gave me the absolution. Once more they have justified the trust imposed in them. They have been true to themselves. They had not the confidence, in themselves or those whom they represented, that they could express in their actions the required measure of non-violence. And so they made the only choice they could honestly make. It was a tremendous sacrifice they made—the sacrifice of the prestige that the Congress had gained in the world for unadulterated non-violence, and the dissolution of the unwritten and un-spoken bond between them and me. But though it is a break in the common practice of a common ideal or policy, there is no break in the friendship of over twenty years' standing.

I am both happy and unhappy over the result. Happy

because I have been able to bear the strain of the break and have been given the strength to stand alone. Unhappy because my word seemed to lose the power to carry with me those whom it was my proud privilege to carry all these many years which seem like yesterday. But I know that, if God shows me the way to demonstrate the efficacy of non-violence of the strong, the break will prove to have been temporary. If there is no way, they will have justified their wisdom in bearing the wrench of letting me go my way alone. If that tragic discovery of my impotence is in store for me, I hope still to retain the faith that has sustained me all these years and to have humility enough to realize that I was not a fit enough instrument to carry the torch of non-violence any further.

But this argument and doubt are based upon the assumption that the members of the Working Committee represent the feeling of the vast majority of Congressmen. They would wish and hope that the vast majority of Congressmen had in them the non-violence of the strong. No one would be more glad than they to discover that they had underrated Congressmen's strength. The probability, however, is that there is no majority but only a good minority which represents the non-violence of the strong. It should be remembered that the matter does not lend itself to argument. The members of the Working Committee had all the argument before them. But non-violence, which is a quality of the heart, cannot come by an appeal to the brain. Therefore what is required is a quiet but resolute demonstration of non-violent strength. The opportunity comes to everyone almost daily. There are communal clashes, there are dacoities, there are wordy duels. In all these things those who are truly non-violent can and will demonstrate it. If it is shown in an adequate measure, it will not fail to infect their surroundings. I am quite clear that there is not a single Congressman who disbelieves in the efficacy of non-violence out of sheer cussedness. Let the Congressmen who believe that the Congress should adhere to non-violence in dealing with internal disorders or external aggression, express it in their daily conduct.

Non-violence of the strong cannot be a mere policy. It must be a creed, or a passion, if 'creed' is objected to. A man with a passion expresses it in every little act of his. Therefore he who is possessed by non-violence will express it in the family circle, in his dealings with neighbours, in his business, in Congress meetings, in public meetings, and in his dealings with opponents. It is because it has not expressed itself in this way among Congressmen that the members of the Working Committee rightly concluded that Congressmen were not ready for non-violent treatment of internal disorders or external aggression. Embarrassment caused by non-violent action would move established authority to yield to popular will. But such action has obviously no play in the face of disorders. We have to court death without retaliation and with no malice or anger toward those who bring about disorder. It is easy enough to see that non-violence required here is of a wholly different type from what the Congress has known hitherto. But it is the only non-violence that is true and that can save the world from self-destruction. This is a certainty sooner or later, sooner rather than later, if India cannot deliver the message of true non-violence to a world which wants to be saved from the curse of wars and does not know how to find the deliverance.

Sevagram, June 24, 1940.

PS. After the foregoing was written and typed, I saw Jawaharlal's statement.[2] His love for and confidence in me peep out of every sentence referring to me. The foregoing does not need any amendment. It is better for the reader to have both the independent reactions. Good must come out of this separation.

'Both Happy and Unhappy'
Harijan, 29 June 1940

---

[1] The resolution of the Working Committee, passed after five days of deliberations, *inter alia* said: 'While the Working Committee hold that the Congress must continue to adhere strictly to the principle of non-violence in their struggle for independence, the Committee cannot ignore the present imperfections and failings in this respect of the human elements they have to deal with. . . . The Committee have deliberated over the problem that has thus arisen and have come to the conclusion that they are unable to go the full length with Gandhiji. But they recognize that he should be free to pursue his great ideal in his own way, and therefore absolve him from responsibility

for the programme and activity which the Congress has to pursue under the conditions at present prevailing in India and the world in regard to external aggression and internal disorder.'

² Jawaharlal Nehru in his statement issued from Bombay on 23 June had said: 'The difference between Gandhiji's approach and that of the Working Committee must be understood and must not lead people to think that there is a break between him and the Congress. The Congress of the past twenty years is his creation and child and nothing can break this bond. I am sure his guidance and wise counsel will always be available to the Congress.'

157. FUNDAMENTALS OF NON-VIOLENCE

[After 18 September 1940]

I hope that all the conversation we had in Bombay has soaked into you. If it has, every problem could be solved by reference to those fundamentals which I tried to put before you. Our non-violence has to begin at home with our children, elders, neighbours and friends. We have to overlook the so-called blemishes of our friends and neighbours and never forgive our own. Then only shall we be able to right ourselves, and as we ascend higher, our non-violence has to be practised among our political associates. We have to see and approach the viewpoints of those who differ from us. We have to be patient with them and convince them of their errors and be convinced of our own. Then proceeding further we have to deal patiently and gently with political parties that have different policies and different principles. We have to look at their criticism from their own standpoint, always remembering that the greater the distance between ourselves and others, the greater the scope for the play of our non-violence; and it is only when we have passed our examination or test in these fields that we can deal with those against whom we are fighting and who have grievously wronged us.

This was one thing we talked about. The other thing I said was that a non-violent man has to keep himself engaged usefully during all waking hours and, therefore, *constructive work is for him what arms are for the violent men.*

Fragment of Letter to Abdul Ghaffar Khan
Harijan, 18 Jan. 1942

158. THE SUPREME LAW

Sevagram,
January 25, 1945

My dear Father Lash,

I am so glad you came. Please tell all our English friends that we all do our duty regardless of result. Has not an English divine said that 'duty will be merit when debt becomes a donation'? Non-violence, translated 'love', is the supreme law for human beings. It knows no exception. I have tried all these years to live by that law and hope to die in that state.

Yours,
M. K. GANDHI

Letter to William Q. Lash
GN 41

159. NON-VIOLENCE ALONE LAWFUL

A straight line is one. Non-violence is a straight line. Lines that are not straight are many. A child who has learnt how to handle a pen can draw as many lines as he wishes. He won't draw a straight line except perhaps by chance. Several readers ask me whether in the violence 'permitted' by me several things mentioned by them could be included. Strange to say all the letters received are in English! The writers should re-read my article and they will at once know why I cannot answer those questions. I am unfit probably for the simple reason that I have never practised violence. Above all I have never permitted violence. I have simply stated two grades of bravery and cowardice. The only thing lawful is non-violence. Violence can never be lawful in the sense meant here, i.e., not according to man-made law but according to the law made by Nature for man. Though violence is not lawful, when it is offered in self-defence or for the defence of the defenceless, it is an act of bravery far better than cowardly submission. The latter befits neither man nor woman. Under violence, there are many stages and varieties of bravery. Every man must judge this for himself. No other person can or has the right.

New Delhi, October 18, 1946

'Notes'
Harijan, 27 Oct. 1946

160. THE NARROW AND STRAIGHT PATH

I would love to attempt an answer to a question which has been addressed to me from more than one quarter of the globe. It is:

How can you account for the growing violence among your people on the part of political parties for the furtherance of political ends? Is this the result of the thirty years of non-violent practice for ending British rule? Does your message of non-violence still hold good for the world? I have condensed the sentiments of my correspondents in my own language.

In answer I must confess my bankruptcy, not that of non-violence. I have already said that the non-violence that was offered during the past thirty years was that of the weak. Whether it is a good enough answer or not is for others to judge. It must be further admitted that such non-violence can have no play in the altered circumstances. India has no experience of the non-violence of the strong. It serves no purpose for me to continue to repeat that the non-violence of the strong is the strongest force in the world. The truth requires constant and extensive demonstration. This I am endeavouring to do to the best of my ability. What if the best of my ability is very little? May I not be living in a fool's paradise? Why should I ask people to follow me in the fruitless search? These are pertinent questions. My answer is quite simple. I ask nobody to follow me. Everyone should follow his or her own inner voice. If he or she has no ears to listen to it, he or she should do the best he or she can. In no case should he or she imitate others sheep-like.

One more question has been and is being asked. If you are sure that India is going the wrong way, why do you associate with the wrong-doers? Why do you not plough your own lonely furrow and have faith that if you are right, your erstwhile friends and followers will seek you out? I regard this as a very fair question. I must not attempt to argue against it. All I can say is that my faith is as strong as ever. It is quite possible that my technique is faulty. There are old and tried precedents to guide one in such a complexity. Only, no one should act mechanically. Hence I can say to all my counsellors that they should have patience with me and even share my belief that there is no hope for the aching world except through the narrow and straight path of non-violence. Millions like me may fail to prove the truth in their own lives, that would be their failure, never of the eternal law.

'Non-Violence'[1]
Harijan, 29 June 1947

[1] Gandhi's written message for the prayer meeting on 15 June 1947.

161. NON-VIOLENCE AND EGOISM

A gentleman writes as follows[1] ...

Such questions are frequently raised. They cannot be brushed aside, either, as being trivial. These problems have been discussed both in the West and the East in books dealing with the deeper meaning of life. In my humble view, there is only one solution to these problems, since they all arise from the same cause. The actions mentioned above certainly involve violence, for every motion or action involves it and, therefore, no action is altogether innocent. The difference between one action and another lies only in the degree of violence involved in either. The very association of the *atman* with the body rests on violence. Every sin is a form of violence, and complete freedom from sin is possible only with the deliverance of the *atman* from the body. A human being, therefore, may keep perfect non-violence as his or her ideal and strive to follow it as completely as possible. But no matter how near it he reaches, he will find some degree of violence unavoidable, in breathing or eating, for instance.

There is life in each grain which we consume. When, there-

fore, we adopt a vegetarian diet and abstain from non-vege-
tarian food we cannot claim that we completely avoid violence. But we prefer the former and regard the violence
involved in it as inescapable. This is why eating for pleasure
must never be indulged in. We should eat only in order that
we may live, and should live only to realize the self. If our
living for this purpose involves any violence, we may be a
party to it as being unable to escape it. We can now see that
if, in spite of all our precautions, there are germs in the water
and bugs in the furniture, we may do whatever we find necessary to get rid of them. I do not believe that it is a divine law
that everyone should act in the same way at certain times and
in certain circumstances.

Non-violence is a quality of the heart. Whether there is
violence or non-violence in our actions can be judged only by
reference to the spirit behind them. Everyone, therefore, who
regards the observance of non-violence as a moral duty should
guide his actions by the principle stated above. I know that
there is a flaw in this reply. One may commit violence as
much as one chooses and then, deceiving oneself and the
world, justify one's actions with the plea of their being unavoidable. This article is not meant for such persons. It is
addressed only to those who believe in the principle of non-
violence and are assailed by moral doubts from time to time.
Such persons will commit even unavoidable violence most
hesitatingly, and limit, not expand, the scope of their activities, so much so that they will not use any of their powers for
selfish ends. They will use all their energies for public service,
dedicating to God everything they do. All the gifts and abilities of a good man, that is, a non-violent, compassionate man,
are for service to others. There is violence always in the attachment to one's ego. When doing anything, one must ask oneself
this question: 'Is my action inspired by egoistic attachment?'
If there is no such attachment, then there is no violence.

'Problem of Non-Violence' (G.)
Navajivan, 6 June 1926

---

[1] The letter is not published here. The correspondent had asked for Gandhi's views
about the impossibility of observing perfect non-violence in practical life, since destruction of insects could never be completely avoided.

162. NON-VIOLENCE AND SELF-PURIFICATION

[Before 23 April 1938]

Everyone who cares to study what is happening at the present moment in our country can see that what we want can be attained if we will but achieve the *mantra* of peace, the creed of non-violence. You cannot breed peace out of no-peace. The attempt is like gathering grapes of thorns or figs of thistles. The more I go into the question, the more forcibly the conclusion is borne in upon me that our first duty is to grasp this fundamental fact. There was a day when I used to flatter myself with the belief that I had mastered the key to learning that lesson. Today I am filled with doubt. I do not know that I have in me purification enough to realize true peace or non-violence. In that frame of mind I cannot think of any other thing, talk of any other thing. But whatever may be my condition, I have no doubt in my mind that there is no *swaraj* without non-violence, nothing that goes by the name of constructive work. Constructive work is a mild aspect of non-violence, but the true test of non-violence lies in acquiring the capacity to meet an innocent and unflinching death in the service of our cause. How to achieve it is the question. I want you to apply your minds to it.

Message to Jaipur Rajya Praja Mandal
Harijan, 4 June 1938

163. NON-VIOLENT ORGANIZATION

Lakki,
[27 October 1938]

The principles on which a non-violent organization is based are different from and the reverse of what obtains in a violent organization. For instance, in the orthodox army, there is a clear distinction made between an officer and a private. The latter is subordinate and inferior to the former. In a non-violent army the general is just the chief servant—first among equals. He claims no privilege over or superiority to the rank and file. You have fondly given the title 'Badshah Khan' to

Khan Saheb. But if in his heart of hearts he actually began to believe that he could behave like an ordinary general, it would spell his downfall and bring his power to an end. He is Badshah in the sense only that he is the truest and foremost Khudai Khidmatgar and excels all other Khudai Khidmatgars in the quality and quantity of service.

The second difference between a military organization and a peace organization is that in the former the rank and file have no part in the choice of their general and other officers. These are imposed upon them and enjoy unrestricted power over them. In a non-violent army, the general and the officers are elected or are as if elected when their authority is moral and rests solely on the willing obedience of the rank and file.

So much for internal relations between the general of a non-violent army and his soldiers. Coming to their relations with the outside world, the same sort of difference is visible between these two kinds of organizations. Just now we had to deal with an enormous crowd that had gathered outside this room. You tried to disperse it by persuasion and loving argument, not by using force and, when in the end we failed in our attempt, we withdrew and sought relief from it by getting behind closed doors in this room. Military discipline knows nothing of moral pressure.

Let me proceed a step further. The people who are crowding outside here are all our friends though they are not Khudai Khidmatgars. They are eager to listen to what we may tell them. Even their indiscipline is a manifestation of their love. But there may be others besides them elsewhere who may not be well disposed towards us, who may even be hostile to us. In armed organizations, the only recognized way of dealing with such persons is to drive them out. Here, to consider the opponent, or, for the matter of that, anybody, even in thought, as your enemy would, in the parlance of non-violence or love, be called a sin. Far from seeking revenge, a votary of non-violence would pray to God that He might bring about a change of heart of his opponent, and if that does not happen he would be prepared to bear any injury that his opponent might inflict upon him, not in a spirit of cowardice or helplessness, but bravely with a smile upon his face. I believe implicitly in the ancient saying that 'non-violence real and complete will melt the stoniest hearts'.

He illustrated his remarks by describing how Mir Alam Khan, his Pathan assailant in South Africa, had ultimately repented and become friendly.

This could not have happened if I had retaliated. My action can be fitly described as a process of conversion. Unless you have felt within you this urge to convert your enemy by your love, you had better retrace your steps; this business of non-violence is not for you.

'What about thieves, dacoits and spoilers of defenceless women?' you will ask. Must a Khudai Khidmatgar maintain his non-violence in regard to them too? My reply is, most decidedly 'Yes'. Punishment is God's, Who alone is the infallible Judge. It does not belong to man 'with judgment weak'. Renunciation of violence must not mean apathy or helplessness in the face of wrongdoing. If our non-violence is genuine and rooted in love, it ought to provide a more effective remedy against wrongdoing than the use of brute force. I certainly expect you to trace out the dacoits, show them the error of their ways and, in so doing, brave even death.

Talk to Khudai Khidmatgars
Harijan, 19 Nov. 1938

164. NON-VIOLENCE AND NON-RETALIATION

Mansehra,
[8 November 1938]

It has become the fashion these days to say that society cannot be organized or run on non-violent lines. I join issue on that point. In a family, when a father slaps his delinquent child, the latter does not think of retaliating. He obeys his father not because of the deterrent effect of the slap but because of the offended love which he senses behind it. That in my opinion is an epitome of the way in which society is or should be governed. What is true of family must be true of society which is but a larger family. It is man's imagination that divides the world into warring groups of enemies and friends. In the ultimate resort it is the power of love that acts even in the midst of the clash and sustains the world.

I am told that the Red Shirts here are Red Shirts only in name. I hope the allegation is baseless. I know that Khan Saheb is seriously disturbed at the infiltration of the Khudai Khidmatgar movement by undesirable and self-seeking elements. I share with him this feeling that mere accession of numbers, unless they are true exponents of the creed which they profess, will only weaken instead of adding strength to the movement.

The Red Shirt movement today has drawn attention of the whole of India and even outside. And yet what it has achieved is only a small fraction of what has to be achieved. I implicitly accept the assurance given by the Khudai Khidmatgars that they are anxious to understand and practise the doctrine of non-violence in full. There are tremendous heights lying before them still to be scaled. The programme of constructive non-violence that I have placed before them is self-acting when it is once started well. Its enforcement will be a sure test too of the earnestness and sincerity of the Khudai Khidmatgars.

Talk to Khudai Khidmatgars
Harijan, 3 Dec. 1938

165. NON-VIOLENT SOCIETY AND GOVERNMENT

I have been very much interested in reading the recent numbers of *Harijan* and your observations on the European crisis and the N.W.F. Province. But there is one aspect of the non-violence problem, which I should have discussed with you at Segaon¹ if there had been time, to which you seldom or never refer. You say that non-violent non-co-operation, as you have developed it, is the answer to the violence which is now threatening the whole world with ruin. There is no doubt as to the immense effect such spirit and action could produce. But must not the non-violent spirit of selfless love for all, enemies and friends alike, express itself, if it is to succeed, in a liberal, democratic and constitutional form of government? Society cannot exist without law and government. International peace cannot exist unless the nations accept a system of constitutional government which will give them unity and law and end anarchy among them. No doubt some day the law of God will be so 'written on the hearts and minds' of men that they become individually the expression of it, and will need no human law or government. But that is the end. The beginning of progress towards that heavenly goal must take the form at first of a willingness among races, religions and nations to unite under a single constitution, through which their unity and membership one of another is established, the laws under which they live are promulgated after public discussion and by some form of majority decision and are enforced, where it is not voluntarily obeyed, not by war but by police force, where persuasion and example have not sufficed. As between sovereign nations the operation of a constructive non-violence spirit must lead to some form of federation. It cannot succeed until it has done so. The proof that it exists effectively will be the appearance of a federal system. Thus the only real solution for the European problem is the federation of its 25 peoples and nations under a single democratic constitution which will create a government which can look at and legislate for the problems of Europe, not as a set of rival and conflicting nations but as a single whole with autonomous parts. In the same way the only solution to the Indian problem is the substitution of a democratic constitution for the control of Great Britain. And what is true for Europe and India is true, in the long run, for the whole world and is the only final method of ending war.

Non-violent non-co-operation may be the best, perhaps the only method of bringing about the change of mind and heart which will make acceptance of a federal democratic constitution by the nation possible. But attainment to democratic federation is the necessary attainment whereby its success is assured and without which it cannot succeed. It is always a matter of interest and indeed of surprise to me that you appear to think that non-violent non-co-operation is enough in itself, and that you never proclaim that a democratic system of government unifying men, races, religions and nations is the goal to which it must lead, though that attainment is only possible as the result of a spiritual change of heart and cannot be reached by force or violence or chicanery.

I do not write this as a kind of indirect argument for the Indian constitution, though it obviously has a bearing on that problem also. The Government of India Act is clearly a very imperfect application of the principle of democratic federation and must necessarily evolve rapidly if it is to work. The main argument I have always urged for it is that in present conditions it represents the only constitutional compromise uniting Provinces, States, Muslims and Hindus which can be made to work and that it has far more seeds of evolution within it than is generally recognized. If your spiritual gospel informed the people, it would rapidly and easily evolve. My object is not to elicit any opinion from you about the constitutional problem but an answer to the larger question set forth in the early part of the letter.

Thus writes Lord Lothian. The letter was received early in January, but urgent matters prevented my dealing earlier with the important question raised in it.

I have purposely refrained from dealing with the nature of government in a society based deliberately on non-violence. All society is held together by non-violence, even as the earth is held in her position by gravitation. But when the law of gravitation was discovered the discovery yielded results of which our ancestors had no knowledge. Even so when society is deliberately constructed in accordance with the law of non-violence, its structure will be different in material particulars from what it is today. But I cannot say in advance what the government based wholly on non-violence will be like.

What is happening today is disregard of the law of non-violence and enthronement of violence as if it were an eternal law. The democracies, therefore, that we see at work in England, America and France are only so called, because they are no less based on violence than Nazi Germany, Fascist Italy or even Soviet Russia. The only difference is that the violence of the last three is much better organized than that of the three democratic powers. Nevertheless we see today a mad race for outdoing one another in the matter of armaments. And if when the clash comes, as it is bound to come one day, the democracies win, they will do so only because they will have the backing of their peoples who imagine that they have a voice in their own government whereas in the other three cases the peoples might rebel against their own dictatorships.

Holding the view that without the recognition of non-violence on a national scale there is no such thing as a constitutional or democratic government, I devote my energy to the propagation of non-violence as the law of our life—individual, social, political, national and international. I fancy that I have seen the light, though dimly. I write cautiously, for I do not profess to know the whole of the Law. If I know the successes of my experiments, I know also my failures. But the successes are enough to fill me with undying hope.

I have often said that if one takes care of the means, the end will take care of itself. Non-violence is the means, the end for every nation is complete independence. There will be an international League only when all the nations, big or small, composing it are fully independent. The nature of that independence will correspond to the extent of non-violence assimilated by the nations concerned. One thing is certain. In a society based on non-violence, the smallest nation will feel as tall as the tallest. The idea of superiority and inferiority will be wholly obliterated.

It follows from this that the Government of India Act is merely a makeshift and has to give way to an Act coined by the nation itself. So far as Provincial Autonomy is concerned, it has been found possible to handle it somewhat. My own experience of its working is by no means happy. The Congress Governments have not that non-violent hold over the people that I had expected they would have.

But the Federal structure is inconceivable to me because it contemplates a partnership, however loose, among dissimilars. How dissimilar the States are is being demonstrated in an ugliness for which I was unprepared. Therefore the Federal structure, as conceived by the Government of India Act, I hold to be an utter impossibility.

Thus the conclusion is irresistible that for one like me, wedded to non-violence, constitutional or democratic government is a distant dream so long as non-violence is not recognized as a living force, an inviolable creed, not a mere policy. While I prate about universal non-violence, my experiment is confined to India. If it succeeds the world will accept it without effort. There is, however, a big BUT. The pause does not worry me. My faith is brightest in the midst of impenetrable darkness.

'Working of Non-Violence'
Harijan, 11 Feb. 1939

---

[1] Lord Lothian was at Segaon from 18 to 20 Jan. 1938.

166. NON-VIOLENT POLICE FORCE

A friend writes as follows[1] . . .

The questions asked in this letter are of the utmost importance and deserve notice. If true *ahimsa* had come into being within us, and if our so-called *satyagraha* movements had been truly non-violent, these questions would not have arisen because they would have been solved.

For one who has never seen the arctic regions an imaginary description of them, however elaborate, can convey but an inadequate idea of the reality. Even so is it with *ahimsa*. If all Congressmen had been true to their creed, we would not be vacillating between violence and non-violence as we are today. The fruits of *ahimsa* would be in evidence everywhere. There would be communal harmony, the demon of untouchability would have been cast out, and, generally speaking, we should have evolved an ordered society. But the reverse is the case just now. There is even definite hostility to the Congress in certain quarters. The word of Congressmen is not always relied on. The Muslim League and most of the Princes have no faith in the Congress and are in fact inimical to it. If Congressmen had true *ahimsa* in them, there would be none of this distrust. In fact the Congress would be the beloved of all.

Therefore I can only place an imaginary picture before the votaries of *ahimsa*.

So long as we are not saturated with pure *ahimsa* we cannot possibly win *swaraj* through non-violence. We can come into power only when we are in a majority or, in other words, when the large majority of people are willing to abide by the law of *ahimsa*. When this happy state prevails, the spirit of violence will have all but vanished and internal disorder will have come under control.

Nevertheless I have conceded that even in a non-violent State a police force may be necessary. This, I admit, is a sign of my imperfect *ahimsa*. I have not the courage to declare that we can carry on without a police force as I have in respect of an army. Of course I can and do envisage a state where the police will not be necessary; but whether we shall succeed in realizing it, the future alone will show.

The police of my conception will, however, be of a wholly different pattern from the present-day force. Its ranks will be composed of believers in non-violence. They will be servants, not masters, of the people. The people will instinctively render them every help, and through mutual co-operation they will easily deal with the ever-decreasing disturbances. The police force will have some kind of arms, but they will be rarely used, if at all. In fact the policemen will be reformers. Their police work will be confined primarily to robbers and dacoits. Quarrels between labour and capital and strikes will be few and far between in a non-violent state, because the influence of the non-violent majority will be so great as to command the respect of the principal elements in society. Similarly there will be no room for communal disturbances. Then we must remember that when such a Congress Government comes into power the large majority of men and women of 21 years and over will have been enfranchised. The rigid and cramped Constitution of today has of course no place in this picture.

Sevagram, August 20, 1940

'My Idea of a Police Force' (G)
Harijanbandhu, 31 Aug. 1940
Harijan, 1 Sept. 1940

---

[1] Not printed here. The correspondent, while conceding the effectiveness of non-violence to meet external aggression, had argued that so long as social injustice and poverty existed internal disturbances were bound to continue and hence also the need for a police force. He had asked Gandhi whether he envisaged such a police force to be maintained for all time.

167. A NON-VIOLENT STATE

A London friend has put seven questions on the working of non-violence. Though similar questions have been dealt with in *Young India* or *Harijan*, it is profitable to answer them in a single article, if perchance the answers may prove helpful.

Q. 1. Is it possible for a modern State (which is essentially based on force) to offer non-violent resistance for countering internal as well as external forces of disorder? Or is it necessary that people wanting to offer non-violent resistance should first of all divest themselves of State-authority and place themselves vis-a-vis the opponent entirely in a private capacity?

A. It is not possible for a modern State based on force, non-violently to resist forces of disorder, whether external or internal. A man cannot serve God and Mammon, nor be 'temperate and furious' at the same time. It is claimed that a State can be based on non-violence, i.e., it can offer non-violent resistance against a world combination based on armed force. Such a State was Ashoka's. The example can be repeated. But the case does not become weak even if it be shown that Ashoka's State was not based on non-violence. It has to be examined on its merits.

Q. 2. Do you think that it would be possible for a Congress government to deal with foreign aggression or internal riots in an entirely non-violent manner?

A. It is certainly possible for a Congress government to deal with 'foreign aggression or internal riots' in a non-violent manner. That the Congress may not share my belief is quite possible. If the Congress changes its course, the change will prove nothing save that the non-violence hitherto offered was of the weak and that the Congress has no faith in State non-violence.

Q. 3. Does not the knowledge that the opponent is wedded to non-violence often encourage the bully?

A. The bully has his opportunity when he has to face non-violence of the weak. Non-violence of the strong is any day stronger than that of the bravest soldier fully armed or a whole host.

Q. 4. What policy would you advocate if a section of the Indian people tries to enforce by sword a selfish measure which is not only repugnant to others but also basically unjust? While it is possible for an unofficial organization to offer non-violent resistance in such a case, is it also possible for the government of the day to do so?

A. The question assumes a case which can never exist. A non-violent State must be broad-based on the will of an intelligent people, well able to know its mind and act up to it. In such a State the assumed section can only be negligible. It can never stand against the deliberate will of the overwhelming majority represented by the State. The government of the day is not outside the people. It is the will of the overwhelming majority. If it is expressed non-violently, it cannot be a majority of one but nearer 99 against one in a hundred.

Q. 5. Is not non-violent resistance by the militarily strong more effective than that by the militarily weak?

A. This is a contradiction in terms. There can be no non-violence offered by the militarily strong. Thus, Russia in order to express non-violence has to discard all her power of doing violence. What is true is that if those, who were at one time strong in armed might, change their mind, they will be better able to demonstrate their non-violence to the world and, therefore, also to their opponents. Those who are strong in non-violence will not mind whether they are opposed by the militarily weak people or the strongest.

Q. 6. What should be the training and discipline for a non-violent army? Should not certain aspects of conventional military training form a part of the syllabus?

A. A very small part of the preliminary training received by the military is common to the non-violent army. These are discipline, drill, singing in chorus, flag-hoisting, signalling and the like. Even this is not absolutely necessary and the basis is different. The positively necessary training for a violent army is an immovable faith in God, willing and perfect obedience to the chief of the non-violent army and perfect inward and outward co-operation between the units of the army.

Q. 7. Is it not better under the existing circumstances that countries like India and England should maintain full military efficiency while resolving to give non-violent resistance a reasonable trial before taking any military step?

A. The foregoing answers should make it clear that under no circumstance can India and England give non-violent resistance a reasonable chance whilst they are both maintaining full military efficiency. At the same time it is perfectly true that all military powers carry on negotiations for peaceful adjustment of rival disputes. But here we are not discussing preliminary peace parleys before appealing to the arbitrament of war. We are discussing a final substitute for armed conflict called war, in naked terms, mass murder.

Simla, May 2, 1946

'Certain Questions'
Harijan, 12 May 1946

168. THE ATOM BOMB AND MORAL STRENGTH

Gandhi Camp, Patna,
April 25, 1947

Sooner or later India is bound to get its freedom. Having made such tremendous sacrifices our earnest endeavour is not going to end in failure. But if the League co-operated with us we could win freedom tomorrow. The League representatives who have joined the Interim Government at present have not done so willingly. It would be a happy union if only it is a sincere union. The world today needs action, not speeches. Our beliefs will have any value only if we put them into practice. Otherwise it is difficult to achieve anything. We have no doubt fought our battle with the weapons of truth and non-violence. Though, I must confess, I have not reached the ideal of my conception—as far as preparing the people on those lines is concerned, but so far as I know my own conscience I have myself striven through thought, word and deed to reach the ideal and am still striving to do so. If unconsciously I have been guilty of a lapse, I am not aware of it. But no society of men can ever be happy at all without following the path of non-violence. This doctrine is not of my invention, it is something that has been followed from time immemorial. A country like Russia which stood by the rights of its people has been caught up in establishing an imperialistic State. How tragic it is! I hold that he who invented the atom bomb has committed the gravest sin in the world of science. The only weapon that can save the world is non-violence. Considering the trend of the world, I might appear a fool to everyone; but I do not feel sorry for it. I rather consider it a great blessing that God did not make me capable of inventing the atom bomb.

It is wrong to say that the people in the West have gone crazy about the atom bomb. There are also people among them who are having second thoughts about it. I can make this assertion in full faith and with conviction that people will be happy and content only where truth and non-violence are followed. Though at present both appear to have disappeared they have not disappeared entirely. You inquired about foreigners. I may say that ultimately they can stay here only if they are willing to stay as Indians. Otherwise there is no place for them here. After India achieves freedom, we have to cultivate friendship with the people of other countries and avoid all discord. We are aware that we might commit many mistakes and face innumerable difficulties in safeguarding our freedom. It is quite possible we may fall short of the expectations of our people. But I see no danger in that. We will learn only through our mistakes and trials. But if the Congress renounces truth and non-violence, its moral strength and its prestige are bound to suffer. But truth and non-violence have to be followed willingly. Then alone can they endure. Nothing done under compulsion will endure. Such rules are not written in a constitution. I can go to the extent of saying that just as it is essential to wear clothes—irrespective of whether they are good or bad—and we have accepted the principle of covering our body, similarly it is imperative that every human being should adopt truth and non-violence.

Talk with Englishmen (G.)
Biharni Komi Agman, pp. 253-4

169. WAR, DEGRADATION, AND ENDURANCE

[8 October 1909]

War with all its glorification of brute force is essentially a degrading thing. It demoralizes those who are trained for it. It brutalizes men of naturally gentle character. It outrages every beautiful canon of morality. Its path of glory is foul with the passions of lust, and red with the blood of murder. This is not the pathway to our goal. The grandest aid to development of strong, pure, beautiful character which is our aim, is the endurance of suffering. Self-restraint, unselfishness, patience, gentleness, these are the flowers which spring beneath the feet of those who accept, but refuse to impose, suffering, and the grim prisons of Johannesburg, Pretoria, Heidelberg and Volksrust are like the four gateways to this garden of God.

Speech at the Emerson Club, London
Indian Opinion, 12 Feb. 1910

170. AFTER-EFFECTS OF WAR

It was not without purpose that I reproduced the main parts of Mr. Page's very able pamphlet on the World War. I hope that the reader followed them with the care and attention the chapters deserved. Mr. Page has proved conclusively that both the parties were equally to blame and that both resorted to barbarous and inhuman practices. We did not need Mr. Page's help to learn that no war of which history has any record took so many lives as this did. Moral loss was greater still. Poisonous forces destructive of the soul (lying and deception) were brought to perfection as much as the forces destructive of the body. The moral results have been as terrible as the physical. It is yet too early to measure the effect on mankind of the collapse of the sexual morality brought about by the War. Vice has usurped the throne of virtue. The brute in man has for the time being gained supremacy.

The after-effects are, perhaps, more terrible than the actual and immediate effects. There is no stability about the government of any single State of Europe. No class is satisfied with its own condition. Each wants to better it at the expense of the rest. War between the States has now become a war within each State.

India has to make her choice. She may try, if she wishes, the way of war and sink lower than she has. In the Hindu–Muslim quarrel, she seems to be taking her first lesson in the art of war. If India can possibly gain her freedom by war, her state will be no better and will be, probably, much worse than that of France or England. Past examples have become obsolete. Not even Japan's comparative progress can be any guide. For, 'the science' of war has made much greater 'progress' since the Russo-Japanese war. Its result can only be studied in the present conditions of Europe. We can safely say that if India throws off the British yoke by the way of war, she must go through the state Mr. Page has graphically described.

But the way of peace is open to her. Her freedom is assured if she has patience. That way will be found to be the shortest even though it may appear to be the longest to our impatient nature. The way of peace insures internal growth and stability. We reject it because we fancy that it involves submission to the will of the ruler who has imposed himself upon us. But the moment we realize that the imposition is only so-called and that through our unwillingness to suffer loss of life or property, we are party to the imposition, all we need do is to change that negative attitude of passive endorsement. The suffering to be undergone by the change will be nothing compared to the physical suffering and the moral loss we must incur in trying the way of war. And the sufferings of war harm both the parties. The sufferings in following the way of peace must benefit both. They will be like the pleasurable travail of a new birth.

Let us not be misled by a hasty generalization of the events of 1920-21. Great as the achievement of that brilliant period was, it was nothing compared to what it might have been, had we been true and had faith. Violence was in the breasts of many of us whilst with our lips we paid homage to non-violence. And, though we were thus false to our creed, so far as we had accepted it, we blamed it and lost faith instead of blaming and correcting ourselves. Chauri Chaura was a symptom of the disease that was poisoning us. Ours was claimed to be a peaceful, non-violent way. We could not sustain the claim in its fulness. The 'enemy's' taunts we need not mind. They saw violence even where there was not a trace of it. But we could not disregard the judgment of the 'still small voice within'. It knew the violence within.

The way of peace is the way of truth. Truthfulness is even more important than peacefulness. Indeed, lying is the mother of violence. A truthful man cannot long remain violent. He will perceive in the course of his search that he has no need to be violent and he will further discover that so long as there is the slightest trace of violence in him, he will fail to find the truth he is searching.

There is no half way between truth and non-violence on the one hand and untruth and violence on the other. We may never be strong enough to be entirely non-violent in thought, word and deed. But we must keep non-violence as our goal and make steady progress towards it. The attainment of freedom, whether for a man, a nation or the world, must be in exact proportion to the attainment of non-violence by each. Let those, therefore, who believe in non-violence as the only method of achieving real freedom, keep the lamp of non-violence burning bright in the midst of the present impenetrable gloom. The truth of a few will count, the untruth of millions will vanish even like chaff before a whiff of wind.

'War Or Peace'
Young India, 20 May 1926

171. THE PATH OF DUTY IN WARTIME

The autobiographical chapter dealing with my participation in the late War continues to puzzle friends and critics. Here is one more letter[1] . . .

No doubt it was a mixed motive that prompted me to participate in the War. Two things I can recall. Though as an individual I was opposed to war, I had no status for offering effective non-violent resistance. Non-violent resistance can only follow some real disinterested service, some heart-expression of love. For instance, I would have no status to resist a savage offering animal sacrifice until he could recognize in me his friend through some loving act of mine or other means. I do not sit in judgment upon the world for its many misdeeds. Being imperfect myself and needing toleration and charity, I tolerate the world's imperfections till I find or create an opportunity for fruitful expostulation. I felt that if by sufficient service I could attain the power and the confidence to resist the Empire's wars and its warlike preparations, it would be a good thing for me who was seeking to enforce non-violence in my own life to test the extent to which it was possible among the masses.

The other motive was to qualify for *swaraj* through the good offices of the statesmen of the Empire. I could not thus qualify myself except through serving the Empire in its life-and-death struggle. It must be understood that I am writing of my mentality in 1914 when I was a believer in the Empire and its willing ability to help India in her battle for freedom. Had I been the non-violent rebel that I am today, I should certainly not have helped but through every effort open to non-violence I should have attempted to defeat its purpose.

My opposition to and disbelief in war was as strong then as it is today. But we have to recognize that there are many things in the world which we do although we may be against doing them. I am as much opposed to taking the life of the lowest creature alive as I am to war. But I continually take such life hoping some day to attain the ability to do without this fratricide. To entitle me in spite of it to be called a votary of non-violence, my attempt must be honest, strenuous and unceasing. The conception of *moksha*, absolution from the need to have an embodied existence, is based upon the necessity of perfected men and women being completely non-violent. Possession of a body like every other possession necessitates some violence, be it ever so little. The fact is that the path of duty is not always easy to discern amidst claims seeming to conflict one with the other.

Lastly, the verse referred to from the *Gita* has a double meaning. One is that there should be no selfish purpose behind our actions. That of gaining *swaraj* is not a selfish purpose. Secondly, to be detached from fruits of actions is not to be ignorant of them, or to disregard or disown them. To be detached is never to abandon action because the contemplated result may not follow. On the contrary, it is proof of immovable faith in the certainty of the contemplated result following in due course.

'Still At It'
Young India, 15 Mar. 1928

¹ Not printed here. The correspondent had asked: 'What impelled you to participate in the War? Was it right to join the War with the hope of gaining something?
I do not know how to reconcile this with the teaching of the *Gita* which says that we
should never act with a view to the fruits of action.'

172. WARS AND EXPLOITATION

It is not without diffidence that I approach the question raised
by Rev. B. de Ligt in his open letter to me with regard to my
attitude towards war. To remain silent at the risk of being
misunderstood is an easy way out of the difficult situation I
find myself in. To say that I made a mistake in participating
in war on the occasions in question would be easier still. But
it would be unfriendly not to answer questions put in the
friendliest manner; and I must not pretend repentance when
I do not feel it. My anxiety to avoid a discussion of the question does not proceed from want of conviction, but it proceeds
from the fear that I may not be able to make my meaning
clear and thereby create an impression about my attitude
towards war which I do not desire. Often do I find language
to be a poor vehicle for expressing some of my fundamental
sentiments. I would therefore urge Mr. B. de Ligt and other
fellow war-resisters not to mind my faulty or incomplete argument and still less to mind my participation in war which
they may be unable to reconcile with my professions about
war. Let them understand me to be uncompromisingly against
all war. If they cannot appreciate my argument, let them
impute my participation to unconscious weakness. For I
would feel extremely sorry to discover that my action was used
by anyone to justify war under certain conditions.

But having said this much I must adhere to the position
taken up in the article which is the subject-matter of Mr. B.
de Ligt's letter. Let the European war resisters appreciate one
vital difference between them and me. They do not represent
exploited nations, I represent the most exploited nation on
earth. To use an unflattering comparison they represent the
cat and I represent the mouse. Has a mouse even the sense of
non-violence? Is it not a fundamental want with him to strive
to offer successful violence before he can be taught to appreciate the virtue, the grandeur, the supremacy of the law of

non-violence—*ahimsa*—in the field of war? May it not be necessary for me as a representative of the mouse tribe to participate in my principal's desire for wreaking destruction even for the purpose of teaching him the superiority of non-destruction?

Here the analogy of the cat and the mouse ends. The mouse has no capacity in him to alter his nature. A human being, however debased or fallen he may be, has in him the capacity of rising to the greatest height ever attained by any human being irrespective of race or colour. Therefore even whilst I may go with my countrymen a long way in satisfying their need for preparation for war, I should do so in the fullest hope of weaning them from war and of their seeing one day its utter futility. Let it be remembered that the largest experiment known to history in mass non-violence is being tried by me even as I seem to be lending myself for the purpose of war. For want of skill the experiment may fail, but the war-resister in Europe should strain every nerve to understand and appreciate the phenomenon going on before him in India of the same man trying the bold experiment in non-violence whilst hobnobbing with those who would prepare for war.

It is part of the plan of non-violence that I should share the feelings of my countrymen if I would ever expect to bring them to non-violence. The striking fact is that India including the educated politician is *nolens volens* driven to the belief that non-violence alone will free the masses from the thraldom of centuries. It is true that all have not followed out the logical consequences of non-violence. Who can? In spite of my boast that I know the truth of non-violence and try my utmost best to practise it, I fail often to follow out the logical conclusions of the doctrine. The working of nature's processes in the human breast is mysterious and baffles interpretation.

This I know that if India comes to her own demonstrably through non-violent means, India will never want to carry a vast army, an equally grand navy and a grander air force. If her self-consciousness rises to the height necessary to give her a non-violent victory in her fight for freedom, the world values will have changed and most of the paraphernalia of war would be found to be useless. Such an India may be a mere day-dream, a childish folly. But such in my opinion is undoubtedly the implication of an India becoming free through non-violence.

When that freedom comes, if it ever does, it will have come through a gentlemanly understanding with Great Britain. But then it will not be an imperialistic haughty Britain manœuvring for world supremacy but a Britain humbly trying to serve the common end of humanity. India will no longer then be helplessly driven into Britain's wars of exploitation but hers will be the voice of a powerful nation seeking to keep under restraint all the violent forces of the world.

Whether all these fanciful ideas are ever realized or not, my own lifeline is cast. I can no longer in any conceivable circumstance take part in Britain's wars. And I have already said in these pages that if India attains (what will be to me so-called) freedom by violent means she will cease to be a country of my pride; that time would be a time for me of civil death. There can therefore never be any question of my participation direct or indirect in any war of exploitation by India.

But I have already pointed out in these pages that fellow war-resisters in the West are participants in war even in peace time inasmuch as they pay for the preparations that are being made for it and otherwise sustain governments whose main occupation is such preparation. Again, all activity for stopping war must prove fruitless so long as the causes of war are not understood and radically dealt with. Is not the prime cause of modern wars the inhuman race for exploitation of the so-called weaker races of the earth?

'A Complex Problem'
Young India, 9 May 1929

173. A SCIENCE OF PEACE

Segaon, Wardha, C. P.,
August 26, 1937

Dear Sister,

Here is my message. You can do with it what you like.

Attainment of real world peace is impossible except for greater scientific precision, greater travail of the soul, greater patience and greater resources than required for the invention and consolidation of the means of mutual slaughter. It cannot be attained by a mere muster-roll signed by millions of mankind desiring peace. But it can, if there is a science of peace, as I hold there is, by a few devoting themselves to the discovery of the means. Their effort being from within will not be showy but then it will not need a single farthing.

Yours sincerely,

M. K. GANDHI

Mrs. Edith Hunter
Secretary, Friends of India Society
47 Victoria Street
London S.W.1

Letter to Edith Hunter
Pyarelal Papers
GN 1534

174. A PEACE BRIGADE

Some time ago I suggested the formation of a Peace Brigade whose members would risk their lives in dealing with riots, especially communal. The idea was that this Brigade should substitute the police and even the military. This reads ambitious. The achievement may prove impossible. Yet, if the Congress is to succeed in its non-violent struggle, it must develop the power to deal peacefully with such situations. Communal riots are engineered by politically minded men. Many of those who take part in them are under the influence of the latter. Surely it should not be beyond the wit of Congressmen to devise a method or methods of avoiding ugly communal situations by peaceful means. I say this irrespective of whether there is or there is not a communal pact. It cannot be that any party seeks to force a pact by violent means. Even if such a pact were a possibility, it would not be worth the paper on which it might be written. For behind such a pact there will be no common understanding. What is more, even after a pact is arrived at, it would be too much to expect that there would never be any communal riots.

Let us therefore see what qualifications a member of the contemplated Peace Brigade should possess.

(1) He or she must have a living faith in non-violence. This is impossible without a living faith in God. A non-violent man can do nothing save by the power and grace of God. Without it he won't have the courage to die without anger, without fear and without retaliation. Such courage comes from the belief that God sits in the hearts of all and that there should be no fear in the presence of God. The knowledge of the omnipresence of God also means respect for the lives of even those who may be called opponents or *goondas*. This contemplated intervention is a process of stilling the fury of man when the brute in him gets the mastery over him.

(2) This messenger of peace must have equal regard for all the principal religions of the earth. Thus, if he is a Hindu, he will respect the other faiths current in India. He must therefore possess a knowledge of the general principles of the different faiths professed in the country.

(3) Generally speaking this work of peace can only be done by local men in their own localities.

(4) The work can be done singly or in groups. Therefore no one need wait for companions. Nevertheless one would naturally seek companions in one's own locality and form a local brigade.

(5) This messenger of peace will cultivate through personal service contacts with the people in his locality or chosen circle, so that when he appears to deal with ugly situations, he does not descend upon the members of a riotous assembly as an utter stranger liable to be looked upon as a suspect or an unwelcome visitor.

(6) Needless to say, a peace-bringer must have a character beyond reproach and must be known for his strict impartiality.

(7) Generally there are previous warnings of coming storms. If these are known, the Peace Brigade will not wait till the conflagration breaks out but will try to handle the situation in anticipation.

(8) Whilst, if the movement spreads, it might be well if there are some whole-time workers, it is not absolutely necessary that there should be. The idea is to have as many good

and true men and women as possible. These can be had only if volunteers are drawn from those who are engaged in various walks of life but have leisure enough to cultivate friendly relations with the people living in their circle and otherwise possess the qualifications required of a member of the Peace Brigade.

(9) There should be a distinctive dress worn by the members of the contemplated Brigade so that in course of time they will be recognized without the slightest difficulty.

These are but general suggestions. Each centre can work out its own constitution on the basis here suggested.

Lest false hopes may be raised, I must warn workers against entertaining the hope that I can play any active part in the formation of Peace Brigades. I have not the health, energy or time for it. I find it hard enough to cope with the tasks I dare not shirk. I can only guide and make suggestions through correspondence or these columns. Therefore let those who appreciate the idea and feel they have the ability, take the initiative themselves. I know that the proposed Brigade has great possibilities and that the idea behind it is quite capable of being worked out in practice.

'Qualifications of a Peace Brigade'
Harijan, 18 June 1938

175. THE UNCONQUERABLE FORCE OF SPIRIT

Why is *Harijan* revived? This question may have occurred to many as it has to me. I may tell the reader that no special effort was made for its revival.[1] An application for the removal of the ban was made on December 3, 1945, and the ban was removed on January 10, 1946. Many readers, including English and American, had all along felt a void, and they began to feel it more after the defeat of the Fascist Powers. The reason for the feeling was obvious. They wanted my reaction, in terms of truth and non-violence, to the various events happening in India, if not in the world. I wished to satisfy this desire.

There have been cataclysmic changes in the world. Do I

still adhere to my faith in truth and non-violence. Has not the atom bomb exploded that faith? Not only has it not done so but it has clearly demonstrated to me that the twins constitute the mightiest force in the world. Before it the atom bomb is of no effect. The two opposing forces are wholly different in kind, the one moral and spiritual, the other physical and material. The one is infinitely superior to the other which by its very nature has an end. The force of the spirit is ever progressive and endless. Its full expression makes it unconquerable in the world. In saying this, I know that I have said nothing new. I merely bear witness to the fact. What is more, that force resides in everybody, man, woman and child, irrespective of the colour of the skin. Only in many it lies dormant, but it is capable of being awakened by judicious training.

It is further to be observed that without the recognition of this truth and due effort to realize it, there is no escape from self-destruction. The remedy lies in every individual training himself for self-expression in every walk of life, irrespective of response by the neighbours. *Harijan* will attempt from week to week to stand up for this truth and illustrate it.

On way to Madura, February 2, 1946

'*Harijan* Revived'
Harijan, 10 Feb. 1946

<hr>

[1] After suspension in August 1942.

176. VICTORS AND VANQUISHED

'Confused' writes: 'I grant that Italy, Germany and Japan have lost their power; but is the loss due to their faith in violence, as you would say, or is it due to their exhaustion brought about by fortunes of war? Will you hold that Britain, Russia and America have been successful because of their non-violence?'

Thus argues a correspondent whom I have paraphrased without diminishing the force of his argument. The questioner has failed to perceive that in the writing quoted by him, I have said nothing about the so-called victorious Powers. But I have said elsewhere that their victory is an empty boast, if they do not learn the lesson while there is time and do not shape their life in accordance with the law of non-violence. I believe wholly in the truth that 'those who take the sword will perish by the sword'. There is no doubt that the victors employed the same means as the vanquished. There was only a question of degree. The victorious parties already seem to be on the verge of quarrelling among themselves. If another war has not already begun, it is because no one is ready to enter upon it. After all men are not machines. They cannot be continually fighting without being reduced to the state of beasts. One has to hope, for the sake of humanity, that they will do some hard thinking and discover the truth that the common man, of whom the world is composed, gains nothing by cutting his fellowman's throat and that the fruits of peace are infinitely superior to those of war. Ingenuity employed in devising methods of destruction lowers, whereas when employed in devising ways of building it befits mankind.

'What Is the Law?'
Harijan, 14 Apr. 1946

XII

Ashram—Experiment with Truth

---

177. *ASHRAM* VOWS AND RULES

February 16, 1916[1]

Mr. Chairman and Dear Friends,

I have so often said that I am not myself fond of hearing my own voice and I assure you that this morning also I retained the same position. It was only, if you will believe me, my great regard for the students, whom I love, whom I respect and who I consider are the hope of future India that moved me to accept this invitation to speak to you this morning. I did not know what subject to choose. A friend has handed me a slip here asking me whether I would enlighten the students on the Benares incident. I fear I shall have to disappoint that friend and those of you who associate yourselves with that view. I don't think that you need lay any stress upon that incident. These are the passing waves which will always come and go. I should therefore this morning fear rather if I can possibly do so and pour my soul out to you with reference to something which I treasure so much above everything else.

To many of the students who came here last year to converse with me, I said I was about to establish an institution—an *ashram*—somewhere in India, and it is about that place that I am going to talk to you this morning. I feel and I have felt during the whole of my public life that what we need, what any nation needs, but we perhaps of all the nations of the world need just now, is nothing else and nothing less than character-building. And this is the view propounded by that great patriot, Mr. Gokhale. As you know, in many of his speeches, he used to say that we would get nothing, we would deserve nothing unless we had character to back what we wished for. Hence his founding of that great body, the Servants of India Society. And as you know, in the prospectus that has been issued in connection with the Society, Mr. Gokhale has deliberately stated that it was necessary to spiritualize the political life of the country. You know also that he used to say so often that our average was less than the average of so many European nations. I do not know whether that statement by him, whom, with pride, I consider to be my political *guru*, has really foundation in fact, but I do believe that there is much to be said to justify it in so far as educated India is concerned; not because we, the educated portion of the community, have blundered, but because we have been creatures of circumstances.

Be that as it may, this is the maxim of life which I have accepted, namely, that no work done by any man, no matter how great he is, will really prosper unless he has a religious backing. But what is religion? the question will be immediately asked. I, for one, would answer, not the religion which you will get after reading all the scriptures of the world; it is not really a grasp by the brain, but it is a heart-grasp. It is a thing which is not alien to us, but it is a thing which has to be evolved out of us. It is always within us, with some consciously so; with others, quite unconsciously. But it is there; and whether we wake up this religious instinct in us through outside assistance or by inward growth, no matter how it is done, it has got to be done if we want to do anything in the right manner and anything that is going to persist.

Our scriptures have laid down certain rules as maxims of life and as axioms which we have to take for granted as self-demonstrated truths. The Shastras tell us that without living according to those maxims, we are incapable even of having a reasonable perception of religion. Believing in these implicitly for all these long years and having actually endeavoured to reduce to practice these injunctions of the Shastras, I have deemed it necessary to seek the association of those who think with me in founding this institution. And I shall venture this morning to place before you the rules that have been drawn up and that have to be observed by everyone who seeks to be a member of that Ashram.

Five of these are known as *yamas*, and the first and the foremost is, the vow of Truth.

Vow of Truth

Not truth simply as we ordinarily understand it, that as far as possible we ought not to resort to a lie, that is to say, not truth which merely answers the saying, 'Honesty is the best policy'—implying that if it is not the best policy, we may depart from it. But here Truth, as it is conceived, means that we have to rule our life by this law of Truth at any cost. And in order to satisfy the definition, I have drawn upon the celebrated illustration of the life of Prahlad.[2] For the sake of Truth, he dared to oppose his own father, and he defended himself, not by retaliation by paying his father back in his own coin, but in defence of Truth, as he knew it, he was prepared to die without caring to return the blows that he had received from his father or from those who were charged with his father's instructions. Not only that: he would not in any way even parry the blows. On the contrary, with a smile on his lips, he underwent the innumerable tortures to which he was subjected, with the result that at last, Truth rose triumphant, not that Prahlad suffered the tortures because he knew that some day or other in his very life-time he would be able to demonstrate the infallibility of the law of Truth. That fact was there; but if he had died in the midst of torture, he would still have adhered to Truth. That is the Truth that I would like us to follow.

There was an incident I noticed yesterday. It was a trifling incident, but I think these trifling incidents are like straws which show which way the wind is blowing. The incident was this: I was talking to a friend who wanted to talk to me aside, and we were engaged in a private conversation. A third friend dropped in and he politely asked whether he was intruding. The friend to whom I was talking said: 'Oh, no, there is nothing private here.' I felt taken aback a little, because, as I was taken aside, I knew that so far as this friend was concerned, the conversation was private. But he immediately, out of politeness, I would call it over-politeness, said there was no private conversation and that he (the third friend) could join. I suggest to you that this is a departure from my definition of Truth. I think that the friend should have, in the gentlest manner possible, but still openly and frankly, said: 'Yes, just now, as you properly say, you would be intruding' without giving the slightest offence to the person if he was himself a gentleman—and we are bound to consider everybody to be a gentleman unless he proves to be otherwise. But I may be told that the incident, after all, proves the gentility of the nation. I think that it is over-proving the case. If we continue to say these things out of politeness, we really become a nation of hypocrites. I recall a conversation I had with an English friend. He was comparatively a stranger. He is a Principal of a College and has been in India for several years. He was comparing notes with me, and he asked me whether I would admit that we, unlike most Englishmen, would not dare to say 'No' when it was 'No' that we meant. And I must admit that I immediately said 'Yes'. I agree with that statement. We do hesitate to say 'No', frankly and boldly, when we want to pay due regard to the sentiments of the person whom we are addressing. In this Ashram, we make it a rule that we must say 'No' when we mean 'No', regardless of consequences. This, then, is the first rule. Then we come to the doctrine of *ahimsa*.

DOCTRINE OF *AHIMSA*

Literally speaking, *ahimsa* means non-killing. But to me it has a world of meaning and takes me into realms much higher, infinitely higher, than the realm to which I would go, if I merely understood by *ahimsa* non-killing. *Ahimsa* really means that you may not offend anybody, you may not harbour an uncharitable thought even in connection with one who may consider himself to be your enemy. Pray notice the guarded nature of this thought; I do not say 'whom you consider to be your enemy', but 'who may consider himself to be your enemy'. For one who follows the doctrine of *ahimsa*, there is no room for an enemy; he denies the existence of an enemy. But there are people who consider themselves to be his enemies, and he cannot help that circumstance. So, it is held that we may not harbour an evil thought even in connection with such persons. If we return blow for blow, we depart from the doctrine of *ahimsa*. But I go further. If we resent a friend's action or the so-called enemy's action, we still fall short of this doctrine. But when I say we should not resent, I do not say that we should acquiesce; but by resenting I mean wishing that some harm should be done to the enemy, or that he should be put out of the way, not even by any action of ours, but by the action of somebody else, or, say, by Divine agency. If we harbour even this thought, we depart from this doctrine of *ahimsa*. Those who join the Ashram have to literally accept that meaning. That does not mean that we practise that doctrine in its entirety. Far from it.

It is an ideal which we have to reach, and it is an ideal to be reached even at this very moment, if we are capable of doing so. But it is not a proposition in geometry to be learnt by heart: it is not even like solving difficult problems in higher mathematics; it is infinitely more difficult than solving those problems. Many of you have burnt the midnight oil in solving those problems. If you want to follow out this doctrine, you will have to do much more than burn the midnight oil. You will have to pass many a sleepless night, and go through many a mental torture and agony before you can reach, before you can even be within measurable distance of this goal. It is the goal, and nothing less than that, you and I have to reach if we want to understand what a religious life means. I will not say much more on this doctrine than this: that a man who believes in the efficacy of this doctrine finds in the ultimate stage, when he is about to reach the goal, the whole world at his feet, not that he wants the whole world at his feet, but it must be so. If you express your love—*ahimsa*—in such a manner that it impresses itself indelibly upon your so-called enemy,

he must return that love. Another thought which comes out
of this is that, under this rule, there is no room for organized
assassinations, and there is no room for murders even openly
committed, and there is no room for any violence even for the
sake of your country, and even for guarding the honour of
precious ones that may be under your charge. After all, that
would be a poor defence of honour.

This doctrine of *ahimsa* tells us that we may guard the
honour of those who are under our charge by delivering *ourselves* into the hands of the man who would commit the sacrilege. And that requires far greater physical and mental
courage than the delivering of blows. You may have some
degree of physical power—I do not say courage—and you
may use that power. But after that is expended, what happens? The other man is filled with wrath and indignation, and
you have made him more angry by matching your violence
against his; and when he has done you to death, the rest of
his violence is delivered against your charge. But if you do not
retaliate, but stand your ground, between your charge and
the opponent, simply receiving the blows without retaliating,
what happens? I give you my promise that the whole of the
violence will be expended on you, and your charge will be left
unscathed. Under this plan of life, there is no conception of
patriotism which justifies such wars as you witness today in
Europe. Then there is the vow of celibacy.

Vow of Celibacy

Those who want to perform national service, or those who
want to have a glimpse of the real religious life, must lead a
celibate life, no matter if married or unmarried. Marriage but
brings a woman closer together [*sic*] with the man, and they
become friends in a special sense, never to be parted either in
this life or in the lives that are to come. But I do not think
that, in our conception of marriage, our lusts should necessarily enter. Be that as it may, this is what is placed before
those who come to the Ashram. I do not deal with that at any
length. Then we have the vow of the control of the palate.

Vow of Control of the Palate

A man who wants to control his animal passions easily does

so if he control his palate. I fear this is one of the most difficult vows to follow. I am just now coming after having inspected the Victoria Hostel. I saw there, not to my dismay, though it should be to my dismay, but I am used to it now, that there are so many kitchens, not kitchens that are established in order to serve caste restrictions, but kitchens that have become necessary in order that people can have the condiments, and the exact weight of the condiments, to which they are used in the respective places from which they come. And therefore we find that for the *Brahmins* themselves there are different compartments and different kitchens catering for the delicate tastes of all these different groups. I suggest to you that this is simply slavery to the palate, rather than mastery over it.

I may say this: Unless we take our minds off from this habit, and unless we shut our eyes to the tea shops and coffee shops and all these kitchens, and unless we are satisfied with foods that are necessary for the proper maintenance of our physical health, and unless we are prepared to rid ourselves of stimulating, heating and exciting condiments that we mix with our food, we will certainly not be able to control the over-abundant, unnecessary, exciting stimulation that we may have. If we do not do that, the result naturally is, that we abuse ourselves and we abuse even the sacred trust given to us, and we become less than animals and brutes. Eating, drinking and indulging passions we share in common with the animals, but have you ever seen a horse or a cow indulging in the abuse of the palate as we do? Do you suppose that it is a sign of civilization, a sign of real life that we should multiply our eatables so far that we do not even know where we are; and seek dish after dish until at last we have become absolutely mad and run after the newspaper sheets which give us advertisements about these dishes? Then we have the vow of non-thieving.

VOW OF NON-THIEVING

I suggest that we are thieves in a way. If I take anything that I do not need for my own immediate use, and keep it, I thieve it from somebody else. I venture to suggest that it is the fundamental law of Nature, without exception, that Nature produces enough for our wants from day to day, and if only everybody took enough for himself and nothing more, there would be no pauperism in this world, there would be no man dying of starvation in this world. But so long as we have got this inequality, so long we are thieving. I am no socialist and I do not want to dispossess those who have got possessions; but I do say that, personally, those of us who want to see light out of darkness have to follow the rule.

I do not want to dispossess anybody. I should then be departing from the rule of *ahimsa*. If somebody else possesses more than I do, let him. But so far as my own life has to be regulated, I do say that I dare not possess anything which I do not want. In India we have got three millions of people having to be satisfied with one meal a day, and that meal consisting of a *chapati* containing no fat in it, and a pinch of salt. You and I have no right to anything that we really have until these three million are clothed and fed better. You and I, who ought to know better, must adjust our wants, and even undergo voluntary starvation in order that they may be nursed, fed and clothed. Then there is the vow of non-possession which follows as a matter of course. Then I go to the vow of *swadeshi*.

Vow of *Swadeshi*

The vow of *swadeshi* is a necessary vow. But you are conversant with the *swadeshi* life and the *swadeshi* spirit. I suggest to you we are departing from one of the sacred laws of our being when we leave our neighbour and go out somewhere else in order to satisfy our wants. If a man comes from Bombay here and offers you wares, you are not justified in supporting the Bombay merchant or trader so long as you have got a merchant at your very door, born and bred in Madras. That is my view of *swadeshi*. In your village, so long as you have got your village-barber, you are bound to support him to the exclusion of the finished barber who may come to you from Madras. If you find it necessary that your village-barber should reach the attainment of the barber from Madras, you may train him to that. Send him to Madras by all means, if you wish, in order that he may learn his calling. Until you do that, you are not justified in going to another barber. That is *swadeshi*.

So, when we find that there are many things that we cannot get in India, we must try to do without them. We may have to do without many things which we may consider necessary, but believe me, when you have that frame of mind, you will find a great burden taken off your shoulders, even as the Pilgrim did in that inimitable book, *Pilgrim's Progress*: There came a time when the mighty burden that the Pilgrim was carrying on his shoulders unconsciously dropped from him, and he felt a freer man than he was when he started on the journey. So will you feel freer men than you are now, immediately you adopt this *swadeshi* life. We have also the vow of fearlessness.

VOW OF FEARLESSNESS

I found, throughout my wanderings in India, that India, educated India, is seized with a paralysing fear. We may not open our lips in public; we may not declare our confirmed opinion in public; we may hold those opinions; we may talk about them secretly; and we may do anything we like within the four walls of our house,—but those are not for public consumption. If we had taken a vow of silence, I would have nothing to say. When we open our lips in public, we say things which we do not really believe in. I do not know whether this is not the experience of almost every public man who speaks in India. I then suggest to you that there is only one Being, if Being is the proper term to be used, Whom we have to fear, and that is God.

When we fear God, we shall fear no man, no matter how high-placed he may be. And if you want to follow the vow of truth in any shape or form, fearlessness is the necessary consequence. And so you find, in the *Bhagavad Gita*, fearlessness is declared as the first essential quality of a *Brahmin*. We fear consequences, and therefore we are afraid to tell the truth. A man who fears God will certainly not fear any earthly consequence. Before we can aspire to the position of understanding what religion is, and before we can aspire to the position of guiding the destinies of India, do you not see that we should adopt this habit of fearlessness? Or shall we over-awe our countrymen even as we are over-awed? We thus see how im-

portant this 'fearlessness vow' is. And we have also the vow
regarding the Untouchables.

Vow Regarding the Untouchables

There is an ineffaceable blot that Hinduism today carries with
it. I have declined to believe that it has been handed to us
from immemorial times. I think that this miserable, wretched,
enslaving spirit of 'untouchableness' must have come to us
when we were in the cycle of our lives, at our lowest ebb, and
that evil has still stuck to us and it still remains with us. It is,
to my mind, a curse that has come to us, and as long as that
curse remains with us, so long I think we are bound to consider that every affliction that we labour under in this sacred
land is a fit and proper punishment for this great and indelible
crime that we are committing. That any person should be
considered untouchable because of his calling passes one's
comprehension; and you, the student world, who receive all
this modern education, if you become a party to this crime, it
were better that you received no education whatsoever.

Of course, we are labouring under a very heavy handicap.
Although you may realize that there cannot be a a single
human being on this earth who should be considered to be
untouchable, you cannot react upon your families, you cannot
react upon your surroundings, because all your thought is
conceived in a foreign tongue, and all your energy is devoted
to that. And so we have also introduced a rule in this Ashram
that we shall receive our education through the vernaculars.

Education through the Vernaculars

In Europe, every cultured man learns, not only his language,
but also other languages, certainly three or four. And even as
they do in Europe, in order to solve the problem of language
in India, we, in this Ashram, make it a point to learn as many
Indian vernaculars as we possibly can. And I assure you that
the trouble of learning these languages is nothing compared
to the trouble that we have to take in mastering the English
language. We never master the English language; with some
exceptions, it has not been possible for us to do so; we can
never express ourselves as clearly as we can in our own mother
tongue. How dare we rub out of our memory all the years of

our infancy? But that is precisely what we do when we commence our higher life, as we call it, through the medium of a foreign tongue. This creates a breach in our life for bridging which we shall have to pay dearly and heavily.

And you will see now the connection between these two things—education and untouchableness—this persistence of the spirit of untouchableness even at this time of the day in spite of the spread of knowledge and education. Education has enabled us to see the horrible crime. But we are seized with fear also and, therefore, we cannot take this doctrine to our homes. And we have got a superstitious veneration for our family traditions and for the members of our family. You say, 'My parents will die if I tell them that I, at least, can no longer partake of this crime.' I say that Prahlad never considered that his father would die if he pronounced the sacred syllables of the name of Vishnu.[3] On the contrary, he made the whole of that household ring, from one corner to another, by repeating that name even in the sacred presence of his father. And so you and I may do this thing in the sacred presence of our parents. If, after receiving this rude shock, some of them expire, I think that would be no calamity. It may be that some rude shocks of the kind might have to be delivered. So long as we persist in these things which have been handed down to us for generations, these incidents may happen. But there is a higher law of Nature, and in due obedience to that higher law, my parents and myself should make that sacrifice, and then we follow hand-weaving.

You may ask: 'Why should *we* use our hands?' and say 'the manual work has got to be done by those who are illiterate. I can only occupy myself with reading literature and political essays.' I think that we have to realize the dignity of labour. If a barber or shoe-maker attends a college, he ought not to abandon the profession of barber or shoe-maker. I consider that a barber's profession is just as good as the profession of medicine.

Last of all, when you have conformed to these rules, I think then, and not till then, you may come to politics and dabble in them to your heart's content, and certainly you will then never go wrong. Politics, divorced of religion, have absolutely no meaning. If the student-world crowd the political platforms of this country, to my mind it is not necessarily a healthy sign of national growth; but that does not mean that you, in your student-life, ought not to study politics. Politics are a part of our being; we ought to understand our national institutions, and we ought to understand our national growth and all those things. We may do it from our infancy. So, in our Ashram, every child is taught to understand the political institutions of our country, and to know how the country is vibrating with new emotions, with new aspirations, with a new life. But we want also the steady light, the infallible light, of religious faith, not a faith which merely appeals to the intelligence, but a faith which is indelibly inscribed on the heart.

First, we want to realize that religious consciousness, and immediately we have done that, I think the whole department of life is open to us, and it should then be a sacred privilege of students and everybody to partake of that whole life, so that, when they grow to manhood, and when they leave their colleges, they may do so as men properly equipped to battle with life. Today what happens is this: much of the political life is confined to student life; immediately the students leave their colleges and cease to be students, they sink into oblivion, they seek miserable employments, carrying miserable emoluments, rising no higher in their aspirations, knowing nothing of God, knowing nothing of fresh air or bright light, and nothing of that real vigorous independence that comes out of obedience to these laws that I have ventured to place before you.

I am not here asking you to crowd into the Ashram, there is no room there. But I say that every one of you may enact that ashram life individually and collectively. I shall be satisfied with anything that you may choose from the rules I have ventured to place before you and act up to it. But if you think that these are the outpourings of a madman, you will not hesitate to tell me that it is so, and I shall take that judgment from you undismayed.

Speech on '*Ashram* Vows' at the YMCA, Madras
Indian Review, February 1916
The Hindu, 16 Feb. 1916

---

[1] The Revd. George Pittendrigh of the Madras Christian College was in the chair.

This was published with the following note by the Editor, *Indian Review*: 'We have received several enquiries from our readers regarding Mr. Gandhi's new organisation, the Satyagrahashram. We are glad to be able to give the following account of the Ashram from a special report of the speech that Mr. Gandhi delivered sometime ago in Madras. The report has since had the benefit of Mr. Gandhi's revision and may, therefore, be taken as an authoritative exposition of the aims and objects of Mr. Gandhi's Satyagrahashram.'

² Prahlad was a devotee of God persecuted by his unbelieving father, the demon king, Hiranyakashipu. Gandhi often spoke of him as an ideal *satyagrahi*.

³ One of the Hindu trinity, regarded as Preserver of the Universe.

178. ACTS OF FELLOWSHIP

Satyagraha Ashram,
Sabarmati,
April 7, 1928

True promotion of Fellowship is to be found in silent acts of fellowship. One such little act, therefore, is more than tons of professions.

Message for 'News Sheet' of the International Fellowship
SN 13172

179. MORAL GROWTH WITHOUT COMPULSION

[25 May 1928]

Chi. Kishorelal,

I have read both your letters carefully.

What I said, and the manner in which I said it, does not seem to have been correctly reported to you.

There is nothing new in the changes I have suggested. I have not made any change in the definition of an Ashram inmate. The only significance of the change is that we should strive hard to follow the ideal which we have always kept before us.

I never put pressure on anyone, and have never wished to do so. I have recently refused to do that on two friends who wish to run separate kitchens for themselves. I, therefore, see no compulsion in regard to anything. I employ earnest argument (with love) and try to explain everything clearly.

I am of the view that those who have joined the Ashram should conform to the moral growth or changes in the Ashram. They cannot say that they will obey certain rules only and that, if new rules are made and applied, it would be breach of contract. No institution can continue to exist on that condition. There can be fixity only about concrete matters, such as salary, period, etc. At the Ashram, however, generally speaking, we have no restrictions other than moral.

Even so, we decided to enforce the rule about *brahmacharya* only after all the inmates had been invited to discuss it and everyone had accepted its necessity. I did say, when reading out this rule, that those who could not or did not wish to observe it, could leave the Ashram.

The common kitchen is functioning satisfactorily at present.

I shall not inflict anything more on you. I have written even this unwillingly. Really speaking, you should not, in your present illness and from that distance, strain yourself thinking about the changes taking place here. Maybe it is morally wrong for you to do so.

How are you now? There is of course no question of your staying at Santa Cruz. You are fit enough to come here. You can take your treatment even here. The climate here is certainly better than there. If, however, you decide to come, I hope you will not think of going away again.

Blessings from
BAPU

Letter to Kishorelal Mashruwala (G.)
SN 11802

180. KNOWLEDGE AND MOTIVE

October 16, 1930

Chi. Bhagwanji,

I have your letter. Your intentions are no doubt pure but one should never be content with one's purity of motive alone. The necessity of knowledge has been accepted for the reason that one may not commit an error in spite of a pure motive. This also you should know for certain that as you achieve purity the Ashram too becomes pure to that extent. The purity of the Ashram is not different from that of any Ashramite. As far as the Ashram goes, there is no one who can surpass Narandas in the matter of rendering help in spiritual difficulties. Totaramji can also help.

Blessings from
BAPU

Letter to Bhagwanji Pandya (G.)
CW 327

181. NEVER LOSE HEART

5 a.m., January 24, 1931

Chi. Mathuradas,

I heard about your request for permission to leave the Ashram. If you have made the request so that you may cultivate greater purity outside, what you have done is all right. But if you have asked for permission to leave the Ashram in despair, thinking that, since you have committed an error once, you are certain to commit more errors in future, then your action is wrong. No one in the world is totally free from shortcomings. We have come together in the Ashram not because we are perfect, but in order that we may know our shortcomings and overcome them. We should not feel unhappy if on some occasion we commit an error. We should feel unhappy only if in committing it we had willingly yielded to a weakness in us or had not been vigilant enough, if we had not struggled, or not sincerely enough, to overcome it. You should never lose heart.

Think over this letter and do what you think proper.

Blessings from
BAPU

Letter to Mathuradas Purushottam (G.)
GN 3752

182. TRUE EDUCATION AND SELF-HELP

July 10, 1932

I will explain in brief one central idea about education which has been dominating my thoughts as I am writing the history of the Ashram. Some persons see a deficiency in the Ashram, namely, absence of any arrangement for education, that is, for literary education. I also can see this deficiency. But it will probably remain as long as the Ashram lasts. I will not here go into the reasons for that.

People see this deficiency because we do not know the true meaning of education and the right method of acquiring it, or we assume that the existing system of imparting education is the right one. According to me, the present idea of education and the method of imparting and receiving it are both faulty.

True education is that which helps us to know the *atman*, our true self, God and Truth. To acquire this knowledge, some persons may feel the need for a study of literature, some for a study of physical sciences and some others for art. But every branch of knowledge should have as its goal knowledge of the self. That is so in the Ashram. We carry on numerous activities with that aim in view. All of them are, in my sense of the term, true education. Those activities can also be carried on without any reference to the goal of knowledge of the self. When they are so carried on, they may serve as a means of livelihood or of something else, but they are not education. In an activity carried on as education, a proper understanding of its meaning, devotion to duty and the spirit of service are necessary. The first necessarily brings about development of the intellect. In doing any piece of work, however small, we should be inspired by a holy aim and, while doing it, we should try to understand the purpose which it will serve and the scientific method of doing it. There is a science of every type of work—whether it be cooking, sanitation, carpentry or spinning. Everybody who does his work with the attitude of a student knows its science or discovers it.

If the inmates of the Ashram understand this, they would see that the Ashram is a great school in which the inmates receive education not for a few hours only but all the time. Every person who lives in the Ashram to attain knowledge of the self—of Truth—is both a teacher and a pupil. He is a teacher in regard to what he knows, and a pupil in regard to anything about which he needs to learn. If we know more than our neighbour about anything, we should willingly share our knowledge with him, and equally willingly receive from him what he knows more than we do. If we thus regularly exchange knowledge with others, we would not feel the absence of teachers, and education would become a painless and spontaneous process. The most important education is the training of character. As we advance in our observance of *yamaniyamas*, our capacity for learning—for knowing Truth— will go on increasing.

What about literary education, then? It is no more a question. The rule for this is the same as for the other activities. The method explained above dispenses with one superstition, namely, that for education we require a separate building known as school and a teacher to teach. When the desire for literary education awakens in us, we should know that we shall have to acquire it through self-help. There is ample scope for this in the Ashram. If I have been able to explain above my idea clearly, literary education should no more be a problem. Those who possess it should take every opportunity to impart it to others and the latter should receive it from them.

'Education' (G.)
MMU/II

183. STAYING IN THE ASHRAM

Mahabaleshwar,
April 26, 1945

Chi. Om Prakash,

Unless you scrupulously follow all the Ashram rules, you will gain nothing by merely staying in the Ashram. You will have to get a certificate from the inmates of the Ashram. If you are hot-tempered, cure yourself of it. The Ashram is the place to overcome temperamental shortcomings. Not everybody can do so. But you must. You have to provide an ideal.

If you do not like the Ashram, it would be futile for you to stay there.

Blessings from
BAPU

Letter to Om Prakash Gupta (H.)
CW 5896

184. IMPERFECT BUT INVALUABLE

October 29, 1945

Chi. Dev,

I have your letter. You will be able to render a lot of service if you remain healthy. I know that though the Ashram is far from perfect there is something in it which is not found elsewhere. We have deliberately given up certain things which are seen at other places.

Sevagram Ashram
Sevagram

Letter to Devprakash Nayyar (H.)
Microfilm (courtesy: National Archives of India)

185. IFS AND BUTS

April 14, 1947

It is futile to argue in terms of *ifs* and *buts*. It is wrong to say that it would have been better if such and such a thing had been done in such and such a way. And this particularly applies to one who claims to be guided by God. Only a person whose heart is pure can claim to be guided by God. I try my best to keep my heart pure. Hence I bring God into the picture.

A Letter (G.)
Biharni Komi Agman, p. 198

Volume Three
Non-Violent Resistance and Social Transformation

XIII

Satyagraha—Non-Violent Resistance

186. THE USE AND SCOPE OF TRUTH-FORCE

[Before 11 July 1914][1]. I shall be at least far away from Phoenix, if not actually in the Motherland, when this Commemoration Issue is published. I would, however, leave behind me my innermost thoughts upon that which has made this special issue necessary. Without Passive Resistance, there would have been no richly illustrated and important special issue of *Indian Opinion*, which has, for the last eleven years, in an unpretentious and humble manner, endeavoured to serve my countrymen and South Africa, a period covering the most critical stage that they will, perhaps, ever have to pass through. It marks the rise and growth of Passive Resistance, which has attracted world-wide attention. The term does not fit the activity of the Indian community during the past eight years. Its equivalent in the vernacular,[2] rendered into English, means Truth-Force. I think Tolstoy called it also Soul-Force or Love-Force, and so it is. Carried out to its utmost limit, this force is independent of pecuniary or other material assistance; certainly, even in its elementary form, of physical force or violence. Indeed, violence is the negation of this great spiritual force, which can only be cultivated or wielded by those who will entirely eschew violence. It is a force that may be used by individuals as well as by communities. It may be used as well in political as in domestic affairs. Its universal applicability is a demonstration of its permanence and invincibility. It can be used alike by men, women, and children.

It is totally untrue to say that it is a force to be used only by the weak so long as they are not capable of meeting violence by violence. This superstition arises from the incompleteness of the English expression. It is impossible for those who consider themselves to be weak to apply this force. Only those who realise that there is something in man which is superior to the brute nature in him, and that the latter always yields to it, can effectively be Passive Resisters. This force is to violence and, therefore, to all tyranny, all injustice, what light is to darkness. In politics, its use is based upon the immutable maxim that government of the people is possible only so long as they consent either consciously or unconsciously to be governed. We did not want to be governed by the Asiatic Act of 1907 of the Transvaal, and it had to go before this mighty force. Two courses were open to us—to use violence when we were called upon to submit to the Act, or to suffer the penalties prescribed under the Act, and thus to draw out and exhibit the force of the soul within us for a period long enough to appeal to the sympathetic chord in the governors or the law-makers. We have taken long to achieve what we set about striving for. That was because our Passive Resistance was not of the most complete type.

All Passive Resisters do not understand the full value of the force, nor have we men who always from conviction refrain from violence. The use of this force requires the adoption of poverty, in the sense that we must be indifferent whether we have the wherewithal to feed or clothe ourselves. During the past struggle, all Passive Resisters, if any at all, were not prepared to go that length. Some again were only Passive Resisters so-called. They came without any conviction, often with mixed motives, less often with impure motives. Some even, whilst engaged in the struggle, would gladly have resorted to violence but for most vigilant supervision. Thus it was that the struggle became prolonged; for the exercise of the purest soul-force, in its perfect form, brings about instantaneous relief. For this exercise, prolonged training of the individual soul is an absolute necessity, so that a perfect Passive Resister has to be almost, if not entirely, a perfect man. We cannot all suddenly become such men, but, if my proposition is correct—as I know it to be correct—the greater the spirit of Passive Resistance in us, the better men we will become. Its use, therefore, is, I think, indisputable, and it is a force which, if it became universal, would revolutionize social ideals and do away with despotisms and the ever-growing militarism under which the nations of the West are groaning and are being almost crushed to death, and which fairly promises to overwhelm even the nations of the East.

If the past struggle has produced even a few Indians who would dedicate themselves to the task of becoming Passive Resisters as nearly perfect as possible, they would not only have served themselves in the truest sense of the term, they would also have served humanity at large. Thus viewed, Passive Resistance is the noblest and the best education. It should come, not after the ordinary education in letters of children, but it should precede it. It will not be denied that a child, before it begins to write its alphabet and to gain worldly knowledge, should know what the soul is, what truth is, what love is, what powers are latent in the soul. It should be an essential of real education that a child should learn that, in the struggle of life, it can easily conquer hate by love, untruth by truth, violence by self-suffering. It was because I felt the force of this truth, that, during the latter part of the struggle, I endeavoured, as much as I could, to train the children at Tolstoy Farm and then at Phoenix along these lines, and one of the reasons for my departure to India is still further to realise, as I already do in part, my own imperfection as a Passive Resister, and then to try to perfect myself, for I believe that it is in India that the nearest approach to perfection is most possible.

'The Theory and Practice of Passive Resistance'
Indian Opinion, Golden Number, 1 Dec. 1914

[1] *En route* to India, Gandhi left Phoenix on 11 July 1914.
[2] *Satyagraha.*

187. READINESS FOR *SATYAGRAHA*

July 27, 1916

In brief, the significance of *satyagraha* consists in the quest for a principle of life. We did not say to anyone in so many words that our fight was in pursuance of this quest. If we had said so, the people there would only have laughed at us. We only made known the secondary aim of our movement, which was that the Government there, thinking us lowly and mean, was making laws to oust us from the country, and that it was right for us to defy these laws and show that we were brave. Suppose the Government passes a law saying that coloured persons shall wear yellow caps; in fact, a law of this kind was made in Rome for the Jews. If the Government intended to treat us in a similar fashion and made a law that appeared to humiliate us, it was for us to make it clear to the Government that we would not obey such a law. If a child says to his father: 'Please put on your turban the wrong side up for me', the father understands that the child wants to have a laugh at his expense and at once obeys the command. But when someone else, with uncharitable motives, says the same thing, he clearly answers, 'Look, brother, so long as my head is on my shoulders, you cannot humiliate me in this manner. You conquer my head first and then make me wear my turban in any fashion you please.'

The Government there in a similar way, thinking the Indians lowly, wanted to treat them as slaves and as far as possible to prevent their coming into the country. And with this end in view, it began inventing ever new laws, such as putting names of Indians in a separate register, making them give finger-prints in the manner of thieves and bandits, forcing them to live in particular areas, forbidding their movement beyond a specified boundary, making rules for them to walk on particular foot-paths and board specified carriages in trains, treating their wives as concubines if they could not produce marriage certificates, levying from them an annual tax of forty-five rupees per capita, etc., etc. Often a disease manifests itself in the body in various forms. The disease in this case, as has been explained, was the evil purpose of the Government of South Africa, and all the rules and regulations mentioned above were the various forms that it took. We, therefore, had to prepare ourselves to fight against these.

There are two ways of countering injustice. One way is to smash the head of the man who perpetrates injustice and to get your own head smashed in the process. All strong people in the world adopt this course. Everywhere wars are fought and millions of people are killed. The consequence is not the progress of a nation but its decline. Soldiers returning from the front have become so bereft of reason that they indulge in various anti-social activities. One does not have to go far for examples. In the Boer War, when the British won a victory at

Mafeking, the whole of England, and London in particular, went so mad with joy that for days on end everyone did nothing but dance night and day! They freely indulged in wickednesses and rowdyism and did not leave a single bar with a drop of liquor in it. *The Times*, commenting, said that no words could describe the way those few days were spent, that all that could be said was that 'the English nation went amafficking [a-Mafeking]'.[1] Pride makes a victorious nation bad-tempered. It falls into luxurious ways of living. Then for a time, it may be conceded, peace prevails. But after a short while, it comes more and more to be realized that the seeds of war have not been destroyed but have become a thousand times more nourished and mighty. No country has ever become, or will ever become, happy through victory in war. A nation does not rise that way, it only falls further. In fact, what comes to it is defeat, not victory. And if, perchance, either our act or our purpose was ill-conceived, it brings disaster to both belligerents.

But through the other method of combating injustice, we alone suffer the consequences of our mistakes, and the other side is wholly spared. This other method is *satyagraha*. One who resorts to it does not have to break another's head; he may merely have his own head broken. He has to be prepared to die himself suffering all the pain. In opposing the atrocious laws of the Government of South Africa, it was this method that we adopted. We made it clear to the said Government that we would never bow to its outrageous laws. No clapping is possible without two hands to do it, and no quarrel without two persons to make it. Similarly, no State is possible without two entities, the rulers and the ruled. You are our sovereign, our Government, only so long as we consider ourselves your subjects. When we are not subjects, you are not the sovereign either. So long as it is your endeavour to control us with justice and love, we will let you to do so. But if you wish to strike at us from behind, we cannot permit it. Whatever you do in other matters, you will have to ask our opinion about the laws that concern us. If you make laws to keep us suppressed in a wrongful manner and without taking us into confidence, these laws will merely adorn the statute-books. We will never obey them. Award us for it what punishment you like, we will put up with it. Send us to prison and we will live there as in a paradise. Ask us to mount the scaffold and we will do so laughing. Shower what sufferings you like upon us, we will calmly endure all and not hurt a hair of your body. We will gladly die and will not so much as touch you. But so long as there is yet life in these our bones, we will never comply with your arbitrary laws.

It all began on a Sunday evening in Johannesburg when I sat on a hillock with another gentleman called Hemchandra. The memory of that day is so vivid that it might have been yesterday. At my side lay a Government *Gazette*. It contained the several clauses of the law concerning Indians. As I read it, I shook with rage. What did the Government take us for? Then and there I produced a translation of that portion of the *Gazette* which contained the said laws and wrote under it: 'I will never let these laws govern me.' This was at once sent for publication to *Indian Opinion* at Phoenix. I did not dream at the time that even a single Indian would be capable of the unprecedented heroism the Indians revealed or that the *satyagraha* movement would gain the momentum it did.

Immediately, I made my view known to fellow-Indians and many of them declared their readiness for *satyagraha*. In the first conflict, people took part under the impression that our aim would be gained after only a few days of suffering. In the second conflict, there were only a very few people to begin with but later many more came along. Afterwards when, on the visit of Mr. Gokhale, the Government of South Africa pledged itself to a settlement, the fight ceased. Later, the Government treacherously refused to honour its pledge; on which a third *satyagraha* battle became necessary. Gokhale at that time asked me how many people I thought would take part in the *satyagraha*. I wrote saying they would be between 30 and 60. But I could not find even that number. Only 16 of us took up the challenge. We were firmly decided that so long as the Government did not repeal its atrocious laws or make some settlement, we would accept every penalty but would not submit. We had never hoped that we should find many fellow-fighters. But the readiness of one person without self-interest to offer himself for the cause of truth and country always has its effect. Soon there were twenty thousand people in the movement. There was no room for them in the prisons, and the blood of India boiled. Many people say that if Lord

Hardinge had not intervened, a compromise would have been impossible. But these people forget to ask themselves why it was that Lord Hardinge intervened. The sufferings of the Canadian Indians were far greater than those of the South African Indians. Why did he not use his good offices there? Where the spiritual might of thousands of men and women has been mustered, where innumerable men and women are eager to lay down their lives, what indeed is impossible? There was no other course open for Lord Hardinge than to offer mediation and he only showed his wisdom in adopting it.

What transpired later is well known to you: the Government of South Africa was compelled to come to terms with us. All of which goes to show that we can gain everything without hurting anybody and through soul-force or *satyagraha* alone. He who fights with arms has to depend on arms and on support from others. He has to turn from the straight path and seek tortuous tracks. The course that a *satyagrahi* adopts in his fight is straight and he need look to no one for help. He can, if necessary, fight by himself alone. In that case, it is true, the outcome will be somewhat delayed. If I had not found as many comrades in the South African fight as I did, all that would have happened is that you would not have seen me here in your midst today. Perhaps all my life would have had to be spent in the struggle there. But what of that? The gain that has been secured would only have been a little late in coming. For the battle of *satyagraha* one only needs to prepare oneself. We have to have strict self-control. If it is necessary for this preparation to live in forests and caves, we should do so.

The time that may be taken up in this preparation should not be considered wasted. Christ, before he went out to serve the world, spent forty days in the wilderness, preparing himself for his mission. Buddha too spent many years in such preparation. Had Christ and Buddha not undergone this preparation, they would not have been what they were. Similarly, if we want to put this body in the service of truth and humanity, we must first raise our soul by developing virtues like celibacy, non-violence and truth. Then alone may we say that we are fit to render real service to the country.

In brief, the aim of the *satyagraha* struggle was to infuse manliness in cowards and to develop the really human virtues,

and its field was the passive resistance against the Government
of South Africa.

Speech on 'The Secret of *Satyagraha* in South Africa'
Satyagraha Ashram, Ahmedabad (H.)
Ramchandra Varma, *Mahatma Gandhi*

[1] The London crowds behaved extravagantly on the relief of Mafeking (17 May
1900).

188. SOUL-FORCE AND *TAPASYA*

[About 2 September 1917]

The force denoted by the term 'passive resistance' and translated into Hindi as *nishkriya pratirodha* is not very accurately
described either by the original English phrase or by its Hindi
rendering. Its correct description is '*satyagraha*'. *Satyagraha* was
born in South Africa in 1908. There was no word in any
Indian language denoting the power which our countrymen
in South Africa invoked for the redress of their grievances.
There was an English equivalent, namely, 'passive resistance',
and we carried on with it. However, the need for a word to
describe this unique power came to be increasingly felt, and
it was decided to award a prize to anyone who could think of
an appropriate term. A Gujarati-speaking gentleman submit-
ted the word '*satyagraha*', and it was adjudged the best.

'Passive resistance' conveyed the idea of the Suffragette
Movement in England. Burning of houses by these women
was called 'passive resistance' and so also their fasting in prison. All such acts might very well be 'passive resistance' but
they were not '*satyagraha*'. It is said of 'passive resistance' that
it is the weapon of the weak, but the power which is the
subject of this article can be used only by the strong. This
power is not 'passive' resistance; indeed it calls for intense
activity. The movement in South Africa was not passive but
active. The Indians of South Africa believed that Truth was
their object, that Truth ever triumphs, and with this definite-
ness of purpose they persistently held on to Truth. They put
up with all the suffering that this persistence implied. With
the conviction that Truth is not to be renounced even unto

death, they shed the fear of death. In the cause of Truth, the prison was a palace to them and its doors the gateway to freedom.

Satyagraha is not physical force. A *satyagrahi* does not inflict pain on the adversary; he does not seek his destruction. A *satyagrahi* never resorts to firearms. In the use of *satyagraha*, there is no ill-will whatever.

Satyagraha is pure soul-force. Truth is the very substance of the soul. That is why this force is called *satyagraha*. The soul is informed with knowledge. In it burns the flame of love. If someone gives us pain through ignorance, we shall win him through love. 'Non-violence is the supreme *dharma*'[1] is the proof of this power of love. Non-violence is a dormant state. In the waking state, it is love. Ruled by love, the world goes on. In English there is a saying, 'Might is Right'. Then there is the doctrine of the survival of the fittest. Both these ideas are contradictory to the above principle. Neither is wholly true. If ill-will were the chief motive-force, the world would have been destroyed long ago; and neither would I have had the opportunity to write this article nor would the hopes of the readers be fulfilled. We are alive solely because of love. We are all ourselves the proof of this. Deluded by modern western civilization, we have forgotten our ancient civilization and worship the might of arms.

We forget the principle of non-violence, which is the essence of all religions. The doctrine of arms stands for irreligion. It is due to the sway of that doctrine that a sanguinary war is raging in Europe.

In India also we find worship of arms. We see it even in that great work of Tulsidas. But it is seen in all the books that soul-force is the supreme power.

Rama stands for the soul and Ravan for the non-soul. The immense physical might of Ravana is as nothing compared to the soul-force of Rama. Ravana's ten heads are as straw to Rama. Rama is a *yogi*, he has conquered self and pride. He is 'placid equally in affluence and adversity', he has 'neither attachment, nor greed nor the intoxication of status'. This represents the ultimate in *satyagraha*. The banner of *satyagraha* can again fly in the Indian sky and it is our duty to raise it. If we take recourse to *satyagraha*, we can conquer our conquerors the English, make them bow before our tremendous soul-force, and the issue will be of benefit to the whole world.

It is certain that India cannot rival Britain or Europe in force of arms. The British worship the war-god and they can all of them become, as they are becoming, bearers of arms. The hundreds of millions in India can never carry arms. They have made the religion of non-violence their own. It is impossible for the *varnashrama* system to disappear from India.

The way of *varnashrama* is a necessary law of nature. India, by making a judicious use of it, derives much benefit. Even the Muslims and the English in India observe this system to some extent. Outside of India, too, people follow it without being aware of it. So long as this institution of *varnashrama* exists in India, everyone cannot bear arms here. The highest place in India is assigned to the *brahmana dharma*—which is soul-force. Even the armed warrior does obeisance to the *Brahmin*. So long as this custom prevails, it is vain for us to aspire for equality with the West in force of arms.

It is our Kamadhenu.² It brings good both to the *satyagrahi* and his adversary. It is ever victorious. For instance, Harishchandra was a *satyagrahi*, Prahlad was a *satyagrahi*, Mirabai was a *satyagrahi*. Daniel, Socrates and those Arabs who hurled themselves on the fire of the French artillery were all *satyagrahis*. We see from these examples that a *satyagrahi* does not fear for his body, he does not give up what he thinks is Truth; the word 'defeat' is not to be found in his dictionary, he does not wish for the destruction of his antagonist, he does not vent anger on him; but has only compassion for him.

A *satyagrahi* does not wait for others, but throws himself into the fray, relying entirely on his own resources. He trusts that when the time comes, others will do likewise. His practice is his precept. Like air, *satyagraha* is all-pervading. It is infectious, which means that all people—big and small, men and women—can become *satyagrahis*. No one is kept out from the army of *satyagrahis*. A *satyagrahi* cannot perpetrate tyranny on anyone; he is not subdued through application of physical force; he does not strike at anyone. Just as anyone can resort to *satyagraha*, it can be resorted to in almost any situation.

People demand historical evidence in support of *satyagraha*. History is for the most part a record of armed activities.

Natural activities find very little mention in it. Only uncommon activities strike us with wonder. *Satyagraha* has been used always and in all situations. The father and the son, the man and the wife are perpetually resorting to *satyagraha*, one towards the other. When a father gets angry and punishes the son, the son does not hit back with a weapon, he conquers his father's anger by submitting to him. The son refuses to be subdued by the unjust rule of his father but he puts up with the punishment that he may incur through disobeying the unjust father. We can similarly free ourselves of the unjust rule of the Government by defying the unjust rule and accepting the punishments that go with it. We do not bear malice towards the Government. When we set its fears at rest, when we do not desire to make armed assaults on the administrators, nor to unseat them from power, but only to get rid of their injustice, they will at once be subdued to our will.

The question is asked why we should call any rule unjust. In saying so, we ourselves assume the function of a judge. It is true. But in this world, we always have to act as judges for ourselves. That is why the *satyagrahi* does not strike his adversary with arms. If he has Truth on his side, he will win, and if his thought is faulty, he will suffer the consequences of his fault.

What is the good, they ask, of only one person opposing injustice; for he will be punished and destroyed, he will languish in prison or meet an untimely end through hanging. The objection is not valid. History shows that all reforms have begun with one person. Fruit is hard to come by without *tapasya*. The suffering that has to be undergone in *satyagraha* is *tapasya* in its purest form. Only when the *tapasya* is capable of bearing fruit do we have the fruit. This establishes the fact that when there is insufficient *tapasya*, the fruit is delayed. The *tapasya* of Jesus Christ, boundless though it was, was not sufficient for Europe's need. Europe has disapproved Christ. Through ignorance, it has disregarded Christ's pure way of life. Many Christs will have to offer themselves as sacrifice at the terrible altar of Europe, and only then will realization dawn on that continent. But Jesus will always be the first among these. He has been the sower of the seed and his will therefore be the credit for raising the harvest.

It is said that it is a very difficult, if not an altogether impossible, task to educate ignorant peasants in *satyagraha* and that it is full of perils, for it is a very arduous business to transform unlettered ignorant people from one condition into another. Both the arguments are just silly. The people of India are perfectly fit to receive the training of *satyagraha*. India has knowledge of *dharma*, and where there is knowledge of *dharma*, *satyagraha* is a very simple matter. The people of India have drunk of the nectar of devotion. This great people overflows with faith. It is no difficult matter to lead such a people on to the right path of *satyagraha*. Some have a fear that once people get involved in *satyagraha*, they may at a later stage take to arms. This fear is illusory. From the path of *satyagraha* [clinging to Truth], a transition to the path of *a-satyagraha* [clinging to untruth] is impossible. It is possible of course that some people who believe in armed activity may mislead the *satyagrahis* by infiltrating into their ranks and later making them take to arms. This is possible in all enterprises. But as compared to other activities, it is less likely to happen in *satyagraha*, for their motives soon get exposed and when the people are not ready to take up arms, it becomes almost impossible to lead them on to that terrible path. The might of arms is directly opposed to the might of *satyagraha*. Just as darkness does not abide in light, soulless armed activity cannot enter the sunlike radiance of soul-force. Many Pathans took part in *satyagraha* in South Africa abiding by all the rules of *satyagraha*.

Then it is said that much suffering is involved in being a *satyagrahi* and that the entire people will not be willing to put up with this suffering. The objection is not valid. People in general always follow in the footsteps of the noble. There is no doubt that it is difficult to produce a *satyagrahi* leader. Our experience is that a *satyagrahi* needs many more virtues like self-control, fearlessness, etc., than are requisite for one who believes in armed action. The greatness of the man bearing arms does not lie in the superiority of the arms, nor does it lie in his physical prowess. It lies in his determination and fearlessness in face of death. General Gordon was a mighty warrior of the British Empire. In the statue that has been erected in his memory he has only a small baton in his hand. It goes to show that the strength of a warrior is not measured by reference to his weapons but by his firmness of mind. A *satya-*

grahi needs millions of times more of such firmness than does a bearer of arms. The birth of such a man can bring about the salvation of India in no time. Not only India but the whole world awaits the advent of such a man. We may in the meanwhile prepare the ground as much as we can through *satyagraha*.

How can we make use of *satyagraha* in the present conditions? Why should we take to *satyagraha* in the fight for freedom? We are all guilty of killing manliness. So long as our learned Annie Besant is in detention, it is an insult to our manhood. How can we secure her release through *satyagraha*? It may be that the government has acted in good faith, that it has sufficient grounds for keeping her under detention. But, at any rate, the people are unhappy at her being deprived of her freedom. Annie Besant cannot be freed through armed action. No Indian will approve of such an action. We cannot secure her freedom by submitting petitions and the like. Much time has passed. We can all humbly inform the Government that if Mrs. Annie Besant is not released within the time limit prescribed by us, we will all be compelled to follow her path. It is possible that all of us do not like all her actions; but we find nothing in her actions which threatens the 'established Government' or the vested interests. Therefore we too by participating in her activities will ask for her lot, that is, we shall all court imprisonment. The members of our Legislative Assembly also can petition the Government and when the petition is not accepted, they can resign their membership. For *swaraj* also, *satyagraha* is the unfailing weapon. *Satyagraha* means that what we want is truth, that we deserve it and that we will work for it even unto death.

Nothing more need be said. Truth alone triumphs. There is no *dharma* higher than Truth. Truth always wins. We pray to God that in this sacred land we may bring about the reign of *dharma* by following *satyagraha* and that this our country may become an example for all to follow.

'*Satyagraha*—Not Passive Resistance' (H.)
Ramchandra Varma, *Mahatma Gandhi*

---

[1] *Ahimsa Paramo Dharmah.*
[2] Mythical cow which yielded whatever one wished.

189. INSTRUCTIONS TO *SATYAGRAHIS*

Satyagraha Camp,
Nadiad,
April 17, 1918

1. The volunteers must remember that, as this is a *satyagraha* campaign, they must abide by truth under all circumstances.

2. In *satyagraha*, there can be no room for rancour; which means that a *satyagrahi* should utter no harsh word about anyone, from a *ravania* to the Governor himself; if someone does so, it is the volunteer's duty to stop him.

3. Rudeness has no place in *satyagraha*. Perfect courtesy must be shown even to those who may look upon us as their enemies and the villagers must be taught to do the same. Rudeness may harm our cause and the struggle may be unduly prolonged. The volunteers should give the most serious attention to this matter and think out in their minds as many examples as possible of the advantages accruing from courtesy and the disadvantages resulting from rudeness and explain them to the people.

4. The volunteers must remember that this is a holy war. We embarked upon it because, had we not, we would have failed in our *dharma*. And so all the rules which are essential for living a religious life must be observed here too.

5. We are opposing the intoxication of power, that is, the blind application of law, and not authority as such. The difference must never be lost sight of. It is, therefore, our duty to help the officers in their other work.

6. We are to apply here the same principle that we follow in a domestic quarrel. We should think of the Government and the people as constituting a large family and act accordingly.

7. We are not to boycott or treat with scorn those who hold different views from ours. It must be our resolve to win them over by courteous behaviour.

8. We must not try to be clever. We must always be frank and straightforward.

9. When they stay in villages, the volunteers should demand the fewest services from the village-folk. Wherever it is possible to reach a place on foot, they should avoid using a vehicle. We must insist on being served the simplest food. Restraining

them from preparing dainties will add grace to the service we render.

10. As they move about in villages, the volunteers should observe the economic condition of the people and the deficiencies in their education and try, in their spare time, to make them good.

11. If they can, they should create opportunities when they may teach the village children.

12. If they notice any violation of the rules of good health, they should draw the villagers' attention to the fact.

13. If, at any place, they find people engaged in quarrelling among themselves, the volunteers should try to save them from their quarrels.

14. They should read out to the people, when the latter are free, books which promote *satyagraha*. They may read out stories of Prahlad, Harishchandra and others. The people should also be made familiar with instances of pure *satyagraha* to be found in the West and in Islamic literature.

15. At no time and under no circumstances is the use of arms permitted in *satyagraha*. It should never be forgotten that in this struggle the highest type of non-violence is to be maintained. *Satyagraha* means fighting oppression through voluntary suffering. There can be no question here of making anyone else suffer. *Satyagraha* is always successful; it can never meet with defeat: let every volunteer understand this himself and then explain it to the people.

MOHANDAS KARAMCHAND GANDHI

'Instructions to Volunteers' (G.)
Kheda Satyagraha

190 THE LAW OF *SATYAGRAHA*

[25 April 1919]

In the first leaflet, I hinted that I would consider the meaning of *satyagraha* in a later number of this series. I feel that the time has now arrived to examine the meaning of *satyagraha*. The word was newly coined some years ago, but the principle which it denotes is as ancient as time. This is the literal meaning of *satyagraha*—insistence on truth, and force derivable from such insistence. In the present movement, we are making use of *satyagraha* as a force: that is to say, in order to cure the evil in the shape of the Rowlatt legislation, we have been making use of the force generated by *satyagraha*, that is, insistence on truth. One of the axioms of religion is, there is no religion other than truth. Another is, religion is love. And as there can be only one religion, it follows that truth is love and love is truth. We shall find too, on further reflection, that conduct based on truth is impossible without love. Truth-force then is love-force. We cannot remedy evil by harbouring ill will against the evil-doer. This is not difficult of comprehension. It is easy enough to understand. In thousands of our acts, the propelling power is truth or love. The relations between father and son, husband and wife, indeed our family relations are largely guided by truth or love. And we therefore consciously or unconsciously apply *satyagraha* in regulating these relations.

If we were to cast a retrospective glance over our past life, we would find that out of a thousand of our acts affecting our families, in nine hundred and ninety-nine we were dominated by truth, that in our deeds, it is not right to say we generally resort to untruth or ill will. It is only where a conflict of interests arises, then arise the progeny of untruth, viz., anger, ill will, etc., and then we see nothing but poison in our midst. A little hard thinking will show us that the standard that we apply to the regulation of domestic relations is the standard that should be applied to regulate the relations between rulers and the ruled, and between man and man. Those men and women who do not recognize the domestic tie are considered to be very like brutes or barbarous, even though they in form have the human body. They have never known the law of *satyagraha*. Those who recognize the domestic tie and its obligations have to a certain extent gone beyond that brute stage. But if challenged, they would say 'what do we care though the whole universe may perish so long as we guard the family interest?' The measure of their *satyagraha*, therefore, is less than that of a drop in the ocean.

When men and women have gone a stage further, they would extend the law of love, i.e., *satyagraha*, from the family to the village. A still further stage away from the brute life is reached when the law of *satyagraha* is applied to provincial life, and the people inhabiting a province regulate their relations by love rather than by hatred. And when as in Hindustan we recognize the law of *satyagraha* as a binding force even between province and province and the millions of Hindustan treat one another as brothers and sisters, we have advanced a stage further still from the brute nature.

In modern times, in no part of the earth have the people gone beyond the nation stage in the application of *satyagraha*. In reality, however, there need be no reason for the clashing of interest between nation and nation, thus arresting the operation of the great law. If we were not in the habit generally of giving no thought to our daily conduct, if we did not accept local custom and habit as matters of course, as we accept the current coin, we would immediately perceive that to the extent that we bear ill will towards other nations or show disregard at all for life, to that extent we disregard the law of *satyagraha* or love, and to that extent we are still not free from the brute nature. But there is no religion apart from that which enables us entirely to rid ourselves of the brute nature. All religious sects and divisions, all churches and temples, are useful only so long as they serve as a means towards enabling us to recognize the universality of *satyagraha*. In India we have been trained from ages past in this teaching and hence it is that we are taught to consider the whole universe as one family. I do wish to submit as a matter of experience that it is not only possible to live the full national life, by rendering obedience to the law of *satyagraha*, but that the fullness of national life is impossible without *satyagraha*, i.e., without a life of true religion. That nation which wars against another has to an extent disregarded the great law of life. I shall never abandon the faith I have that India is capable of delivering this truth to the whole world, and I wish that all Indians, men and women, whether they are Hindus or Mahomedans, Parsis, Christians or Jews, will share with me this unquenchable faith.

M. K. GANDHI

'*Satyagraha*: Its Significance'
Satyagraha Leaflet Series, No. 6
Gandhi Smarak Sangrahalaya, New Delhi
(Courtesy: H. S. L. Polak)

191. ESSENTIALS OF *SATYAGRAHA*

Lahore,
January 25, 1920

Dear Mr. ....[1]

I have drawn the distinction between passive resistance as understood and practised in the West and *satyagraha* before I had evolved the doctrine of the latter to its full logical and spiritual extent. I often used 'passive resistance' and '*satyagraha*' as synonymous terms: but as the doctrine of *satyagraha* developed, the expression 'passive resistance' ceases even to be synonymous, as passive resistance has admitted of violence as in the case of suffragettes and has been universally acknowledged to be a weapon of the weak. Moreover passive resistance does not necessarily involve complete adherence to truth under every circumstance. Therefore it is different from *satyagraha* in three essentials: *Satyagraha* is a weapon of the strong; it admits of no violence under any circumstance whatever; and it ever insists upon truth. I think I have now made the distinction perfectly clear.

Yours sincerely,

To
Madanpalli (P. O.)

A letter
SN 7071

---

[1] The addressee's name is illegible.

192. FORM AND SUBSTANCE

The Ashram,
Sabarmati,
May 31, 1926

Dear Friend,

I have your letter. I fully appreciate your struggle. But I have no doubt that if the humiliations you may be suffering purify you, they may to that extent and only to that extent benefit your fellows. My non-resistance is activitized resistance in a different plane. Non-resistance to evil does not mean absence of any resistance whatsoever but it means not resisting evil with evil but with good. Resistance, therefore, is transferred to a higher and absolutely effective plane.

Capitalism, therefore, is to be resisted not with the ways open to capitalism but with absolutely new weapons. If only employees will realize the power within them, they will not, as they do today, merely change the form but they will radically change the substance. And for this desirable reform the power comes from within. One does not need to wait till the rest have made the commencement. One person making the beginning will in the end be enough to destroy the system. But I am free to confess that in the intervening period, one may have to put up with estrangement and much worse, which, however, is the lot of almost every reformer.

Yours sincerely,

Wilhelm Wartenberg, Esq.
Hamburg 23
Bitterstr 134 II
Germany

Letter to Wilhelm Wartenberg
SN 12471

193. RULES FOR *SATYAGRAHIS*

Satyagraha literally means insistence on truth. This insistence arms the votary with matchless power. This power or force is connoted by the word *satyagraha*. *Satyagraha*, to be genuine, may be offered against parents, against one's wife or one's children, against rulers, against fellow-citizens, even against the whole world.

Such a universal force necessarily makes no distinction between kinsmen and strangers, young and old, man and woman, friend and foe. The force to be so applied can never be physical. There is in it no room for violence. The only force of universal application can, therefore, be that of *ahimsa* or love. In other words, it is soul-force.

Love does not burn others, it burns itself. Therefore, a

satyagrahi, i.e., a civil resister, will joyfully suffer even unto death.

It follows, therefore, that a civil resister, whilst he will strain every nerve to compass the end of the existing rule, will do no intentional injury in thought, word or deed to the person of a single Englishman. This necessarily brief explanation of *satyagraha* will perhaps enable the reader to understand and appreciate the following rules:

AS AN INDIVIDUAL

1. A *satyagrahi*, i.e., a civil resister, will harbour no anger.
2. He will suffer the anger of the opponent.
3. In so doing he will put up with assaults from the opponent, never retaliate; but he will not submit, out of fear of punishment or the like, to any order given in anger.
4. When any person in authority seeks to arrest a civil resister, he will voluntarily submit to the arrest, and he will not resist the attachment or removal of his own property, if any, when it is sought to be confiscated by authorities.
5. If a civil resister has any property in his possession as a trustee, he will refuse to surrender it, even though in defending it he might lose his life. He will, however, never retaliate.
6. Non-retaliation excludes swearing and cursing.
7. Therefore a civil resister will never insult his opponent, and therefore also not take part in many of the newly coined cries which are contrary to the spirit of *ahimsa*.
8. A civil resister will not salute the Union Jack, nor will he insult it or officials, English or Indian.
9. In the course of the struggle if anyone insults an official or commits an assault upon him, a civil resister will protect such official or officials from the insult or attack even at the risk of his life.

AS A PRISONER

10. As a prisoner, a civil resister will behave courteously towards prison officials, and will observe all such discipline of the prison as is not contrary to self-respect; as for instance, whilst he will *salaam*[1] officials in the usual manner, he will not perform any humiliating gyrations and refuse to shout 'Vic-

tory to *Sarkar*'[2] or the like. He will take cleanly cooked and cleanly served food, which is not contrary to his religion, and will refuse to take food insultingly served or served in unclean vessels.

11. A civil resister will make no distinction between an ordinary prisoner and himself, will in no way regard himself as superior to the rest, nor will he ask for any conveniences that may not be necessary for keeping his body in good health and condition. He is entitled to ask for such conveniences as may be required for his physical or spiritual well-being.

12. A civil resister may not fast for want of conveniences whose deprivation does not involve any injury to one's self-respect.

AS A UNIT

13. A civil resister will joyfully obey all the orders issued by the leader of the corps, whether they please him or not.

14. He will carry out orders in the first instance even though they appear to him insulting, inimical or foolish, and then appeal to higher authority. He is free before joining to determine the fitness of the corps to satisfy him, but after he has joined it, it becomes a duty to submit to its discipline, irksome or otherwise. If the sum total of the energy of the corps appears to a member to be improper or immoral, he has a right to sever his connection, but being within it, he has no right to commit a breach of its discipline.

15. No civil resister is to expect maintenance for his dependents. It would be an accident if any such provision is made. A civil resister entrusts his dependents to the care of God. Even in ordinary warfare wherein hundreds of thousands give themselves up to it, they are able to make no previous provision. How much more, then, should such be the case in *satyagraha*? It is the universal experience that in such times hardly anybody is left to starve.

IN COMMUNAL FIGHTS

16. No civil resister will intentionally become a cause of communal quarrels.

17. In the event of any such outbreak, he will not take

sides, but he will assist only that party which is demonstrably in the right. Being a Hindu he will be generous towards Mussalmans and others, and will sacrifice himself in the attempt to save non-Hindus from a Hindu attack. And if the attack is from the other side, he will not participate in any retaliation but will give his life in protecting Hindus.

18. He will, to the best of his ability, avoid every occasion that may give rise to communal quarrels.

19. If there is a procession of *satyagrahis* they will do nothing that would wound the religious susceptibilities of any community, and they will not take part in any other processions that are likely to wound such susceptibilities.

'Some Rules of *Satyagraha*' (G.)
Navajivan, 23 Feb. 1930
Young India, 27 Feb. 1930

---

[1] Salute.
[2] Government.

194. BASIC ASSUMPTIONS OF *SATYAGRAHA*

Utmanzai,
October 14, 1938

An esteemed correspondent, who has for years been following, as a student, the non-violent action of the Congress and who ultimately joined the Congress, expresses certain doubts with lucid argument. Whilst the argument is helpful to me it is unnecessary to reproduce it here. He lays down three basic assumptions and argues that India is hardly able to satisfy these assumptions under all circumstances. We may, he says, scrape through with the English because they are lovers of liberty, are few in number, and their democratic instinct, more or less developed, restrains them from lengths to which autocrats will go.

If non-violence has all these limitations, it is not of much value or it has as much value as any other remedy, including violence, may have. But I have presented it as a never-failing remedy against tyranny. Limitations it has, but they are all applicable to the user and therefore under his control.

The suggested basic assumptions are:

1. Complete unity of the people in their desire and demand for freedom;

2. Complete appreciation and assimilation of the doctrine in all its implications by the people as a whole, with consequent control over one's natural instincts for resort to violence either in revenge or as a measure of self-defence; and (this is the most important of all)

3. Implicit belief that the sight of suffering on the part of multitudes of people will melt the heart of the aggressor and induce him to desist from his course of violence.

For the application of the remedy of non-violence complete unity is not an indispensable condition. If it was, the remedy would possess no special virtue. For complete unity will bring freedom for the asking. Have I not said repeatedly in the columns of *Young India* and these columns that even a few true *satyagrahis* would suffice to bring us freedom? I have maintained that we would require a smaller army of *satyagrahis* than that of soldiers trained in modern warfare, and the cost will be insignificant compared to the fabulous sums devoted by nations to armaments.

Nor is the second assumption necessary. *Satyagraha* by the vast mass of mankind will be impossible if they had all to assimilate the doctrine in all its implications. I cannot claim to have assimilated all its implications nor do I claim even to know them all. A soldier of an army does not know the whole of the military science; so also does a *satyagrahi* not know the whole science of *satyagraha*. It is enough if he trusts his commander and honestly follows his instructions and is ready to suffer unto death without bearing malice against the so-called enemy.

The third assumption has to be satisfied. I should word it differently, but the result would be about the same.

My friend says there is no historical warrant for the third assumption. He cites Ashoka as a possible exception. For my purpose, however, Ashoka's instance is unnecessary. I admit that there is no historical instance to my knowledge. Hence it is that I have been obliged to claim uniqueness for the experiment. I have argued from the analogy of what we do in families or even clans. Humankind is one big family. And if the love expressed is intense enough, it must apply to all mankind. If individuals have succeeded even with savages, why should not a group of individuals succeed with a group, say, of savages? If we can succeed with the English, surely it is merely an extension of faith to believe that we are likely to succeed with less cultured or less liberally-minded nations. I hold that if we succeed with the English with unadulterated non-violent effort, we must succeed with the others; which is the same thing as saying that if we achieve freedom with non-violence, we shall defend it also with the same weapon. If we have not achieved that faith, our non-violence is a mere expedient, it is alloy, not pure gold. In the first place we shall never achieve freedom with doubtful non-violence, and in the second, even if we do, we shall find ourselves wholly unprepared to defend the country against an aggressor. If we have doubt about the final efficacy of non-violence, it would be far better for the Congress to revise its policy and invite the nation to a training in arms. A mass organization like the Congress will be untrue to its charge if, not knowing its own mind, it misled the people into a false belief. It would be an act of cowardice. As I have said before, because we cease to pin our faith to non-violence, we do not necessarily become violent. We merely throw off the mask and be natural. It would be a perfectly dignified course to adopt. The lesson learnt during the past seventeen years will still not be thrown away.

Now I am in a position to state what, in my opinion, are basic assumptions underlying the doctrine of *satyagraha*:

1. There must be common honesty among *satyagrahis*.

2. They must render heart discipline to their commander. There should be no mental reservation.

3. They must be prepared to lose all, not merely their personal liberty, not merely their possessions, land, cash, etc., but also the liberty and possessions of their families, and they must be ready cheerfully to face bullets, bayonets, or even slow death by torture.

4. They must not be violent in thought, word or deed towards the 'enemy' or among themselves.

'What are Basic Assumptions?'
Harijan, 22 Oct. 1938

195. TIMING AND COOLNESS IN *SATYAGRAHA*

Delhi,
March 15, 1939

Satyagraha does not begin and end with civil disobedience. Let us do a little more *tapascharya* which is the essence of *satyagraha*. Suspension thus conceived can never do harm to the movement. The opponent will find that his battery is exhausted when we do not act up to his expectations, refuse to have any firework displays or put ourselves at his disposal for brutal assaults of his *goondas*.[1] We must meet all his provocative and repressive measures with a coolness and an exemplary self-restraint even at the risk of being charged with cowardice. If there is no cowardice in us, we are safe; ours will ultimately be reckoned an act of rare bravery.

Meanwhile we should watch how things shape themselves. I am thinking out new plans of conducting the movement in view of the terrorist methods that some States seem to have adopted. We have to develop that technique of rendering futile the employment of hired hooligans against peaceful citizens.

An able general always gives battle in his own time on the ground of his choice. He always retains the initiative in these respects and never allows it to pass into the hands of the enemy.

In a *satyagraha* campaign the mode of fight and the choice of tactics, e.g., whether to advance or retreat, offer civil resistance or organize non-violent strength through constructive work and purely selfless humanitarian service, are determined according to the exigencies of the situation. A *satyagrahi* must carry out whatever plan is laid out for him with a cool determination giving way to neither excitement nor depression.

For a *satyagrahi* there can be only one goal, viz., to lay down his life performing his duty whatever it may be. It is the highest he can attain. A cause that has such worthy *satyagrahi* soldiers at its back can never be defeated.

Discussion with Philipose about Travancore
Harijan, 27 May 1939

---

[1] Ruffians.

196. *SATYAGRAHA* AND WORLD PEACE

Sevagram,
March 29, 1941

Deep inside me I have an ever growing faith that in the midst of this universal destruction due to bloodshed, I am carrying on an absolutely innocuous struggle which, however, is pregnant with great potentialities.

The movement, for the conduct of which I am responsible, may prove a vain effort, if I represent no one but myself; and if I remain true to my faith, I may be satisfied, but so far as world peace is concerned, the effort will prove inadequate in terms of the present. For producing the desired result during the lifetime of the present generation, it will be necessary to give an unmistakable demonstration that a substantial part of the nation is behind the effort. Much more has to happen before such a demonstration becomes possible. The present movement is a humble attempt in that direction.

Man can only make an honest attempt. In a *satyagraha* movement, the saying that God is the giver of the result is literally true. Therefore, it is faith that sustains me and it is faith that must sustain the other *satyagrahis*. We have only begun the battle. The real test, the real suffering, has yet to come. Let me repeat for the thousandth time that, in this long and arduous struggle, quality alone will count, never quantity. In this there is no room for hatred, certainly not for camouflage.

Despite my being the originator of this struggle, I venture to say that only through it can we hope for permanent world peace. Peace can never come through war.

'The Only Way Towards World Peace' (H.)
The Hindu, 6 May 1941
Sarvodaya, May 1941

197. *SATYAGRAHA* AND ARMED RESISTANCE

Poona,
March 6, 1946

A friend has gently posed the question as to what a *satyagrahi* should do to prevent looting by *goondas*. If he had understood the secret of *satyagraha*, he would not have put it.

To lay down one's life, even alone, for what one considers to be right, is the very core of *satyagraha*. More no man can do. If a man is armed with a sword, he might lop off a few heads but ultimately he must surrender to superior force or else die fighting. The sword of the *satyagrahi* is love and the unshakeable firmness that comes from it. He will regard as brothers the hundreds of *goondas* that confront him and instead of trying to kill them he will choose to die at their hands and thereby live.

This is straight and simple. But how can a solitary *satyagrahi* succeed in the midst of a huge population? Hundreds of hooligans were let loose on the city of Bombay for arson and loot. A solitary *satyagrahi* will be like a drop in the ocean. Thus argues the correspondent.

My reply is that a *satyagrahi* may never run away from danger, irrespective of whether he is alone or in the company of many. He will have fully performed his duty, if he dies fighting. The same holds good in armed warfare. It applies with greater force in *satyagraha*. Moreover the sacrifice of one will evoke the sacrifice of many and may possibly produce big results. There is always this possibility. But one must scrupulously avoid the temptation of a desire for results. Here I am indicating only a possibility. May no one regard results as a temptation.

I believe that every man and woman should learn the art of self-defence in this age. This is done through arms in the West. Every adult man is conscripted for army training for a definite period. The training for *satyagraha* is meant for all, irrespective of age or sex. The more important part of the training here is mental, not physical. There can be no compulsion in mental training. The surrounding atmosphere no doubt acts on the mind but that cannot justify compulsion.

It follows that shopkeepers, traders, mill-hands, labourers, farmers, clerks, in short everyone ought to consider it his or her duty to get the necessary training in *satyagraha*.

Satyagraha is always superior to armed resistance. This can only be effectively proved by demonstration, not by argument. It is the weapon that adorns the strong. It can never adorn the weak. By weak is meant the weak in mind and spirit, not in body. That limitation is a quality to be prized and not a defect to be deplored.

One ought also to understand one of its other limitations. It can never be used to defend a wrong cause.

Satyagraha brigades can be organized in every village and in every block of buildings in the cities. Each brigade should be composed of those persons who are well-known to the organizers. In this respect *satyagraha* differs from armed defence. For the latter the State impresses the service of everybody. For a *satyagraha* brigade only those are eligible who believe in *ahimsa* and *satya*. Therefore an intimate knowledge of the persons enlisted is necessary for the organizers.

'*Satyagraha* in Face of Hooliganism' (G.)
Harijan, 17 Mar. 1946

198. *SATYAGRAHA* AND SELFISHNESS

New Delhi,
October 3, 1947

Brothers and Sisters,

I find *satyagraha* being carried on it many places in the country. I really wonder if what people describe as *satyagraha* is *satyagraha* or *duragraha*. What is happening in the country is that people talk of one thing and act quite to the contrary. Today every employee, whether belonging to the Post Office or the Telegraph Office, or the Railways or to the Indian States, must examine wherever he is trying to offer *satyagraha*, whether it stands for truth or untruth. If it is for untruth, there is no need to offer it and if it is for truth it should surely be offered under all circumstances. Whatever is done with a selfish motive cannot be called *satyagraha*. That would be like insisting on untruth. I have explained quite a few conditions for *satyagraha*. I have said that two things are essential in *satyagraha*. One is that the point on which we insist should be truth and another that our insistence should be necessarily non-violent.

Those who are carrying on *satyagraha* today should act with due deliberation. If the basic thing is not truth and there is recourse to force in pressing for the demand, then it would be well to give it up. If the thing is poisonous, if it is *duragraha* and an untruth and if we go on demanding what we possibly cannot get, then let me tell you that we cannot remain non-violent in making such a demand. This cannot be non-violence, it is only violence. It is impossible that anyone should make an unjust demand and at the same time claim to be non-violent.

If I am in charge of the refugee camps I would tell the people living in those camps that they must clean their places themselves. Should. they only play cards and dice and gamble or simply remain idle? I know there is not enough food and water for them. But if for that reason they start refusing to do any work, they will fall a prey to vices. And then there are not just half a dozen persons in those camps. Thousands are living in those camps. No one can say when they will be able to return to their homes. We shall certainly provide food for them; but let them at least do some work to earn it. They can start by cleaning their camps and then offer to do other jobs like spinning, weaving, carpentry, smithery, tailoring, etc. There are plenty of things one can find to do in India. These people may have been millionaires yesterday; but today they have lost their millions. Such things happen often in the world. Then it becomes necessary to begin afresh and start working. If somebody comes and says that he was once a millionaire and cannot work, all our plans will be upset. We cannot then succeed. Very respectfully I would like to say that we cannot proceed that way.

Whatever work we carry on should be ideal from every point of view. It should be clean and there should be nothing shoddy. Let me tell you that our difficulties are likely to be solved to a great extent if people do their own work. And if we get absorbed in our work our anger will also subside. The desire for revenge in our hearts will also die out. Goodness lies in recognizing evil as evil and then meeting it with goodwill. Therein lies the good of the country. We will not inflict suffering on anyone but will try to make others happy by undergoing hardships ourselves. If we do this, we shall be acting not only for the good of India but of the world. Today the world is watching how India is conducting herself. Now is the real moment of our test. We have attained independence. What are we going to do now?

Speech at Prayer Meeting (H.)
Prarthana Pravachan, Vol. I, pp. 374-6

199   LOYALTY AND *SATYAGRAHA*

New Delhi,
November 28, 1947

A friend asked me· the other day whether I shared the opinion often expressed that as between nationalism and religion, the former was superior to the latter. I said that the two were dissimilars and that there could be no comparison between dissimilars. Each was equal to the other in its own place. No man who values his religion as also his nationalism can barter away the one for the other. Both are equally dear to him. He renders unto Caesar that which is Caesar's and unto God that which is God's. And if Caesar, forgetting his limits, oversteps them, a man of God does not transfer his loyalty to another Caesar, but knows how to deal with the usurpation. A rehearsal of this difficulty gave rise to *satyagraha*.

Take a homely illustration. Suppose I have mother, wife and daughter. All the three must be equally dear to me in their own places. It is a vulgar error to think that a man is entitled to forsake his mother and his daughter for the sake of his wife. He dare not do the converse. And if any of the three oversteps her limits, the law of *satyagraha* comes to his assistance for the restoration of the equilibrium of the three forces.

'No Comparison Possible'
Harijan, 7 Dec. 1947

200.   SUBMISSION TO THE PENALTY OF DISOBEDIENCE

[Motihari,]
April 18, 1917

Mr. Gandhi appeared before the District Magistrate on Wednesday, the 18th instant. He read the statement printed below, and being asked to plead and finding that the case was likely to be unnecessarily prolonged, pleaded guilty. The Magistrate would not award the penalty but postponed judgement till 3 p.m. Meanwhile he was asked to see the Superintendent and then the District Magistrate. The result was that he agreed not to go out to the villages, pending instructions from the Government as to their view of his mission. The case was then postponed up to Saturday, April 21.

With the permission of the Court, I would like to make a brief statement showing why I have taken the very serious step of seemingly disobeying the order made under Section 144 of the Criminal Procedure Code. In my humble opinion, it is a question of difference of opinion between the local administration and myself. I have entered the country with motives of rendering humanitarian and national service. I have done so in response to a pressing invitation to come and help the *ryots*, who urge they are not being fairly treated by the indigo planters. I could not render any help without studying the problem. I have, therefore, come to study it with the assistance, if possible, of the administration and the planters. I have no other motive and I cannot believe that my coming here can in any way disturb the public peace or cause loss of life. I claim to have considerable experience in such matters. The administration, however, have thought differently. I fully appreciate their difficulty, and I admit too, that they can only proceed upon information they receive. As a law-abiding citizen, my first instinct would be, as it was, to obey the order served upon me. I could not do so without doing violence to my sense of duty to those for whom I have come. I feel that I could just now serve them only by remaining in their midst. I could not, therefore, voluntarily retire. Amid this conflict of duty, I could only throw the responsibility of removing me from them on the administration.

I am fully conscious of the fact that a person, holding in the public life of India a position such as I do, has to be most careful in setting examples. It is my firm belief that in the complex constitution under which we are living, the only safe and honourable course for a self-respecting man is, in the circumstances such as face me, to do what I have decided to do, that is, to submit without protest to the penalty of disobedience. I have ventured to make this statement not in any way in extenuation of the penalty to be awarded against me, but to show that I have disregarded the order served upon me, not for want of respect for lawful authority, but in obedience of the higher law of our being—the voice of conscience.

'Statement Before the Court'
The Leader, 22 Apr. 1917

201. CIVIL DISOBEDIENCE AND MASS *SATYAGRAHA*

Bombay,
April 18, 1919

It is not without sorrow that I feel compelled to advise the temporary suspension of civil disobedience. I give this advice not because I have less faith now in its efficacy, but because I have, if possible, greater faith than before. It is my perception of the law of *satyagraha* which impels me to suggest the suspension. I am sorry, when I embarked upon a mass movement, I underrated the forces of evil and I must now pause and consider how best to meet the situation. But whilst doing so, I wish to say that from a careful examination of the tragedy at Ahmedabad and Viramgam, I am convinced that *satyagraha* had nothing to do with the violence of the mob and that many swarmed round the banner of mischief raised by the mob, largely because of their affection for Anasuyabai and myself. Had the Government in an unwise manner not prevented me from entering Delhi and so compelled me to disobey their order, I feel certain that Ahmedabad and Viramgam would have remained free from the horrors of the past week. In other words, *satyagraha* has neither been the cause nor the occasion of the upheaval. If anything, the presence of *satyagraha* has acted as a check even so slight upon the previously existing lawless elements. As regards events in the Punjab, it is admitted that they are unconnected with the *satyagraha* movement.

In the course of the *satyagraha* struggle in South Africa, several thousands of indentured Indians had struck work. This was a *satyagraha* strike and therefore entirely peaceful and voluntary. Whilst the strike was going on, a strike of European miners, railway employees, etc., was declared. Overtures were made to me to make common cause with the European strik-

ers. As a *satyagrahi*, I did not require a moment's consideration to decline to do so. I went further and for fear of our
strike being classed with the strike of Europeans in which
methods of violence and use of arms found a prominent place,
ours was suspended and *satyagraha* from that moment came to
be recognized by the Europeans of South Africa as an honourable and honest movement—in the words of General
Smuts, a constitutional movement. I can do no less at the
present critical moment. I would be untrue to *satyagraha*, if I
allowed it by any action of mine to be used as an occasion for
feeding violence for embittering relations between the English
and the Indians. Our *satyagraha* must therefore now consist in
ceaselessly helping the authorities in all the ways available to
us as *satyagrahis* to restore order and to curb lawlessness. We
can turn the tragedies going on before us to good account if
we could but succeed in gaining the adherence of the masses
to the fundamental principles of *satyagraha*.

Satyagraha is like a banyan tree with innumerable branches.
Civil disobedience is one such branch, *satya* (truth) and *ahimsa*
(non-violence) together make the parent trunk from which all
innumerable branches shoot out. We have found by bitter
experience that whilst in an atmosphere of lawlessness, civil
disobedience found ready acceptance. *Satya* and *ahimsa*, from
which alone civil disobedience can worthily spring, have com-
manded little or no respect. Ours then is a Herculean task,
but we may not shirk it. We must fearlessly spread the doctrine of *satya* and *ahimsa* and then, and not till then, shall we
be able to undertake mass *satyagraha*.

My attitude towards the Rowlatt legislation remains un-
changed. Indeed, I do feel that the Rowlatt legislation is one
of the many causes of the present unrest. But in a surcharged
atmosphere, I must refrain from examining these causes. The
main and only purpose of this letter is to advise all *satyagrahis*
to temporarily suspend civil disobedience, to give Government
effective co-operation in restoring order and by preaching and
practice to gain adherence to the fundamental principles mentioned above.

Press Statement on Suspension of Civil Disobedience
The Hindu, 21 Apr. 1919

202. LOYALTY AND DISLOYALTY

There is no halfway house between active loyalty and active disloyalty. There is much truth in the late Justice Stephen's remark that a man to prove himself not guilty of disaffection must prove himself to be actively affectionate. In these days of democracy there is no such thing as active loyalty to a person. You are therefore loyal or disloyal to institutions. When, therefore, you are disloyal you seek not to destroy persons but institutions. The present State is an institution which, if one knows it, can never evoke loyalty. It is corrupt. Many of its laws governing the conduct of persons are positively inhuman. Their administration is worse. Often the will of one person is the law. It may safely be said that there are as many rulers as there are districts in this country. These, called Collectors, combine in their own persons the executive as well as the judicial functions. Though their acts are supposed to be governed by laws in themselves highly defective, these rulers are often capricious and regulated by nothing but their own whims and fancies. They represent not the interests of the people but those of their foreign masters or principals. These (nearly three hundred) men form an almost secret corporation, the most powerful in the world. They are required to find a fixed minimum of revenue, they have therefore often been found to be most unscrupulous in their dealings with the people.

This system of government is confessedly based upon a merciless exploitation of unnumbered millions of the inhabitants of India. From the village Headmen to their personal assistants these satraps have created a class of subordinates who, whilst they cringe before their foreign masters, in their constant dealings with the people act so irresponsibly and so harshly as to demoralize them and by a system of terrorism render them incapable of resisting corruption. It is then the duty of those who have realized the awful evil of the system of Indian Government to be disloyal to it and actively and openly to preach disloyalty. Indeed, loyalty to a State so corrupt is a sin, disloyalty a virtue.

The spectacle of three hundred million people being cowed down by living in the dread of three hundred men is demoralizing alike for the despots as for the victims. It is the duty of those who have realized the evil nature of the system, however attractive some of its features may, torn from their context, appear to be, to destroy it without delay. It is their clear duty to run any risk to achieve the end.

But it must be equally clear that it would be cowardly for three hundred million people to seek to destroy the three hundred authors or administrators of the system. It is a sign of gross ignorance to devise means of destroying these administrators or their hirelings. Moreover they are but creatures of circumstances. The purest man entering the system will be affected by it and will be instrumental in propagating the evil. The remedy therefore naturally is not being enraged against the administrators and therefore hurting them, but to non-co-operate with the system by withdrawing all the voluntary assistance possible and refusing all its so-called benefits. A little reflection will show that civil disobedience is a necessary part of non-co-operation. You assist an administration most effectively by obeying its orders and decrees. An evil administration never deserves such allegiance. Allegiance to it means partaking of the evil. A good man will therefore resist an evil system or administration with his whole soul. Disobedience of the law of an evil State is therefore a duty. Violent disobedience deals with men who can be replaced. It leaves the evil itself untouched and often accentuates it. Non-violent, i.e., civil, disobedience is the only and the most successful remedy and is obligatory upon him who would dissociate himself from evil.

There is danger in civil disobedience only because it is still only a partially tried remedy and has always to be tried in an atmosphere surcharged with violence. For when tyranny is rampant much rage is generated among the victims. It remains latent because of their weakness and bursts in all its fury on the slightest pretext. Civil disobedience is a sovereign method of transmuting this undisciplined life-destroying latent energy into disciplined life-saving energy whose use ensures absolute success. The attendant risk is nothing compared to the result promised. When the world has become familiar with its use and when it has had a series of demonstrations of its successful working, there will be less risk in civil disobedience than there is in aviation, in spite of that science having reached a high stage of development.

'Duty of Disloyalty'
Young India, 27 Mar. 1930

203. BLOODLESS NON-CO-OPERATION

I have most carefully read the manifesto[1] addressed by Sir Narayan Chandavarkar and others dissuading the people from joining the non-co-operation movement. I had expected to find some solid argument against non-co-operation, but to my great regret I have found in it nothing but distortion (no doubt unconscious) of the great religions and history. The manifesto says that 'non-co-operation is deprecated by the religious tenets and traditions of our motherland, nay, of all the religions that have saved and elevated the human race'. I venture to submit that the *Bhagavad Gita* is a gospel of non-co-operation between forces of darkness and those of light. If it is to be literally interpreted, Arjuna representing a just cause was enjoined to engage in bloody warfare with the unjust Kauravas.[2] Tulsidas[3] advises the *Sant* (the good) to shun the *Asant* (the evil-doers). The *Zend-Avesta* represents a perpetual duel between Ormuzd and Ahriman, between whom there is no compromise. To say of the Bible that it taboos non-co-operation is not to know Jesus, a prince among passive resisters, who uncompromisingly challenged the might of the Sadducees and the Pharisees and for the sake of truth did not hesitate to divide sons from their parents. And what did the Prophet of Islam do? He non-co-operated in Mecca in a most active manner so long as his life was not in danger and wiped the dust of Mecca off his feet when he found that he and his followers might have uselessly to perish, and fled to Medina and returned when he was strong enough to give battle to his opponents.

The duty of non-co-operation with unjust men and kings is as strictly enjoined by all the religions as is the duty of co-operation with just men and kings. Indeed most of the scriptures of the world seem even to go beyond non-co-operation and prefer violence to effeminate submission to a wrong. The

Hindu religious tradition, of which the manifesto speaks, clearly proves the duty of non-co-operation. Prahlad[4] dissociated himself from his father, Mirabai[5] from her husband, Bibhishan[6] from his brutal brother.

The manifesto speaking of the secular aspect says, 'The history of nations affords no instance to show that it [non-co-operation] has, when employed, succeeded and done good.' One most recent instance of brilliant success of non-co-operation is that of General Botha who boycotted Lord Milner's reformed councils and thereby procured a perfect constitution for his country. The Dukhobours[7] of Russia offered non-co-operation, and a handful though they were, their grievances so deeply moved the civilized world that Canada offered them a home where they form a prosperous community. In India instances can be given by the dozen, in which in little principalities the *raiyats*[8] when deeply grieved by their chiefs have cut off all connection with them and bent them to their will. I know of no instance in history where well managed non-co-operation has failed.

Hitherto I have given historical instances of bloodless non-co-operation. I will not insult the intelligence of the reader by citing historical instances of non-co-operation combined with violence, but I am free to confess that there are on record as many successes as failures in violent non-co-operation. And it is because I know this fact that I have placed before the country a non-violent scheme in which, if at all worked satisfactorily, success is a certainty and in which non-response means no harm. For if even one man non-co-operates, say, by resigning some office, he has gained, not lost. That is its ethical or religious aspect. For its political result naturally it requires polymerous support. I fear therefore no disastrous result from non-co-operation save for an outbreak of violence on the part of the people whether under provocation or otherwise. I would risk violence a thousand times than risk the emasculation of a whole race.

'Crusade Against Non-Co-operation'
Young India, 4 Aug. 1920

[1] Signed by Sir Narayan Chandavarkar, Gokuldas K. Parekh, Phiroze Sethna, C. V. Mehta, Jamnadas Dwarkadas, K. Natarajan, H. P. Mody, Uttumlal K. Trivedi,

B. C. Dalvi, Mawji Govindji, N. M. Joshi, Kanji Dwarkadas and others and published in *The Bombay Chronicle*, 30 July 1920.

    [2] Sons of King Dhritarashtra and cousins of the Pandavas.

    [3] The great Hindi poet; author of *Ramacharitamanasa*, a Hindi version of the *Ramayana*.

    [4] Devotee of Vishnu, was persecuted by his disbelieving father, the demon king Hiranyakashipu. Gandhi often spoke of him as the ideal *satyagrahi*.

    [5] A medieval saint-poetess of Rajasthan; queen of Mewar, she spent her days in devotions to Krishna, incurring her husband's displeasure.

    [6] The virtuous brother of Ravana. He tried long and hard to convert Ravana but, failing in his attempts, went over to Rama before the great battle began.

    [7] 'Spirit-wrestlers'; a non-conformist Russian sect which emigrated to Canada in 1898.

    [8] Tenants.

204. NON-CO-OPERATION AND SOCIAL REFORM

A gentleman writes . . .[1]

The principle which we have applied to the system of British Government is applicable here also. If the people co-operate in order not to allow that system to continue, its foundation will go; it will crumble right today. Similarly, if one wishing to end the empire of evil customs offers non-co-operation that empire will certainly crack up. The question naturally arises as to what purpose will be served if only one person non-co-operates thus. One answer to this is that he who launches non-co-operation wins and becomes free from faults, and the empire is weakened to the extent of the loss of his co-operation. A house does not collapse if a single brick is removed, but everyone realizes that from the day the brick came off, the house has certainly begun to get weakened. While it is difficult for the first brick to get loose, it is not so for the second brick to fall away or get removed.

Every reform in the world has been initiated by the efforts of one man. Today even an appropriate atmosphere has been created in respect of evil customs like child-marriage, etc. Those who regard them as evil customs are lax only in regard to acting against them. If we today try to take an opinion poll, the majority will hold that customs like child-marriage and spending lavishly on marriages are evil, and costly dresses of foreign material are reprehensible and evil. Majority opinion can be had against other such evil customs. Despite this, they have not disappeared because those who are opposed to them are truly speaking weak and, while they are brave in bragging, they are afraid to act. That cowardice will disappear only when a number of people refrain from attending such functions even by putting themselves to trouble.

'How to Tackle Evil Customs' (G.)
Navajivan, 14 Mar. 1926

[1] The correspondent had asked how one could rid one's caste of customs like child-marriage, use of costly foreign dresses and lavish expenditure on marriages.

205. SOCIAL BOYCOTT AND SOCIAL SERVICE

Non-co-operation being a movement of purification is bringing to the surface all our weaknesses as also excesses of even our strong points. Social boycott is an age-old institution. It is coeval with caste. It is the one terrible sanction exercised with great effect. It is based upon the notion that a community is not bound to extend its hospitality or service to an excommunicate. It answered when every village was a self-contained unit, and the occasions of recalcitrancy were rare. But when opinion is divided, as it is today, on the merits of non-co-operation, when its new application is having a trial, a summary use of social boycott in order to bend a minority to the will of the majority is a species of unpardonable violence. If persisted in, such boycott is bound to destroy the movement. Social boycott is applicable and effective when it is not felt as a punishment and accepted by the object of boycott as a measure of discipline. Moreover, social boycott to be admissible in a campaign of non-violence must never savour of inhumanity. It must be civilized. It must cause pain to the party using it, if it causes inconvenience to its object. Thus, depriving a man of the services of a medical man, as is reported to have been done in Jhansi, is an act of inhumanity tantamount in the moral code to an attempt to murder.

I see no difference in murdering a man and withdrawing

medical aid from a man who is on the point of dying. Even the laws of war, I apprehend, require the giving of medical relief to the enemy in need of it. To deprive a man of the use of an only village-well is notice to him to quit that village. Surely, non-co-operators have acquired no right to use that extreme pressure against those who do not see eye to eye with them. Impatience and intolerance will surely kill this great religious movement. We may not make people pure by compulsion. Much less may we compel them by violence to respect our opinion. It is utterly against the spirit of democracy we want to cultivate.

There are no doubt serious difficulties in our way. The temptation to resort to social boycott is irresistible when a defendant, who submits to private arbitration, refuses to abide by its award. Yet it is easy to see that the application of social boycott is more than likely to arrest the splendid movement to settle disputes by arbitration which, apart from its use as a weapon in the armoury of non-co-operation, is a movement fraught with great good to the country. People will take time before they accommodate themselves to private arbitration. Its very simplicity and inexpensiveness will repel many people even as palates jaded by spicy foods are repelled by simple combinations. All awards will not always be above suspicion. We must therefore rely upon the intrinsic merits of the movement and the correctness of awards to make itself felt.

It is much to be desired if we can bring about a complete *voluntary* boycott of law courts. That one event can bring about *swaraj*. But it was never expected that we would reach completion in any single item of non-co-operation. Public opinion has been so far developed as to recognize the courts as signs not of our liberty but of our slavery. It has made it practically impossible for lawyers to practise their profession and be called popular leaders.

Non-co-operation has greatly demolished the prestige of law courts and to that extent of the Government. The disintegrating process is slowly but surely going on. Its velocity will suffer diminution if violent methods are adopted to hasten it. This Government of ours is armed to the teeth to meet and check forces of violence. It possesses nothing to check the mighty forces of non-violence. How can a handful of Englishmen resist a voluntary expression of opinion accompanied by the voluntary self-denial of thirty crores of people?

I hope, therefore, that non-co-operation workers will beware of the snares of social boycott. But the alternative to social boycott is certainly not social intercourse. A man who defies strong, clear public opinion on vital matters is not entitled to social amenities and privileges. We may not take part in his social functions such as marriage feasts, we may not receive gifts from him. But we dare not deny social service. The latter is a duty. Attendance at dinner parties and the like is a privilege which it is optional to withhold or extend. But it would be wisdom to err on the right side and to exercise the weapon even in the limited sense described by me on rare and well-defined occasions. And in every case the user of the weapons will use it at his own risk. The use of it is not as yet in any form a duty. No one is entitled to its use if there is any danger of hurting the movement.

'Social Boycott'
Young India, 16 Feb. 1921

206. THE WEAPON OF LABOUR

March 15, 1918[1]

As the weapon of the rich is money, that of the workers is their labour. Just as a rich man would starve if he did not employ his wealth, even so if the worker did not employ his wealth—did not work—he would also starve. One who does not work is not a worker. A worker who is ashamed of working has no right to eat. If, therefore, the workers desire to fulfil their pledge in this great struggle, they should learn to do some work or other. Those who collect funds and, remaining idle, maintain themselves out of them do not deserve to win. Workers are fighting for their pledge. Those who want food without working for it do not, it may be said, understand what a pledge means. He alone can keep his pledge who can feel shame or has self-respect. Is there anyone who will not look down on those who desire to be maintained on public funds without doing any work? It behoves us, therefore, that we maintain ourselves by doing some work. If a worker does not work, he is like sugar which has lost its sweetness. If the sea-water lost its salt, where would we get our salt from? If the worker did not work, the world would come to an end.

This struggle is not merely for a 35 per cent increase; it is to show that workers are prepared to suffer for their rights. We are fighting to uphold our honour. We have launched on this struggle in order to better ourselves. If we start using public funds improperly, we shall grow worse and not better. Consider the matter from any angle you choose, you will see that we must maintain ourselves by our own labour. Farhad[2] broke stones for the sake of Shirin, his beloved. For the workers, their pledge is their Shirin. Why should they not break stones for its sake? For the sake of truth, Harishchandra[3] sold himself; why should workers not suffer hardships for upholding their pledge? For the sake of their honour, Imam Hassan and Hussain suffered greatly. Should we not be prepared even to die for our honour? If we get money while we remain idle at home and fight with that money, it would be untrue to say that we are fighting.

We hope, therefore, that every worker will work to maintain himself so that he may be able to keep his oath and remain firm. If the struggle lengthens, it will be because of weakness on our part. So long as the mill-owners believe that workers will not take to any labour and, therefore, will eventually succumb, they will have no compassion and will continue to resist the demand. So long as they are not convinced that workers will never give in, they will not be moved by compassion and will continue to oppose the workers even at the sacrifice of their own profits. When, however, they feel certain that the workers will, under no circumstances, give up their resolve, they will show compassion enough and welcome the workers back. Today the employers believe that the workers will not do any manual labour and so are bound to succumb soon. If the workers depend on others' money for their maintenance, the mill-owners will think that the source is bound to be exhausted sooner or later, and so will not take the workers seriously. If, on the other hand, workers who have no other means of subsistence begin to do manual work, the employers will see that they will lose their workers unless they grant the 35 per cent increase forthwith. Thus, it is for us to shorten or lengthen the struggle. We shall be free the sooner by enduring greater suffering just now. If we flinch from suffering, the struggle is bound to be protracted. Those who have weakened will, we hope, consider all these points and become strong again.

Some workers are inclined to believe that those who have weakened cannot be persuaded to become strong. This is a wrong impression altogether. It is the duty of us all—yours and ours—to try, with gentleness, to persuade those who have weakened for one reason or another. It is also our duty to educate those who do not know what the struggle means. What we have been saying is that we may not use threats, tell lies, or resort to violence, or exert pressure in any manner to keep anyone away from work. If, despite persuasion, anyone resumes work, that is no reason for us to lose heart. Even if only one person holds out, we shall never forsake him.

'Ahmedabad Mill-Hands' Strike',
Leaflet No. 14 (G.)
Ek Dharmayuddha

---

[1] This leaflet was issued on the day Gandhi commenced his fast.

[2] Central figure in a Persian poem.

[3] Legendary king of Ayodhya who went through many ordeals for the sake of truth.

207. FASTING AND TRUE *SATYAGRAHA*

[12 September 1926]

There are many forms of *satyagraha*, of which fasting may or may not be one, according to the circumstances of the case. A friend has put the following poser:

A man wants to recover money another owes him. He cannot do so by going to law as he is a non-co-operator, and the debtor in the intoxication of the power of his wealth pays him no heed, and refuses even to accept arbitration. If in these circumstances, the creditor sits *dharna* at the debtor's door, would it not be *satyagraha*? The fasting creditor seeks to injure no one by his fasting. Ever since the golden age of Rama, we have been following this method. But I am told you regard this as intimidation. If you do, will you kindly explain?

I know the correspondent. He has written from the purest motive. But I have no doubt that he is mistaken in his interpretation of *satyagraha*. *Satyagraha* can never be resorted to for personal gain. If fasting with a view to recovering money is to be encouraged, there would be no end of scoundrels blackmailing people by resorting to the means. I know that many such people are to be met with in the country. It is not right to argue that those who rightly resort to fasting need not be condemned because it is abused in a few cases. Any and everyone may not draw his own distinction between fasting—*satyagraha*—true and false. What one regards as true *satyagraha* may very likely be otherwise. *Satyagraha*, therefore, cannot be resorted to for personal gain, but only for the good of others. A *satyagrahi* should always be ready to undergo suffering and pecuniary loss. That there would not be wanting dishonest people to reap an undue advantage from the boycott of lawcourts practised by good people was a contingency not unexpected at the inception of non-co-operation. It was then thought that the beauty of non-co-operation lay just in taking those risks.

But *satyagraha* in the form of fasting cannot be undertaken as against an opponent. Fasting can be resorted to only against one's nearest and dearest, and that solely for his or her good.

In a country like India, where the spirit of charity or pity is not lacking, it would be nothing short of an outrage to resort to fasting for recovering money. I know people who have given away money, quite against their will, but out of a false sense of pity. The *satyagrahi* has, therefore, to proceed warily in a land like ours. It is likely that some men may succeed in recovering money due to them by resorting to fasting; but instead of calling it a triumph of *satyagraha*, I would call it a triumph of *duragraha* or violence. The triumph of *satyagraha* consists in meeting death in the insistence on truth. A *satyagrahi* is always unattached to the attainment of the object of *satyagraha*; one seeking to recover money cannot be so unattached. I am therefore clear that fasting for the sake of personal gain is nothing short of intimidation and the result of ignorance.

'*Satyagraha*—True and False' (G.)
Navajivan, 12 Sept. 1926
Young India, 30 Sept. 1926

208. CONSTRUCTIVE AND PARLIAMENTARY WORK

Sodepur,
December 18, 1945

Dear Sister,

I was happy to read your letter. Your Hindi is not in any way inferior to mine.

Everyone should do some constructive work over and above parliamentary work. And the aim of parliamentary work should also be to advance constructive work.

Yours,
M. K. GANDHI

Shri Anasuyabai Kale
Anand Bhavan
Dhantoli
Nagpur

Letter to Anasuyabai Kale (H.)
From a copy of the Hindi: *Pyarelal Papers*

209. NEED FOR BOLD CONSTRUCTIVE WORKERS

May 13, 1947

Independence is now as good as come. But it is only political independence. Let not anyone think that once the British quit India there will be more comfort and convenience and the Constructive Programme would become superfluous. But from the prevailing atmosphere it seems that for at least a decade after independence our condition would continue to deteriorate. This political freedom no doubt will remove the restraints over us and we shall be able to accomplish our cherished aims. Real hard work will have to be done only after independence. Unless poverty and unemployment are wiped out from India, I would not agree that we have attained freedom. Real wealth does not consist in jewellery and money, but in providing for proper food, clothes, education, and creating healthy conditions of living for every one of us. A country can be called prosperous and free only when its citizens can easily earn enough to meet their needs. But today the situation is so tragic that on the one hand there are people who roll in pomp and luxury and on the other there are people who do not have enough clothes to cover their bodies and who live on the brink of starvation. Today men are sitting idle having no work to do. A man should have full opportunity to develop himself. That will happen only when there is an awakening among the constructive workers.

The country does need politicians. But now when it is necessary to work hard for the prosperity of the country we need devoted constructive workers. I am convinced that people who are wedded to machinery are going to be disillusioned. Everyone, if only after being disillusioned, will have to ply the *charkha*. One has to be self-reliant in everything. If people do not start working of their own free will, time and circumstances will make them do so. But right now I find it suffocating to see the manner in which we are marching towards freedom. I find no light anywhere. Now that the British are contemplating transfer of power every community is keen on grabbing it. But, if we do not do our duty, we will be giving a chance for the people to say that slavery was better than this freedom. To the extent the constructive workers are bold and fearless, these qualities would be reflected in their actions and through their work spread in the atmosphere. If the nation breathes such a healthy air, it would definitely grow healthy. So, the time has come for every constructive worker to gird up his loins and plunge into action. Let him put this moment to good use and justify the life God has granted him.

'Advice to Constructive Workers' (G.)
Biharni Komi Agman, pp. 346–7

XIV

Swaraj—Freedom and Self-Rule

---

210. INDEPENDENCE AND DECENTRALIZATION

Panchgani
July 21, 1946

Q. You have said in your article in the *Harijan* of July 15, under the caption 'The Real Danger', that Congressmen in general certainly do not know the kind of independence they want. Would you kindly give them a broad but comprehensive picture of the Independent India of your own conception?

A. I do not know that I have not, from time to time, given my idea of Indian independence. Since, however, this question is part of a series, it is better to answer it even at the risk of repetition.

Independence of India should mean independence of the whole of India, including what is called India of the States and the other foreign powers, French and Portuguese, who are there, I presume, by British sufferance. Independence must mean that of the people of India, not of those who are today ruling over them. The rulers should depend on the will of those who are under their heels. Thus, they have to be servants of the people, ready to do their will.

Independence must begin at the bottom. Thus, every village will be a republic or panchayat having full powers. It follows, therefore, that every village has to be self-sustained and capable of managing its affairs even to the extent of defending itself against the whole world. It will be trained and prepared to perish in the attempt to defend itself against any onslaught from without. Thus, ultimately, it is the individual who is the unit. This does not exclude dependence on and willing help from neighbours or from the world. It will be free and voluntary play of mutual forces. Such a society is necessarily highly cultured in which every man and woman knows what he or she wants and, what is more, knows that no one should want anything that others cannot have with equal labour.

This society must naturally be based on truth and non-violence which, in my opinion, are not possible without a living belief in God, meaning a self-existent, all-knowing living Force which inheres every other force known to the world and which depends on none and which will live when all other forces may conceivably perish or cease to act. I am unable to account for my life without belief in this all-embracing living Light.

In this structure composed of innumerable villages, there will be ever-widening, never-ascending circles. Life will not be a pyramid with the apex sustained by the bottom. But it will be an oceanic circle whose centre will be the individual always ready to perish for the village, the latter ready to perish for the circle of villages, till at last the whole becomes one life composed of individuals, never aggressive in their arrogance but ever humble, sharing the majesty of the oceanic circle of which they are integral units.

Therefore the outermost circumference will not wield power to crush the inner circle but will give strength to all within and derive its own strength from it. I may be taunted with the retort that this is all Utopian and, therefore, not worth a single thought. If Euclid's point, though incapable of being drawn by human agency, has an imperishable value, my picture has its own for mankind to live. Let India live for this true picture, though never realizable in its completeness. We must have a proper picture of what we want, before we can have something approaching it. If there ever is to be a republic of every village in India, then I claim verity for my picture in which the last is equal to the first or, in other words, no one is to be the first and none the last.

In this picture every religion has its full and equal place. We are all leaves of a majestic tree whose trunk cannot be shaken off its roots which are deep down in the bowels of the earth. The mightiest wind cannot move it.

In this there is no room for machines that would displace human labour and that would concentrate power in a few hands. Labour has its unique place in a cultured human family. Every machine that helps every individual has a place. But I must confess that I have never sat down to think out what that machine can be. I have thought of Singer's sewing machine. But even that is perfunctory. I do not need it to fill in my picture.

ç. Do you believe that the proposed Constituent Assembly could be used for the realization of your picture?

A. The Constituent Assembly has all the possibilities for the realization of my picture. Yet I cannot hope for much, not because the State Paper holds no such possibilities but because the document, being wholly of a voluntary nature, requires the common consent of the many parties to it. These have no common goal. Congressmen themselves are not of one mind even on the contents of Independence. I do not know how many swear by non-violence or the *charkha* or, believing in decentralization, regard the village as the nucleus. I know on the contrary that many would have India become a first-class military power and wish for India to have a strong centre and build the whole structure round it. In the medley of these conflicts I know that if India is to be leader in clean action based on clean thought, God will confound the wisdom of these big men and will provide the villages with the power to express themselves as they should.

Q. If the Constituent Assembly fizzles out because of the 'danger from within', as you have remarked in the above-mentioned article, would you advise the Congress to accept the alternative of general country-wide strike and capture of power, either non-violently or with the use of necessary force? What is your alternative in that eventuality if the above is not approved by you?

A. I must not contemplate darkness before it stares me in the face. And in no case can I be party, irrespective of non-violence, to a universal strike and capture of power. Though, therefore, I do not know what I should do in the case of a breakdown, I know that the actuality will find me ready with an alternative. My sole reliance being on the living Power which we call God, He will put the alternative in my hands when the time has come, not a minute sooner.

'Independence'
Harijan, 28 July 1946

211. *SWARAJ* AND COMPLETE INDEPENDENCE

December 28, 1926[1]

You are seeking to inculcate a spirit of complete independence among those who are divided amongst themselves. A wise man does not attempt to take a bigger bite than he can digest. Supposing complete independence was something infinitely superior to *swaraj*, even then I suggest to you to be patient and attain what is possible at the present moment and then mount further steps. One step is now enough for me, but coming to the rock-bottom, I suggest to you that *swaraj* includes complete independence, and because it included this, Mr. Jinnah and Pandit Malaviya resisted it, and Mr. Jinnah even went out. We want to make it absolutely clear that we want to remain within the Empire if it may be possible. Why do you lose all faith in human nature and in yourself? Why do you lose faith in your ability to bend down the haughtiness of the Englishmen and make them serve you? If you have repugnance against the white skin, do you want to drive away every Englishman and not keep any, even for teaching you English? Take the instance of South Africa; there is that haughty nation the Dutch Boer. Even they do not bring in such a resolution. General Hertzog has returned from London completely converted. He knows, if he wants to declare independence today he can get it. I shall not be satisfied with any constitution that we may get from the British Parliament unless it leaves that power with us also. So that if we choose to declare independence we could do so. Do not impair the effect that the word carries. Do not limit its interpretation. Who knows, somebody may give us a still better definition and is, I would say, undefinable.

Speech at Congress Session, Gauhati
The Searchlight, 2 Jan. 1927

[1] Gandhi was speaking on the Independence Resolution in the Subjects Committee.

212. *SWARAJ*, FREEDOM, AND INDEPENDENCE

It is said that the Independence Resolution is a fitting answer to Lord Birkenhead. If this be a serious contention, we have little notion of the answer that we should make to the appointment of the Statutory Commission and the circumstances attending the announcement of the appointment. The act of appointment needs, for an answer, not speeches, however heroic they may be, not declarations, however brave they may be, but corresponding action adequate to the act of the British Minister, his colleagues and his followers. Supposing the Congress had passed no resolution whatsoever, but had just made a bonfire of every yard of foreign cloth in its possession, and induced a like performance on the part of the whole nation, it would have been some answer, though hardly adequate, to what the act of appointment means. If the Congress could have brought about a strike of every Government employee beginning with the Chief Judges and ending with the petty peons, not excluding soldiers, that act would have been a fairly adequate answer. It would certainly have disturbed the comfortable equanimity with which the British ministers and those concerned are looking upon all our heroics.

It may be said this is merely a counsel of perfection which I should know is not capable of execution. I do not hold that view. Many Indians who are not speaking today are undoubtedly preparing in their own manner for the happy day when every Indian now sustaining the system of Government which keeps the nation in bondage, will leave the denationalizing service. It is contended that it is courage, it is undoubtedly wisdom, to restrain the tongue whilst one is unprepared for action. Mere brave speech without action is letting off useless steam. And the strongest speech shed its bravery when, in 1920, patriots learnt to court imprisonment for strong speeches. Speech is necessary for those who are dumbstruck. Restraint is necessary for the garrulous. The English administrators chaff us for our speech and occasionally betray by their acts their contempt of our speeches and thereby tell us more effectively than by words: 'Act if you dare.' Till we can take up the challenge, every single threatening speech or gesture of ours is, in my opinion, a humiliation, and admission of

impotence. I have seen prisoners in chains spitting forth oaths
only to provide mirth for their jailors.

Moreover, has independence suddenly become a goal in
answer to something offensive that some Englishman has
done? Do men conceive their goals in order to oblige people
or to resent their action? I submit that, if it is a goal, it must
be declared and pursued irrespective of the acts or threats of
others.

Let us, therefore, understand what we mean by independence. England, Russia, Spain, Italy, Turkey, Chile, Bhutan
have all their independence. Which independence do we
want? I must not be accused of begging the question. For, if
I were told that it is Indian independence that is desired, it
is possible to show that no two persons will give the same
definition. The fact of the matter is that we do not know
our distant goal. It will be determined not by our definitions
but by our acts, voluntary and involuntary. If we are
wise, we will take care of the present and the future will
take care of itself. God has given us only a limited sphere of
action and a limited vision. Sufficient unto the day is the good
thereof.

I submit that *swaraj* is an all-satisfying goal for all time. We
the English-educated Indians often unconsciously make the
terrible mistake of thinking that the microscopic minority of
English-speaking Indians is the whole of India. I defy anyone
to give for independence a common Indian word intelligible
to the masses. Our goal at any rate may be known by an
indigenous word understood of the three hundred millions.
And we have such a word in 'swaraj' first used in the name of
the nation by Dadabhai Naoroji.[1] It is infinitely greater than
and includes independence. It is a vital word. It has been
sanctified by the noble sacrifices of thousands of Indians. It is
a word which, if it has not penetrated the remotest corner of
India, has at least got the largest currency of any similar
word. It is a sacrilege to displace that word by a foreign
importation of doubtful value. This Independence Resolution
is perhaps the final reason for conducting Congress proceedings in Hindustani and that alone. No tragedy like that of the
Independence Resolution would then have been possible. The
most valiant speakers would then have ornamented the native

meaning of the word '*swaraj*' and attempted all kinds of definitions, glorious and inglorious. Would that the independents would profit by their experience and resolve henceforth to work among the masses for whom they desire freedom and taboo English speech in its entirety in so far as mass meetings such as the Congress are concerned.

Personally, I crave not for 'independence', which I do not understand, but I long for freedom from the English yoke. I would pay any price for it. I would accept chaos in exchange for it. For the English peace is the peace of the grave. Anything would be better than this living death of a whole people. This Satanic rule has well-nigh ruined this fair land materially, morally and spiritually. I daily see its law-courts denying justice and murdering truth. I have just come from terrorized Orissa. This rule is using my own countrymen for its sinful sustenance. I have a number of affidavits swearing that, in the district of Khurda, acknowledgments of enhancement of revenue are being forced from the people practically at the point of the bayonet. The unparalleled extravagance of this rule has demented the Rajas and the Maharajas who, unmindful of consequences, ape it and grind their subjects to dust. In order to protect its immoral commerce, this rule regards no means too mean, and in order to keep three hundred millions under the heels of a hundred thousand, it carries a military expenditure which is keeping millions in a state of semi-starvation and polluting thousands of mouths with intoxicating liquor.

But my creed is non-violence under all circumstances. My method is conversion, not coercion; it is self-suffering, not the suffering of the tyrant. I know that method to be infallible. I know that a whole people can adopt it without accepting it as its creed and without understanding its philosophy. People generally do not understand the philosophy of all their acts. My ambition is much higher than independence. Through the deliverance of India, I seek to deliver the so-called weaker races of the earth from the crushing heels of Western exploitation in which England is the greatest partner. If India converts, as it can convert, Englishmen, it can become the predominant partner in a world commonwealth of which England can have the privilege of becoming a partner if she chooses. India has the right, if she only knew, of becoming the predominant partner by reason of her numbers, geographical position and culture inherited for ages. This is big talk, I know. For a fallen India to aspire to move the world and protect weaker races is seemingly an impertinence. But in explaining my strong opposition to this cry for independence, I can no longer hide the light under a bushel. Mine is an ambition worth living for and worth dying for. In no case do I want to reconcile myself to a state lower than the best for fear of consequences. It is, therefore, not out of expedience that I oppose independence as my goal. I want India to come to her own and that state cannot be better defined by any single word than '*swaraj*'. Its content will vary with the action that the nation is able to put forth at a given moment. India's coming to her own will mean every nation doing likewise.

'Independence v. *Swaraj*'
Young India, 12 Jan. 1928

¹ In his presidential address at the Calcutta Congress in 1906, Dadabhai Naoroji used the word '*swaraj*' as a synonym for 'self-government'.

213. A LIFE-AND-DEATH STRUGGLE

Oxford,¹
October 24, 1931

Sir Gilbert Murray ... seemed to be very much perturbed over what he thought were most dangerous manifestations of non-violent revolution and nationalism. 'I find myself today in greater disagreement with you than even Mr. Winston Churchill', he said. Gandhi said:

You want co-operation between nations for the salvaging of civilization. I want it too, but co-operation presupposes free nations worthy of co-operation. If I am to help in creating or restoring peace and goodwill and resist disturbances thereof I must have ability to do so and I cannot do so unless my country has come to its own. At the present moment, the very movement for freedom in India is India's contribution to peace. For so long as India is a subject nation, not only she is a danger to peace, but also England which exploits India. Other nations may tolerate today England's Imperialist policy and her exploitation of other nations, but they certainly do not appreciate it; and they would gladly help in the prevention of England becoming a greater and greater menace every day. Of course you will say that India free can become a menace herself. But let us assume that she will behave herself with her doctrine of non-violence, if she achieves her freedom through it, and for all her bitter experience of being a victim to exploitation.

The objection about my talking in terms of revolution is largely answered by what I have already said about nationalism. But my movement is conditioned by one great and disturbing factor. You might of course say that there can be no non-violent rebellion and there has been none known to history. Well, it is my ambition to provide an instance, and it is my dream that my country may win its freedom through non-violence. And, I would like to repeat to the whole world times without number that I will not purchase my country's freedom at the cost of non-violence. My marriage with non-violence is such an absolute thing that I would rather commit suicide than be deflected from my position. I have not mentioned truth in this connection, simply because truth cannot be expressed except by non-violence. So, if you accept the conception, my position is sound. . . .

You may be justified in saying that I must go more warily, but, if you attack the fundamentals, you have to convince me. And I must tell you that the boycott may have nothing to do with nationalism even. It may be a question of pure reform, as without being intensely nationalistic, we can refuse to purchase your cloth and make our own. A reformer cannot always afford to wait. If he does not put into force his belief he is no reformer. Either he is too hasty or too afraid or too lazy. Who is to advise him or provide him with a barometer? You can only guide yourself with a disciplined conscience, and then run all risks with the protecting armour of truth and non-violence. A reformer could not do otherwise.

Q. Would not India wait some time before she launched on the difficult task of self-government? If we send out our soldiers, we have to be responsible for their lives, and so may it not be that the sooner you get an Indian army the better? The Muslim community said last year in a united voice that they did not want responsibility at the centre. How are we to judge?

A. The long and the short of it is that you will not trust us. Well, give us the liberty to make mistakes. If we cannot handle our affairs today, who is to say when we will be able to do so? I do not want you to determine the pace. Consciously or unconsciously you adopt the role of divinity. I ask you for a moment to come down from that pedestal. Trust us to ourselves. I cannot imagine anything worse happening than is happening today, a whole humanity lying prostrate at the feet of a small nation.

And what is this talk of being responsible for the lives of your soldiers? I issue a notice to all foreigners to enlist for military service in India, and if some Britishers will come, will you prevent them? If they will enlist, we should be responsible for their lives, as any other Government whom they serve would be. The key to self-government is without doubt the control of the army.

As regards a united demand, I must say, what I have now said several times, that you cannot have a united demand from a packed Conference. It is my case that the Congress represents the largest number of Indians. The British Ministers know it. If they do not know it, I must go back to my country and have as overwhelming an opinion as possible. We had a life-and-death struggle. One of the noblest of Englishmen[2] tried us and did not find us wanting. In consequence he opened the jail gates and appealed to the Congress to go to the Round Table Conference. We had long talks and negotiations during which we exercised the greatest patience and there was a Settlement under which the Congress agreed to be represented on the Round Table Conference. The Settlement was respected by Government more in its breach than its observance, and after much hesitation I agreed to come, if only to keep my word of honour given to that Englishman. On coming here I find that I had miscalculated the forces arrayed against India and the Congress. But that does not dismay me. I must go and qualify myself and prove by suffering that the whole country wants what it asks for. Hunter has said that success on the battle-field was the shortest cut to power. Well, we worked for success on a different battle-field. I am trying to touch your heart instead of your body. If I do not succeed this time, I shall succeed next time.

Talk at Oxford
Young India, 12 Nov. 1931

¹ Those present at the talk included Dr. Gilbert Murray, Dr. Gilbert Slater, Prof. Reginald Coupland, and Dr. Datta.
² Lord Irwin, as Viceroy of India.

214. *SWARAJ* AND EXPLOITATION

[23 February 1935]

I am afraid I must repeat the gospel to you and remind you that, when you demand *swaraj*, you do not want *swaraj* for yourself alone, but for your neighbour, too. The principle is neither metaphysical nor too philosophical for comprehension. It is just good common sense. If you love thy neighbour as thyself, he will do likewise with you.

What you say about the difficulties of a worker in the villages is too true,¹ but we have got to falsify it. We have to be true villagers without their shortcomings and failings, and I am quite sure that, when we do so, there would be no difficulty for an honest labourer to earn a living wage. But let no one come and tell me: 'I have a mother, three widowed sisters, a brother who has to be sent to England to be called to the Bar, another reading in Muir College and a third to be sent to the Indian Sandhurst.' Sure enough, work in the villages will not give such a one a 'living'! But it is possible to earn a genuine living for all the members of one's family, if all those members also will work, as do all the members in a peasant's family.

There is a conflict of interest between capital and labour, but we have to resolve it by doing our own duty. Just as pure blood is proof against poisonous germs, so will labour, when it is pure, be proof against exploitation. The labourer has but to realize that labour is also capital. As soon as labourers are properly educated and organized and they realize their strength, no amount of capital can subdue them. Organized and enlightened labour can dictate its own terms. It is no use vowing vengeance against a party because we are weak. We have to get strong. Strong hearts, enlightened minds and willing hands can brave all odds and remove all obstacles. No, 'Love thy neighbour as thyself' is no counsel of perfection. The capitalist is as much a neighbour of the labourer as the latter is a neighbour of the former, and one has to seek and win the willing co-operation of the other. Nor does the principle mean that we should accept exploitation lying down. Our internal strength will render all exploitation impossible.

Speech at Meeting of Village Workers, Nagpur
Harijan, 1 Mar. 1935

¹ A worker had said that he had found it very difficult to live like a villager in a village and make both ends meet.

215. VILLAGE *SWARAJ*

Sevagram,
July 18, 1942

Q. In view of the situation that may arise at any moment in India, would you give an outline or skeleton of a village *swaraj* committee, which could function in all village matters in the absence of, and without relying upon, an overhead Government or other organization? In particular, how would you ensure that the Committee should be fully representative and that it would act impartially, efficiently and without favour or fear? What should be the scope of authority and the machinery to enforce its commands? And what should be the manner in which a committee or an individual member of it could be removed for corruption, inefficiency or other unfitness?

A. My idea of village *swaraj* is that it is a complete republic, independent of its neighbours for its own vital wants, and yet interdependent for many others in which dependence is a necessity. Thus every village's first concern will be to grow its own food crops and cotton for its cloth. It should have a reserve for its cattle, recreation and playground for adults and children. Then if there is more land available, it will grow *useful* money crops, thus excluding *ganja*, tobacco, opium and the like. The village will maintain a village theatre, school and public hall. It will have its own waterworks, ensuring clean water supply. This can be done through controlled wells or tanks. Education will be compulsory up to the final basic course. As far as possible every activity will be conducted on the co-operative basis. There will be no castes such as we have today with their graded untouchability. Non-violence with its technique of *satyagraha* and non-co-operation will be the sanction of the village community. There will be a compulsory service of village guards who will be selected by rotation from the register maintained by the village.

The government of the village will be conducted by a Panchayat of five persons annually elected by the adult villagers, male and female, possessing minimum prescribed qualifications. These will have all the authority and jurisdiction required. Since there will be no system of punishments in the accepted sense, this Panchayat will be the legislature, judiciary and executive combined to operate for its year of office. Any village can become such a republic today without much interference even from the present Government whose sole effective connection with the villages is the exaction of the village revenue. I have not examined here the question of relations with the neighbouring villages and the centre if any. My purpose is to present an outline of village government. Here there is perfect democracy based upon individual freedom. The individual is the architect of his own government. The law of non-violence rules him and his government. He and his village are able to defy the might of a world. For the law governing every villager is that he will suffer death in the defence of his and his village's honour.

The reader may well ask me—I am asking myself while penning these lines—as to why I have not been able to model Sevagram after the picture here drawn. My answer is: I am making the attempt. I can see dim traces of success though I can show nothing visible. But there is nothing inherently impossible in the picture drawn here. To model such a village may be the work of a lifetime. Any lover of true democracy and village life can take up a village, treat it as his world and sole work, and he will find good results. He begins by being the village scavenger, spinner, watchman, medicine man and schoolmaster all at once. If nobody comes near him, he will be satisfied with scavenging and spinning.

'Question Box'
Harijan, 26 July 1942

216. INDEPENDENT INDIA OF MY DREAM

Kafilatali,
February 12, 1947

Independent India, as conceived by me, will have all Indians belonging to different religions living in perfect friendship. There need be no millionaires and no paupers; all would belong to the State, for the State belonged to them. I will die in the act of realizing this dream. I would not wish to live to see India torn asunder by civil strife.

From Speech at Prayer Meeting
The Hindu, 15 Feb. 1947

217. SELF-GOVERNMENT AND GOOD GOVERNMENT

June 6, 1947

I am replying to your letter today itself. You are gravely mistaken in assuming that as soon as *swaraj* comes prosperity will flood the country. If, before assuming that, you had used your imagination a bit to see that after 150 years of slavery, we would need at least half that much time to cleanse our body-politic of the virus that has infiltrated every cell and pore of our being during our subjection, you would not have found it necessary to ask me. I am sure you will understand what I mean, namely, that far greater sacrifices will be needed after the attainment of self-government to establish good government and raise the people than were required for the attainment of freedom by means of *satyagraha*.

'A Letter' (G.)
Bihar Pachhi Dilhi, p. 81

218. BEYOND PARTIES AND ISMS

June 7, 1947

Today the rulers are not foreigners but our own countrymen. If we do not work in perfect harmony with them, our newly-won freedom will be in danger. Let all people sit together and find a proper solution to problems on which there are differences. But our greatest defect is that, as soon as we differ from somebody ever so slightly, or a misunderstanding arises, instead of meeting the person concerned and trying to find a solution we take him to task publicly. This creates a great mental gulf between people, leading to antagonism. Parties and isms are only results of such differences. One fruit of this poison we have seen in the coming into existence of Pakistan. Are we not satisfied even with that?

You have simply not understood what socialism means. The Russian type of socialism will not suit India at all. Even in Russia their policies have not succeeded completely. Why don't you try to save the country from the calamity which has befallen it today? So long as this communal virus has not been eradicated, socialism will never come. Note down and remember, all of you, these words of an old man. The people will want to see our work and our sacrifices; they will judge our labour and look for perfection of character in us. But you wish to pay no attention to these things. On the one hand, hundreds of thousands of our brothers and sisters have become homeless. If now you incite the people and exploit these riots to establish new parties or spread your isms, rest assured God will never forgive this terrible crime of betrayal of the country.

Discussion with Socialist Workers (G.)
Bihar Pachhi Dilhi, pp. 4–5

XV

Swadeshi—Self-Reliance

219. THE MEANING OF *SWADESHI*

We examined the balance-sheet of the last year. We were unhappy at the thought that we had to follow an alien calendar in making our calculations. No cause for unhappiness would remain if *swadeshi* were to replace everything foreign. We can easily attain happiness if we exert ourselves to that end during the year that has just commenced. *Swadeshi* carries a great and profound meaning. It does not mean merely the use of what is produced in one's own country. That meaning is certainly there in *swadeshi*. But there is another meaning implied in it which is far greater and much more important. *Swadeshi* means reliance on our own strength. We should also know what we mean by 'reliance on our own strength'. 'Our strength' means the strength of our body, our mind and our soul. From among these, on which should we depend? The answer is brief. The soul is supreme, and therefore soul-force is the foundation on which man must build. Passive resistance or *satyagraha* is a mode of fighting which depends on such force. That, then, is the only real key to success for the Indians.

During this year a good deal will depend on the Transvaal and Natal. The Transvaal fight is continuing. In Natal, the issue of licences will come up. If the Indians in the Transvaal give up their fight, that will have an immediate adverse effect in Natal, because the course of events in Natal during the coming year will largely be determined by this movement. Nothing will be gained by submitting petitions to the Natal Government. How, then, may anything be gained? The Transvaal provides the answer to this. That is to say, the

answer to the question as to what this year has in store for us
will be provided by whether or not the Indians in the Transvaal fight to the last.

It may be hoped that a community from among which
2,000 men have been to gaol will never accept defeat, though
there may be some traitors in it. Looking at the matter in this
light, every Indian will find that what the new year will bring
lies entirely in his own hands.

'New Year' (G.)
Indian Opinion, 2 Jan. 1909

220. *SWADESHI* AND MASS AWAKENING

[8 April 1919]

The following is the text of the *swadeshi* vow:

With God as my witness, I solemnly declare that from today I shall
confine myself, for my personal requirements, to the use of cloth
manufactured in India from Indian cotton, silk or wool and I shall
altogether abstain from using foreign cloth, and I shall destroy all
foreign cloth in my possession.

For a proper observance of the pledge, it is really necessary
to use only hand-woven cloth made out of hand-spun yarn.
Imported yarn, even though spun out of Indian cotton and
woven in India, is not *swadeshi* cloth. We shall reach perfection
only when our cotton is spun in India on indigenous
spinning-wheels and yarn so spun is woven on similarly made
handlooms. But requirements of the foregoing pledge are met,
if we all only use cloth woven by means of imported machinery from yarn spun from Indian cotton by means of similar
machinery.

I may add that covenanters to the restricted *swadeshi* referred to here will not rest satisfied with *swadeshi* clothing
only. They will extend the vow to all other things as far as
possible.

I am told that there are in India English-owned mills which
do not admit Indian share-holders. If this information be true,

I would consider cloth manufactured in such mills to be foreign cloth. Moreover, such cloth bears the taint of ill will. However well made such cloth may be, it should be avoided. The majority do not give thought to such matters. All cannot be expected to consider whether their actions promote or retard the welfare of their country, but it behoves those, who are learned, those who are thoughtful, whose intellects are trained or who are desirous of serving their country, to test every action of theirs, whether public or private, in the manner aforesaid, and when ideals which appear to be of national importance and which have been tested by practical experience should be placed before the people as has been said in the Divine Song, 'the multitude will copy the actions of the enlightened'. Even thoughtful men and women have not hitherto generally carried on the above-mentioned self-examination. The nation has therefore suffered by reason of this neglect. In my opinion, such self-examination is only possible where there is religious perception.

Thousands of men believe that by using cloth woven in Indian mills, they comply with the requirements of the *swadeshi* vow. The fact is that most fine cloth is made of foreign cotton spun outside. Therefore the only satisfaction to be derived from the use of such cloth is that it is woven in India. Even on handlooms for very fine cloth only foreign yarn is used. The use of such cloth does not amount to an observance of *swadeshi*. To say so is simple self-deception. *Satyagraha*, i.e., insistence on truth, is necessary even in *swadeshi*. When men will say, 'we shall confine ourselves to pure *swadeshi* cloth, even though we may have to remain satisfied with a mere loin cloth', and when women will resolutely say, 'we shall observe pure *swadeshi* even though we may have to restrict ourselves to clothing just enough to satisfy the sense of modesty', then shall we be successful in the observance of the great *swadeshi* vow. If a few thousand men and women were to take the *swadeshi* vow in this spirit, others will try to imitate them so far as possible. They will then begin to examine their wardrobes in the light of *swadeshi*. Those who are not attached to pleasures and personal adornment, I venture to say, can give a great impetus to *swadeshi*.

Generally speaking, there are very few villages in India

without weavers. From time immemorial, we have had village farmers and village weavers, as we have village carpenters, shoemakers, blacksmiths, etc., but our farmers have become poverty-stricken and our weavers have patronage only from the poor classes. By supplying them with Indian cloth spun in India, we can obtain the cloth we may need. For the time being it may be coarse, but by constant endeavours, we can get our weavers to weave out of fine yarn and so doing we shall raise our weavers to a better status, and if we would go a step still further, we can easily cross the sea of difficulties lying in our path. We can easily teach our women and our children to spin and weave cotton, and what can be purer than cloth woven in our own home? I tell it from my experience that acting in this way we shall be saved from many a hardship, we shall be ridding ourselves of many an unnecessary need, and our life will be one song of joy and beauty. I always hear divine voices telling me in my ears that such life was a matter of fact once in India, but even if such an India be the idle dream of the poet, it does not matter. Is it not necessary to create such an India now, does not our *purushartha* lie therein?

I have been travelling throughout India. I cannot bear the heart-rending cry of the poor. The young and old tell me, 'We cannot get cheap cloth, we have not the means wherewith to purchase dear cloth. Everything is dear—provisions, cloth and all. What are we to do?' And they heave a sigh of despair. It is my duty to give these men a satisfactory reply. It is the duty of every servant of the country, but I am unable to give a satisfactory reply. It should be intolerable for all thinking Indians that our raw materials should be exported to Europe and that we have to pay heavy prices therefor. The first and the last remedy for this is *swadeshi*. We are not bound to sell our cotton to anybody and when Hindustan rings with the echoes of *swadeshi*, no producer of cotton will sell it for its being manufactured in foreign countries. When *swadeshi* pervades the country, everyone will be set a-thinking why cotton should not be refined and spun and woven in the place where it is produced, and when the *swadeshi mantra* resounds in every ear, millions of men will have in their hands the key to the economic salvation of India. Training for this does not require hundreds of years. When the religious sense is awakened, people's thoughts undergo a revolution in a single moment. Only selfless sacrifice is the *sine qua non*.

The spirit of sacrifice pervades the Indian atmosphere at the present moment. If we fail to preach *swadeshi* at this supreme moment, we shall have to wring our hands in despair. I beseech every Hindu, Mussulman, Sikh, Parsi, Christian and Jew, who believes that he belongs to this country, to take the *swadeshi* vow and to ask others also to do likewise. It is my humble belief that if we cannot do even this little for our country, we are born in it in vain. Those who think deep will see that such *swadeshi* contains pure economics. I hope that every man and woman will give serious thought to my humble suggestion. Imitation of English economics will spell our ruin.

'The *Swadeshi* Vow—II'
The Bombay Chronicle, 18 Apr. 1919
New India, 22 Apr. 1919

221.   *SWADESHI* AND MACHINERY

[14 September 1919]

I have observed that this doubt is felt by many people, and accordingly I have given the reply too. Pure *swadeshi* is not at all opposed to machinery. The *swadeshi* movement is meant only against the use of foreign cloth. There is no objection to weaving mill-made cloth. But I do not myself wear mill-made cloth and in the explanations to the *swadeshi* vow I have certainly suggested that it should be the ideal of every Indian to wear hand-spun and hand-woven cloth. If, fortunately for India, crores of people happen to translate this ideal into practice, the mills may perhaps have to suffer some loss. But if the whole of India makes that pure resolve, I am sure that even our mill-owners would welcome that resolve, respect its purity and associate themselves with it. But it takes long to outgrow inveterate habits. There is thus room in the country for both the mill industry and the handloom weaving. So let mills increase as also spinning-wheels and handlooms. And I should think that these latter are no doubt machines. The handloom is a miniature weaving mill. The spinning-wheel is a miniature spinning-mill. I would wish to see such beautiful little mills in every home. But the country is fully in need of the hand-spinning and hand-weaving industry.

Agriculturists in no country can live without some industry to supplement agriculture. And in India, which is entirely dependent on favourable monsoons, the spinning-wheel and the handloom are like Kamadhenus.[1] This movement is thus intended in the interests of 21 crore peasants of India. Even if we have sufficient mills in the country to produce cloth enough for the whole country, we are bound to provide our peasantry, daily being more and more impoverished, with some supplementary industry, and that which can be suitable to crores of people is hand-spinning and hand-weaving. Opposition to mills or machinery is not the point. What suits our country most is the point. I am not opposed to the movement of manufacturing machines in the country, nor to making improvements in machinery. I am only concerned with what these machines are meant for. I may ask, in the words of Ruskin, whether these machines will be such as would blow off a million men in a minute or they will be such as would turn waste lands into arable and fertile land. And if legislation were in my hands, I would penalize the manufacture of labour-saving machines and protect the industry which manufactures nice ploughs which can be handled by every man.

'*Swadeshi* v. Machinery?'
Young India, 17 Sept. 1919

---

[1] Kamadhenu is the mythical cow which bestowed anything one wished for.

222 *SWADESHI* AND *SWARAJ*

The Congress resolution has rightly emphasized the importance of *swadeshi* and thereanent of greater sacrifice by merchants.

India cannot be free so long as India voluntarily encourages or tolerates the economic drain which has been going on for the past century and a half. Boycott of foreign goods means no more and no less than boycott of foreign cloth. Foreign cloth constitutes the largest drain voluntarily permitted by us. It means sixty crores of rupees annually paid by us for piece-goods. If India could make a successful effort to stop that drain, she can gain *swaraj* by that one act.

India was enslaved for satisfying the greed of the foreign cloth manufacturer. When the East India Company came in, we were able to manufacture all the cloth we needed, and more for export. By processes that need not be described here, India has become practically wholly dependent upon foreign manufacture for her clothing.

But we ought not to be dependent. India has the ability to manufacture all her cloth if her children will work for it. Fortunately India has yet enough weavers to supplement the out-turn of her mills. The mills do not and cannot immediately manufacture all the cloth we want. The reader may not know that, even at the present moment, the weavers weave more cloth than the mills. But the latter weave five crore yards of fine foreign counts, equal to forty crore yards of coarser counts. The way to carry out a successful boycott of foreign cloth is to increase the output of yarn. And this can only be done by hand-spinning.

To bring about such a boycott, it is necessary for our merchants to stop all foreign importation, and to sell out, even at a loss, all foreign cloth already stocked in India, preferably to foreign buyers. They must cease to speculate in cotton, and keep all the cotton required for home use. They must stop purchasing all foreign cotton.

The mill-owners should work their mills not for their profits but as a national trust and therefore cease to spin finer counts, and weave only for the home market.

The householder has to revise his or her ideas of fashion and, at least for the time being, suspend the use of fine garments which are not always worn to cover the body. He should train himself to see art and beauty in the spotlessly white *khaddar* and to appreciate its soft unevenness. The householder must learn to use cloth as a miser uses his hoard.

And even when the householders have revised their tastes

about dress, somebody will have to spin yarn for the weavers. This can only be done by everyone spinning during spare hours either for love or money.

We are engaged in a spiritual war. We are not living in normal times. Normal activities are always suspended in abnormal times. And if we are out to gain *swaraj* in a year's time, it means that we must concentrate upon our goal to the exclusion of everything else. I therefore venture to suggest to the students all over India to suspend their normal studies for one year and devote their time to the manufacture of yarn by hand-spinning. It will be their greatest act of service to the motherland, and their most natural contribution to the attainment of *swaraj*. During the late War our rulers attempted to turn every factory into an arsenal for turning out bullets of lead. During this war of ours, I suggest every national school and college being turned into a factory for preparing cones of yarns for the nation. The students will lose nothing by the occupation: they will gain a kingdom here and hereafter. There is a famine of cloth in India. To assist in removing this dearth is surely an act of merit. If it is sinful to use foreign yarn, it is a virtue to manufacture more *swadeshi* yarn in order to enable us to cope with the want that would be created by the disuse of foreign yarn.

The obvious question asked would be, 'If it is so necessary to manufacture yarn, why not pay every poor person to do so?' The answer is that hand-spinning is not, and never was, a calling like weaving, carpentry, etc. Under the pre-British economy of India, spinning was an honourable and leisurely occupation for the women of India. It is difficult to revive the art among the women in the time at our disposal. But it is incredibly simple and easy for the school-goers to respond to the nation's call. Let no one decry the work as being derogatory to the dignity of man or of students. It was an art confined to the women of India because the latter had more leisure. And being graceful, musical, and as it did not involve any great exertion, it had become the monopoly of women. But it is certainly as graceful for either sex as is music, for instance. In hand-spinning is hidden the protection of women's virtue, the insurance against famine, and the cheapening of prices. In it is hidden the secret of *swaraj*. The revival of hand-spinning is the least penance we must do for the sin of our forefathers in having succumbed to Satanic influences of the foreign manufacturer.

The school-goers will restore hand-spinning to its respectable status. They will hasten the process of making *khaddar* fashionable. For no mother, or father, worth the name will refuse to wear cloth made out of yarn spun by their children. And the scholars' practical recognition of art will compel the attention of the weavers of India. If we are to wean the Punjabi from the calling not of a soldier but of the murderer of innocent and free people of other lands, we must give back to him the occupation of weaving. The race of the peaceful *julahis*[1] of the Punjab is all but extinct. It is for the scholars of the Punjab to make it possible for the Punjabi weaver to return to his innocent calling.

I hope to show in a future issue how easy it is to introduce this change in the schools and how quickly, on these terms, we can nationalize our schools and colleges. Everywhere the students have asked me what new things I would introduce into our nationalized schools. I have invariably told them I would certainly introduce spinning. I feel, so much more clearly than ever before, that, during the transition period, we must devote exclusive attention to spinning and certain other things of immediate national use, so as to make up for past neglect. And the students will be better able and equipped to enter upon the new course of studies.

Do I want to put back the hand of the clock of progress? Do I want to replace the mills by hand-spinning and hand-weaving? Do I want to replace the railway by the country cart? Do I want to destroy machinery altogether? These questions have been asked by some journalists and public men. My answer is: I would not weep over the disappearance of machinery or consider it a calamity. But I have no design upon machinery as such. What I want to do at the present moment is to supplement the production of yarn and cloth through our mills, save the millions we send out of India, and distribute them in our cottages. This I cannot do unless and until the nation is prepared to devote its leisure hours to hand-spinning. To that end we must adopt the methods I have ventured to suggest for popularizing spinning as a duty rather than as a means of livelihood.

'The Secret of *Swaraj*'
Young India, 19 Jan. 1921

<hr>

[1] Weavers.

223. THE DOCTRINE OF *SWADESHI*

Swadeshi is the law of laws enjoined by the present age. Spiritual laws, like Nature's laws, need no enacting; they are self-acting. But through ignorance or other causes man often neglects or disobeys them. It is then vows are needed to steady one's course. A man who is by temperament a vegetarian needs no vow to strengthen his vegetarianism. For, the sight of animal food, instead of tempting him, would only excite his disgust. The law of *swadeshi* is ingrained in the basic nature of man but it has today sunk into oblivion. Hence the necessity for the vow of *swadeshi*. In its ultimate and spiritual sense *swadeshi* stands for the final emancipation of the human soul from its earthly bondage. For, this earthly tabernacle is not its natural or permanent abode, it is a hindrance in its onward journey, it stands in the way of its realizing its oneness with other lives. A votary of *swadeshi* therefore, in his striving to identify himself with the entire creation, seeks to be emancipated from the bondage of the physical body.

If this interpretation of *swadeshi* be correct, then it follows that its votary will as a first duty dedicate himself to the service of his immediate neighbours. This involves exclusion or even sacrifice of the interests of the rest but the exclusion or the sacrifice would be apparent only. Pure service of one's neighbours can never, from its very nature, result in disservice to those who are remotely situated, rather the contrary. 'As with the individual so with the universe' is an unfailing principle which we would do well to lay to heart. On the other hand, a man who allows himself to be lured by 'the distant scene' and runs to the ends of the earth for service is not only foiled in his ambition but fails in his duty towards his neighbours also. Take a concrete instance. In the particular place where I live I have certain persons as my neighbours, some relations and dependents. Naturally, they all feel, as they have a right to, that they have a claim on me and look to me for help and support. Suppose now I leave them all at once and set out to serve people in a distant place. My decision would throw my little world of neighbours and dependents out of gear while my gratuitous knight-errantry would more likely than not disturb the atmosphere in the new place. Thus a culpable neglect of my immediate neighbours and an unintended disservice to the people whom I wish to serve would be the first fruits of my violation of the principles of *swadeshi*.

It is not difficult to multiply such instances. That is why the *Gita* says: 'It is better to die performing one's duty or *swadharma*, but *paradharma*, or another's duty, is fraught with danger.'[1] Interpreted in terms of one's physical environment this gives us the law of *swadeshi*. What the *Gita* says with regard to *swadharma* equally applies to *swadeshi* also, for *swadeshi* is *swadharma* applied to one's immediate environment.

It is only when the doctrine of *swadeshi* is wrongly understood that mischief results, e.g., it would be a travesty of the doctrine of *swadeshi*, if to coddle my family I set about grabbing money by all means fair or foul. The law of *swadeshi* requires me no more than to discharge my legitimate obligations towards my family by just means, and the attempt to do so will reveal to me the Universal Code of Conduct. The practice of *swadeshi* can never do harm to anyone and if it does it is not *swadharma* but egotism that moves me.

There may come occasions when a votary of *swadeshi* may be called upon to sacrifice his family at the altar of universal service. Such an act of willing immolation will then constitute the highest service rendered to the family. 'Whosoever wants to save his life will lose it, and whosoever loses his life for the Lord's sake will find it', holds good for the family group no less than the individual. Take another instance. Supposing there is an outbreak of the plague in my village and in trying to serve the victims of the epidemic I, my wife and children and all the rest of my family are wiped out of existence, then in inducing those dearest and nearest to join me I will not have acted as the destroyer of my family but on the contrary as its truest friend. In *swadeshi* there is no room for selfishness, or if there is selfishness in it, it is of the highest type which is not different from the highest altruism. *Swadeshi* in its purest form is the acme of universal service.

It was by following this line of argument that I hit upon *khadi* as a necessary and the most important corollary of the principle of *swadeshi* in its application to society. 'What is the kind of service', I asked myself, 'that the teeming millions of India most need at the present time, that can be easily understood and appreciated by all, that is easy to perform and will at the same time enable the crores of our semi-starved countrymen to live', and the reply came that it is the universalization of *khadi* or the spinning-wheel alone that can fulfil these conditions.

Let no one suppose that the practice of *swadeshi* through *khadi* would harm the foreign mill-owners. A thief who is weaned from his vice or is made to return the property that he has stolen is not harmed thereby, on the contrary he is the gainer consciously in the one case, unconsciously in the other. Similarly if all the opium addicts or the drunkards in the world were to shake themselves free from their vice, the canteen keepers or the opium vendors who would be deprived of their customers could not be said to be losers. They would be the gainers in the truest sense of the word. The elimination of the 'wages of sin' is never a loss either to the individual concerned or to society; it is pure gain.

It is the greatest delusion to suppose that the duty of *swadeshi* begins and ends with merely spinning so much yarn anyhow and wearing *khadi* made from it. *Khadi* is the first indispensable step towards the discharge of *swadeshi dharma* towards society. One often meets men who wear *khadi* but in all other things indulge their taste for foreign manufactures with a vengeance. Such men cannot be said to be practising *swadeshi*. They are simply following the fashion. A votary of *swadeshi* will carefully study his environment and try to help his neighbours wherever possible by giving preference to local manufactures even if they are of an inferior grade or dearer in price than things manufactured elsewhere. He will try to remedy their defects but will not give them up because of their defects and take to foreign manufactures.

But even *swadeshi* like any other good thing can be ridden to death if it is made a fetish. That is a danger that must be guarded against. To reject foreign manufactures merely because they are foreign and to go on wasting national time and money to promote manufactures in one's country for which it is not suited would be criminal folly and a negation of the *swadeshi* spirit. A true votary of *swadeshi* will never harbour ill-will towards the foreigner, he will not be moved by antagonism towards anybody on earth. Swadeshism is not a cult of hatred. It is a doctrine of selfless service that has its roots in the purest *ahimsa*, i.e., love.

'The Law of *Swadeshi*'
Navajivan, 31 Apr. 1931 (G.)
Young India, 18 June 1931

[1] *Bhagavad Gita*, III. 35.

224. SELF-RELIANCE AND *AHIMSA*

June 15, 1947

Only the self-reliant man can progress towards success in any task. This is as true of a country as of a man. At present we have no faith in *ahimsa* because we have no self-reliance. It has become second nature with us in every matter to look to other people or other nations. As a result we have become so weak in body, mind and resources that we cannot protect even our own selves. That is why I tell Rajendrababu every day that it is better for us to starve than to import even a single grain of food from outside. But mine is a voice in the wilderness. Or could it be that I am growing too old and therefore losing my grip over things?

'A Letter' (G.)
Bihar Pachhi Dilhi, p. 142.

XVI

Sarvodaya—Non-Violent Social Transformation

225. THE-GREATEST-GOOD-OF-ALL PRINCIPLE

A constant reader of *Young India* sends the following ...[1]

I reproduce this letter for it helps me to elucidate my own position. If such a very careful reader of *Young India*, as I know this correspondent is, misunderstands my position as is evident from his letter, how many more occasional readers must have done likewise? Several readers did draw my attention to the danger of a misunderstanding arising owing to the traditional hardness of our hearts which makes us prone to seize every opportunity of doing violence. One can only be—one ought to be—most careful in the handling of delicate problems; but no fear of misuse of statements can be permitted to stop a free and honest discussion of fundamental truths. For me, I shall learn to be and do right only by prayerful discussion, elucidation and interchange of views. This letter I have quoted is an instance in point. The discussion has brought to light an honest misunderstanding of difference between the correspondent and myself in the interpretation of the same principle.

Whilst I am of opinion that Dr. Blazer was well acquitted, according to the test laid down by me, he was wrong in taking the life of his daughter. It betrayed want of faith in the humanity of those around him. There was no warrant for him to suppose that the daughter would not have been cared for by others. The position in the case of dogs under the circumstances assumed by me is materially different from the position in which Dr. Blazer found himself. Nor am I able to subscribe to the view that an idiot has no soul. I believe that even the lower creation have souls.

Weightier still is the difficulty which another earnest reader puts and which may be thus summarized:

I appreciate the position you have taken up. It is the only true position. But does not your argument after all resolve itself into the utilitarian doctrine of the greater good of the greater number? And if that is your position, wherein does the doctrine of non-violence differ from the utilitarian which makes no pretence to non-violence and which will not hesitate to destroy life if the destruction would lead to the greater good of the greater number?

In the first place even though the outward act may be the same, its implications will vary according to the motive prompting it. Thus as non-violence in the West stops at man and, even then, only where possible, there is no compunction felt either over subjecting animals to vivisection for the supposed greater good of mankind or over heaping up most destructive armaments also in the name of the same doctrine of utility. A votary of non-violence, on the other hand, might have done one act of destruction in common with the utilitarian, but he would prefer to die rather than make himself party to vivisection or to an endless multiplication of armaments.

The fact is that a votary of *ahimsa* cannot subscribe to the utilitarian formula. He will strive for the greatest good of all and die in the attempt to realize the ideal. He will therefore be willing to die so that the others may live. He will serve himself with the rest, by himself dying. The greatest good of all inevitably includes the good of the greater number, and therefore he and the utilitarian will converge at many points in their career but there does come a time when they must part company, and even work in opposite directions. The utilitarian to be logical will never sacrifice himself. The absolutist will even sacrifice himself. The absolutist, when he kills a dog, does so either out of weakness or in rare cases for the sake of the dog himself. That it is a dangerous thing to decide what is or is not good for the dog, and that he may therefore make grievous mistakes is irrelevant to the fact of the motive prompting the act. The absolutist's sphere of destruction will be always the narrowest possible. The utilitarian's has no limit. Judged by the standard of non-violence the late War was wholly wrong. Judged by the utilitarian standard each party has justified it according to its idea of utility. Even the Jallianwala Bagh massacre was justified by its perpetrators on the grounds of utility. And precisely on the same ground the anarchist justifies his assassinations. But none of these acts can possibly be justified on the greatest-good-of-all principle.

'The Greatest Good of All'
Young India, 9 Dec. 1926

---

[1] The correspondent enclosed a newspaper cutting which carried a report of how a Dr Blazer had chloroformed his imbecile daughter because he felt there would be no one to look after her once he was dead. It also carried the report of a French actress who shot her lover at his own request as he was suffering from an incurable disease. The jury in both cases acquitted the accused.

226. THE PRINCIPLE OF NON-POSSESSION

Yeravda Mandir,
Tuesday morning, August 26, 1930

Chi. Narandas,

Non-possession is allied to non-stealing. A thing not originally stolen must nevertheless be classified as stolen property if we possess it without needing it. Possession implies provision for the future. A seeker after truth, a follower of the law of love, cannot hold anything against tomorrow. God never stores for the morrow; He never creates more than what is strictly needed for the moment. If, therefore, we repose faith in His providence, we should be assured that He will give us every day our daily bread, meaning everything we require. Saints and men of faith have always found justification for it from their experience. Our ignorance or negligence of the Divine Law, which gives to man from day to day his daily bread and no more, has given rise to inequalities with all the miseries attendant upon them. The rich have a superfluous store of things which they do not need, and which are therefore neglected and wasted; while millions starve to death for want of sustenance. If each retained possession only of what he needed, no one would be in want and all would live in contentment. As it is, the rich are discontented no less than the poor. The poor man would fain become a millionaire, and the millionaire a multi-millionaire. The poor are not content if they get their daily needs. They have a right, however, to get enough for their daily needs and it is the duty of society to help them to satisfy them. The rich should take the initiative in dispossession with a view to universal diffusion of the spirit of contentment. If only they keep their own property within moderate limits, the starving will be easily fed and will learn the lesson of contentment along with the rich.

Perfect fulfilment of the ideal of non-possession requires that man should, like the birds, have no roof over his head, no clothing and no stock of food for the morrow. He will indeed need his daily bread, but it will be God's business, and not his, to provide it. Only very very few, if any at all, can reach this ideal. We ordinary seekers may not be repelled by the seeming impossibility. But we must keep the ideal constantly before us, and in the light thereof critically examine our possessions and try to reduce them. Civilization, in the real sense of the term, consists not in the multiplication, but in the deliberate and voluntary reduction of wants. This alone promotes real happiness and contentment, and increases the capacity for service. Judging by this criterion, we find that in the Ashram we possess many things the necessity for which cannot be proved, and we thus tempt our neighbours to steal. If people try, they can reduce their wants and, as the latter diminish, they become happier, more peaceful and healthier. From the standpoint of pure truth, the body, too, is a possession. It has been truly said that desire for enjoyment creates bodies for the soul and sustains them. When this desire vanishes, there remains no further need for the body and man is free from the vicious cycle of births and deaths. The soul is omnipresent; why should she care to be confined within the cage-like body, or do evil and even kill for the sake of that cage? We thus arrive at the ideal of total renunciation and learn the use of the body for the purposes of service so long as it exists, so much so that service, and not bread, becomes for us the staff of life. We eat and drink, sleep and wake, for service alone. Such an attitude of mind brings us real happiness and the beatific vision in the fulness of time. Let us all examine ourselves from this standpoint.

We should remember that non-possession is a principle applicable to thoughts as well as to things. A man who fills his brain with useless knowledge violates that inestimable principle. Thoughts which turn us away from God or do not turn us towards Him are unnecessary possessions and constitute impediments in our way. In this connection we may consider the definition of knowledge contained in Chapter XIII of the *Gita*. We are there told that humility, *amanitvam*, etc., constitute knowledge and that all the rest is ignorance. If this is true—and there is no doubt that it is true—much that we hug today as knowledge is ignorance pure and simple, and therefore only does us harm instead of conferring any benefit. It makes the mind wander and even reduces it to a vacuity, and discontent flourishes in endless ramifications of evil. Needless to say, this is not a plea for inertia. Every moment of our life should be filled with mental or physical activity, but that activity should be *sattvik*, tending towards truth. One who has consecrated his life to service cannot be idle for a single moment. But we have to learn to distinguish between good activity and evil activity. This discernment goes naturally with a single-minded devotion to service.

Blessings from
Bapu

Letter to Narandas Gandhi (G.)
MMU/I

227. *YAJNA*, WELFARE, AND SERVICE

Tuesday morning, Diwali,
October 21, 1930

Chi. Narandas,

My blessings to all the friends there. My *Vandemataram* and due regards to everyone. May we be filled with greater spirit of service during the next year, and become fitter instruments and more awake to our duty in that regard.

We make frequent use of the word '*yajna*'. We have raised spinning to the rank of a daily *mahayajna*. It is therefore necessary to think out the various implications of the term '*yajna*'. '*Yajna*' means an act directed to the welfare of others, done without desiring any return for it, whether of a temporal or spiritual nature. 'Act' here must be taken in its widest sense, and includes thought and word, as well as deed. 'Others' embraces not only humanity, but all life. Therefore, and also from the standpoint of *ahimsa*, it is not a *yajna* to sacrifice lower animals even with a view to serving humanity. It does not matter that animal sacrifice is supposed to find a place in the Vedas. It is enough for us that such sacrifice cannot stand the fundamental tests of Truth and Non-violence. I readily admit my incompetence in Vedic scholarship. But the incompetence, so far as this subject is concerned, does not worry me because, even if the practice of animal sacrifice be proved to have been a feature of Vedic society, it can form no precedent for a votary of *ahimsa*.

From this definition of *yajna* it follows that a primary sacrifice must be an act which conduces the most to the welfare of the greatest number in the widest area, and which can be performed by the largest number of men and women with the least trouble. It will not, therefore, be a *yajna*, much less a *mahayajna*, to wish or to do ill to anyone else even in order to serve a so-called higher interest. And the *Gita* teaches, and experience testifies, that all action that cannot come under the category of *yajna* promotes bondage.

The world cannot subsist for a single moment without *yajna* in this sense and, therefore, the *Gita*, after having dealt with true wisdom in the second chapter, takes up in the third the means of attaining it and declares in so many words that *yajna* came with Creation itself. This body, therefore, has been given us only in order that we may serve all Creation with it. And therefore, says the *Gita*, he who eats without offering *yajna* eats stolen food. Every single act of one who would lead a life of purity should be in the nature of *yajna*. *Yajna* having come to us with our birth, we are debtors all our lives and thus for ever bound to serve the universe. And even as a bondslave receives food, clothing and so on from the master whom he serves, so should we gratefully accept such gifts as may be assigned to us by the Lord of the universe. What we receive must be called a gift; for as debtors we are entitled to no consideration for the discharge of our obligations. Therefore we may not blame the Master if we fail to get it. Our body is His to be cherished or cast away according to His will. This is not a matter for complaint or even pity; on the contrary, it is a natural and even a pleasant and desirable state, if only we realize our proper place in God's scheme.

We do indeed need strong faith, if we would experience this supreme bliss. 'Do not worry in the least about yourself, leave all worry to God',—this appears to be the commandment in all religions. This need not frighten anyone. He who devotes himself to service with a clear conscience will day by day grasp the necessity for it in greater measure and will continually grow richer in faith. The path of service can hardly be trodden by one who is not prepared to renounce self-interest and to recognize the conditions of his birth. Any service rendered by such a person will be tainted by selfishness. But, then, men of such utter selfishness are rare in this world. Consciously or unconsciously, every one of us does render some service or other. If we cultivate the habit of doing this service deliberately, our desire for service will steadily grow stronger and will make not only for our own happiness but also for that of the world at large.

Blessings from
BAPU

Letter to Narandas Gandhi (G.)
MMU/I

228 *YAJNA* AND RENUNCIATION

Tuesday morning, October 28, 1930

Chi. Narandas,

I wrote about *yajna* last week, but feel like writing more about it. It will perhaps be worthwhile further to consider a principle which has been created along with mankind. *Yajna* is duty to be performed, or service to be rendered, all the twenty-four hours of the day, and hence a maxim like 'The powers of the good are always exercised for a benevolent purpose' is inappropriate, if benevolence has any taste of favour about it. To serve without desire is to favour not others, but ourselves even as in discharging a debt we serve only ourselves, lighten our burden and fulfil our duty. Again, not only the good, but all of us are bound to place our resources at the disposal of humanity. And if such is the law, as evidently it is, indulgence ceases to hold a place in life and gives way to renunciation. For human beings renunciation itself is enjoyment. This is what differentiates man from the beast. Some object that life thus understood becomes dull and devoid of art, and leaves no room for the householder. But I think in saying this they misinterpret the word 'renunciation'. Renunciation here does not mean abandoning the world and retiring into the forest.

The spirit of renunciation should rule all the activities of life. A householder does not cease to be one if he regards life as a duty rather than as an indulgence. A cobbler, a cultivator, a tradesman or a barber may be inspired in their work or activities either by the spirit of renunciation or merely by the desire for self-indulgence. A merchant who carries on his business in a spirit of sacrifice will have crores passing through his hands, but he will, if he follows the law, use his abilities for service. He will, therefore, not cheat or speculate, will lead a simple life, will not injure a living soul and will lose millions rather than harm anybody. Let no one run away with the idea that this type of merchant exists only in my imagination. Fortunately for the world, he does exist in the West as well as in the East. It is true such merchants may be counted on one's fingers but the type ceases to be imaginary as soon as even one living specimen can be found to answer to it. All of us know of a philanthropic tailor in Wadhwan. I know of one such barber. Every one of us knows of such a weaver.[1] And if we go deeply into the matter, we shall come across men in every walk of life who lead dedicated lives. No doubt these sacrificers obtain their livelihood by their work. But livelihood is not their objective, but only a by-product of their vocation. Motilal was a tailor at first, and continued as a tailor afterwards. But his spirit was changed and his work was transmuted into worship. He began to think about the welfare of others and his life became artistic in the real sense of the term.

A life of sacrifice is the pinnacle of art and is full of true joy. Such life is the source of ever fresh springs of joy which never dry up and never satiate. *Yajna* is not *yajna* if one feels it to be burdensome or annoying. Self-indulgence leads to destruction and renunciation to immortality. Joy has no independent existence. It depends upon our attitude to life. One man will enjoy theatrical scenery, another the ever new scenes which unfold themselves in the sky. Joy, therefore, is a matter of education. We shall delight in things which we have been taught to delight in as children. And illustrations can be easily cited of different national tastes.

Again, many sacrificers imagine that they are free to receive from the people everything they need and many things they do not need, because they are rendering disinterested service. Directly this idea sways a man, he ceases to be a servant and becomes a tyrant over the people. One who would serve others will not waste a thought upon his own comforts, which he leaves to be attended to or neglected by his Master on high. He will not, therefore, encumber himself with everything that comes his way; he will take only what he strictly needs and leave the rest. He will be calm, free from anger and unruffled in mind even if he finds himself inconvenienced. His service, like virtue, is its own reward, and he will rest content with it.

Again, one dare not be negligent in service or be behind-hand with it. He who thinks that he must be diligent only in his personal business, and unpaid public business may be done in any way and at any time he chooses, has still to learn the very rudiments of the science of sacrifice. Voluntary service of others demands the best of which one is capable, and must take precedence over service of self. In fact, the pure devotee consecrates himself to the service of humanity without any reservation whatever.

Blessings from
BAPU

Letter to Narandas Gandhi (G.)
MMU/I

[1] The allusion probably is to Kabir.

229. OVER-INDULGENCE AND THE NEEDS OF ALL
June 17, 1932

I, for one, daily realize this truth from experience, that Nature provides for the needs of every living creature from moment to moment, and I also see that, voluntarily or involuntarily, knowingly or unknowingly, we violate this great law every moment of our lives. All of us can see that, in consequence of our doing so, on the one hand large numbers suffer through over-indulgence and, on the other, countless people suffer through want. Our endeavour, therefore, is to save mankind from the calamity of widespread starvation, on the one hand, and, on the other, destruction of food-grains by the American millionaires through a false understanding of economic laws. It is true, of course, that it is impossible at present to live in perfect conformity with this natural law. But that need not worry us.

Letter to Chhaganlal Joshi
Mahadevbhaini Diary, Vol. I, p. 224

230. *SARVODAYA*, NON-VIOLENCE, AND *TAPASCHARYA*

Segaon,[1]
July 21, 1938

Sarvodaya is impossible without *satyagraha*. The word *satyagraha* should be understood here in its etymological sense. There can be no insistence on truth where there is no non-violence. Hence, the attainment of *sarvodaya* depends upon the attainment of non-violence. The attainment of non-violence in its turn depends upon *tapascharya*. *Tapascharya*, again, should be pure. Ceaseless effort, discretion, etc., should form part of it. Pure *tapascharya* leads to pure knowledge. Experience shows that although people talk of non-violence, many are mentally so lazy that they do not even take the trouble of familiarizing themselves with the facts. Take an example. India is a poor country. We wish to do away with poverty. But how many people have made a study of how this poverty came about, what its implications are, how it can be removed, etc.? A devotee of non-violence should be full of such knowledge.

It is the duty of *Sarvodaya* to create such means and not to enter into controversies. Editors of *Sarvodaya* should forget Gandhism. There is no such thing as Gandhism. I have not put anything new before India; I have only presented an ancient thing in a new way. I have tried to utilize it in a new field. Hence my ideas cannot be appropriately called Gandhism. We shall adopt truth wherever we find it, praise it wherever we see it, and pursue it. In other words, in every sentence of *Sarvodaya*, we should catch a glimpse of non-violence and knowledge.

'What is *Sarvodaya*?' (H.)
GN 7680

[1] Message for the first issue of *Sarvodaya*, a journal published by D. B. Kalelkar and Dada Dharmadhikari.

231. POSSESSIONS AND THE SOCIAL STRUCTURE

Sevagram
February 9, 1942

Q. Why can't you see that whilst there is possession it must be defended against all odds? Therefore your insistence that violence should be eschewed in all circumstances is utterly unworkable and absurd. I think non-violence is possible only for select individuals.

A. This question has been answered often enough in some form or other in these columns as also in those of *Young India*. But it is an evergreen. I must answer it as often as it is put, especially when it comes from an earnest seeker as this one does. I claim that even now, though the social structure is not based on a conscious acceptance of non-violence, all the world over mankind lives and men retain their possessions on the sufferance of one another. If they had not done so, only the fewest and the most ferocious would have survived. But such is not the case. Families are bound together by ties of love, and so are groups in the so-called civilized society called nations. Only they do not recognize the supremacy of the law of non-violence. It follows, therefore, that they have not investigated its vast possibilities. Hitherto out of sheer inertia, shall I say, we have taken it for granted that complete non-violence is possible only for the few who take the vow of non-possession and the allied abstinences.

Whilst it is true that the votaries alone can carry on research work and declare from time to time the new possibilities of the great eternal law governing man, if it is the law, it must hold good for all. The many failures we see are not of the law but of the followers, many of whom do not even know that they are under that law willy-nilly. When a mother dies for her child she unknowingly obeys the law. I have been pleading for the past fifty years for a conscious acceptance of the law and its zealous practice even in the face of failures. Fifty years' work has shown marvellous results and strengthened my faith. I do claim that by constant practice we shall come to a state of things when lawful possession will command universal and voluntary respect. No doubt such possession will not be tainted. It will not be an insolent demonstration of the inequalities that surround us everywhere. Nor need the problem of unjust and unlawful possessions appal the votary of non-violence. He has at his disposal the non-violent weapon of *satyagraha* and non-co-operation which hitherto has been found to be a complete substitute of violence whenever it has been applied honestly in sufficient measure. I have never claimed to present the complete science of non-violence. It does not lend itself to such treatment. So far as I know no single physical science does, not even the very precise science of mathematics. I am but a seeker, and I have fellow-seekers like the questioner whom I invite to accompany me in the very difficult but equally fascinating search.

'Question Box'
Harijan, 22 Feb. 1942

232. TEST OF NON-ATTACHMENT

November 5, 1947

... If self-control has taken root in one's heart, why should one wear saffron robes or withdraw oneself into the forests? And one whose heart is not firm is not likely to gain anything whether he goes to a forest or anywhere else. I believe that the man who observes self-control in thought, word and deed in the midst of the world is verily a great ascetic. If things do not bind us, if we are not attached to things even when they are easily available, that, according to me, is a greater test of our detachment than mere withdrawal to a lonely forest.

Fragment of a Letter (G.)
Dilhiman Gandhiji, Vol. I, p. 200

233. WOMEN OF THE WORLD MUST UNITE

New Delhi,
July 18, 1947

If only the women of the world would come together they could display such heroic non-violence as to kick away the atom bomb like a mere ball. Women have been so gifted by God. If an ancestral treasure lying buried in a corner of the house unknown to the members of the family were suddenly discovered, what a celebration it would occasion. Similarly, women's marvellous power is lying dormant. If the women of Asia wake up, they will dazzle the world. My experiment in non-violence would be instantly successful if I could secure women's help.

Message to Chinese Women (G.)
Bihar Pachhi Dilhi, p. 354

234. REMOVAL OF EXPLOITATION

Satyagraha Ashram,
Sabarmati,
March 20, 1928

There can be no living harmony between races and nations unless the main cause is removed, namely, exploitation of the weak by the strong. We must revise the interpretation of the so-called doctrine of 'the survival of the fittest'.

M. K. GANDHI

Message to Marcelle Capy
SN 13117

235. EQUALITY OF TREATMENT

March 16, 1932

It is possible and necessary to treat human beings on terms of equality, but this can never apply to their morals. One would be affectionate and attentive to a rascal and to a saint; but one cannot and must not put saintliness and rascality on the same footing.

Fragment of a Letter
The Diary of Mahadev Desai, Vol. I, p. 15

236. NEED FOR A CHARTER OF DUTIES

[Before 16 April 1940]

RECEIVED YOUR CABLE.[1] HAVE CAREFULLY READ YOUR FIVE AR-
TICLES.[2] YOU WILL PERMIT ME TO SAY YOU ARE ON THE WRONG
TRACK. I FEEL SURE THAT I CAN DRAW UP A BETTER CHARTER OF
RIGHTS THAN YOU HAVE DRAWN UP. BUT OF WHAT GOOD WILL IT
BE? WHO WILL BECOME ITS GUARDIAN? IF YOU MEAN PROPAGANDA
OR POPULAR EDUCATION YOU HAVE BEGUN AT THE WRONG END.
I SUGGEST THE RIGHT WAY. BEGIN WITH A CHARTER OF DUTIES
OF MAN (BOTH D AND M CAPITALS) AND I PROMISE THE RIGHTS
WILL FOLLOW AS SPRING FOLLOWS WINTER. I WRITE FROM EX-
PERIENCE. AS A YOUNG MAN I BEGAN LIFE BY SEEKING TO ASSERT
MY RIGHTS AND I SOON DISCOVERED I HAD NONE NOT EVEN OVER
MY WIFE. SO I BEGAN BY DISCOVERING AND PERFORMING MY DUTY
BY MY WIFE MY CHILDREN FRIENDS COMPANIONS AND SOCIETY
AND I FIND TODAY THAT I HAVE GREATER RIGHTS, PERHAPS THAN
ANY LIVING MAN I KNOW. IF THIS IS TOO TALL A CLAIM THEN I
SAY I DO NOT KNOW ANYONE WHO POSSESSES GREATER RIGHTS
THAN I.

Cable to H. G. Wells[3]
The Hindustan Times, 16 April 1940

[1] H. G. Wells had sought Gandhi's opinion on the 'Rights of Man' drawn up by him.

[2] Published in *The Hindustan Times*.

[3] Herbert George Wells (1866-1946); English novelist, sociological writer and his-
torian; author of *The Time Machine, The War of the Worlds, The Shape of Things to
Come, The Outline of History, The Invisible Man*, and various other works.

237. EQUAL DISTRIBUTION THROUGH NON-VIOLENCE

In last week's article on the Constructive Programme I mentioned equal distribution of wealth as one of the 13 items.

The real implication of equal distribution is that each man shall have the wherewithal to supply all his natural needs and no more. For example, if one man has a weak digestion and requires only a quarter of a pound of flour for his bread and another needs a pound, both should be in a position to satisfy their wants. To bring this ideal into being the entire social order has got to be reconstructed. A society based on non-violence cannot nurture any other ideal. We may not perhaps be able to realize the goal, but we must bear it in mind and work unceasingly to near it. To the same extent as we progress towards our goal we shall find contentment and happiness, and to that extent too shall we have contributed towards the bringing into being of a non-violent society.

It is perfectly possible for an individual to adopt this way of life without having to wait for others to do so. And if an individual can observe a certain rule of conduct, it follows that a group of individuals can do likewise. It is necessary for me to emphasize the fact that no one need wait for anyone else in order to adopt a right course. Men generally hesitate to make a beginning if they feel that the objective cannot be had in its entirety. Such an attitude of mind is in reality a bar to progress.

Now let us consider how equal distribution can be brought about through non-violence. The first step towards it is for him who has made this ideal part of his being to bring about the necessary changes in his personal life. He would reduce his wants to a minimum, bearing in mind the poverty of India. His earnings would be free of dishonesty. The desire for speculation would be renounced. His habitation would be in keeping with the new mode of life. There would be self-restraint exercised in every sphere of life. When he has done all that is possible in his own life, then only will he be in a position to preach this ideal among his associates and neighbours.

Indeed at the root of this doctrine of equal distribution must lie that of the trusteeship of the wealthy for the superfluous wealth possessed by them. For according to the doctrine they may not possess a rupee more than their neighbours. How is this to be brought about? Non-violently? Or should the wealthy be dispossessed of their possessions? To do this we would naturally have to resort to violence. This violent action cannot benefit society. Society will be the poorer, for it will lose the gifts of a man who knows how to accumulate wealth. Therefore the non-violent way is evidently superior. The rich man will be left in possession of his wealth, of which he will use what he reasonably requires for his personal needs and will act as a trustee for the remainder to be used for the society. In this argument honesty on the part of the trustee is assumed.

As soon as a man looks upon himself as a servant of society, earns for its sake, spends for its benefit, then purity enters into his earnings and there is *ahimsa* in his venture. Moreover, if men's minds turn towards this way of life, there will come about a peaceful revolution in society, and that without any bitterness.

It may be asked whether history at any time records such a change in human nature. Such changes have certainly taken place in individuals. One may not perhaps be able to point to them in a whole society. But this only means that up till now there has never been an experiment on a large scale in non-violence. Somehow or other the wrong belief has taken possession of us that *ahimsa* is pre-eminently a weapon for individuals and its use should therefore be limited to that sphere. In fact this is not the case. *Ahimsa* is definitely an attribute of society. To convince people of this truth is at once my effort and my experiment. In this age of wonders no one will say that a thing or idea is worthless because it is new. To say it is impossible because it is difficult is again not in consonance with the spirit of the age. Things undreamt of are daily being seen, the impossible is ever becoming possible. We are constantly being astonished these days at the amazing discoveries in the field of violence. But I maintain that far more undreamt of and seemingly impossible discoveries will be made in the field of non-violence. The history of religion is full of such examples. To try to root out religion itself from society is a wild goose chase. And were such an attempt to succeed, it would mean the destruction of society. Superstition, evil customs and other imperfections creep in from age to age and mar religion for the time being. They come and go. But religion itself remains, because the existence of the world in a broad sense depends on religion. The ultimate definition of religion may be said to be obedience to the law of God. God and His law are synonymous terms. Therefore God signifies an unchanging and living law. No one has ever really found Him. But *avatars* and prophets have, by means of their *tapasya*, given to mankind a faint glimpse of the eternal Law.

If, however, in spite of the utmost effort, the rich do not become guardians of the poor in the true sense of the term and the latter are more and more crushed and die of hunger, what is to be done? In trying to find the solution to this riddle I have lighted on non-violent non-co-operation and civil disobedience as the right and infallible means. The rich cannot accumulate wealth without the co-operation of the poor in society. Man has been conversant with violence from the beginning, for he has inherited this strength from the animal in his nature. It was only when he rose from the state of a quadruped (animal) to that of a biped (man) that the knowledge of the strength of *ahimsa* entered into his soul. This knowledge has grown within him slowly but surely. If this knowledge were to penetrate to and spread amongst the poor, they would become strong and would learn how to free themselves by means of non-violence from the crushing inequalities which have brought them to the verge of starvation.

I scarcely need to write anything about non-co-operation and civil disobedience, for the readers of *Harijanbandhu* are familiar with these and their working.

'Equal Distribution'
Harijanbandhu, 24 Aug. 1940
Harijan, 25 Aug. 1940

238. BALANCED GROWTH

Sevagram,
August 23, 1946

One of the complaints that has been made by one of you is that too much emphasis is laid here on manual work. I am a firm believer in the educative value of manual work. Our present educational system is meant for strengthening and perpetuating the imperialist power in India. Those of you who have been brought up under it have naturally developed a taste for it and so find labour irksome. No one in Government schools or colleges bothers to teach the students how to clean the roads or latrines. Here cleanliness and sanitation form the very Alpha and Omega of your training. Scavenging is a fine art you should take pains to learn. Persistent questioning and healthy inquisitiveness are the first requisite for acquiring learning of any kind. Inquisitiveness should be tempered by humility and respectful regard for the teacher. It must not degenerate into impudence. The latter is the enemy of receptivity of mind. There can be no knowledge without humility and the will to learn.

Useful manual labour, intelligently performed, is the means *par excellence* for developing the intellect. One may develop a sharp intellect otherwise too. But then it will not be a balanced growth but an unbalanced distorted abortion. It might easily make of one a rogue and a rascal. A balanced intellect presupposes a harmonious growth of body, mind and soul. That is why we give to manual labour the central place in our curriculum of training here. An intellect that is developed through the medium of socially useful labour will be an instrument for service and will not easily be led astray or fall into devious paths. The latter can well be a scourge. If you grasp that essential point, the money spent by your respective governments in sending you here for training will have been well spent.

Address to Trainees of Basic Teachers' Camp
Harijan, 8 Sept. 1946

239. THE DUTY OF CITIZENSHIP OF THE WORLD

[Before 8 June 1947]

All rights to be deserved and preserved come from duty well done. Thus the very right to live accrues to us only when we do the duty of citizenship of the world. From this very fundamental statement perhaps it is easy enough to define the duties

of man and woman and correlate every right to some corresponding duty to be first performed. Every other right can be
shown to be a usurpation hardly worth fighting for.

'A Letter' (G.)
Harijan, 8 June 1947
Harijanbandhu, 8 June 1947

240. BOLSHEVISM AND NON-VIOLENCE

It is my good fortune and misfortune to receive attention in
Europe and America at the present moment. It is my good
fortune in that my message is being studied and understood
in the West. It is my misfortune in that it is also being either
unconsciously exaggerated or wilfully distorted. Every truth is
self-acting and possesses inherent strength. I therefore remain
unperturbed even when I find myself grossly misrepresented.
A kind European friend has sent me a warning which shows,
if the information given to him be true, that I am being either
wilfully or accidentally misunderstood in Russia. Here is the
message:

The Russian representative at Berlin, Mr. Krestinsky, would be
asked by the Minister for Foreign Affairs to give an official welcome
to Gandhi (?) and to 'profit by the situation to undertake Bolshevik
propagandist activities among his followers'. Besides, Krestinsky
would be given the task of inviting Gandhi to come to Russia. He
is authorized to give a subsidy for the publication of propagandist
literature among the oppressed peoples of Asia; and he is to found,
for the purposes of the Oriental Club and Secretariat, a purse in the
name of Gandhi, for students who are of his ideas (of the ideas of
Gandhi or of those of Moscow?). Finally three Hindus would be
enlisted in this work. All this is published in the Russian newspapers
like the *Rul* of Oct. 18th.

The message gives the clue to the reports that I was likely
to be invited to visit Germany and Russia. I need not say that

I have received no such invitation at all, nor have I the slightest desire to visit these great countries. I am conscious of the fact that the truth for which I stand has not yet been fully accepted by India. It has not yet been fully vindicated. My work in India is still in the experimental stage. In such circumstances any foreign adventure on my part would be altogether premature. I should be fully satisfied if the experiment demonstrably succeeds in India.

My path is clear. Any attempt to use me for violent purposes is bound to fail. I have no secret methods. I know no diplomacy save that of truth. I have no weapon but non-violence. I may be unconsciously led astray for a while but not for all time. I have therefore well-defined limitations, within which alone I may be used. Attempts have been made before now to use me unlawfully more than once. They have failed each time so far as I am aware.

I am yet ignorant of what exactly Bolshevism is. I have not been able to study it. I do not know whether it is for the good of Russia in the long run. But I do know that in so far as it is based on violence and denial of God, it repels me. I do not believe in short-violent-cuts to success. Those Bolshevik friends who are bestowing their attention on me should realize that however much I may sympathize with and admire worthy motives, I am an uncompromising opponent of violent methods even to serve the noblest of causes. There is, therefore, really no meeting ground between the school of violence and myself. But my creed of non-violence not only does not preclude me but compels me even to associate with anarchists and all those who believe in violence. But that association is always with the sole object of weaning them from what appears to me to be their error. For experience convinces me that permanent good can never be the outcome of untruth and violence. Even if my belief is a fond delusion, it will be admitted that it is a fascinating delusion.

'My Path'
Young India, 11 Dec. 1924

241. THE BOLSHEVIK IDEAL AND EXPROPRIATION

Q. What is your opinion about the social economics of Bolshevism and how far do you think they are fit to be copied by our country?

A. I must confess that I have not yet been able fully to understand the meaning of Bolshevism. All that I know is that it aims at the abolition of the institution of private property. This is only an application of the ethical ideal of non-possession in the realm of economics and if the people adopted this ideal of their own accord or could be made to accept it by means of peaceful persuasion there would be nothing like it. But from what I know of Bolshevism it not only does not preclude the use of force but freely sanctions it for the expropriation of private property and maintaining the collective State ownership of the same. And if that is so I have no hesitation in saying that the Bolshevik regime in its present form cannot last for long. For it is my firm conviction that nothing enduring can be built on violence. But be that as it may there is no questioning the fact that the Bolshevik ideal has behind it the purest sacrifice of countless men and women who have given up their all for its sake, and an ideal that is sanctified by the sacrifices of such master spirits as Lenin cannot go in vain: the noble example of their renunciation will be emblazoned for ever and quicken and purify the ideal as time passes.

'My Notes' (G.)
Navajivan, 21 Oct. 1928
Young India, 15 Nov. 1928

242. AVOIDING CLASS WAR

If you will benefit the workers, the peasant and the factory hand, can you avoid class war?

I can, most decidedly, if only the people will follow the non-violent method. The past twelve months have abundantly shown the possibilities of non-violence adopted even as a policy. When the people adopt it as a principle of conduct, class war becomes an impossibility. The experiment in that direction is being tried in Ahmedabad. It has yielded most satisfactory results and there is every likelihood of its proving conclusive. By the non-violent method we seek not to destroy the capitalist, we seek to destroy capitalism. We invite the capitalist to regard himself as trustee for those on whom he depends for the making, the retention and the increase of his capital. Nor need the worker wait for his conversion. If capital is power, so is work. Either power can be used destructively or creatively. Either is dependent on the other. Immediately the worker realizes his strength, he is in a position to become a co-sharer with the capitalist instead of remaining his slave. If he aims at becoming the sole owner, he will most likely be killing the hen that lays golden eggs.

Inequalities in intelligence and even opportunity will last till the end of time. A man living on the banks of a river has any day more opportunity of growing crops than one living in an arid desert. But if inequalities stare us in the face the essential equality too is not to be missed. Every man has an equal right to the necessaries of life even as birds and beasts have. And since every right carries with it a corresponding duty and the corresponding remedy for resisting any attack upon it, it is merely a matter of finding out the corresponding duties and remedies to vindicate the elementary fundamental equality. The corresponding duty is to labour with my limbs and the corresponding remedy is to non-co-operate with him who deprives me of the fruit of my labour. And if I would recognize the fundamental equality, as I must, of the capitalist and the labourer, I must not aim at his destruction. I must strive for his conversion.

My non-co-operation with him will open his eyes to the wrong he may be doing. Nor need I be afraid of someone else taking my place when I have non-co-operated. For I expect to influence my co-workers so as not to help the wrongdoing of the employer. This kind of education of the mass of workers is no doubt a slow process, but as it is also the surest, it is necessarily the quickest. It can be easily demonstrated that destruction of the capitalist must mean destruction in the end of the worker and as no human being is so bad as to be beyond redemption, no human being is so perfect as to warrant his destroying him whom he wrongly considers to be wholly evil.

'Questions and Answers'
Young India, 26 Mar. 1931

243. THE CRAZE FOR MACHINERY

Mr. Henry Eaton writes from California . . .[1]

This letter betrays two superstitions. One of them is that India is unfit to govern herself because she cannot defend herself and is torn with internal dissensions. The writer gratuitously assumes that if Britain withdraws Russia is ready to pounce upon India. This is an insult to Russia. Is Russia's one business to rule over those peoples who are not ruled by Britain? And if Russia has such nefarious designs upon India, does not the writer see that the same power that will oust the British from domination is bound to prevent any other domination? If the control is handed to India's representatives by agreement, there must be some condition whereby Britain will guarantee protection from foreign aggression as a penance for her conscious or unconscious neglect during all these past years to fit India for defending herself.

Personally, even under agreement, I should rely more upon the capacity of the nation to offer civil resistance to any aggressor as it did last year with partial success in the case of the British occupier. Complete success awaits complete assimilation of non-violence in thought, word and deed by the nation. An ocular demonstration of the success of nationwide *satyagraha* must be a prelude to its worldwide acceptance and hence as a natural corollary to the admission of the futility of armament. The only antidote to armament which is the visible symbol of violence is *satyagraha*, the visible symbol of non-violence. But the writer is oppressed also by the fear of our dissensions. In the first place they are grossly exaggerated in transmission to the West. In the second place, they are hardened during foreign control. Imperial rule means *divide et impera*. They must therefore melt with the withdrawal of the frigid foreign rule and the introduction of the warmth-giving sunshine of real freedom.

The second superstition is harder still. I mean that about the spinning-wheel. This is shared by some even in India. The writer begs the question when he calls the method of machinery enlightened and that of the hand ignorant. It has still to be proved that displacement of the hand by the machine is a blessing in every case. Nor is it true that that which is easy is better than that which is hard. It is still less proved that every change is a blessing or that everything old is fit only to be discarded.

I hold that the machinery method is harmful when the same thing can be done easily by millions of hands not otherwise occupied. It is any day better and safer for the millions spread in the seven hundred thousand villages of India scattered over an area nineteen hundred miles long and fifteen hundred broad that they manufacture their clothing in their own villages even as they prepare their own food. These villages cannot retain the freedom they have enjoyed from time immemorial, if they do not control the production of prime necessaries of life. Western observers hastily argue from Western conditions that what may be true of them must be true of India where conditions are different in so many material respects. Applications of the laws of economics must vary with varying conditions.

The machinery method is no doubt easy. But it is not necessarily a blessing on that account. The descent to a certain place is easy but dangerous. The method of the hand is a blessing, in the present case at any rate, because it is hard. If the craze for the machinery method continues, it is highly likely that a time will come when we shall be so incapacitated and weak that we shall begin to curse ourselves for having forgotten the use of the living machines given to us by God. Millions cannot keep themselves fit by games and athletics. And why should they exchange the useful, productive, hardy occupations for the useless, unproductive and expensive games and exercises? They are all right today for a change and recreation. They will jar upon us when they become a necessary occupation in order that we may have the appetite for eating the food in the production of which we had no hand or part.

Lastly, I do not subscribe to the belief that everything old is bad. Truth is old and difficult. Untruth has many attractions. But I would gladly go back to the very old Golden Age of Truth. Good old brown bread is any day superior to the pasty white bread which has lost much of its nutritive value in going through the various processes of refinement. The list of old and yet good things can be endlessly multiplied. The spinning-wheel is one such thing, at any rate, for India.

When India becomes self-supporting, self-reliant and proof against temptations and exploitation, she will cease to be the object of greedy attraction for any power in the West or the East and will then feel secure without having to carry the burden of expensive armament. Her internal economy will be India's strongest bulwark against aggression.

'Superstitions Die Hard'
Young India, 2 July 1931

---

[1] The letter is not reproduced here.

244. LABOUR FRANCHISE AND TRUSTEESHIP

October 6, 1934

My Dear Srirangasayi,

I have your letter. It is refreshing to know that the Socialist Party in Andhra appreciates all the amendments suggested by me. I say the Socialist Party because I take it that your letter is representative of the Party's opinion as you have signed it in your capacity as Secretary. But you know in what unmeasured terms the meeting in Banaras has condemned the amendments. Even when I first conceived spinning franchise as a token of the dignity of labour and its universal recognition, a friend had shown me a booklet containing the constitution of the Soviets and drawn my attention to the fact that in

Russia labour franchise had a definite place. But here I do not know whether you represent the general body of Socialists. What about those who have passed the resolutions of condemnation?

You take exception to my wish that the rich should regard themselves as trustees for the whole of society rather than as owners of the wealth they might possess. Of course, it is an uphill task, but by no means impossible. Indeed I see definite signs of that idea spreading and being accepted. You suggest that the poor should be regarded as trustees for the rich. But you forget that it is implied in the proposition I have laid down. Because, have I not said that labour is as much capital as metal? Therefore, workers, instead of regarding themselves as enemies of the rich, or regarding the rich as their natural enemies, should hold their labour in trust for those who are in need of it. This they can do only when, instead of feeling so utterly helpless as they do, they realize their importance in human economy and shed their fear or distrust of the rich. Fear and distrust are twin sisters born of weakness. When labour realizes its strength it won't need to use any force against moneyed people. It will simply command their attention and respect.

Letter to B. Srirangasayi
The Hindu, 11 Oct. 1934

245. SOCIALISTS AND VIOLENCE

[Before 22 March 1935]

Dear Madeleine,

I have just read your letter to Pyarelal. Thank God I am about to observe complete silence, thus I can reply to your letter immediately. Yes, I ought to write a complete letter in reply to the long letter of the Sage.[1] But the very adjective 'complete' frightens me. I have no time to compose a letter which will do sufficient justice to this letter from there. I must try to do it during my days of silence. Your question is simple. My opposition is to socialism as it is interpreted here in its official programme. I can have nothing to say against the theory or the philosophy of socialism. The programme as it is put here cannot be achieved without violence. The socialists here do not exclude violence under all circumstances whatsoever. They would take to arms openly if they saw there was a chance to usurp power by it. There are in the programme some details into which I need not enter. I wonder if this reply will answer your difficulties. However, you must write about your difficulties more concretely.

Love to you both.

BAPU

Letter to Madeleine Rolland
CW 9737

¹ Romain Rolland.

246. PROPER USE OF MACHINERY

[Before 22 June 1935]¹

GANDHIJI: Is not this wheel a machine?²

[SOCIALIST:] I do not mean this machine, but I mean bigger machinery.

Do you mean Singer's sewing machine? That too is protected by the village industries movement, and for that matter any machinery which does not deprive masses of men of the opportunity to labour, but which helps the individual and adds to his efficiency, and which a man can handle at will without being its slave.

But what about the great inventions? You would have nothing to do with electricity?

Who said so? If we could have electricity in every village home, I should not mind villagers plying their implements and tools with the help of electricity. But then the village communities or the State would own power-houses, just as they have their grazing pastures. But where there is no electricity and no machinery, what are idle hands to do? Will you give them work, or would you have their owners cut them down for want of work?

I would prize every invention of science made for the benefit of all. There is a difference between invention and invention. I should not care for the asphyxiating gases capable of killing masses of men at a time. The heavy machinery for work of public utility which cannot be undertaken by human labour has its inevitable place, but all that would be owned by the State and used entirely for the benefit of the people. I can have no consideration for machinery which is meant either to enrich the few at the expense of the many, or without cause to displace the useful labour of many.

But even you as a socialist would not be in favour of an indiscriminate use of machinery. Take printing-presses. They will go on. Take surgical instruments. How can one make them with one's hands? Heavy machinery would be needed for them. But there is no machinery for the cure of idleness but this. I can work it whilst I am carrying on this conversation with you, and am adding a little to the wealth of the country. This machine no one can oust.

'A Discussion'
Harijan, 22 June 1935

¹ A socialist holding a brief for machinery asked Gandhi if the village industries movement was not meant to oust all machinery.

² Gandhi was just then spinning.

247. ENLIGHTENED ANARCHY

Political power, in my opinion, cannot be our ultimate aim. It is one of the means used by men for their all-round advancement. The power to control national life through national representatives is called political power. Representatives will become unnecessary if the national life becomes so perfect as to be self-controlled. It will then be a state of enlightened anarchy in which each person will become his own ruler. He will conduct himself in such a way that his behaviour will not hamper the well-being of his neighbours. In an ideal State there will be no political institution and therefore no political power. That is why Thoreau has said in his classic statement that that government is the best which governs the least.

'Enlightened Anarchy—A Political Ideal' (H.)
Sarvodaya, Jan. 1939

248. TRUSTEESHIP AND NON-VIOLENCE

May 6, 1939

I am either unable to understand your theory of trusteeship or my reason cannot grasp it. Will you kindly explain it?

It is the same thing whether you are unable to understand it or your reason does not accept it. How can I explain such an important principle in a few minutes? Still I shall try to explain it in brief. Just imagine that I have a crore of rupees in my possession. I can either squander the amount in dissipation or take up the attitude that the money does not belong to me, that I do not own it, that it is a bequest, that it has been put in my possession by God and that only so much of it is mine as is enough for my requirements. My requirements also should be like those of the millions. My requirements cannot be greater because I happen to be the son of a rich man. I cannot spend the money on my pleasures. The man who takes for himself only enough to satisfy the needs customary in his society and spends the rest for social service becomes a trustee.

Ever since the idea of socialism became popular in India, we have been confronted with the question as to what our attitude should be towards the Princes and millionaires. The socialists say that the Princes and the millionaires should be done away with, that all must become workers. They advocate confiscation of the properties of all these people and say that they should be given the same wages as everyone else—from Rs. 5 to eight annas a day or Rs. 15 a month. So much for what the socialists say. We too assert that the rich are not the owners of their wealth whereas the labourer is the owner of his labour. He is, therefore, from our point of view, richer than the rich. A zamindar can be recognized as the owner of

one, two or ten *bighas* of land. That is to say, of as much as
may be necessary for his livelihood. We also want that his
wages should not be higher than those of the labourer, that
he should maintain himself on eight annas a day and use the
rest of his wealth for the welfare of society. But we would not
take away his property by force. This is the most important
point. We also wish that the Princes and the millionaires too
should do manual work and maintain themselves on eight
annas a day, considering the rest of their property as national
trust.

At this point it may be asked as to how many trustees of
this type one can really find. As a matter of fact, such a
question should not arise at all. It is not directly related to
our theory. There may be just one such trustee or there may
be none at all. Why should we worry about it? We should
have the faith that we can, without violence or with so little
violence that it can hardly be called violence, create such a
feeling among the rich. We should act in that faith. That is
sufficient for us. We should demonstrate through our endeavour that we can end economic disparity with the help of
non-violence. Only those who have no faith in non-violence
can ask how many trustees of this kind can be found.

You may say that such a thing can never happen. You may
consider it as something not in keeping with human nature.
But I cannot believe that you are not able to understand it or
that your reason cannot grasp it.

Answers to Questions at Gandhi Seva Sangh Meeting,
    Brindaban—II (H.)
Gandhi Seva Sanghke Panchama Varshik Adhiveshan (Brindaban, Bihar)ka
    Vivaran, pp. 50-9

249. BUILDING A STATELESS SOCIETY

New Delhi,
September 6, 1946

Shri Shankarrao Deo writes:

People find it strange that men who once called themselves *satyagra-*
his should, on becoming Ministers, resort to the use of the army and

the police. They feel it is a violation of *ahimsa*, whether accepted as a creed or as a policy. It would seem they are right. This contradiction between the belief and the practice of Congress Ministers confuses our workers and they find it difficult to face the critics, inside the Congress and those outside the Congress who want to make capital out of it.

By and large the *ahimsa* of the Congress has been the *ahimsa* of the weak. This was the only thing possible under the prevailing conditions in India.... I admit that there can be no objection to people who accept *ahimsa* only as a policy accepting positions of power. Thus many Congressmen have accepted positions in the Government and you have permitted them to do so.... But having won power through *ahimsa*, how should we practise *ahimsa* in such a way that government becomes redundant? If you do not suggest a way, *satyagraha* will be deemed to be an insufficient means for the end we seek.

I think the answer is easy. For some time now I have been saying that the words 'truth and non-violence' should be removed from the Congress constitution. If we proceed on the assumption that whether these words are removed from the Congress constitution or not we certainly have become removed from truth and *ahimsa*, we shall be able to judge independently whether a certain action is right or wrong.

I am convinced that so long as the army or the police continues to be used for conducting the administration, we shall remain subservient to the British or some other foreign power, irrespective of whether the power is in the hands of the Congress or others. Let us suppose that Congress ministries do not have faith in *ahimsa*. Let us suppose further that Hindus, Muslims and others seek protection from the army or the police. In that case they will continue to get such protection. Then these Congress Ministers who are votaries of *ahimsa* and do not like to seek help from the army or the police may resign. This means that so long as people have not learnt to settle their quarrels themselves, *goondaism* will continue and we shall never be able to generate the true strength of *ahimsa* in us.

Now the question is how to generate such strength. I answered this question in the *Harijan* of August 4 in my reply to a letter from Ahmedabad. So long as we do not develop the strength to die bravely, with love in our hearts, we cannot develop in us the non-violence of the brave.

Would there be State power in an ideal society or would such a society be Stateless? I think the question is futile. If we continue to work towards the building of such a society, to some extent it is bound to be realized and to that extent people will benefit by it. Euclid has defined a straight line as having no breadth, but no one has yet succeeded in drawing such a line and no one ever will. Still we can progress in geometry only by postulating such a line. This is true of every ideal.

We might remember though that a Stateless society does not exist anywhere in the world. If such a society is possible it can be established first only in India. For attempts have been made in India towards bringing about such a society. We have not so far shown that supreme heroism. The only way is for those who believe in it to set the example.

'Congress Ministries and *Ahimsa*' (H.)
Harijan, 15 Sept. 1946
Harijan Sevak, 15 Sept. 1946

250. TRUSTEESHIP AND THE STATE

Q. Is it possible to defend by means of non-violence anything which can only be gained through violence?

A. It followed from what he had said above that what was gained by violence could not only not be defended by non-violence but the latter required the abandonment of the ill-gotten gains.

Q. Is the accumulation of capital possible except through violence whether open or tacit?

A. Such accumulation by private persons was impossible except through violent means but accumulation by the State in a non-violent society was not only possible, it was desirable and inevitable.

Q. Whether a man accumulates material or moral wealth he does so only through the help or co-operation of other members of society. Has he then the moral right to use any of it mainly for personal advantage?

A. No, he has no moral right.

Q. How would the successor of a trustee be determined? Will he only have the right of proposing a name, the right of finalization being vested in the State?

A. As he had said yesterday, choice should be given to the original owner who became the first trustee, but the choice must be finalized by the State. Such arrangement puts a check on the State as well as the individual.

Q. When the replacement of private by public property thus takes place through the operation of the theory of trusteeship, will the ownership vest in the State, which is an instrument of violence or in associations of a voluntary character like village communes and municipalities, which may of course derive their final authority from State-made laws?

A. That question involved some confusion of thought. Legal ownership in the transformed condition vested in the trustee, not in the State. It was to avoid confiscation that the doctrine of trusteeship came into play retaining for the society the ability of the original owner in his own right. Nor did he, the speaker, hold that the State must always be based on violence. It might be so in theory but the practice of the theory demanded a State which would for the most part be based on non-violence.

'Gandhiji on Trusteeship'
Harijan, 16 Feb. 1947

251. THE SOCIALIST IDEAL

Gandhi Camp, Patna,
April 15, 1947

Socialism is a term of the modern age but the concept of socialism is not a new discovery. Lord Krishna preaches the same doctrine in the *Gita*. One need have in one's possession only what one requires. It means that all men are created by God and therefore entitled to an equal share of food, clothing and housing. It does not require huge organizations for the realization of this ideal. Any individual can set about to realize it. First of all, in order to translate this ideal into our lives we should minimize our needs, keeping in mind the poorest of the poor in India. One should earn just enough to support oneself and one's family. To have a bank balance would thus be incompatible with this ideal. And whatever is earned should be earned with the utmost honesty. Strict restraint has to be kept over small matters in our lives. Even if a single individual enforces this ideal in his life, he is bound to influence others. Wealthy people should act as trustees of their wealth. But if they are robbed of this wealth through violent means, it would not be in the interest of the country. This is known as communism. Moreover, by adopting violent means we would be depriving society of capable individuals.

Talk with Manu Gandhi (G.)
Biharni Komi Agman, pp. 201–2

252. TRUSTEES AND PARTNERS
Gandhi Camp, Patna,
April 18, 1947

Zamindars or capitalists will not be able to survive if they continue to suppress peasants and labourers. Now you should behave towards them not as their masters but as partners and friends, and act as their trustees; then alone can you survive. For a long time during the British regime you have been exploiting the labourers and peasants. Therefore I advise you in your own interest that if you do not see the writing on the wall, it will be difficult for you to adjust.

Talk with Zamindars (G.)
Biharni Komi Agman, p. 222

253. WORLD FEDERATION, DEMOCRACY, AND *RAMARAJYA*

New Delhi,
July 4, 1947

Brothers and Sisters,

Some people ask me if what has happened and what is happening and the Dominion Status that we are about to get will lead to *Ramarajya*. Those who put the question are usually sarcastic and I have to admit that I cannot say that all this will lead to *Ramarajya*. All the signs I see are against it. The country has been divided and there will be two Dominions and, if they are hostile to each other, how can we expect the establishment of *Ramarajya*? Of course Dominion Status does not imply subservience to the British. It is as good as independence. But the other Dominions in the British Commonwealth are more or less of the same race. Since India is an Asian country, how can it remain a Dominion? If all the countries of the world were to become such Dominions, that would be a different matter and then *Ramarajya* could be brought about. But what has come about cannot lead to *Ramarajya* or the Kingdom of God. The British Government had originally intended to transfer power to Indian hands by June 30, 1948. But now they have decided that the sooner they get out the better it would be. But how can they do that? So they came to the conclusion that if Dominion Status were granted to the divided India there would be no risks because then they would still have links with us.

I do not want India to be a frog in the well, unaware of what happens outside the well. Jawaharlal and other leaders have said that we will not be hostile to any country. We shall have friendship for all including the British. Do they then want a world federation? As I said at the Asian Relations Conference, a world federation is possible of realization and in that case it would not be necessary for countries to maintain armed forces. Some countries today describe themselves as democratic but of course one does not become a democrat by simply saying so. What is the need for an army where there is rule by the people? Where the army rules the people cannot rule. There can be no world federation of countries ruled by armies. The military dictatorships of Germany and Japan had tried to inveigle various countries into friendship with them. But the deception did not last long. Today I look around and find *Ramarajya* nowhere.

People ask me if the rule of the sword and the bullet that prevails today is not the result of my teaching of truth and non-violence for thirty-two years. But does this then mean that for thirty-two years I have prevailed through lies and hypocrisy? Does it mean that the millions of people who imbibed the lesson of *ahimsa* from me have after thirty-two years suddenly become liars and murderers? I have admitted that our *ahimsa* was the *ahimsa* of the weak. But in reality weakness and *ahimsa* cannot go together. It should therefore be described not as *ahimsa* but as passive resistance. But the *ahimsa* I advocated was not the *ahimsa* of the weak while passive resistance is only for the weak. Then passive resistance is a preparation for active and armed resistance. As a result the violence the people had been harbouring in their hearts has now suddenly erupted.

Our passive resistance has not been a complete failure. We have all but won our freedom. The violence we see today is the violence of cowards. There is also such a thing as the violence of the brave. If four or five men enter into a fight and die by the sword, there is violence in it but it is the violence of the brave. But when ten thousand armed men attack a village of unarmed people and slaughter them along with their wives and children it is the violence of cowards. America unleashed its atom bomb over Japan. That was the violence of the cowards. The non-violence of the brave is a thing worth seeing. I want to see that non-violence before I die. For this we should have inner strength. It is a unique weapon. If people had realized its beauty, all the life and property that have been lost would never have been lost.

If people had learnt the lesson of *ahimsa* which I had been trying to impart to them over the last 32 years, there would have been no need at present for rationing of food and cloth. If we are thoughtful in consuming food and cloth, there can be no scarcity of either in India. If people learnt to live truthfully and help each other, there would be no need for us to look towards the Civil Service. The late Mr. Montagu had described the Civil Service as a wooden structure. Civil servants do not consider themselves servants of the people nor are they employed for the service of the people. They are here somehow to keep the foreign rule going. Ensconced in their offices they issue orders through peons. If we could learn to stand on our feet and give up dependence on the Civil Service, there would be no need in India either for rationing or for the Civil Service today. Some kind of civil service no doubt will be needed for running the administration. If civil servants could change with the times and run the administration to serve the people, then a truly democratic regime could be brought about.

Speech at Prayer Meeting (H.)
Prarthana Pravachan, Vol. I, pp. 217-20

254. LEADERS AND LAWS

July 6, 1947

We shall never be able to raise the standard of public life through laws. We are not made that way. Only if the lives of the leaders, both private and public, are perfect will they be able to produce any effect on the people. Mere preaching will have no effect.

'A Letter' (G.)
Bihar Pachhi Dilhi, p. 285

255. CONVERSION TO SOCIALISM

New Delhi,
July 6, 1947

Socialism is a beautiful word and so far as I am aware in socialism all the members of society are equal—none low, none high. In the individual body the head is not high because it is the top of the body, nor are the soles of the feet low because they touch the earth. Even as members of the individual body are equal, so are the members of society. That is socialism.

In it the prince and the peasant, the wealthy and the poor, the employer and the employee are all on the same level. In terms of religion there is no duality in socialism. It is all unity.

Looking at society all the world over there is nothing but duality or plurality. Unity is conspicuous by its absence. This man is high, that one is low, that one is a Hindu, that one a Muslim, third a Christian, fourth a Parsi, fifth a Sikh, sixth a Jew. Even among these there are sub-divisions. In the unity of my conception there is perfect unity in the plurality of designs.

In order to reach this state we may not look on things philosophically and say that we need not make a move until all are converted to socialism. Without changing our life we may go on giving addresses, forming parties and hawk-like seize the game when it comes our way. This is no socialism. The more we treat it as game to be seized, the further it must recede from us.

Socialism begins with the first convert. If there is one such, you can add zeros to the one and the first zero will account for ten and every addition will account for ten times the previous number. If, however, the beginner is a zero, in other words, no one makes the beginning, multiplicity of zeros will also produce zero value. Time and paper occupied in writing zeros will be so much waste.

This socialism is as pure as crystal. It, therefore, requires crystal-like means to achieve it. Impure means result in an impure end. Hence the prince and the peasant will not be equalized by cutting off the prince's head, nor can the process of cutting off equalize the employer and the employee. One cannot reach truth by untruthfulness. Truthful conduct alone can reach truth. Are not non-violence and truth twins? The answer is an emphatic 'no'. Non-violence is embedded in truth and *vice versa*. Hence has it been said that they are faces of the same coin. Either is inseparable from the other. Read the coin either way. The spelling of words will be different. The value is the same. This blessed state is unattainable without perfect purity. Harbour impurity of mind or body and you have untruth and violence in you.

Therefore, only truthful, non-violent and pure-hearted socialists will be able to establish a socialistic society in India and the world. To my knowledge there is no country in the world which is purely socialistic. Without the means described above the existence of such a society is impossible.

'Who Is A Socialist?' (G.)
Harijan, 13 July 1947
Harijanbandhu, 13 July 1947

256. SOCIALISM AND *SATYAGRAHA*

New Delhi,
July 13, 1947

Truth and *ahimsa* must come alive in socialism. This can only be possible when there is a living faith in God. Mere mechanical adherence to truth and *ahimsa* is likely to break down at the critical moment. Hence have I said that truth is God.

This God is a living Force. Our life is of that Force. That Force resides in the body, but is not the body. He who denies the existence of that great Force denies to himself access to its inexhaustible power and thus remains impotent. He is like a rudderless ship which, tossed about here and there, perishes without making any headway. Many find themselves in this plight. The socialism of such people does not reach anywhere, what to say of the millions.

If such be the case, why is there no socialist who believes in God? If there are such socialists why have they not made any progress? Also there have been many believing in God; why is it they have not succeeded in bringing socialism?

There is no effective answer to this. Nevertheless, it is possible to say that it has perhaps never occurred to a believing socialist that there is any connection between his socialism and his belief in God. Equally, men of God perhaps never felt any need for socialism. Superstitions have flourished in the world in spite of godly men and women. In Hinduism which believes in God, untouchability has, till of late, held undoubted sway.

The nature of this Divine Force and its inexhaustible power have been matters of incessant quest.

My claim is that in the pursuit of that quest lies the discovery of *satyagraha*. It is not, however, claimed that all the laws of *satyagraha* have already been formulated. I cannot say either that I myself know all the laws. This I do assert that every worthy object can be achieved through *satyagraha*. It is the highest and the most potent means, the most effective weapon. I am convinced that socialism will not be reached by any other means.

Satyagraha can rid society of all evils, political, economic and moral.

'Socialism' (G.)
Harijan, 20 July 1947
Harijanbandhu, 20 July 1947

257. ERASING 'I' AND 'MINE'

The following condensed report of Sjt. Satis Chandra Mukerjee's speech delivered at a peace meeting the other day at Darbhanga will be read with interest and profit . . .[1]

If we could erase the 'I's' and the 'Mine's' from religion, politics, economics, etc., we shall soon be free and bring heaven upon earth.

'The Curse of "I" and "Mine" '
Young India, 23 Sept. 1926

---

[1] The writer's thesis was that the feeling of 'I' and 'mine' was responsible for much of the communal intolerance and violence in the country, and that, indeed, a true understanding of all religions was possible only through regard for the universal virtues, Truth, Non-violence, etc.

258. SERVICE AND SELF-REALIZATION

May 16, 1932

Bhai,

Ask for anything only in the sacrificial spirit.

A *guru* is one who guides us to righteousness by his own righteous conduct.

True development consists in reducing ourselves to a cipher.

Selfless service is the secret of life. To rise above passions is the highest ideal.

The sages mainly from their own experiences have laid down rules of thought and conduct.

A *rishi* is one who has realized himself. *Sannyasa* according to *Gita* is the renunciation of actions prompted by desire.

Only one who has his body under control is a man. Beauty because of its quality of inwardness cannot be experienced in the physical sense.

All your questions have been answered.

BAPU

A Letter (H.)
CW 9122

259. LIVING FOR THE SAKE OF SERVICE

July 29, 1947

Anybody who wishes to serve always finds enough for his needs. He can indulge in no luxuries, of course. If, therefore, you wish to live in the Ashram for the sake of service, you should be content with whatever you get. Otherwise you should leave the Ashram and find a job. A person like you should have no difficulty in finding one. There is no third course open to a public servant.

'A Letter' (G.)
Bihar Pachhi Dilhi, p. 440

260. RENUNCIATION, NOT ASCETICISM

March 17, 1945

Asceticism in the English sense is not needed at the present time. But there is all the need for renunciation. Read the

Ishavasya[1] and reflect on it. Realize the inner meaning of renunciation. It has been explained in the *Gita*.[2]

Blessings from
BAPU

Note to Gope Gurbuxani (H.)
GN 1328

[1] The reference is to verse 1 of this Upanishad.
[2] The addressee had asked: 'How far are asceticism and renunciation beneficial in life?'

261. JOY THROUGH SILENCE

January 28, 1946

Today is my day of silence. Therefore I am not able to speak to you. You must please excuse me. What a good thing is silence! I have personal experience of it. The joy one derives from silence is unique. How good it will be, if everyone observed silence for some time every day! Silence is not for some great men; I know that whatever one person is able to do can be done by everyone, given the effort. There is a saying amongst us that through silence everything can be achieved. There is much truth in this saying.

Speech Read out at Prayer Meeting, Madras
The Hindu, 30 Jan. 1946

262. HUMANITY AND THE KINGDOM OF HEAVEN

April 15, 1946

In a moment of introspection the poet asks himself:

O man, why have you left off taking God's name? You have not given up anger or lust or greed, but you have forgotten truth. What a tragedy to save worthless pennies and to let go the priceless gem of God's love! Why would you not, O fool, renounce all vanities and throw yourself on the grace of God alone?

This does not mean that if one has wealth, it should be thrown away and wife and children should be turned out of doors. It simply means that one must give up attachment to these things and dedicate one's all to God and make use of His gifts to serve Him only. It also means that if we take His name with all our being we are automatically weaned from all lust, untruth and baser passions.

In the first *shloka* of *Ishopanishad* that is repeated every day at the beginning of the prayer, one is asked to dedicate everything to God and then use it to the required extent. The principal condition laid down is that one must not covet what belongs to another. These two maxims contain the quintessence of the Hindu religion.

In another *shloka* which is recited during the morning prayer it is said:

I do not ask for temporal power, nor do I ask to go to heaven, nor even to attain *nirvana*. What I ask for is that I may be able to relieve the pain of those who are in pain.

The pain might be physical, mental or spiritual. Spiritual pain due to slavery to one's passions is sometimes greater even than physical.

But God does not come down in person to relieve suffering. He works through human agency. Therefore, prayer to God to enable one to relieve the sufferings of others must mean a longing and readiness on one's part to labour for it.

The prayer, you will note, is not exclusive. It is not restricted to one's own caste or community. It is all-inclusive. It comprehends the whole of humanity. Its realization would thus mean the establishment of the Kingdom of Heaven on earth.

Speech at Prayer Meeting
Hindustan Times, 16 Apr. 1946
Harijan, 28 Apr. 1946

263. UNIVERSAL SERVICE

On the Train,
July 31, 1947

Chi. Amrit,

Your last words were penetrating. Personal service when it merges into universal service is the only service worth doing. All else is rubbish.

Keep well and cheer up.

The journey is going well. Not a soul at the stations. Hence the night undisturbed.

Love.

BAPU

Letter to Amrit Kaur
CW 3706

264. A TALISMAN

[August 1947]

I will give you a talisman. Whenever you are in doubt, or when the self becomes too much with you, apply the following test. Recall the face of the poorest and the weakest man whom you may have seen, and ask yourself if the step you contemplate is going to be of any use to him. Will he gain anything by it? Will it restore him to a control over his own life and destiny? In other words, will it lead to *swaraj* for the hungry and spiritually starving millions?

Then you will find your doubts and yourself melting away.

M. K. GANDHI[1]

'A Note'
From a facsimile: *Mahatma*, Vol. VIII, p. 89

---

[1] The signature is in the Devanagari and Bengali scripts.

Chronology

M. K. Gandhi (1869–1948)

1869	2 Oct.	Mohandas Karamchand Gandhi was born into a Vaishya family at Porbander in Kathiawar, Gujarat; the youngest of three sons of Karamchand Gandhi, Prime Minister in Porbander, Rajkot, and Vanakner States, and his fourth wife Putlibai.
1876		Goes to Rajkot with parents; attends primary school there until twelfth year. Betrothal to Kasturbai, daughter of Gokuldas Makanji.
1882		Marries Kasturbai Makanji.
1884		Experiments in meat-eating and agnosticism.
1888	Spring	Birth of Harilal.
	4 Sept.	Despite disapproval of caste elders, sails for England to study.
	6 Nov.	Enrols as law student at Inner Temple, London.
1889	Nov.	Meets H. P. Blavatsky and Annie Besant of the Theosophical Society. Becomes acquainted with the *Bhagavad Gita, The Light of Asia*, and the Sermon on the Mount.
1890	19 Sept.	Becomes executive member of the London Vegetarian Society.
1891	26 Mar.	Enrols as associate member of the London Theosophical Society.
	10 June	Called to the Bar and enrols in the High Court of London.
	12 June	Sails for India.
1892	Spring	Birth of Manilal.
	14 May	Receives permission to practise law in Kathiawar. Fails to establish successful practice. Settles in Rajkot as legal draughtsman.

S. AFRICA?

1893	Apr.	Sails for South Africa as legal adviser to Dada Abdullah & Company.
	June	Ordered off train to Pretoria. Makes resolve to resist racial discrimination nonviolently.
	July	Kicked off footpath near President Kruger's house, but refuses to sue the assailant.
1894	Apr.	Studies religious literature, including the Bible, the Koran, and Tolstoy's *The Kingdom of God is Within You.*
	22 Aug.	Organizes Natal Indian Congress.
	3 Sept.	Enrolled as barrister in the High Courts of Natal and the Transvaal over opposition of European lawyers.
1895	Apr.	Visits Trappist monastery near Durban.
	May	Appeals to Natal Assembly and to Lord Ripon against re-indenture clause in Indian Immigration Bill.
	16 Dec.	Issues *The Indian Franchise: An Appeal to Every Briton in South Africa.*
1896	5 June	Sails for India. Addresses meetings on behalf of Indians in South Africa.
	30 Nov.	Sails for South Africa with his family.
1897	13 Jan.	Arrives in Durban and is attacked by a mob.
	20 Jan.	Declines to prosecute assailants.
	May	Birth of Ramdas.
1898		Petitions local and Imperial authorities regarding discriminatory laws.
1899	Dec.	Organizes Indian Ambulance Corps to serve in the Boer War.
1900	22 May	Birth of Devadas.
1901	18 Oct.	Sails with family to India.

1901	27 Dec.	Offers resolution on South Africa at Indian National Congress.
1902	Feb.	Stays with Gokhale for a month in Calcutta. Fails to establish successful law practice in Rajkot. Moves to Bombay where he pursues legal work.
	20 Nov.	Returns with family to South Africa in response to call to champion Indian cause against anti-Asiatic legislation in the Transvaal.
1903	Feb.	Enrols as Attorney of Supreme Court of the Transvaal. Opens law office in Johannesburg.
	4 June	Launches *Indian Opinion*.
1904	Oct.	Reads Ruskin's *Unto This Last*.
	Dec.	Founds the Phoenix Settlement near Durban.
1905	May	Begins learning Tamil.
	9 Aug.	Calls for revision of Bill levying poll tax against Natal Indians.
	19 Aug.	Calls for united opposition to Bengal partition and supports boycott of British goods.
1906	12 May	Advocates Home Rule for India.
	June–July	Engages in ambulance work during Zulu Rebellion. Vow of chastity.
	11 Sept.	Addresses mass meeting of Indians at Empire Theatre in Johannesburg calling for withdrawal of Asiatic Registration Bill.
	3 Oct.	Sails for England to seek redress from British government.
	7 Nov.	Addresses members of Parliament.
	Dec.	Returns to South Africa.
1907	Jan.–Feb.	Writes series of eight articles on 'Ethical Religion'.
	14 July	Calls upon Indians not to submit to re-registration.
	31 July	Explains significance of Passive Resistance. General Strike follows.

1907 28 Dec.   Conducts his own trial and appears in defence of pickets; ordered to leave Transvaal within forty-eight hours. Later, speaks at meeting in Government Square.

1908 10 Jan.   Adopts term '*Satyagraha*' in place of 'Passive Resistance'.
                Sentenced to two months' imprisonment. Released on 31 January along with all other *satyagrahis*.

      10 Feb.   Assaulted and nearly killed by Mir Alam Khan and other Pathans. Appeals from his sick-bed that assailants be forgiven, and asks Asiatics to give their finger-prints voluntarily.

      16 Aug.   Addresses mass meeting and encourages the burning of registration certificates.

      23 Aug.   Mass meeting in Johannesburg in which more registration certificates are burnt. Mir Alam, Gandhi's assailant, and other Pathans admit their error and resolve 'to fight to the end'.

      7 Oct.   Arrested at Volksrust for entering Transvaal without registration certificate. Sentenced to two months' hard labour. Released on 12 December.

1909 16 Jan.   Arrested again at Volksrust for failing to produce registration certificate. On deportation, returns and is re-arrested but released on bail.

      25 Feb.   Arrested at Volksrust on same charge. Sentenced to three months. Released on 24 May.

      23 June   Sails for England.

      10 July   Arrives in London. With assistance of Lord Ampthill, seeks to educate influential British leaders.

      13 Nov.   Returns to South Africa. *En route* writes *Hind Swaraj* and translates Tolstoy's 'Letter to a Hindoo'.

1910 4 Apr.   Sends Tolstoy a copy of *Indian Home Rule* (*Hind Swaraj*).

      8 May   Tolstoy replies that Passive Resistance is of greatest importance for India and humanity.

1910   30 May   Establishes Tolstoy Farm Ashram on 1,100 acres provided by Herman Kallenbach.

1911   22 Apr.   Smuts agrees to assurances demanded by Indians in reciprocation of suspension of *Satyagraha* Movement.

1912   22 Oct.   Gokhale arrives in Cape Town. Gandhi accompanies him during a five-week tour.
Gives up European dress and milk and restricts his diet to fresh and dried fruit.

1913   Apr.   Kasturbai joins the *Satyagraha* struggle.

15 Sept.   *Satyagraha* is revived. Party of twelve men and four women, including Kasturbai Gandhi, leave Durban for Volksrust.

23 Sept.   Kasturbai is arrested along with other *satyagrahis*. Sentenced to three months' imprisonment at hard labour.

28 Oct.   Leads march from Newcastle with 1,700 *satyagrahis*.

6 Nov.   With 2,221 marchers, arrives at Volksrust border. Arrested at Palmford railway station. Others cross the border.

7 Nov.   At Volksrust, released on bail and rejoins 2,037 marchers.

8 Nov.   Arrested at Standerton, released on recognition. March continues.

9 Nov.   Arrested at Teakworth and taken to Balfour.

11 Nov.   Sentenced at Dundee to nine months' imprisonment at hard labour on charges of inducing a strike.

18 Dec.   Released. From time of release till settlement takes only one meal a day and wears indentured labourer's dress.

1914   13 Jan.   Begins negotiations with General Smuts, resulting in a compromise on 22 January.

22 Jan.   Suspends *Satyagraha* following agreement with Smuts.

1914	18 July	Sails for London *en route* to India, leaving South Africa for the last time.
	6 Aug.	Arrives in England two days after World War I begins.
	8 Aug.	Given reception at Hotel Cecil by English and Indian friends; Jinnah, Lala Lajpat Rai, Sarojini Naidu are among those present.
	13 Aug.	Organizes Ambulance Corps of Indian students in London.
	19 Dec.	Owing to ill health sails for India. Begins learning Bengali.
1915	9 Jan.	Arrival in Bombay. Awarded Kaiser-i-Hind Gold Medal for ambulance services.
	3 Mar.	At Poona meeting to mourn death of Gokhale.
	7 Apr.	Goes to Rishikesh, and visits Swargashram.
	20 May	Establishes Satyagraha Ashram (later known as Sabarmati Ashram) at Ahmedabad.
	Sept.	Admits untouchable family to Satyagraha Ashram.
1916		Tours India and Burma, travelling third class on railway.
	6 Feb.	Speaks at Benares University.
	21 Oct.	At Bombay Provincial Conference held at Ahmedabad, Gandhi proposes election of Jinnah as President.
	26 Dec.	Attends Indian National Congress at Lucknow.
	29 Dec.	Presides over All-India Common Script and Common Language Conference in Lucknow.
1917		Idea of using spinning-wheel to produce handmade cloth on large scale takes root in his mind.
	10 Apr.	Begins working with problems of indigo farmers in Champaran, leading to a workers' resolution in August.
	31 Aug.	Tells Mahadev Desai, 'I have got in you the man I wanted.'

1917	3 Oct.	Champaran Committee reaches compromise with planters.
1918	20 Feb.	Presides over annual gathering of Bhagini Samaj in Bombay, speaking on women's education.
	22 Feb.	Leads *Satyagraha* campaign on behalf of mill workers in Ahmedabad. Settlement reached 18 March.
	22 Mar.	Inaugurates Kheda *Satyagraha* in Nadiad. Successfully terminated 29 June.
	27 Apr.	Attends Viceroy's War Conference at Delhi, addressing it in Hindustani. Tours to raise recruits for British armed forces.
	14 Nov.	Opening of Gujarat Swadeshi Store.
1919	24 Feb.	Notifies Viceroy of *Satyagraha* Pledge.
	Mar.	Issues first '*Satyagraha* Leaflet', quoting Thoreau.
	19 Mar.	Speaks at meeting of Madras Labour Union, B. P. Wadia presiding.
	6 Apr.	Inaugurates all-India *Satyagraha* Movement: country-wide *hartal*.
	7 Apr.	First issue of *Satyagrahi* released without registration.
	10–12 Apr.	Arrested on way to Delhi for refusal to comply with order not to enter the Punjab. Outbreaks of violence in several towns accompany his escort back to Bombay.
	13 Apr.	Massacre at Amritsar.
	14 Apr.	Commencement of three-day penitential fast. Leads *Satyagraha* campaign against Rowlatt Act. Confesses his 'Himalayan miscalculation' regarding mass *Satyagraha*. Martial law declared in Punjab.
	18 Apr.	Suspends *Satyagraha*.
	Sept.	Assumes editorship of *Navajivan*.
	Oct.	Assumes editorship of *Young India*.

1919	4 Nov.	Received in Golden Temple at Amritsar.
	24 Nov.	Presides over all-India Khilafat Conference at Delhi.
1920	2 Apr.	Rabindranath Tagore visits Sabarmati Ashram.
	1 Aug.	Addresses letter to Viceroy, returning Kaiser-i-Hind, Zulu War, and Boer War medals.
	31 Aug.	Takes pledge to wear *khadi* for life.
	8 Sept.	Special session of Indian National Congress accepts his programme of non-co-operation to secure redress of Punjab and Khilafat wrongs.
	Dec.	Nagpur Congress session adopts his resolution declaring object of Congress to be attainment of *Swaraj* by legitimate and peaceful means.
1921	30 Mar.	In Vijayanagaram, pleads for Hindi to be made lingua franca of India.
	Apr.	Launches programme to set up twenty *lakhs* of *charkhas* in the country.
	31 July	Leads campaign for complete boycott of foreign cloth. Presides over huge bonfire at Bombay.
	31 Oct.	Takes vow of daily spinning.
	19 Nov.	Fasts for five days as protest against communal riots.
	Dec.	Mass *Satyagraha* campaign begins. Invested with full powers by Congress. Many Congress leaders arrested.
1922	4 Feb.	Riots at Chauri Chaura.
	12 Feb.	Commences five-day fast as protest against violence. Abandons plan of *Satyagraha* Movement.
	10 Mar.	Arrested for sedition at Sabarmati. Sentenced to six years' imprisonment.
1923	26 Nov.	In prison begins writing *Satyagraha in South Africa*.
1924	12 Jan.	Operated upon for appendicitis.

1924	4 Feb.	Ordered released from prison.
	12 Feb.	Requests Mahomed Yakub to desist from moving Assembly resolution recommending award of Nobel Peace Prize to him.
	18 May	In first public appearance after release from gaol, presides over Buddha Jayanti celebrations in Bombay.
	17 Sept.	Begins twenty-one-day fast on behalf of Hindu–Muslim unity. Ends fast on 8 October.
1925	15 Feb.	Inaugurates a national school and a Jain hostel at Rajkot.
	2 July	Bakr-i-Id day riots break out in Kidderpore, Calcutta. Gandhi, with Abul Kalam Azad, visits trouble spots, pacifies both communities.
	22 Sept.	Founds All-India Spinners' Association.
	7 Nov.	Madeleine Slade (Mirabehn) joins the Ashram at Sabarmati.
	24 Nov.	Announces seven days' fast for misdeeds of Ashram inmates.
	29 Nov.	Begins writing *The Story of My Experiments With Truth*.
1927	Jan.–Nov.	Extensive *khadi* tour through North and South India.
	Nov.	Visits Ceylon.
1928	12 Feb.	Bardoli peasants refuse to pay taxes as an act of *Satyagraha*. Gandhi presides over successful settlement on 6 August.
	Dec.	Moves resolution at Calcutta Congress in favour of Independence if Dominion Status is not granted by end of 1929.
1929	3 Feb.	Completes *The Story of My Experiments With Truth*.
	4 Mar.	Arrested for burning foreign cloth. Released later on personal recognition.
	20 Aug.	Declines Congress Presidentship. Suggests Jawaharlal Nehru instead.

1929	27 Dec.	Declares for complete Indian independence at Lahore Congress.
1930	26 Jan.	Declaration of Independence prepared by him is proclaimed all over India.
	12 Mar.	Begins Salt March from Sabarmati to Dandi.
	6 Apr.	Breaks salt law on the beach at Dandi. Launches *Satyagraha* throughout India.
	18 Apr.	Riots at Chittagong.
	5 May	Arrested at Karadi and imprisoned at Yeravda gaol without trial. *Hartal* all over India. Over 100,000 are gaoled before close of year.
1931	26 Jan.	Released together with other Congress leaders.
	4 Mar.	Gandhi-Irwin Pact signed.
	8 Apr.	At Amritsar, discusses with Sikhs solutions to communalism..
	2 Aug.	Opens family temple of Chinubhai Madhavlal to untouchables in Ahmedabad.
	12 Sept.	Arrives in London to attend Round Table Conference, to meet with British leaders and elucidate the need for India's complete independence.
	26 Sept.	Talks with representatives of cotton industry.
	27 Sept.	Receives deputations from unemployed workers at Bradford.
	9 Oct.	Meets Madame Montessori.
	23 Oct.	Addresses a gathering at Eton College.
	24 Oct.	Delivers a talk to Oxford dons.
	6 Nov.	Mr and Mrs George Bernard Shaw call on Gandhi.
	14 Dec.	Sails to India after visiting Romain Rolland in Switzerland.
1932	4 Jan.	Arrested in Bombay after his draft resolution for resumption of *Satyagraha* is adopted by the Congress Working Committee. Detained at Yeravda gaol.

1932	20 Sept.	Begins fast unto death as protest against separate electorates for untouchables.
	24 Sept.	Yeravda Pact signed by high and low caste Hindus in the presence of Gandhi.
	26 Sept.	Concludes fast.
1933	Feb.	While in prison, founds the Harijan Sevak Sangh and *Harijan*.
	8 May	Begins fast 'for the purification of self and associates'. Is released from gaol.
	9 May	Announces suspension of *Satyagraha* Movement for six weeks and calls on Government to withdraw its Ordinances.
	29 May	Breaks fast after twenty-one days.
	26 July	Announces disbanding of Satyagraha Ashram, Ahmedabad. Prepares to march to Ras with thirty-three companions on 1 August.
	1 Aug.	Arrested and sentenced to one year's imprisonment for disobeying restraint order.
	16 Aug.	Begins fast because he is not allowed to work for untouchables while in prison. Four days later removed to hospital.
	23 Aug.	Released unconditionally from prison.
1933-4	Nov.-June	Extensive tour on behalf of *Harijans* in North and South India, last month of which is undertaken on foot.
1934	25 June	Escapes bomb attempt on his life.
	17 Sept.	Announces decision to retire from politics from 1 October to engage in development of village industries, Harijan service, and education through basic crafts.
	24 Oct.	Inaugurates All-India Village Industries Association.
	30 Oct.	Resigns from Congress.

1936 30 Apr. Settles at Sevagram near Wardha in the Central Provinces, making it his headquarters.

1937 22 Oct. Presides over Educational Conference at Wardha.

1938 3–5 Feb. Attends Congress Working Committee at Wardha.

      Oct. Tours North-west Frontier.

1939 3 Mar. Commences fast unto death at Rajkot to secure local ruler's adherence to his promise to reform administration. Ends 7 March on Viceroy's intervention.

      23 July Writes letter to Hitler (undelivered).

1940   Attends frequent Congress Working Committee Meetings where he plays an active role.

      Oct. Suspends *Harijan* and allied weeklies following official demand for pre-censorship on the subject of *Satyagraha*.

      17 Oct. Launches limited civil disobedience campaign in protest against India's enforced participation in World War II.

1941 13 Dec. Completes *Constructive Programme: Its Meaning and Place*.

1942 18 Jan. Revives *Harijan* and weekly journals.

      27 Mar. Meets Sir Stafford Cripps in New Delhi. Later declares his proposals to be a 'post-dated cheque'.

      8 Aug. Launches 'Quit India' Movement.

      9 Aug. Arrested and taken to Aga Khan's Palace, Poona.

      15 Aug. Death of Mahadev Desai from heart failure in Aga Khan's Palace.

1943 10 Feb. Begins twenty-one-day fast as an appeal for justice. Ends on 3 March.

1944 22 Feb. Death of Kasturbai Gandhi while in prison at Poona.

      6 May Released from prison because of ill health.
Devotes himself to Constructive Programme.

1944	9 Sept.	Begins talks with Jinnah.
	27 Sept.	Announces breakdown of talks with Jinnah.
1945	17 Mar.	Declares Vinoba Bhave and Kishorelal Mashruwala as his successors in Sevagram Ashram.
	25 June	Attends Simla Conference.
	19 Dec.	Lays foundation stone of C. F. Andrews Memorial Hospital at Shantiniketan.
1945-6	Dec.-Jan.	Tours Bengal and Assam.
1946	Jan.-Feb.	Tours South India for anti-untouchability and the learning of Hindustani.
	10 Feb.	Once again revives *Harijan* and allied journals.
	Apr.	Participates in political talks with Cabinet Mission in Delhi.
	5-12 May	Attends Simla Conference.
	23 June	Advises Congress not to enter Interim Government proposed by Viceroy.
	24 June	Meets Cabinet Mission.
	29 June	Leaves Delhi for Poona by rail. Attempts made to derail train *en route*.
	7 July	Addresses Congress meeting at Bombay.
	16 Aug.	Four days' rioting starts in Calcutta as the consequence of 'Direct Action' called by Muslim League.
	27 Aug.	Cables warning to British Government against repetition of 'Bengal Tragedy'.
	15 Oct.	Muslim League enters Interim Government.
	Nov.	Tours riot-torn East Bengal on foot for four months.
1947	2 Jan.	Says: 'All around me is utter darkness.'
	3-29 Jan.	Leaves Srirampur on walking tour. Tours riot-affected areas in Bihar.

1947	29 Mar.	Lord Mountbatten, last Viceroy of India, arrives in India.
	1-2 Apr.	Addresses Asian Relations Conference in Delhi.
	15 Apr.	With Jinnah, issues joint appeal for communal peace.
	5 May	Denies that communal division of India is inevitable.
	2 June	Viceroy's Partition plan revealed. Congress Working Committee accepts.
	6 June	Writes to Mountbatten to persuade Jinnah to settle amicably all outstanding points with Congress.
	12 June	Addresses Congress Working Committee.
	15 Aug.	British India divided into two self-governing dominions; Gandhi rejoices for the deliverance from British rule, while deploring India's partition. Mass migration of Hindus and Muslims accompanied by widespread violence.
	1 Sept.	In Calcutta begins fast unto death. Fast broken after local peace is restored four days later.
1948	13 Jan.	Begins fast in New Delhi on behalf of communal unity.
	17 Jan.	Central Peace Committee formed and decides on 'Peace Pledge'.
	18 Jan.	Ends fast.
	20 Jan.	Bomb explosion at Birla House.
	30 Jan.	Struck by an assassin's bullet while on his way to evening prayer meeting. With hands folded in prayer and a gesture of forgiveness, he passed from this life with the words 'Hey Ram, Hey Ram' on his lips.

Bibliography

Primary Sources

COLLECTED WORKS

The Collected Works of Mahatma Gandhi (ninety volumes), New Delhi: Publications Division of the Government of India, Navajivan, 1958-84.

BOOKS BY GANDHI

Hind Swaraj, Ahmedabad: Navajivan, 1938.
Satyagraha in South Africa (translated by V. G. Desai), Ahmedabad: Navajivan, 1928.
The Story of My Experiments With Truth (translated by Mahadev Desai), Ahmedabad: Navajivan; Volume I, 1927; Volume II, 1929.
The Constructive Programme: Its Meaning and Place, Ahmedabad: Navajivan, 1941.
Ashram Observances in Action, Ahmedabad: Navajivan, 1955.
Discourses on the Gita, Ahmedabad: Navajivan, 1960.
A Guide to Health, Madras: S. Ganesan, 1921. Ahmedabad: Navajivan, 1967.

JOURNALS EDITED BY GANDHI

Indian Opinion, Natal, South Africa (1903-14).
Young India, Ahmedabad, India (1919-32).
Navajivan, Ahmedabad, India (1919-31).
Harijan, Ahmedabad, India (1933-48).

COLLECTIONS OF WRITINGS BY GANDHI

Bapu's Letters to Mira (1928-48), Ahmedabad: Navajivan, 1949.
Cent Per Cent Swadeshi, Madras; G. A. Natesan, 1933.
Conversations of Gandhiji (edited by Chandrashankar Shukla), Bombay: Vora & Co., 1949.

More Conversations of Gandhiji (edited by Chandrashankar Shukla), Bombay: Vora & Co., 1950.

Delhi Diary, Ahmedabad: Navajivan, 1948.

The Economics of Khadi, Ahmedabad: Navajivan, 1941.

Ethical Religion, Madras: S. Ganesan, 1922.

For Pacifists, Ahmedabad: Navajivan, 1949.

From Yeravda Mandir: Ashram Observances (translated by V. G. Desai), Ahmedabad: Navajivan, 1932.

Gandhiji's Correspondence with the Government, 1942–1944, Ahmedabad: Navajivan, 1945.

Gokhale: My Political Guru, Ahmedabad: Navajivan, 1958.

Hindu Dharma, Ahmedabad: Navajivan, 1950.

History of Satyagraha Ashram, Madras: G. A. Natesan, 1933.

India of My Dreams, Ahmedabad: Navajivan, 1947.

Letters to Manibehn Patel, Ahmedabad: Navajivan, 1963.

Letters to Rajkumari Amrit Kaur, Ahmedabad: Navajivan, 1961.

The Medium of Instruction (edited by Bharatan Kumarappa), Ahmedabad: Navajivan, 1954.

My Appeal to the British, New York: John Day Company, 1942.

'My Dear Child': Letters to Esther Faering, Ahmedabad: Navajivan, 1956.

Non-Violence in Peace and War, Ahmedabad: Navajivan; Part I, 1945; Part II, 1949.

The Rowlatt Bills and Satyagraha, Madras: G. A. Natesan, 1919.

Sarvodaya, Ahmedabad: Navajivan, 1951.

Satyagraha, Ahmedabad: Navajivan, 1951.

Selected Letters, Ahmedabad: Navajivan, 1962.

Self-Restraint v. Self-Indulgence, Ahmedabad: Navajivan, 1947.

Socialism of My Conception, Bombay: Bharatiya Vidya Bhavan, 1957.

Speeches and Writings, Madras: G. A. Natesan, 1933.

To a Gandhian Capitalist, Bombay: Hind Kitabs, 1951.

To Ashram Sisters, Ahmedabad: Navajivan, 1952.

Unto This Last, Ahmedabad: Navajivan, 1951.

Untouchability, Ahmedabad: Navajivan, 1954.

Women and Social Injustice, Ahmedabad: Navajivan, 1942.

Secondary Sources

ANDREWS, C. F., *Mahatma Gandhi's Ideas*, London: George Allen, 1929.

    Mahatma Gandhi: His Own Story, New York: The Macmillan Company, 1930.

—— *Mahatma Gandhi at Work*, New York: The Macmillan Company, 1931.

ASHE, GEOFFREY, *Gandhi: A Study in Revolution*, London: Heinemann, 1968.

BIRLA, G. D., *In the Shadow of the Mahatma*, Bombay: Orient Longmans, 1955.

BONDURANT, JOAN, *Conquest of Violence*, Berkeley: University of California Press, 1965.

BROWN, D. M., *The White Umbrella: Indian Political Thought From Manu to Gandhi*, Berkeley: University of California Press, 1958.

BROWN, JUDITH M., *Gandhi's Rise to Power: Indian Politics 1915-1922*, Cambridge: Cambridge University Press, 1972.

—— *Gandhi and Civil Disobedience: The Mahatma in Indian Politics 1928-1934*, Cambridge: Cambridge University Press, 1977.

CATLIN, GEORGE, *In the Path of Mahatma Gandhi*, London: Macdonald & Co., 1948.

CHARPENTIER, MARIE VICTOIRE, *Gandhi*, Paris: Edition France-Empire, 1969.

DATTA, DHIRENDRA MOHAN, *The Philosophy of Mahatma Gandhi*, Madison: University of Wisconsin Press, 1961.

DESAI, MAHADEV, *Gandhiji in Indian Villages*, Madras: S. Ganesan, 1927.

—— *Gandhiji in Ceylon*, Madras: S. Ganesan, 1928.

—— *The Story of Bardoli*, Ahmedabad: Navajivan, 1929.

—— *The Nation's Voice*, Ahmedabad: Navajivan, 1932.

—— *The Gita According to Gandhi*, Ahmedabad: Navajivan, 1946.

DESAI, VALJI GOVINDJI (ed.), *The Diary of Mahadev Desai*, Ahmedabad: Navajivan, 1953.

DHAWAN, G., *The Political Philosophy of Mahatma Gandhi*, Ahmedabad: Navajivan, 1951.

DIWAKAR, R. R., *Satyagraha—Its Technique and Theory*, Bombay: Hind Kitabs, 1946.

DIWAN, ROMESH, LUTZ, MARK, *Essays in Gandhian Economics*, New Delhi: Gandhi Peace Foundation, 1985.

DOKE, J. J., *M. K. Gandhi: An Indian Patriot in South Africa* (introduction by Lord Ampthill), London: The London Indian Chronicle, 1909.

ELWIN, VERRIER, *Mahatma Gandhi*, London: Golden Vista Press, 1932.

ERIKSON, ERIK H., *Gandhi's Truth*, New York: Norton, 1969.

FISCHER, LOUIS, *The Life of Mahatma Gandhi*, New York: Harper & Brothers, 1950.

GANDHI, MANUBEHN, *The Miracle of Calcutta*, Ahmedabed: Navajivan, 1959.

—— *Last Glimpses of Bapu*, Delhi: Shiva Lal Agarwala, 1962.

GEORGE, S. K., *Gandhi's Challenge to Christianity*, London: Allen & Unwin, 1939.

GREGG, RICHARD B., *The Power of Non-Violence*, Ahmedabad: Navajivan, 1938.

HORSBURGH, H. J. N., *Non-Violence and Aggression*, London: Oxford University Press, 1971.

HUNT, JAMES D., *Gandhi in London*, New Delhi: Promilla, 1978.

HUTTENBACK, ROBERT A., *Gandhi in South Africa: British Imperialism and The Indian Question, 1860–1914*, Ithaca: Cornell University Press, 1971.

IYER, RAGHAVAN N., *The Moral and Political Thought of Mahatma Gandhi*, New York: Oxford University Press, 1973. Galaxy Paperback, 1979. Second edition: Santa Barbara: Concord Grove Press, 1983.

—— *Utilitarianism and All That*, London: Chatto & Windus, 1960. Second edition: Santa Barbara: Concord Grove Press, 1983.

—— *Parapolitics: Toward the City of Man*, New York, Oxford: Oxford University Press, 1979. Second edition: Santa Barbara: Concord Grove Press, 1986.

KRIPALANI, J. B., *Gandhian Thought*, Bombay: Orient Longmans, 1961.

—— *Gandhi: His Life and Thought*, New Delhi: Publications Division of the Government of India, 1975.

KYTLE, CALVIN, *Gandhi, Soldier of Non-Violence: His Effect on India and the World Today*, New York: Grosset & Dunlap, 1969.

LANZA DEL VASTO, JOSEPH J., *Gandhi to Vinoba: The New Pilgrimage* (translated from the French by Philip Leon), London: Rider, 1956.

LEYS, WAYNE, and RAO, P.S.S.R., *Gandhi and America's Educational Future*, Carbondale: Southern Illinois University Press, 1969.

MAURER, HERRYMON, *Great Soul*, New York: Doubleday, 1948.

MUZUMDAR, HARIDAS T., *Gandhi Versus the Empire*, New York: Universal Publishing Co., 1932.

NAESS, ARNE, *Gandhi and the Nuclear Age*, Totowa: Bedminster Press, 1965.

NAG, KALIDAS, *Tolstoy and Gandhi*, Patna: Pustak Bhandar, 1950.

NAMBOODIRIPAD, E. M. S., *The Mahatma and the Ism*, New Delhi: People's Publishing House, 1958.

NANDA, B. R., *Mahatma Gandhi*, London: Allen & Unwin, 1958.

NIKAM, N. A., *Gandhi's Discovery of Religion: A Philosophical Study*, Bombay: Bharatiya Vidya Bhavan, 1963.

OSTERGAARD, GEOFFREY, Nonviolent Revolution in India, New Delhi: Gandhi Peace Foundation, 1985.

——, and CURRELL, M., *The Gentle Anarchists*, Oxford: Clarendon Press, 1971.

PANTER-BRICK, SIMONE, *Gandhi Against Machiavellism: Non-Violence in Politics* (translated by D. Leon), London: Asia Publishing House, 1966.

PAYNE, ROBERT, *The Life and Death of Mahatma Gandhi*, New York: E. P. Dutton & Co., 1969.

POLAK, H. S. L., BRAILSFORD, H. N., PETHICK-LAWRENCE, FREDERICK, *Mahatma Gandhi*, London: Odhams Press, 1949.

POLAK, MILLIE GRAHAM, *Mr. Gandhi: The Man*, Bombay: Vora & Co., 1950.

POWER, PAUL F., *Gandhi on World Affairs*, Washington: Public Affairs Press, 1960.

PRABHU, R. K., and RAO, U. R. (eds.), *The Mind of Mahatma Gandhi*, Ahmedabad: Navajivan, 1967.

PRASAD, RAJENDRA, *Satyagraha in Champaran*, Ahmedabad: Navajivan, 1949.

PYARELAL, *The Epic Fast*, Ahmedabad: Mohanlal Maganlal Bhatt, 1932.

—— *Mahatma Gandhi: The Last Phase*, Ahmedabad: Navajivan; Volume I, February 1956; Volume II, February 1958.

—— *Mahatma Gandhi: The Early Phase*, Ahmedabad: Navajivan, 1965.

RADHAKRISHNAN, S. (ed.), *Mahatma Gandhi: Essays and Reflections*, London: Allen & Unwin, 1938.

—— *Mahatma Gandhi—100 Years*, New Delhi: Gandhi Peace Foundation, 1968.

RAMACHANDRAN, G., and MAHADEVAN, T. K. (eds.), *Gandhi: His Relevance for Our Times*, Bombay: Bharatiya Vidya Bhavan, 1964.

RAO, V. K. R. V., *The Gandhian Alternative to Western Socialism*, Bombay: Bharatiya Vidya Bhavan, 1970.

Reflections on 'Hind Swaraj' by Western Thinkers, Bombay: Theosophy Company, 1948.

REYNOLDS, REGINALD, *To Live in Mankind—A Quest for Gandhi*, London: Andre Deutsch, 1951.

ROLLAND, ROMAIN, *Mahatma Gandhi*, London: Allen & Unwin, 1924.

ROTHERMUND, INDIRA, *The Philosophy of Restraint*, Bombay: Popular Prakashan, 1963.

SHARMA, JAGDISH, *Mahatma Gandhi: A Descriptive Bibliography*, New Delhi: S. Chand & Co., 1955.

SHARP, GENE, *Gandhi As a Political Strategist*, Boston. Porter Sargent, 1979.

SHIRER, WILLIAM LAURENCE, *Gandhi: A Memoir*, New York: Simon & Schuster, 1979.

SHUKLA, C., *Gandhi's View of Life*, Bombay: Bharatiya Vidya Bhavan, 1954.

SPRATT, PHILIP, *Gandhism: An Analysis*, Madras: Huxley Press, 1939.

TENDULKAR, D.G., *Mahatma* (eight volumes), New Delhi: Publications Division of the Government of India, 1951-1954.

   Gandhi in Champaran, New Delhi: Publications Division of the Government of India, 1957.

WATSON, FRANCIS, and BROWN, MAURICE (eds.), *Talking of Gandhiji*, Calcutta: Orient Longmans, 1957.

Index